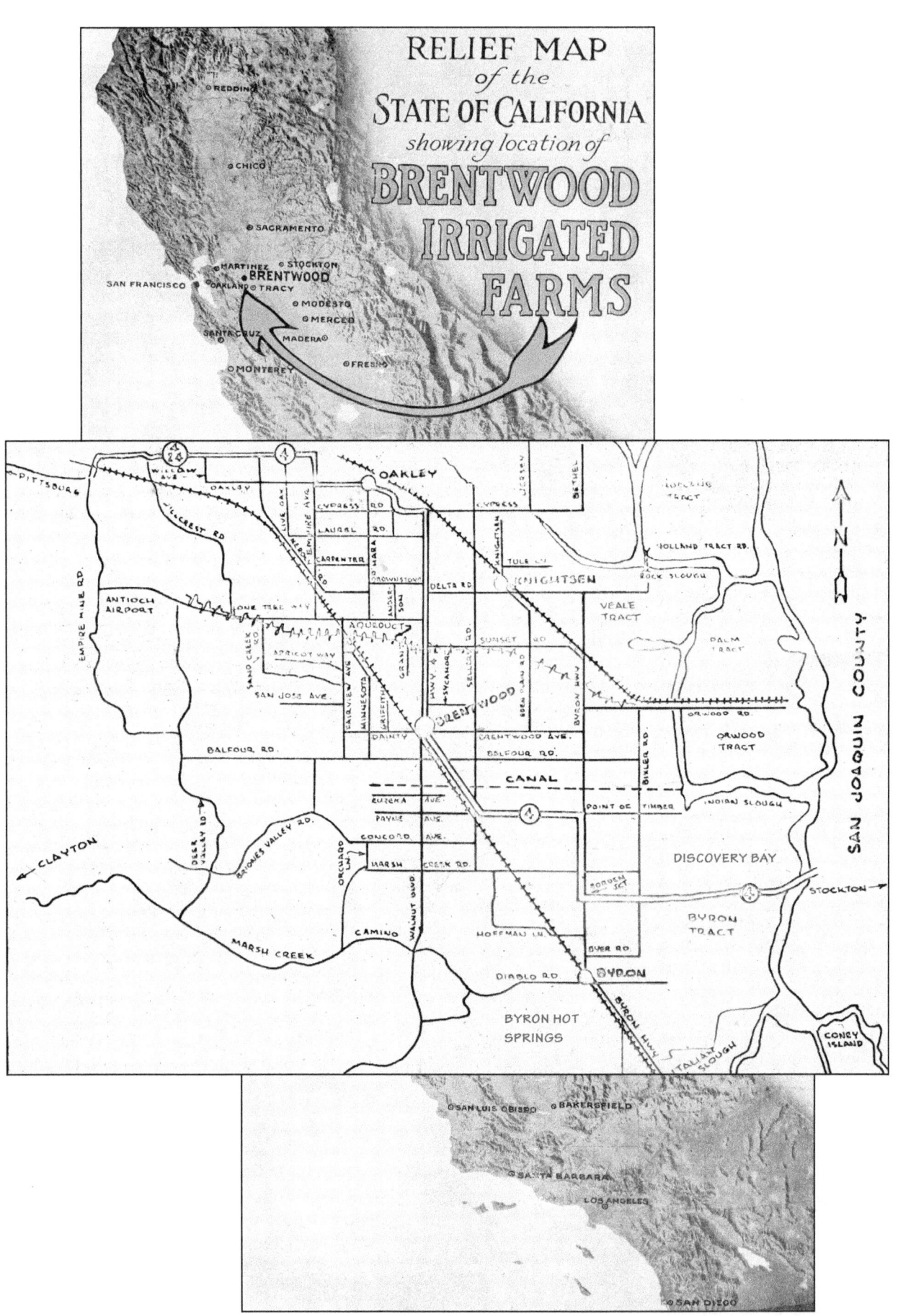

FOOTPRINTS IN THE SAND

Second Edition

Revised and Expanded

KATHY LEIGHTON

Published by Byron Hot Springs, San Francisco, California
www.byronhotsprings.com

Author copyright © 2021, 2001 Kathy Leighton. All rights reserved

No part of this publication may be reproduced, stored in a retrieval system, or transmitted in any form by any means, electronic, mechanical, or photocopying, recording, or otherwise without the permission of the author.

ISBN: 978-0-578-80055-4

Library of Congress Control Number: 2021932420

Cover design by Leigh McLellan
Front cover image by Chantelle Leighton

Frontispiece: *Top and bottom*: Relief Map of the State of California showing location of Brentwood Irrigated Farms brochure cover. (Private collection.) *Center*: Map of eastern Contra Costa County indicating the Delta communities of Brentwood, Byron, Oakley, Knightsen, Bethel Island, and Discovery Bay (East Contra Costa Historical Society research room archives.)

Second Edition: Reprinted and revised

Printed in the United States of America in compliance with the Lacey Act by Ingram® Lightning Source®

For general information, reviews, and corrections, please contact historian@byronhotsprings.com

Disclaimer: All errors and omissions are the responsibility of the author.

"Lives of great men all remind us
we can make our lives sublime,
And, departing, leave behind us
FOOTPRINTS ON THE SANDS OF TIME."

Henry Wadsworth Longfellow

This book is dedicated to
my grandmother, Cassie Armstrong, who gave me a love of history,
my parents, Barbara & Oliver Armstrong, who gave me all there was to give,
my husband, Bill for his immeasurable love, support and patience,
my children Brandon, Barrett and Chantelle for giving my life purpose,
my grandchildren, Cody, Ty, Dylan and Ryan who give me optimism for the future,
and U'geni for her friendship.

CONTENTS

Preface — vii
Introduction to the First Edition — ix
Introduction to the New Edition — x
Acknowledgments — xii

EAST CONTRA COSTA COUNTY

East Contra Costa Indians	2
Mount Diablo	4
View from Mount Diablo—1923	6
Indian Burial Site Uncovered at Los Vaqueros	8
Contra Costa County Wildlife 1850	10
Contra Costa County in 1772	12
John Marsh: A Villain or a Hero?	14
Doctor John Marsh Murdered 1856	16
Bidwell-Bartleson Party	18
Pioneers Travel to California	20
Wagons to Contra Costa County	22
Point of Timber	24
Early Stage Lines	26
History of the Grange	27
Cattlemen of East Contra Costa	29
The Wheat Boom	31
History of Farming in East Contra Costa	33
Coal Mining in East Contra Costa	35
Early Law Enforcement	37
Railroad History	39
Union Cemetery and Brentwood Funeral Home	41
Pioneer Doctors of East Contra Costa	43
The One-Room Schoolhouse	45
Education in East Contra Costa—L.U.H.S.	49
East County Churches	52
Catholic Churches of East Contra Costa	54
Businessmen Come to East County	56
Early Banks of East Contra Costa	58
East Contra Costa Floods, Fires and Earthquakes	60
Headlines from the Contra Costa Gazette	62
Remember the Windmills	63
Women of East Contra Costa	65
Street Name Origins	67
Did You Know?	69

Roller Skating	71
East Contra Costa Historical Society	73

BRENTWOOD

Brentwood Timeline	76
Joseph F. Carey & Soloman Davis	80
The Post Office	82
The Men with the Badge	84
Brentwood Newspapers	86
Brentwood City Park	88
City of Brentwood Park Timeline	90
Brentwood Fire Department	92
Brentwood Hotels	95
Sweeney's History	97
John Fletcher	99
Judge Robert Wallace	100
The Shafer Family	101
Cakebread: Pioneer Coalminer—Wheat Farmer	103
James Ball Dainty	105
Robert Garwood Dean—Pioneer Entrepreneur	107
The Prewetts Pioneer Family	109
Jeremiah Morgan	111
W.A. Davis—Brentwood's First Drug Store	112
Barkley History	113
Simon Taylor Barkley	115
Walter Hinebaugh's Memories	118
Coates Hall—Colonel Robert Coates	120
Balfour, Guthrie & Company	122
Hercules Logan—Brentwood Contractor	124
Oscar Starr—Inventor	126
Henry Cowell Family	128
Apricot Festival	130
H. P. Garin Company	132
Civic, Fraternal and Farm Organizations in the 1930s	134
Robert Frederick—Major General	136
Brentwood Incorporates	138
Brentwood Incorporates—Part II	140
Brentwood 1951—A City on the Move	142
Brentwood Women's Club	144
Brentwood Masonic Lodge	146
American Legion Has a Long History	148
Lions Club	150
Rotary	152
Brentwood Clubs	153

BYRON

Byron Timeline	156
Early Byron History—Founded 1878	160
How Byron Got It's Name	162
Henry Wilkening—Byron Founder	164
Wild Idol	166
Early Mercantile Stores	168
Louis and Moritz Grunauer—Early Businessmen	170
Byron Hot Springs School	172
Doctor James Hammond—Pioneer Physician	174
Judge Henry G. Krumland	176
Fred M. Holway	178
Alonzo Plumley	180
Byron Train Wreck	182
The Byron Times	185
Byron in 1912	188
Byron Fuel Industry	190
Byron-Bethany Irrigation Company	192
Byron-Discovery Bay Fire Protection District Timeline	194
The Byron Fire of 1923	198
Silica Sand	200
Pioneer Families Paved the Way to Byron	202
Alexander T. Taylor	204
Alpheus Richardson	206
McCabe—Pioneer Family	207
John Samuel Armstrong	204
Wills Family—Mabel and Edna	209
John Smith Netherton—Pioneer	214
Frank Cabral—Early Sheep Rancher	216
George Cople—Pioneer Wheat Farmer	218
Byron Grieves the Loss of an "Old Timer"—Leo Thomas	220
Cassie Harper Armstrong	222
Nick Papadakos	224
Ellen Hosie Ladd	226
Byron Holiday Yard, a Family Event	228
Bethany	229
Marsh Creek Springs Park	231
Reflecting on the Hot Springs	233
A Mecca for Tourists from Every Part of California	235
Hot Springs Vacation 1905	237
Prisoners of War at Byron Hot Springs	239

DISCOVERY BAY

Discovery Bay Timeline	242
Discovery Bay History	244

THE DELTA

History of the Delta	247
East Contra Costa Landings	249
Tracts and Islands of the Delta	251
A Cruise through the Delta	253

BETHEL ISLAND

Bethel Island Timeline	256
Bethel Island	259
Bethel Island Fire Protection District Timeline	261
Bethel Island Fire Protection District History	265

KNIGHTSEN

Knightsen Timeline	268
Knightsen Founded in 1898	271
George W. Knight	273
Samuel and Sarah Sellers	275
Sheriff Veale's Record of Achievements	277
Frederick Babbe—Early Landing Developer	279
The Christian Heidorn Family—Knightsen Pioneers	280
Oakley-Knightsen Fire Protection District Time Line	282

OAKLEY

Oakley Timeline	286
Oakley History	291
Oakley Pioneers	293
Oakley Fire Department	295
Oakley's Holy Ghost Festival	296
John Augusto & Joseph Augusta	297
Salvadore Dal Porto	299

Index	300
About the East Contra Costa Historical Society & Museum	305
About the Author	306

PREFACE

COMMITTEES:
CHAIR: TRANSPORTATION
BUDGET
INSURANCE
VETERANS AFFAIRS
SUBCOMMITTEE NO. 1 ON HEALTH AND HUMAN SERVICES

California Legislature

December 15, 2020

Dear Reader,

    Kathy Leighton time-travels. One day she is homesteading the eastern Contra Costa County foothills near Byron with her great-great grandfather Samuel. The next day finds her scorekeeping a cribbage game in 1901 that will determine the name of the last Contra Costa Township. Will it be "Dewey" or "Oak Leigh?" Randolph C. Marsh won the hand from Joel D. Wightman hence the right to name the town, "Oakley." Sadly, Kathy cannot remember the final cribbage score

    For over forty year's Kathy has captured the biographies, stories and times of our ancestors in the 11th Assembly district. She is a 7th generation citizen of Byron carrying on her family's legacy of service. Capturing history and writing it for the current generation and those to follow is only part of her story. She and her husband of over 50 years, Bill Leighton, have owned a road construction business, nurtured 3 children to maturity and helped launch the next generation. Outside the home and business, Kathy has served on numerous local commissions and boards. The short list includes the Contra Costa County Central Committee, Byron Airport Commission, Byron Municipal Advisory Council (MAC), John Marsh Historic Trust, Contra Costa County Historical Society, founding chairperson of the East Contra Costa Historical Committee and numerous election committees.

    For her service to community, Kathy has been honored locally as a 2015 "Graduate of Distinction" by her alma mater, Liberty Union High School. Her legislative efforts resulted in further honor as 2001 "California Legislature Woman of the Year" as nominated by past Assemblywoman Lynne Leach, 11th Assembly District. To this list, I add our District's acknowledgement and thanks.

    Perhaps Kathy Leighton's lasting contribution to our community is this compilation of history-based articles written for the local newspapers. It is this work that she is justly most proud. It leaves a lasting record of our San Joaquin River Delta. If not for Kathy's effort, research and writing our history would not be as accessible today for students, parents, residents, or planning departments. History counts. *Footprints in the Sand* should be on everyone's reading list. Good job, Kathy!

Sincerely,

Jim Frazier
Assembly Member, District 11

INTRODUCTION
to the First Edition

This is not a history book. Instead a collection of short stories relating to East Contra Costa County that have appeared in local publications over the past few years. I am not a writer, just a women who happened to get hooked on local history.

My ancestors settled in the shadow of Mount Diablo well over a century ago. In 1991, I decided to research my roots and write a "short" biography of the Armstrong and the Barkley families for my grandchildren. As I started researching my forefathers I found myself curious about why they settled in East Contra Costa County; how they overcame the hardships of the 1800's; and what impact they had on the community they lived in. I found I couldn't research my own family without collecting information about other early settlers and general information about this region of California. Before long I had accumulated volumes of information. What had started out as a genealogy project soon developed into my own personal passion for regional history.

I have made every effort to tell the story of our past as factual as possible. However, I have had to rely on old timers memories, often very selective; old newspapers, journals and personal letters, written to reflect the incident as the writer saw it; early Contra Costa County history books and my own family folklore as I remember it.

The story begins with the Native Americans that lived throughout the Delta area; the Spanish Explorers, the early ranchos and the vaqueros tending the cattle; the trappers, mountain men and wilderness wanders that ventured west; the arrival of John Marsh; the forty-niners seeking their fortune in the gold fields; the wheat farmers planting their roots in the rich fertile soil; the railroad companies laying track that linked East Contra Costa County to Stockton and San Francisco; the merchants and businessmen that built the towns; and finally those early settlers that came with their families to be a part of developing this region of California.

If someone would have asked me to make a list of things I would never do in this lifetime ten years ago writing a book would definitely have been on that list. I'm still not sure what gave me the audacity to tackle it. Footprints in the Sand is ready to go off to the printer. I thought I'd be elated, but instead I have mixed feelings. There are concerns about the numerous families and organizations that played a role in the early development of East Contra Costa County not mentioned in the stories that follow.

This book is intended to share merely a glimpse of life as it was. These words are fragments only — fragments that give us some feeling of life as it was lived by our forefathers — not a complete picture certainly, but rather little pieces of time. I hope you enjoy reading Footprints in the Sand as much as I have enjoyed writing it.

INTRODUCTION
to the New Edition

Local history and family genealogy have always been my passion. Still, the idea of writing a book on 19th and early 20th Century life in eastern Contra Costa County seemed too daunting. It would not have seemed possible to my 20, 30, or 40 year-old self. Yet, here it is, *Footprints in the Sand,* in a new and revised edition.

According to the popular proverb, "There is only one way to eat an elephant: a bite at a time." So, too, there is only one way to write a local history book, "One article at a time." Creating this original book was accomplished exactly this way. It is the result of over a decade of researching and writing history columns for local newspapers. Weekly columns for the *Brentwood News, Antioch Ledger, Contra Costa Times, Brentwood Bee, and Discovery Bay Clipper* appeared in the papers from 1989 to 2001. The City of Brentwood and the East Contra Costa Historical Society urged compilation of these articles into a hardback book. I cobbled them together, edited, wrote an introduction, table of contents and an index. Voila! The elephant was eaten and the book written.

Each article explored a unique community event, pioneer, profession, natural wonder, or benchmark. Native Americans lived in their San Joaquin Delta paradise, John Marsh purchased his Rancho del los Méganos, Yankee farmers settled in Point of Timber, railroads arrived, towns established, communities grown and babies born. Researching the life and times of the communities is the most fun of all. I am still amazed at the resiliency, the inventiveness, the toughness of our forefathers and foremothers to emigrate from "the States" to the California Delta. Some went directly to the gold mines. Others established businesses in San Francisco. A few sought escape from the 1906 Great Earthquake and Fire and sanctuary in East County. All found East Contra Costa County where they left their indelible footprints in our society and created who we are today.

My family homesteaded in the Byron foothills seven generations ago. The eighth generation, my grandchildren, is now asking questions. Why are there so many Armstrongs? Answer: Great grandparents Samuel and Mary had 10 children, most stayed in the area and there are now lots of cousins. Why is the street named "Balfour?" Answer: Balfour Guthrie & Co was the large British agricultural concern that developed present day Brentwood. Why is Knightsen called Knightsen? Answer: the name combines town founder George *Knight* and his wife's maiden name, Christen*sen*, hence Knight-sen.

Inquiring new residents have the same questions. Brentwood had a population of 1,500, 2,300, or 2,800 residents in 1965 depending on which of the three city limit signs you believed as you entered town. The City of Brentwood today (2020) has in excess of 65,000 residents as consistently posted on the many city limit signs. The demographics have also changed dramatically. East Contra Costa County is known primarily for agricultural production from the 1870s through the 1960s. "Manufacturing" at the time, our main economic activity, meant grain harvesting, vegetable and fruit packing, and nut hulling. These were the primary export products from the area that brought prosperity to the community. Today, the primary export product is the commuter/ wage earner traveling west into the Bay Area or Silicon Valley. The wages earned by the commuter return to the community and with it prosperity. Current resident age is also a factor. The individuals chronicled in these have mostly passed. Their legacy survives in a few long-time, living residents, grandchildren and great-grandchildren still in the area.

This new, revised edition of the original *Footprints in the Sand* answers many of these historical questions. The following pages offer many new articles on topics of historic interest and additional images to complement the stories. The table of contents is expanded with new articles integrated into the communities to which they apply. The index is also expanded to include not just original pioneer family names but topic areas of interest. Publication as a perfect bound paperback will make it more affordable, hence accessible, to the reading public.

There is an apologia for the dated nature of the history as written herein. These articles were originally researched and written in the late 20th Century. As such, they are woefully lacking in the cultural, age, gender, and racial diversity we have come to expect and embrace in today's scholarship. Our communities of Brentwood, Byron, Oakley, Knightsen, Bethel Island, Discovery Bay, and the Far East islands have a rich immigrant and emigrant history. Our area of California was paradise to its indigenous peoples. Berms dug by Asian Americans helped drain the swampland, levees completed by Azoreans created the islands, cattle herded by Californios fed the 49ers, russet potatoes grown by Nisei farmers later removed to WWII internment camps and only one African American lived in the area to tell his tale. There are some great stories yet to be researched and written about these people and their contributions to our shared history. Regrettably, I must leave those articles to *Footprints in the Sand,* volume II.

My sincere appreciation to those individuals who assisted in the revisions and additions to this book: Gretchen Tovar, RoseAnne Yanes, Magdalena Northcut, and Carol Jensen. The outstanding cover design is the creative inspiration of my dear daughter, Chantelle. Thank you friends and family.

…Until Next time.

Kathy Leighton
Byron, California
January 12, 2021

ACKNOWLEDGMENTS

The author wishes to thank the City of Brentwood for underwriting this effort. Their patience in seeing the completion of this project and their foresight in recognizing the importance of recording the annals of East Contra Costa County for the residents is much appreciated.

I would also like to thank the Delta Parents Association at Willow Wood School and the Laurel and Jim Depolo family for their generous donation toward this publication. Their generosity is much appreciated.

A special thank you is extended to Jeannine Gendar, Sharon Marsh and Steve Herrick for their editorial ministrations, Barbara Bonnickson for the encouragement that spurred the undertaking in the first place, and especially my husband, Bill, for his perpetual support and putting up with "one more project".

Sharon Mushrush helped from Footprints inception. She has read more drafts of the manuscript than I care to admit I wrote. Without her computer skills, developmental suggestions, and the hours she spent scanning photos and compiling stories this project would not have ever been completed.

I have found that the memories of our past truly are locked in the hearts and souls of the people who lived and shared the experience of developing the Diablo Valley. I have been blessed with the opportunity of interviewing many old timers. A special thanks goes to those that willingly shared the stories of their youth. To many stories are lost forever because no one bothered to record them and unfortunately over the years much history has been carted to the dumps, burned, or ruined by the elements.

While researching East Contra Costa County I have accumulated volumes of information. In writing this book I have been deeply indebted to many people and there is no way in which they can all be thanked enough. Some have granted me interviews and others have loaned photographs, scrapbooks, and family memorabilia. If I thanked everyone that helped with this publication, my acknowledgments would be longer than the text itself. The most immediate thanks are due- - -

Bob Abney	Josephine & Vern Allen	Barbara & Oliver Armstrong
Mary Jane Barnes	Zelma Dainty Beaman	Barbara Boar
Charlie Bohakel	Barbara Bonnickson	JoAnn Byer
Helen & Dick Cakebread	City of Brentwood	Clayton Historical Society
Lynn Clousing	Contra Costa Co. Historical Society	Chick Cowen
Pyron Crosslin	Vern Currier	Carolyn DeMartini
Bob Doran	Bob Fletcher	Dave Fowler
Harry Green	Bob Gromm	Agnes Hannum
Jack Harrison	Steve Herrick	Carol Jensen
Sandra Kelly	Ellen Hosie Ladd	John Mackenzie
Betty Maffei	Sharon Marsh	Martinez Historical Society
Julie Mattes	Mickie Moore	Nick Papadakas
Reddie & Ed Prewett	Louise & Clarence Reynolds	Lois Ricioli
Blair Rixon	John Rodriques	Jess Santos
Vera Thomas	Tracy Historical Society	Ugeni
Mark White	Dorothy Yule	Brentwood Library

EAST CONTRA COSTA COUNTY

EAST CONTRA COSTA INDIANS

Thousands of years before Spanish explorers ventured to East Contra Costa County the rolling green hills and plains were scattered with villages populated by California Indians. Indians were present in the area at least three thousand years prior to the arrival of John Marsh, the first white settler in the area. Marsh came to build his home near what is now Brentwood. Professor Kroeber of the University of California at Berkeley estimated the state's Indian population in 1769 at the time of the Spanish arrival at between 133,000 and 150,000. By 1900 the number had dropped to about 16,000.

As we drive through East County today we see tracts of homes, farms, highways, railroads, and shopping centers. Along rivers we notice marinas and boat docks. In the foothills there are wind mills, electric power poles, and cattle ranches. These are all a part of our man-made environment. Two hundred years ago, the hills were covered with grass and groves of oak trees. In the valley area there were many rivers and streams filled with fish and flowing freely over the land. Huge flocks of ducks flew in the skies while herds of antelope and elk grazed the land.

Giant Oak in the shadow of Mt Diablo

Contra Costa County was home to the Miwok, the Costanoan, and the Yokut Indian Tribes. The Indians of Contra Costa County were primarily a peaceful and friendly people. Their villages were located along the shores of the Delta and in the foothills under the shadows of Mount Diablo

The Indians were short, broad-shouldered, strong, hard-working people who chose to wear their straight coarse black hair long. Little clothing was worn during the winter months, and nakedness was often accepted during the warm summer months. Each member of a tribe served an important purpose within the village. Men hunted and fished for food. They also made and repaired their weapons and tools. Women gathered plants, prepared food, built houses, wove baskets, and created home furnishings. Children were responsible for the gathering of firewood and spent much of their time watching and learning from the elders of the Tribe.

Male members of the Tribe would hunt deer and small game for their village. The Indians diet included a variety of plants, roots, insects and fish. Mushrooms were gathered in the spring and fall, greens were gathered in the spring, and seeds were gathered in late summer and early fall. Women and children would harvest acorns from the local oaks (the most important food crop) in late September. Preparation of the acorns into a type of mush was a tedious task at best.

Prior to cooking, the acorns were cracked, the kernels cleaned of their inner skins, and the nuts pounded in a mortar. The resulting flour was leached with water to rid it of the tannins which gave the flour a bitter taste. Finally, the resulting dough was mixed with water in a cooking basket and boiled with hot stones to make mush.

An Indian family could consume 1000 to 2000 pounds of acorns a year. Often the underbrush around the oak trees would be burned to reveal acorns which had previously fallen to the ground. Acorn granaries were constructed of upright poles and deerbrush bound with grapevines and thatched with conifer boughs to keep the rain out. The floor was usually two to three feet above the ground to prevent spoilage. A granary might hold five or six hundred pounds of acorns and other seeds and nuts.

The main weapon for hunting or making war was the bow and arrow. Bows were generally crafted from incense cedar or California nutmeg with a string made of twisted sinew or milkweed. Arrow shafts were feathered and tipped with obsidian points.

Women wove baskets for many different purposes including carrying loads, harvesting grass seeds, transporting infants, and winnowing acorns. Acorn mush and other food was cooked in tightly woven baskets filled with water into which hot stones were placed.

Indian housing varied from tribe to tribe. Some dug a hole 2 to 12 feet deep with a sod roof or lived in the Vasco Caves near Byron. Others constructed a cone shaped hut made of willow stakes and tule weeds.

"Sweat houses" or "temescals" to cure illnesses were common place. These inverted bowl-like structures, 40 feet in diameter, were made of tree branches and poles and covered with a layer of earth. A large fire would be built in the middle of the sweat house, which had a hole in the top to let the smoke out. The Indians would enter the house and perspire for several hours before rushing to a nearby stream and jumping in, a practice thought to drain sickness out of the body.

Religious beliefs differed among the Tribes. The earth was believed to have been formed by the eagle and the coyote. Burials were very religious with the deceased buried in certain positions to fend off evil spirits or to keep the soul within the body. Some Indians believed it an insult to the deceased and their family to mention the deceased after burial.

Destruction of the Indians can be attributed to several factors, including diseases, declining birth rate, high infant mortality, and warfare. The main cause however was diseases brought by the white man, sometimes intentionally.

During the fall of 1833 a cholera epidemic recked havoc with the Indian Villages of Contra Costa County. The death rate was of so high that survivors did not have time to bury their dead. Measles and smallpox also left their mark. In 1838 a smallpox epidemic took another high toll within the Indian population.

J.J. Warner, a fur trapper who traveled through the San Joaquin Valley in 1833, wrote a newspaper account of the cholera epidemic. As he traveled south he wrote: "The banks of the Sacramento and San Joaquin, and the numerous tributaries of these rivers were studded with Indian villages from one to twelve hundred inhabitants each." Later that year on his trip north Warner witnessed the following: "Death had obtained a victory. Not one female did we see. The first struck down (by cholera) were buried. But the increasing dead gave not time to the living to dispose of their departed fellows. The decaying bodies compelled us nightly to pitch our tents in the open prairie."

The American Indians have long since disappeared from East Contra Costa. However, I can't help but wonder that their spirits still lay heavy over the Diablo Valley, their unassuming beliefs, ways of life, and eternal respect for the lands upon which they lived have definitely left footprints in chapters of our past that we should perhaps reflect on every now and then. Until Next Time....

MOUNT DIABLO

Snowstorm 1922, Scene of Marsh Creek below Mt Diablo

Indians residing in the canyons and ravines of Mount Diablo, as well as early explorers and pioneers, relied on the summit as a landmark. There is evidence of Indians living throughout the Mount Diablo region as far east as what is now Vasco Road. These first Californians found the mountain abundant with wildlife, seeds, acorns, sweet clover, roots, and other everyday necessities.

Several legends exist about how Mount Diablo (mountain of the devil) came upon its name. The reference to "diablo" or devil can be traced back to 1804, when a Spanish military expedition visited the area in search of runaway Mission Indians. At a willow thicket, or "monte," near what is today Concord the soldiers encountered a village of Indians and surrounded them, but after nightfall the Indians all escaped, unseen. Angry and confused, the Spanish called the site Monte del Diablo. Later, English-speaking newcomers mistakenly assumed the word "monte" to mean "mountain" and applied the title to this beautiful East Bay peak.

Don Pedro Fages is credited with having been the first white man to explore this region of California and in 1772 he described the mountain in his journals. In 1776, Don Juan Bautista de Anza and his party passed through the foothills that surround the mountain. Members of his party named the mountain "Sierra de los Bolbones" after the Indian tribe they encountered residing on the mountain.

On July 18, 1851 (one year after California became a state) Leander Ransome of the California General Land Office established the Mount Diablo Meridian. The marker he placed on the summit established the east-west base line and the north-south meridian line for surveying northern and central California as well as Nevada.

As early as 1874, a recreation area was established atop Mount Diablo. Joseph H. Hall, an early settler of the region, built "Mountain House" an elegant sixteen-room hotel, about one mile from the summit. Daily stagecoaches brought guests from the surrounding area and beyond to enjoy the serenity and vast views.

Mountain House offered its guests an observation platform and telescope; a wonderful dining room; and most importantly, a serene and beautiful retreat. Many pioneer couples chose this location to exchange their wedding vows, and celebrities from all over Europe and America were regular visitors to the mountain. In those days, it was widely held that you hadn't seen the West until you had experienced the sunrise, sunset, or full moon from the upper slopes of Mount Diablo.

For many years the hotel was successful. In 1891, two toll roads that brought guests to the summit were closed in response to complaints from local ranchers about traffic through their pasturelands. It wasn't until 1915 that a new 23-mile road, Mount Diablo Scenic Boulevard, was opened to the public. Horse-drawn wagons and horseless carriages transported sightseers up the mountain. Toll rates were expensive for the time. An automobile with two passengers was $1.00; a two-horse vehicle $1.50; a four-horse vehicle $2.00; a hiker 25¢; a horse or cow 10¢; and
sheep 2-1/2¢ each.

Thousands of people hiked to the summit of Mount Diablo to take in the awesome view. On a clear day, it was possible to see 35 of California's 58 counties. Visitors could see Mount Shasta, Mount Lassen, Yosemite's Half Dome, and over six hundred miles of the Sierra Nevada.

Mount Diablo became a state park and game refuge in 1921. In 1930, the residents of California approved a $6 million bond issue to improve their state parks, thus allowing additional acreage to be added to Mount Diablo State Park.

In 1939, the State Department of Parks, using rock quarried from the mountain, built a museum on the summit. The museum included an octagonal observatory tower upon which the original beacon was mounted. The beacon (a ten-million candlepower aerial navigation beacon) was so powerful that it was used as a navigational aid by ships one hundred miles out at sea.

Mount Diablo has seen many changes in the past two hundred years. Although the developed valleys in her shadow have been overlaid with concrete, the mountain remains preserved for future generations. Wildlife is still in abundance; coastal blacktailed deer, raccoons, squirrels, gray fox, bobcats, mountain lions, eagles and many other native animals make the mountain their home. Visitors still walk among the California oaks, grasslands, and extensive areas of chaparral. Campsites, picnic areas, and guided hikes are available daily.

Through the years, Mount Diablo has played an important role in the history of Contra Costa County as a prominent landmark, guiding travelers passing through this region of California on their journeys. Until Next Time....

VIEW FROM MOUNT DIABLO - 1923

A few weeks ago, I had the opportunity to spend the afternoon at the new San Francisco Library's History Center doing some research. This facility is a real treasure. It is not only beautiful to look at but also well staffed with pleasant, good-natured employees that offered me lots of assistance.

I spent hours researching early editions of the *San Francisco Examiner,* gleaning out information about East Contra Costa. I came home with piles of data to add to my collection of local history. One of the articles that I found particularly interesting was printed in the November 4, 1923, Automotive section of the *Examiner*. This section of the paper offered readers information about areas that they could tour in their new horseless carriages. The column by E. V. Weller was titled "Delightful Tours To Be Encountered Off Traveled Ways." It offered the reader a great opportunity to peak through a window of time into the other side of yesterday.

"Good roads, pleasant vista and a minimum of traffic are to be encountered by the motorist who leaves the beaten path in the Contra Costa hill country. Along the banks of Sand Creek, through the Alhambra Valley and beside the placid stream of Marsh Creek, you will discover panoramas ever changing and ever pleasant. The range of hills that culminates in the bleak crag of "Diablo" shuts off the cool breezes from the bay and makes the little district ideal for the autumn picnicking tourist."

"Forgotten in the network of paving that threads the county, little crossroads and laterals afford an easy afternoon's drive that will furnish as much in the way of scenic entertainment as many a trip of more impressive mileage. Too frequently the motorist, out for a Sunday's outing, clings to the concrete trail with a thousand and one of his fellow drivers simply because he doesn't want to flounder around blazing paths over uncharted grounds."

Pete Schermer, Andrew DeMartini
P.G. Moody, Paul DeMartini and Mr. Gassner

"Here's the prescription for a day's outing that will insure a day of pleasure. Ferry to Oakland, drive out San Pablo Avenue to Pinole, turn here to the Alhambra Creek Road and follow this winding hill road to the concrete highway. You'll continue on into the town of Concord, then on over pavement to Pittsburg and Antioch. Turn off the highway here toward Mount Diablo over the Sand Creek Road until you encounter Marsh Creek. Here you will swing back to Concord again where you have the alternative of returning by way of Martinez and the Franklin Canyon Road or by way of the Tunnel Road into Berkeley and Oakland."

"The Marsh Creek Road affords the tourist a wonderful view of Diablo, the highest mountain in the bay area. It is a view that is different than the aspect of the Bay Shore side and it is even more inspiring than that from Danville or the Dublin Canyon Road. This is said to be the trail over which Fremont came when he named the Golden Gate. The earliest settlers in Contra Costa County established their headquarters in this little chain of valleys, and it is still one of the great agricultural sections of the country."

"Mount Diablo towers 3,869 feet from the level of the bay, and from its lofty crest, a wonderful panorama of the bay district is revealed. The outstanding natural feature of the East Bay district is this sentinel peak of the rugged hills that slope to the bay. Overlooking the fruitful valleys that border the San Joaquin as well as the more distant borderlands of the Sacramento, it offers a view at once diversified and picturesque."

"Its name, derived from the rocky, barren appearance of its higher slopes, fails to convey any terrors into the regions that lie about its base, as on every side there are orchards and farms and wide awake villages that are growing only as California villages can grow. Thirty miles away, across the bay, is Mt. Tamalpais. Sixty miles to the north, at the head of the Napa Valley, is Mt. St. Helena and far to the south is Mt. Hamilton, lair of stargazers."

Here is the way a writer described the vista from the slopes of "Diablo" in the early 1890's: "The wheat fields seem to be contracted to small squares, the orchards into still smaller ones; and the nearest farmhouses appear hardly larger than bird cages. San Francisco is reduced to a picture; but with a powerful glass, the spars of ships that line the waterfront look like a forest of dead trees where a fire has lapped up every green thing. By way of relief, some ships, like toys, are seen coming in and going out with white specks of canvas which seem to kiss the water. But the view which is printed as it were on the very soul is that beheld looking across the great San Joaquin Valley, beyond all the towns and villages that dot the plain, inner mixing with tilth of fields and emerald squares of vineyard to the western slope of the Sierras, and beyond to the great domes and peaks lifted up from 10,000 to 15,000 feet above the sea, clad in eternal white, watching in serene majesty over all the peaceful and fruitful valleys."

I took my grandsons, Cody and Ty, to the summit of Mount Diablo not long ago to feed the chipmunks and enjoy a bit of nature. I'm not sure whether to blame my aging eyes or the smog-filled skies, but I couldn't see the Bay, or San Francisco, and there were definitely no sailing ships coming or going.

I can't help but wonder what E. V. Weller would think of how we have developed Contra Costa County in the past 75 years. In 1923 Mount Diablo and the foothills around it were more densely timbered than now, game was abundant and life in general moved at a much slower pace. Where thousands of homes are spread across the landscape today, small towns and golden seas of wheat fields once prevailed. In the name of progress we have marched behind our bulldozers, raiding the land, turning quaint little villages into sprawling cities. Until Next Time....

INDIAN BURIAL SITE UNCOVERED AT LOS VAQUEROS PROJECT

A Miwok and Ohlone Indian burial ground has been located near Vasco Road on the Los Vaqueros water project property. One hundred and forty human skeletons as well as arrowheads, mortars, crystals, stone tools, pottery, beads, shells and numerous other artifacts have been exhumed from the site, dating back as early as 500 B.C.

The unearthed human bones and artifacts were removed from the Vasco site and studied at Sonoma State University. Dr. Dave Frederickson, an archaeologist and the Sonoma State representative on the project said, "The Los Vaqueros site is filling in a period of time we know very little about in this area. Many of the secrets of the Vasco region and the peoples that lived there for centuries will be lost under the waters of the Los Vaqueros Reservoir, but the research that is in progress today will tell us much about the Native Americans that resided in this region of California."

According to Gary Darling, the project manager, the Contra Costa County Water District has been doing cultural studies of the area since 1982. There is evidence that the Los Vaqueros locality was home to the Ohlone, the Bay Miwok, the Plains Miwok, and the Northern Valley Yokuts. To date the district has spent several million dollars on the cultural studies. Archaeologists studied the prehistoric period when the area was used by Native Americans; the adobe homes and artifacts from the Spanish/Mexican ranchero era; and the period when the Euro-American settlers established their homes in these foothills.

Vasco Road - 1931

There was an extensive Indian population in this region of California. This was not wilderness, or at least, not an unpopulated wilderness. As late as 1772, when the Spanish explored the Mount Diablo area, they found thousands of Native Americans settled throughout the Vasco territory. The arrival of the white man was the beginning of the end for the Indian's way of life. They brought with them cholera. smallpox and other diseases, and hundreds of Native Americans died. By the end of the nineteenth century, Contra Costa had towns, farms and industry, but the true natives of the county were very nearly extinct.

We often underestimate how advanced the Native Americans were. By examining areas like the Vasco site, researchers can begin to understand how these people lived. Tools, carved of bone or stone, provide us with a glimpse into their workshop. Animal bones tell us about their diet, shells and stones not normally found in the Vasco region tell us that these people traveled to the coast and Napa Valley to acquire some of their needs, or perhaps they traded with neighboring tribes. Travel was no small item for the Indians, as they had neither horse nor wheel.

It is believed that the Vasco territory was Mother Nature's "marketplace" for many different tribes. The Vasco foothills were covered in oak trees, which were the mainstay of the Native American diet and economy. The area offered berries, bulbs, roots, clover grass, buckeyes and peppery tasting bay nuts. There was an abundance of game like squirrel, tule elk, deer, antelope and waterfowl, and the streams ran off the mountain with sweet fresh water. Because of the plentiful oak woodland it was possible to harvest a year's supply of acorns in a week.

For many years when Indian remains were discovered at construction sites they were either quickly covered over or shipped to a museum or university. That has changed. State laws protect archaeological sites, and in 1991, President Bush signed the Native American Graves Repartriation and Protection Act. Today developers are required to work with Indian representatives, making sure Native American heritage is preserved and the dead are treated respectfully. Developers must check for archaeological artifacts before breaking ground.

Andres Galvan, a Native American consultant for the Ohlone tribe, is actively involved in the Vasco site. He will be working very closely with the Contra Costa Water District throughout the excavation of the entire project. "This is a significant site because it helps clarify these people and fills in gaps in their history." he said. It is of particular interest that amoung the skeletons exhumed there were both male and female, young and old. This gives researchers an opportunity to determine causes of death (in childbirth, old age and illness). "We can tell that people died mostly the same way they die today." Galvan said.

The archaeologists are hoping to glean all the information the site can offer them before the area is interred under the waters of the reservoir.

One of the problems that occurs when the public learns of arechaeological finds like the one on the Los Vaqueros site is that, too often, people go souvenir hunting. These sites are protected by federal law, and out of respect for the Native Americans we ask that you not attempt to cross fences and trespass onto Contra Costa Water District Property. Until Next Time....

Footnote: This article was written in July of 1995

CONTRA COSTA COUNTY WILDLIFE 1850

Early settlers of Contra Costa County could never have imagined what the county would look like in the 1990's. It is equally difficult for us to visualize what this area looked like in the 1850's. As I research the chapters of our past, I find the transformation of this region very interesting: from frontier to modern times; open range to fenced pastures; use of wagon trains to the arrival of the iron horse; from dry farming to irrigated pastures; from makeshift and make-do to more convenient, easier ways; and from the abundant supply of wildlife that roamed freely over the terrain to an almost complete loss of wildlife in Contra Costa County today.

If we could transport ourselves to a time when not a house or a fence could be seen, when groves of oak, big leaf maple, California laurel, pine and buckeye covered the land as far as one could see, we would find wildflowers decorating the hills and valleys in the spring, and a rich supply of flourishing wildlife. We would see an abundance of California quail, ducks, geese, doves, and other wildlife everywhere. In fact, the wild geese along the riverbanks were said to have created a great nuisance for the early farmers. Immense flocks of ducks or geese would move into a field of grain, leaving the field bare as they ascended to their next target. Early settlers often hired men to ride horses through their grain fields, scaring the intruding birds away with their shotguns.

Large flocks of pelicans, both gray and white, were common in the lagoons and tule swamps, as were cranes and many other water birds. The rivers were filled with an endless supply of salmon, and beaver and otters would often be seen.

According to Captain Kimball, a pioneer of Antioch, herds of elk roamed over the San Joaquin plains. He recalled on the first day of his arrival in Contra Costa County, in 1849, coming across a herd of eighty elk grazing between Antioch and Oakley and shooting a fine heifer weighing four hundred pounds.

The plains were covered with wild cattle, which sprang from stock introduced by the mission fathers. These were slaughtered for their hides and tallow in the 1840's and used as the only acceptable currency in this area.

The foothills were filled with herds of deer and antelope as well as elk. They could be seen feeding on clover grass, and being good swimmers, they were often sighted fording the Delta waters to reach the green grasses on a local island.

Coyote, fox, and badgers were a familiar sight to early settlers. They would approach farms in search of food and steal eggs and chickens from the roost. If you traveled into the timberland around Mount Diablo you would have probably seen a mountain lion or a bobcat.

Grizzly bears were so abundant that Dr. John Marsh once said he could have one caught by his vaqueros anytime that he wished. The bears often killed Marsh's cattle and horses, as well as elk, deer and antelope.

As a rider traveled from Point of Timber to Eden Plain, squirrels, gophers, rabbits, skunks, raccoons and other small critters could be seen scampering about.

Traces of the wildlife once freely roaming Contra Costa County can still be found on the 19,000 acres of Mount Diablo State Park. The Park not only offers visitors a fabulous view of the valleys below, but also has become a refuge for what wildlife remains. Black-tailed deer, raccoons, ground squirrels, and gray foxes are often seen. Bobcats, mountain lions, badgers, coyotes, deer mice, cottontail rabbits, black-tailed hares, and many other animals now call the mountain their home. An occasional golden eagle can still be seen flying in the clear blue skies above the summit, allowing us a glimpse of what the early settlers viewed on the other side of yesterday.

For hundreds of years Indians living in this region of California survived on the resources of the land. They fished the streams, feasted on rabbit or venison, and in winter found comfort under a bearskin blanket. Then, the mission fathers, the trappers and mountain men, and finally the early settlers brought civilization to California.

View along the South Slope of Mount Diablo

We now find ourselves in the midst of a network of asphalt freeways, sub-divisions, and shopping centers. Sound walls block out not only sound, but also our view of Mount Diablo. For the good of the public we have taken streams that once ran openly through the countryside and rerouted their waters through concrete pipes. All of this has been done for the purpose of covering much of our rich, fertile farmland with pink condominiums and large shopping centers. Isn't progress grand? Until Next Time....

CONTRA COSTA COUNTY IN 1772

The first Europeans to settle in California were Spanish missionaries who claimed the land for their use, built missions and ranches, and attempted to convert the native Indians to Catholicism.

Don Pedro Fages and Father Juan Crespi are credited with being the first Europeans to explore the Sacramento-San Joaquin River Delta and portions of the great interior of California in 1772. Fages was a Catalonian lieutenant originally from Guissona, Spain, and Crespi was a native of the Island of Majorca, off the eastern coast of Spain in the Mediterranean Sea.

The explorers joined together in March 1772 to lead a sixteen-man expedition comprised of twelve foot soldiers, a muleteer, and an Indian guide. The group marched from Monterey to San Francisco Bay in search of a way to cross the bay to Marin County and with the ultimate goal of establishing a mission at Point Reyes.

Fages and Crespi believed that if they traveled far enough eastward they would find a route to Point Reyes without crossing the bay. The expedition set up camp within the boundaries of Contra Costa County several times. They first camped near a creek where El Cerrito is located today, continuing on to Pinole Creek, where they established another camp, then on to Crockett and Alhambra Creek.

Failing to find a way to cross the bay, the explorers headed inland, traveling to the top of Willow Pass, where they could easily view the Delta and Central Valley as well as the snow-capped Sierra Nevada to the east. The expedition moved on to Kirker Pass near Pittsburg and camped at a location between present-day Antioch and Pittsburg.

Fages and Crespi never went farther inland than Antioch, but in 1776, Captain Don Juan Bautista de Anza followed the earlier explorers' route as far as Antioch. He then continued on along the eastern slope of Mount Diablo, traveling through Deer Valley, near Brentwood, and on toward Tracy, passing through the Byron area. De Anza kept a diary that described in great detail this region of California. He wrote about seeing six Indian villages, an abundant supply of wildlife, and beautiful valleys green with grass and thickly covered with wildflowers. The area was the domain of an estimated thirty thousand native Indians, including Yokuts, Miwok and Costanoans. These tough, enduring people sustained themselves on edible plants and wild game including antelope, tule elk, deer, beaver, raccoon, salmon and waterfowl. After the arrival of white men the Indian population declined from diseases brought by the Europeans which were previously unknown to the Indians. A cholera epidemic struck in 1833, followed by a smallpox epidemic in 1838.

Mount Diablo and the surrounding foothills were more densely timbered than today, and game was inexhaustible; elk and deer were common and an occasional grizzly contributed a spice of danger for the hunter. Wild ducks and geese literally swarmed in the lowland marshes, while the yip of coyotes, now seldom heard, was incessant through the night.

In 1821, Mexico gained its independence from Spain and claimed California for its own. Mexicans began moving into California territories claiming land and establishing huge ranchos.

Fur trappers were next to arrive in the Delta, claiming the lands as their private hunting preserve from roughly 1830 to 1845. Jedediah Smith was the first white man to come overland to California in 1826. He trapped otter and beaver, selling his pelts to the Hudson Bay Company at Fort Vancouver. Smith was followed by another American trapper, Captain Joseph R. Walker, who was also eager to explore the Delta region.

Trappers did not come to settle and raise families, but pioneers wishing to set up households in the West soon followed them. Dr. John Marsh was the first American to settle in Contra Costa County when, in 1837, he purchased Rancho Los Meganos from José Noriega.

View of Mount Diablo from the South

From 1846 to 1848, the United States was at war with Mexico over ownership of California and the area that is now known as Arizona and New Mexico. This conflict became known as the Mexican-American War. The Americans won the war and claimed the lands—just in time for the Gold Rush.

By the 1850's, men headed west seeking their fortunes in the gold fields, while others were planting their roots in the rich fertile soil of East Contra Costa. Early settlers acquired land by preemption and homesteading. Preemption, under U.S. public land law, gave settlers first right to purchase lands they settled on, not exceeding a quarter section. Many of the first settlers paid $2.50 per acre. Until Next Time....

JOHN MARSH: A VILLAIN OR A HERO?

On Marsh Creek Road, a few miles from Brentwood, stands an abandoned stone house built nearly a century and a half ago. The structure was once the home of Doctor John Marsh, the first U.S. citizen to build a permanent home in Contra Costa County. Marsh's life was filled with endless contradictions: he was an introspective scholar, a great adventurer, a friend to the Indians, uncivil to the Spaniards, and a recluse who invited hundreds to come and live in his county.

John Marsh can be traced to many different locations in the chapters of our country's history, beginning in Massachusetts, where he was born, then his prep days at Phillips Academy, Andover, and college at Harvard, where he graduated. He taught at the first school in Fort Snelling, Minnesota, and in Prairie du Chien, Wisconsin, he fell in love with a young Indian woman who bore him a son. He then went on to Davenport, Iowa; New Salem, Illinois; St. Louis and Independence, Missouri, where he was a general merchant; Santa Fe, New Mexico; and finally a rancho in the shadows of Mount Diablo.

Marsh not only had tremendous impact on this region of California, but also left footprints in the history of our nation from the Atlantic to the Pacific. He was one of the greatest of our early pioneers and one of the few wilderness wanderers who could boast of an alma mater. He was witness to the treaty that terminated the Black Hawk War and transferred an immense tract of land from the hands of the Indians to those of the white man. He was instrumental in starting the prairie schooners rolling across the continent, and in freeing California from the last of her Mexican governors. Marsh was a key player in paving the way for California's acquisition by the United States.

John Marsh arrived in California in 1836 and presented his Harvard diploma to the governor, who in turn gave him a license to practice medicine. The diploma was written in Latin, and the governor, presumably unable to read Latin, accepted Marsh's word that it was a medical degree. Although Marsh had not graduated from Harvard as a doctor, he was not a complete hypocrite, having received some medical training at Harvard and more at Fort Snelling. His medical experience met a dire need in a land where doctors were rare.

Doctor Marsh practiced medicine in the Los Angeles area for nearly a year. He saved his money, then headed north hoping to buy a ranch, which at the time was very difficult for a non-Californian to do. Marsh, not only a foreigner, but also a non-Catholic, found it necessary to be baptized a Catholic before he could purchase any land. In December 1837, after being baptized, he purchased the beautiful Rancho Los Meganos from José Noriega for five hundred dollars. The rancho extended from Mount Diablo to the San Joaquin River and consisted of 17,000 acres.

John and Abby Marsh with Daughter, Alice

Marsh continued his medical practice after moving north. Being the only doctor in the area, he found that his services were in great demand. His fee system was very simple. He charged patients one cow for every mile traveled to care for them. Cowhides were selling for two dollars each, and though his fees were exorbitant he had no shortage of patients, and soon one of the largest cattle herds in California. This enabled him to erect his own little empire beneath the grassy slopes of Mount Diablo.

It is said that he was uncivil and discourteous to his Spanish neighbors, but kind and helpful to local Indians, teaching them gardening and simple crafts, and giving them medical care without charge. In return for his kindness, the natives built Marsh an adobe house, a crude, dirt-floored four-room structure on the banks of Marsh Creek, across from their village. With help from the natives, Marsh planted a vineyard and an orchard and sowed a field of wheat.

With an eye on the future, Marsh solicited immigration to California from the East. Longing to see California become part of the United States, he wrote glowingly of its attributes and attractions to friends in the East. The letters were widely published in newspapers and encouraged other early pioneers to cross the Sierra Nevada into the San Joaquin Valley.

The first immigrant wagon train, Bidwell-Bartleson, arrived at the Marsh rancho in 1841, and the settling of California as we know it today began. Marsh welcomed the immigrants effusively, fed them tortillas made from his precious seed wheat, and told them to help themselves to a cow for breakfast. In the first of a series of incidents between Marsh and Bidwell, the immigrants mistakenly barbecued Marsh's prize ox, and the infuriated Marsh thought Bidwell was responsible for the misdeed. He requested that the pioneers leave the premises immediately.

By the 1840's Marsh had developed a large agricultural enterprise, supplying San Francisco, Stockton and nearby mining towns with beef, grain, grapes and other produce. When gold was first discovered, Marsh went into the Sierra and returned with $40,000 in gold from selling cattle for thirty to forty dollars a head, chickens for three or four dollars each, eggs for four dollars a dozen and grapes for 86 cents a pound. However, he decided more money could be realized by supplying miners with other necessary supplies, so he constructed a wharf at the river's edge and shipped goods to the miners at a great profit.

In 1851 Marsh met and married Abigail Smith Tuck, a frail, deeply religious schoolteacher from Massachusetts who had come to California to recover her health in the warm, dry climate. They first lived in the adobe where Marsh had resided for more than ten years, but Marsh decided to build his bride a magnificent home of the finest stone available, a home that would be the showplace of California.

While the stone house was under construction, a daughter, Alice, was born. Abby never recovered from childbirth; the heat of the valley took its toll, and Abby died before the house was completed.

In September of 1856, three neighboring ranch hands murdered Doctor John Marsh over a pay dispute. He was originally buried on his ranch near the stone house, but in 1873 his body was moved to Mountain View Cemetery in Oakland where he was laid to rest near his wife.

In researching the history of Marsh it is interesting to note that he is remembered either as an unkind, miserable hermit or the extreme opposite. John Bidwell, a fellow pioneer, called him "the meanest man in California." Historian Walton Ben Bean described Marsh as a "morose, greedy, and indeed miserly man." But historian George D. Lyman refers to Marsh as "one of our greatest early adventurers" and "a hero neglected by historians." Which was he, a villain or a hero? In reality he was probably a little of both. He was human. Until Next Time....

DOCTOR JOHN MARSH MURDERED 1856

While doing some research at the Martinez Museum, I found a report about "Crimes and Punishment in Contra Costa County 1850-1900" written by Peter Selo in the early 1960s. Selo's report gave a detailed portrayal of this county's early judicial system and offered a glimpse into life on the other side of yesterday. Among the crimes he wrote about was a revealing report of the murder of Doctor John Marsh in 1856.

Marsh was the first white man to settle in Contra Costa County when he purchased the Los Meganos Rancho in 1837. He is remembered as a colorful and enigmatic pioneer of this region of California and definitely a key-player in the early development of East Contra Costa County.

John Marsh's home was located only a few miles from present day Brentwood. His rancho was noted for one of the largest cattle herds in Northern California. Dr. Marsh would often hire outside laborers to work around the rancho, and in September 1856, hired five Mexicans to cut some wood. When it came time to pay them an argument arose over their wages. Marsh paid two of the workers $3 each but refused to pay the other three. The three distressed laborers left Marsh's rancho together riding toward Robert Livermore's Ranch a few miles away.

The following day Dr. Marsh started out in his buggy bound for Martinez where he planned to board a schooner to San Francisco for the purpose of selling one hundred head of cattle. Marsh was known to make regular business trips to the city taking a carpetbag containing clothes, paperwork, and personal effects. According to Charles Marsh, the doctor's son, his father's bag that day contained $45 in gold coins, several two dollar gold pieces, and a silver Mexican coin valued at four or five dollars.

Around dusk, just outside of Martinez, Dr. Marsh was confronted by Jose Antonio Olivas, one of the three unpaid laborers he had dealt with the day before. Olivas asked Marsh for the wages that he felt were due him. The doctor told Olivas that upon his return from the city he would pay him as he didn't have any funds with him to settle up now. Olivas rode off and Marsh continued on his way.

A few minutes later, Olivas was joined by his two companions, Felipe Moreno and Juan Garcia. The three young men were enraged by the treatment they had received from Marsh and discussed killing the good doctor, but decided to only rob him. With tempers flaring they immediately took off in pursuit of Doctor Marsh and upon overtaking him Olivas, at the command of Moreno, stopped the doctor's horse while Garcia stood alongside and Moreno jumped into the buggy.

The doctor, surprised by what was happening, asked his assailants if they intended to kill him. Olivas told Marsh that they merely wanted to be paid, but Moreno shouted they would only be satisfied with his death. He slashed the doctor's face with his knife and dragged him out of his buggy.

Olivas later claimed to have endeavored to help the doctor, but Marsh, fearing another wound, struck him and a confrontation ensued. Dr. Marsh was a strong man and was getting the better of the fight when Olivas called to Moreno for help. Moreno stabbed the doctor in the left side and Marsh fell to the ground. The doctor attempted to rise but yielded to the mortal wound and fell into a ditch along side the roadway, dead.

Garcia and Moreno rifled the doctor's pockets and ransacked the buggy to be certain nothing had been overlooked. Before leaving the scene, Moreno slashed Dr. Marsh's throat to be sure he was dead. The three men proceeded to split what they had taken, mounted their horses, and road off disappearing into the night. Moreno ended up with Doctor Marsh's watch and Olivas took the carpetbag.

The day after the murder George Williams found Dr. Marsh's buggy and took it to Robert Borden's stable in Martinez. Williams and Borden set out in search of Dr. Marsh. Finding his body in the roadside ditch they reported it to the Sheriff.

Meanwhile, Olivas had stopped at the home of Edward LeGrange. LeGrange was alerted when he saw Marsh's carpetbag in the possession of Olivas and took him to the Sheriff in Walnut Creek. The county instantly held a Coroner's Inquest, presided over by R.A. Madison, Justice of the Peace of the First District. At the time, a Justice of the Court presided as the County did not have a Coroner. The inquest determined that, indeed, Dr. John Marsh had been murdered. Jose Antonio Olivas, unwilling to shoulder the full responsibility of the crime, implicated Felipe Moreno and Juan Garcia.

At Olivas' confession, he informed the Sheriff that he thought the other two men may have gone to the ranch of Ignacio Sibrian. They had both been employed by Sibrian. The Sheriff and a companion, John Smith, rode to the Sibrian ranch only to discover that the two men had indeed been there but left the prior day. Although the murderers were not caught at the time, further evidence was obtained from some of Sibrian's cowboys who stated that both men had boasted about what they had done to Dr. Marsh. A manhunt to find Moreno and Garcia was begun.

John Marsh Home built 1856

Jose Antonio Olivas was tried on December 19, 1856 in the Seventh District Court (Solano County) and acquitted of the crime. Felipo Moreno changed his name to Don Castro and settled in Sacramento where he was captured ten years after the crime. He was returned to Contra Costa County to stand trial. On November 20, 1866 Moreno was arraigned (Moreno couldn't speak English so F.H. Mathews acted as an interpreter) and entered a plea of not guilty. Because of a crowded court schedule and a number of postponements Moreno's trial did not begin until almost a year later.

On November 22, 1867 the trial of Felipo Moreno began. Records indicate that public feelings against Moreno must have been very keen because Judge Dwinell, acting on the motion of the defendant's attorney, M.S. Chase, excluded all spectators from the court room. From a potential panel of 40 jurors it took attorney's three days to pick a jury of twelve men. On the afternoon of November 28, 1867, the third day of the trial, the jury finally returned its verdict; guilty of murder in the second degree. Moreno received a sentence of life in the State Prison after a motion for a new trial was denied. Juan Garcia, the third man involved in Marsh's murder, was never found.

Dr. John Marsh was originally buried at his rancho, but in 1873 his body was exhumed and moved to the Mountain View Cemetery in Oakland where he was laid to rest near his wife.

Today there is a historical landmark where Dr. John Marsh was murdered. It may be seen near the railroad overpass as you are going toward Martinez on Pacheco Blvd. Until Next Time....

BIDWELL-BARTLESON PARTY

THE FIRST EMIGRANT TRAIN TO CALIFORNIA

The Bidwell-Bartleson party made the first planned overland emigration west to California in 1841, arriving at John Marsh's rancho (near Brentwood) on November 3. A sturdy company of men and women including a Methodist minister and a group of Jesuit missionaries and their mountaineer guide left Westport, Missouri, on May 18, 1841. Their journey offered them an endless list of trials and tribulations. They encountered a tornado and hailstorms, Indians, stampeding buffalo and difficult river crossings.

John Marsh, the first native-born American to live permanently in Contra Costa County, settled in the shadow of Mount Diablo in 1837 on a 17,000-acre rancho he had purchased. Shortly after establishing himself in California he started writing letters to friends in the East, praising the rich soil, fine climate and vast land that the West had to offer. His description of California made it seem like a paradise, and his letters were published in the newspapers in Independence. John Marsh has been credited with providing the inspiration that set the great emigration movement to the West in motion.

The Bidwell-Bartleson wagon train traveled under the guidance of Thomas "Broken Hand" Fitzpatrick, an experienced mountain man. The journey's first days along the Platt River, through South Pass and on to Soda Springs in Utah, were untroubled. Upon reaching Soda Springs, the turning point to the Willamette Valley or California, half of the original party and the guide took the Fort Hall Road toward Oregon; some turned back to Missouri; and the remaining 32 continued toward California. Bidwell and his companions headed west with no guide, no compass and nothing but the sun to direct them. They had learned from John Marsh's letters the latitude of San Francisco Bay, and they thought the sun was sufficient to guide them there.

The westbound troop experienced hostile Indians, shortages of supplies, disagreements within the company and encounters with the wildlife that provided suspense, terror and adventure for every mile of the journey. By the time they were confronted by the Sierra Nevada, they were travel-weary; horses and oxen were on their last legs and tempers were short. After almost six months on the trail they found themselves in the San Joaquin Valley.

When the wagon train arrived at Marsh's rancho they were welcomed by John Marsh, fed tortillas made from Marsh's precious seed wheat, and told to help themselves to a cow for breakfast. By mistake the immigrants barbecued Marsh's prize ox, causing Marsh to become furious. He immediately became uncivil, especially toward Bidwell, who he thought was responsible for the misdeed. Marsh charged them for the food and services he had so generously offered and demanded they leave the premises immediately.

Many of the Bidwell-Bartleson party pioneers definitely left footprints in California's early history. John Bidwell was the founder of Chico and ran on the Prohibitionist ticket for president in 1892; Charles Weber was the founder of Stockton; Josiah Belden was the first U.S. mayor of San Jose; Benjamin Kelsey became a farmer in the Clear Lake region; and Robert Thomas founded the Tehama Ranch in what is now known as Tehama County.

John Bidwell was 21 years old when he started his trek west. He had left his home in Ohio a year earlier with $75, the clothes on his back and a pocket knife. He had heard talk of bountiful California, and in the winter of 1840 joined a California Emigrant Society.

John Bartleson returned to Missouri in 1842. He died there in 1848. Bartleson was the elected captain of the wagon train. The choice was under duress: he threatened to pull out with his contingent if not elected party commander.

Nancy Kelsey, age eighteen, traveled with her husband, Benjamin, and one-year-old daughter, Ann. The Kelseys left their home in Kentucky to seek their fortune in the new frontier. Nancy and Ann became the first American mother and child to reach California via the Oregon Trail. It was considered almost rash for a woman to venture on so perilous a journey, but Nancy said, "Where my husband goes, I can go. I can better endure the hardships of the journey than the anxieties for an absent husband."

Talbot H. Green was the assumed name of Paul Geddes. Green was a bank embezzler and carried a brick disguised as lead that was actually the missing gold bullion from his bank. History remembers him as charming and intelligent, and a most agreeable trail companion. Green Street in San Francisco was named for him.

Nicholas Dawson, a schoolteacher from Ohio, left home at the age of nineteen. One night while on the journey west, Dawson wandered from camp and was captured by Cheyennes, who took his mule and his clothes. They left him to find his way back to the wagon train in his underwear. He was known as "Cheyenne Dawson" forever after.

Joseph Chiles had been a farmer in Missouri before heading west at the age of 31. Between 1841 and 1855 Chiles made seven journeys across the continent, often acting as a scout for other emigrants and cutting new trails to California.

Charles M. Weber was born in Germany in 1814 and immigrated to America in 1836, joining the Bidwell-Bartleson Party in 1841. He worked for John Sutter when he first arrived in California. Weber is credited with planting the first garden in California, an interest that became a lifelong passion. He received a patent for 48,747 acres, and founded and named the present town of Stockton in 1846.

The pioneers that came west with the Bidwell-Bartleson Party and those that were to follow them were primarily men that wanted to mold their own destiny. The journey west tested the courage and determination of all who came. Until Next Time….

PIONEERS TRAVEL TO CALIFORNIA

America is a country founded on a love of independence. During the 1800s the greatest opportunites and freedom were to be found in the vast lands of California. Farmers, hunters, miners, artists, adventurers, missionaries, and shopkeepers all ventured west in search of a new life. Some hoped to strike it rich in the gold fields, while others simply wanted to plant their roots in the fertile soil of California. They all helped carve a new state out of the wilderness, and many settled in East Contra Costa.

In 1862 the Homestead Act was established, and the government offered to deed 160 acres of land (a quarter of a square mile) free of charge to any adult male that settled certain land, improved it, and lived on it for at least five years. The Homestead Act, though often abused for speculative purposes, helped make the family farm an American institution. Many of the early settlers to East Contra Costa homesteaded.

The long journey to California tested a pioneers courage, endurance and determination. As I research the history of East Contra Costa, it has been interesting to note the various modes of travel chosen by the pioneers who settled this region of California.

CAPE HORN:

Most early settlers from the East tried to reach California by sea. There were several ways to get to the West via the ocean. One was to sail on a clipper for the six-month, 15,000-mile voyage around Cape Horn to San Francisco. With the discovery of gold in California, the rush west began and all available ships (many just leaky tubs) were pressed into service carrying eager prospectors to the West Coast, where they would travel inland to the gold fields.

The Cape Horn route was originally thought the safest and most comfortable way to travel. However, as demand for passage increased, so did prices, while accommodations grew crowded and uncomfortable. In their haste to reach California, groups of easterners often pooled their funds to charter a ship, often an aged, unseaworthy wreck whose condition was concealed by a fresh coat of paint. Such vessels were no match for the brutal winds and heavy seas around Cape Horn, and many perished in the swirling waters off Tierra del Fuego.

Some of East Contra Costa's pioneers that traveled via Cape Horn were: Robert G. Dean, wheat farmer and the first president of Bank of Brentwood, 1850; Henry Wilkening, the first resident and post master of Byron, 1854; Robert Cakebread, farmer in the Marsh Creek area, 1857; and Christopher Heidorn, pioneer merchant and farmer, 1868.

ISTHMUS OF PANAMA:

Settlers could also sail through the Isthmus of Panama, portage overland to the Pacific, and board another vessel for the northward journey. If everything went without a hitch, the Panama route was by far the fastest; ticket agents promised arrival in California in six weeks, but few of those traveling via Panama made it in anything close to that time, and many never made it at all. During the jungle trip across the Isthmus and the long wait in Panama City for a ship's passage, malaria, yellow fever, or cholera often struck pioneers.

Pioneers that settled in the Brentwood or Byron area having arrived via the Isthmus of Panama: George Shafer, farmer and blacksmith, 1851; Thomas Murphy, farmer Round Valley, 1856; Richard Veale, farmer Eden Plain, 1857; Colburn Preston, farmer Point of Timber, 1864; and Louis Grunauer, one of the first businessmen in Brentwood, 1868.

OVERLAND TRAILS:

Those early settlers who were unable to afford passage on a ship or who preferred solid ground underfoot had a choice of several overland trails. Most popular was the Oregon Trail, which was nothing more than a pair of ruts cut into the earth by the thousands of wagons moving west. My great grandfather, Simon Taylor Barkley, chose this route when he traveled west in the 1860's.

The Oregon Trail entailed 2,400 miles across prairies, the enormous desert beyond, the treacherous Rocky Mountains, more desert, then, and on through the Sierra Nevada, attempting to arrive in California before winter storms made the mountains impassable. Pioneers found a full measure of hardship along the way---starvation, disease, thirst, and Indian harassment.

Jacob & Henriette Grueninger
Early Settlers of the Vasco Region

Most early settlers of the area came on overland trails. Some local pioneers that traveled to California overland were: Jeremiah Morgan, grain farmer, Morgan Territory, 1849; John S. Netherton, farmer, 1850; Joseph Carey, the first blacksmith in Brentwood, 1853; Thomas McCabe, wheat farmer at Point of Timber, 1853; George Cople, farmer at Point of Timber, 1854; and John Richard Byer, farmer, Brentwood area 1863.

By the 1870s many of the families moving west traveled on the railroad. In 1869 the transcontinental railroad was completed, uniting the East and West with two bands of steel, reducing the five or six month overland trip by wagon train was reduced to eight days by rail.

It is the pioneer families, the ordinary people---men, women, and children--- who established permanent homes and farmed the land that are real heroes of the great western adventure. They proved that with courage and hard work anything is possible. East Contra Costa history is filled with endless stories of ordinary people that lived extraordinary lives. Until Next Time....

WAGONS TO CONTRA COSTA COUNTY

Many early settlers of Contra Costa County came West by way of wagon train. These first emigrants from the East found unsettled wilderness and underwent unbelievable hardships traveling to California. Most pioneers were not well-to-do; they were men of ordinary means, with perhaps a wife and four or five children.

Most decisions and preparations were made before actually heading westward. Selecting a wagon and draft animals, deciding what supplies were needed for the journey, and most important, choosing which route to travel, often took months of preparation. There were several routes to California, the two most commonly traveled during the 1850's and 1860's were the Oregon Trail and the Santa Fe Trail.

The average wagon was usually constructed of hardwood such as maple, hickory or oak measuring ten by four feet and could carry loads of as much as 2,500 pounds. It was necessary for the wagon to be strong enough to carry the pioneers and their belongings across more than two thousand miles of jolting wilderness. Since wagons traveled only about two miles an hour, the trip took months to complete. Emigrants stocked their wagons high with food, clothes, and a few family treasures. The wagons were fitted with canvas covers stretched over wooden frames to protect their cargo, and provide a reasonably snug shelter against prairie storms. From a distance these slow moving vehicles with white canvas topping looked like ships on the plains, which is how they acquired the nickname of "prairie schooners." Linseed oil was used to waterproof the canvas, pockets and slings were sewn into the inner surface of the fabric for extra storage, and a plow, hoe and other farm tools often tied to the outside of the wagon.

Selecting the best draft animals to pull the wagon was an issue of concern. Horses were expensive, so most were reserved for saddle riding. The real choice was between oxen or mules, and a good case could be made for or against either. Most pioneer families that I've researched chose oxen because they could pull heavier loads, they would eat anything, they didn't run away at night, they were cheaper than mules ($50 apiece against $90 for a mule), and they were less often stolen by Indians.

The pioneers faced great miseries on the trail. The weather was too dry or too wet, too cold or too hot. When the sun burned down upon them there were great clouds of dust. When it rained they were drenched and then slept in the mud on the wet ground beneath the wagon. Storms could break with awesome speed, creating lighting that could kill men and animals.

During the trip people had little privacy and no sanitary facilities. The journey was especially hard for women because they were expected to cook, wash, mend clothes and the wagon canvas, take care of the children, and doctor the family. Women and children also spent part of the day walking in choking dust behind the wagons, picking up dried buffalo droppings to use in place of wood for fuel. Men repaired harnesses and wagons, cared for the animals, planned the route with the wagon train captain, hunted game and stood guard at night.

The hardships did not end when the pioneers reached their goal. Because of the length of the overland trip, most early settlers reached California in the fall. Despite their exhaustion, they had to build a shelter and start clearing fields.

Gradually, settlements grew into villages, then into towns. Areas like Point of Timber, Eden Plain, Morgan Territory, Briones Valley, Deer Valley and the Vasco have all but been forgotten. Only a few old-timers and an occasional history buff are left in East Contra Costa to reflect on the amazing families that struggled to settle this region of California.

A few of the East Contra Costa pioneer families that traveled to California via wagon train:

Joseph W. Carey: Carey is credited with being one of Brentwood's first residents and businessmen, and postmaster in 1889. He and his younger brother, Levy Carey, crossed the plains in a wagon drawn by oxen in 1853. The Carey brothers mined for several years before settling in the East Contra Costa area in 1862.

William Hammond: Hammond was a scout for Kit Carson and had made four trips across the plains before joining a wagon train in 1860, and moving his family to California. William was the father of James Hammond, a well-known doctor in the Byron area for many years, and of Harry Hammond, the distinguished editor and owner of the *Byron Times* newspaper.

Ferdinand Hoffman: Hoffman was a native of Prussia, immigrating to New York in 1847. In 1850, he and his brother, Christian, joined a wagon train, arriving in California six months later. They were among the first settlers of the Byron and the Knightsen areas and two of the first to plant wheat in this region of California. Hoffman Lane is named for this pioneer family.

Jeremiah Morgan: Morgan was born in the Cherokee Nation, on the banks of the Tennessee River, Alabama. In March 1849, he and six companions outfitted a wagon with an oxen team and crossed the trackless plains, rugged mountains, and waterless deserts to California. He mined for gold for several years before returning to the East to bring his family west. In 1853, he again undertook the overland journey to the Golden State. In 1856, while hunting for bear on Mount Diablo, Morgan discovered the tract of land which today is know as Morgan Territory (off Marsh Creek Road), and claimed and fenced ten thousand acres.

Alonzo Plumley: Alonzo and Julia Plumley were newlyweds in 1853 when they left their families in Illinois and traveled for more than five months via prairie schooner to Contra Costa County. Like many of their neighbors they planted their roots deep in the rich soil of this region of California and engaged in general farming and stock raising. The Plumleys had twelve children and did much to aid in the early expansion of this area.

Lazarus Barkley, my great grandfather, Simon Barkley's older brother, made the overland journey from Iowa to California in 1853, first working in the gold fields, and later settling in Eden Plain, where he grew wheat for many years. I have a copy of a daily journal Lazarus kept during his trek across the plains, mountains, and deserts to Contra Costa that reveals many of the hardships the early pioneers experienced during their quest to reach California.

Matthew Sullenger: My great-great-grandfather, Matthew Sullenger, was born in North Carolina and traveled to California with his brother, John, in 1852. The Sullengers crossed the plains via the Oregon Trail in a covered wagon. They first went to the mines in search of gold and both later became farmers in the Deer Valley area.

Immigrants that chose not to travel overland to California could take passage on a sailing ship from New York or Boston for a six-month, 13,000-mile sea voyage around Cape Horn. Pressed for time, the voyager could also save three months—and risk yellow fever—by taking the short cut across the isthmus of Panama.

The early settlers underwent incredible hardships to travel to California. Those that survived the journey west and managed to establish themselves in this new land definitely left footprints in the chapters of our past. Until Next Time….

POINT OF TIMBER

Long before the towns of Byron and Brentwood were established in 1878, Point of Timber and Point of Timber Landing were the main trading and shipping centers of East Contra Costa.

Point of Timber was a busy little hamlet located where Bay Cities Building Supply is today, one-half mile east of Union Cemetery on Highway 4. Its name was derived from a peculiar belt of timber covering this section of land that grew in a large v-shape. As early as the 1850's the main road from the San Joaquin Valley to Antioch followed the shore of the marsh lands through East Contra Costa and past Point of Timber. Wild cattle roamed free throughout this region before early settlers arrived.

There was a post office established at Point of Timber in 1869 and the community offered Wolfe, Kahn & Co. general store, a blacksmith shop, cobbler, lumber yard, Methodist Episcopal church, stage stop and several other businesses. The area's first school, referred to in early history books as "Pioneer School" was located at Point of Timber as early as 1864 and later became the Excelsior School.

The Point of Timber Grange #14, Patrons of Husbandry organized in 1873 as an outgrowth of the Farmers Protection Club. Grange Hall was one of the main buildings in the Point of Timber region and was an all-purpose building utilized as a church, lodge, and dance hall. The hall was built in 1877 on a site donated by Silvester Wills at the corner of Marsh Creek Road and Byron Highway.

Thomas McCabe harvester in the Point of Timber Region - 1890's

Grains, the staff of life, were raised in the section and by the mid-1860's wheat, oats, and barley flourished from season to season. Jabe Wilson is credited with sowing the first grain in the district in 1862.

Farmers depended on natural rainfall to nurture their crops until 1914, when the Byron-Bethany Irrigation project was founded. Early settlers raising these heavy crops in the fertile soil of East Contra Costa were faced with a challenge, physically and financially, getting their harvest to market.

The Delta was a slow moving, freshwater swamp, a natural tidal marsh over deep peat bog. From late fall until spring, water covered a great portion of this region and rigs were frequently seen stuck in three or four feet of water. There are now over 1,100 miles of man-made levees holding back the waters of the Sacramento and San Joaquin Rivers.

Originally Point of Timber Landing was built by local farmers for shipment of cattle and grain to market. Other landings were also built all along the riverbanks and shipping became big business, with the river as the road transporting crops to market.

Prior to the building of Point of Timber Landing in the early 1860's, settlers used Babbe's Landing, which was in the Knightsen area where Burrough's Dairy is located today. In 1881 a tule fire destroyed Point of Timber Landing. Local farmers banded together and built a new facility in 1884. They built a ¾ mile canal, 36 feet wide and 4 ½ feet deep, through the tules from Indian Sough to the new site. At high tide the canal furnished over 6 feet of water and at low tide 2 feet. The company hired Chinese laborers to dig the peat land, removing soil with wheelbarrows to create a canal that would allow schooners to land on high ground. This landing was located about two and a half miles east of Union Cemetery. Later, barges took the place of schooners.

In my historic research, I have been fortunate in falling heir to many old papers and documents about Byron and the outlying areas of days gone by. Among these papers I found a biography written by Virginia Boltzen in 1940. Virginia was the daughter of Captain C. W. Lent, the first man to run a passenger boat from Point of Timber to Stockton.

Lent's boat opened the opportunity for locals to do their shopping in Stockton and return the same day. Captain Lent made the Stockton trip every Saturday and would carry 15 to 25 passengers at a time. The trip took an average of three hours and was a great accommodation in those days.

Point of Timber is all but forgotten today. It is hard to imagine a time when this busy little community was the heart of East Contra Costa. Until Next Time….

EARLY STAGE LINES

The stagecoach was designed to carry passengers over rough and rugged terrain. The stage-line era in California began in 1849 and was replaced with the railroad between 1869 and 1880.

The first settlers of East Contra Costa County were isolated. Long before Brentwood or Byron were founded, Point of Timber was the center of activity in this region of California. Caswell and Durwood Wright ran a stage line from Banta to Antioch in the early 1870's. The coach ran twice a week, stopping at Point of Timber to pick up fresh horses.

I remember my grandmother Cassie Armstrong telling me great stories about my great-great-grandmother Mary Ann Armstrong traveling to San Francisco to visit family in the early 1870's. The Armstrongs had settled in the Byron foothills, where the Byron airport is located today. On the days Mary Ann traveled she would rise at 4:30 a.m., hook up the spring wagon and make her way over dusty, rutted roads more than three miles to Point of Timber, where she would board a stage bound for Antioch. In Antioch she would embark on a schooner to Martinez, then travel by train to Berkeley, where she would connect with a ferry that delivered her to the waterfront of San Francisco after sundown. The railroad arrived in East County in 1878, making travel much easier.

By 1865 there were a hundred or more local stage lines operating within California, and three transcontinental mail stages transporting mail and passengers from the east.

Have you ever thought about what traveling by stage would be like? The big screen and television have led us to believe that passengers arrived at their destinations squeaky-clean and rested. The reality is that roads were bumpy and dusty. It was not uncommon for a roadway to be blocked by a fallen tree; a creek bed to be impassable; a stage to get stuck in the mud; or a coach wheel to need repair between stations. Passengers were often asked to assist.

Passengers were given a list of basic rules to follow if they were going to ride the stage.

Basic rules for stage passengers:
1. The premium seat on the stage is the forward one, next to the driver. If you have a tendency toward stage sickness when riding backwards, you'll get over it quicker in this seat and receive less jolts and jostling.
2. If the stage team runs away or you're pursued by highwaymen, stay in the coach and take your chances. Don't jump out, for you could get injured.
3. In cold weather refrain from drinking spirits, for you are subject to freezing if you're under the influence.
4. If you are drinking from a bottle, pass it around. It is the only polite thing to do.
5. Don't smoke a strong cigar or pipe on the stage, especially when women or children are present. If chewing tobacco, spit to leeward side.
6. Don't swear or smoke or flop on other passengers when sleeping. Let other passengers share the coach robes provided for cold weather.
7. Don't shoot firearms for pleasure while en route, as it scares the horses.
8. Don't discuss politics or religion. Don't point out sites where robberies or Indian attacks took place.
9. While at stations don't lag at washbasins or privies. Don't grease hair with oil or tallow, as travel is very dusty.
10. Don't imagine you are going on a picnic, for stage travel is inconvenient. Expect annoyances, discomfort and hardships. Tolerate them with fortitude!

With the ease of travel we experience today it is hard to imagine the difficult conditions the early settlers contended with on the other side of yesterday. Until Next Time....

HISTORY OF THE GRANGE

In 1867, farmers nationwide developed an organization called the Patrons of Husbandry, or the Grange. The Grange was originally planned to help early farm families cope with the loneliness of farm life. Many early settlers felt a lack of community and missed the sociability of village life. People in areas like Point of Timber, a stopping-off point between Antioch and Banta located between today's Brentwood and Byron (approximately where Bay Cities Building Materials is located on Highway 4) found themselves very isolated from the outside world. There were few opportunities to see people other than their own families, although most would occasionally travel by wagon or buggy to Antioch.

The Grange was founded by a clerk in the U.S. Department of Agriculture, Oliver Kelley, who had been raised in Minnesota and knew well the hardships of farm life. Kelley wanted to establish a national organization with a chapter in every farm community to meet the recreational, cultural and social needs of its membership, as well as create an opportunity for farmers to exchange ideas about better ways of farming. By 1872, there were Granges in fourteen states and a national membership of over 800,000.

The Point of Timber Grange #14 was organized May 21, 1873, as an outgrowth of the Point of Timber Farmers Protective Club, which had been established a few years earlier. The first officers were: R. G. Dean, Master; M. A. Walton, Overseer; J. H. Baldwin, Lecturer; J. B. Henderson, Steward; A. Richardson, Assistant Steward; A. Plumley, Chaplain; Thomas McCabe, Treasurer; Joseph W. Carey, Secretary; and C. M. Carey, Gatekeeper. The Grange, Good Templar Lodge, Methodist Church, and Terpsichore all met in the small Pioneer Schoolhouse at Point of Timber for many years.

Reaping the Crop

Members of the organization built a handsome, commodious hall on the corner of Marsh Creek Road and Byron Highway (across from the Excelsior School) in 1877. According to the *Contra Costa Gazette* (August 1877), Silvester Monroe Wills donated one-half acre of land for this hall. Wills had purchased 160 acres of farmland from Joseph Carey, who had homesteaded this parcel in the early 1860's. Grange Hall served as the heart of the Point of Timber region, being utilized for dances, voting, receptions, community meetings, church activities, school functions, and more until the railroad came through and the towns of Byron and Brentwood were established.

Although the Grange was established as a social club, by the early 1870's it had become quite political. Farmers had many complaints and decided they needed to organize and unite in order to hold their own against railroads, bankers and monopolies.

Farmers found that many aspects of their lives were out of their control. They had to deal with the banks to buy their land and on the railroads to get their grain and livestock to market. The railroads also owned most of the grain warehouses and stockyards.

Early farmers fought bugs, floods and dry spells to get their crops ready for market. They spent months planting, harvesting and raising livestock. After struggling to prepare their products for market, they did not want the railroad and bank to take away their hard-earned profits. By banking together in cooperatives, they could sell their products to city markets, thus avoiding the middlemen, and they could purchase machinery and other goods in large quantities at a low wholesale price.

On a local level, the Grange was an active part of most of the early development of East Contra Costa. They participated in addressing water problems; constructing Point of Timber Landing on Indian Slough; purchasing seed at reduced rates; banding together to help elect legislators to represent their views in Sacramento; and generally helping their neighbors.

Contra Costa County had numerous Granges. The communities of Martinez, Danville, Pacheco, Walnut Creek, and Clayton each offered a Grange for their residents. The Martinez Grange, organized in 1875, advertised that they would help their members deal with purchasing all kinds of agricultural implements and general merchandise. They also offered to ship grain and other merchandise to and from foreign and domestic ports as factor and broker; to supply and maintain warehousing and a wharf near Martinez for the storage of grain and other products; and to reserve or transmit and ship products.

Hauling Sugar Beets - 1919

In 1887, the Point of Timber Grange was moved to Brentwood, a growing railroad town six miles from Point of Timber. It was felt that this move would provide a more central location for a larger number of Grange members from all parts of East Contra Costa County.

On February 2, 1932, the original Grange became Diablo Valley Grange, still located in Brentwood. The Diablo Valley organization was very involved with many of the agricultural problems of the time.

Collectively, the county Granges offered farm families a wonderful opportunity to join together and help form the foundation of this region of California. They offered both business and social programs. From the 1920's to the 1960's the Grange offered many scholarships for young people (primarily in agriculture and home economics education), raised money for charities and donated many gifts and materials to people in need.

Nationally, the Granges banded together and helped pass laws to regulate the railroad. Other laws set fair prices for storing and shipping grain. These laws were known as Granger Laws. The Grange was so powerful nationwide that many of its members were elected to political offices. This organization has definitely left footprints in the chapters of America's past. Until Next Time....

CATTLEMEN OF EAST CONTRA COSTA

During the 1770's a few hundred head of longhorn, or Andalusian, cattle originally brought to Mexico as early as 1519 by the Spanish conquerors, were introduced into California and cared for by mission padres. For many years, without a market for beef, hundreds of calves were born into larger and larger herds. Fifty years after their introduction, many cattle had wandered off to become wild, and thousands belonged to mission, presidio, pueblo, and rancho.

California was a great place to raise cattle. Contra Costa County offered miles and miles of good pastureland. Natural springs and cool streams in the foothills of Mount Diablo allowed the cattle to grow fat on wild oats, sweet clover, and alfilaria. Primary predators were coyote and bear; coyotes would often drag off calves, and a bear could kill a grown cow.

Few trading ships brought goods to the area, and early settlers found it necessary to make everything. Cattle played a crucial part in the settlers' lives. As food, cattle offered early Californians meat, milk, cheese, and butter. Beef spoiled quickly in the heat, so much of it was cut into strips and dried. Fresh meat was roasted on a stick over an open fire or in an iron pot on the clay floor inside the rancho. Fat, or tallow, was used for cooking, and provided settlers with their only source of light: tallow oil was used for their lanterns and candles. Fat was also mixed with lye from wood ash to make soap.

Hides were used in many ways: seats of chairs; bed mattresses; doors; window shutters; boots, shoes and saddles; hats and clothing; bridles and reins. At harvest time, grain was stored in large leather bags made from tanned hides.

Doctor John Marsh purchased the beautiful Rancho Los Meganos from José Noriega in 1837, for $500. The rancho extended from Mount Diablo to the San Joaquin River and was four leagues long and three wide. Here and there, Marsh found bands of wild mustangs and herds of untamed, spotted cattle, which had sprung from peacefully grazing stock introduced by the mission fathers. With purchase of the rancho Marsh acquired fine meadows, ranges and water sources for grazing, but he lacked funds to purchase cattle. To obtain stock he began a medical practice. His fees were considered large, as he charged patients one cow for every mile he traveled to care for them. Cowhides were selling for two dollars each and though his fees were exorbitant, there was no shortage of patients. Soon cattle bearing the doctor's brand on ear and rump began to make their appearance on the ranges of Los Meganos, and as the years went by his herds multiplied. By the mid-1850's Marsh owned over six thousand head of cattle. His cattle were exported to mining towns and markets in San Francisco where there was a great demand for beef.

When people from eastern and midwestern states began to settle in California during the late 1840's, there were still great herds of wild cattle. The land was open, unfenced rangeland, where each ranchero marked his cattle with his own brand during an annual roundup.

The Vasco region, near Byron, was definitely affected by the cattle industry. An influx of miners and settlers created a near instant demand for meat, which resulted in a fundamental change in cattle raising. Improved cross-herd stock began to replace the original Spanish longhorns, which had become lank and tough through neglect and freedom of roaming the open range. Early settlers captured many of the wild cattle from the open range of Contra Costa; they then imported Devon, Hereford and Shorthorn cattle to breed out the longhorn variety and produce a larger, more marketable species. The longhorn gradually disappeared and today only a few are left.

The Los Vaqueros area was devoted to cattle raising throughout the 1850's and 1860's, with thousands of head of stock grazing the foothills near Byron. A group of eighty Basques emigrated from Buenos Aires to California in the early 1850's. The Sunol brothers and early Basque settlers were the primary cattlemen in this region. The Basques gave their name to this region of California, which was to be known locally as "the Basco" or "the Vasco." Most of these early settlers had prospered in the Argentine cattle industry and continued in the same enterprise when settling in California. Vasco ranches supplied beef to mining towns during the Gold Rush, but when easily accessible placer deposits of gold were played out, many of the miners realized that farming offered a far more stable source of income, and planted their roots in East Contra Costa. These early farmers raised wheat and barley throughout the Byron area.

For many years, the Vasco operated under a free-range system. When farmers began settling in the same territory, roaming livestock became a threat to vulnerable crops, and by the 1870's, fencing laws were passed with barbed wire introduced to fence rangeland.

Stock raising has remained a principal part of life in the Vasco since the California Rancho days. Louis Peres acquired property held by the Sunol Brothers in 1864. Peres owned a wholesale cattle-butchering business in San Francisco. By 1880, Peres owned 17,752 acres in the Vasco. Landholdings on this scale incurred heavy taxes and he leased parcels to tenant farmers to offset his costs.

Peres' tenants were independent operators; they paid Peres a portion of each year's crop as rent. The main crops were wheat, grain, barley, cattle, hogs and poultry. Some of these early tenants were: Sylvain Bordes, Frank Viala, Johnson Righter, Fred Dickhoff, Louis Cumming, George Easton, and James Andrews. The Vasco reached its maximum population around 1900, with at least seventeen households residing there.

In 1881, Charles McLaughlin acquired Louis Peres' holdings in the Vasco region. McLaughlin was killed in 1883, leaving the property to his wife, Kate. Kate McLaughlin died in 1888, and left the large estate to her two nieces, Kate Dillion and Mary Crocker.

Oscar Starr purchased a 7,883-acre parcel from Mary Crocker in 1935 and Edith Ordway bought the western portion of the Starr Ranch in 1948. Both Starr and Ordway operated one of the finest cattle ranches in Contra Costa County for many years, with a beautiful residence to house foremen and ranch hands, corrals, and many notable improvements.

By the 1950's, Louis B. Souza and Anthony Pimental had the largest cattle ranch in Eastern Contra Costa. They owned the Los Vaqueros Ranch (approximately 7,000 acres), raising over a thousand head of Hereford cattle each year.

The history of cattle in the Byron area is interesting indeed. The early cattlemen of East Contra Costa definitely engraved their indelible brand on the chapters of our past.
Until Next Time....

THE WHEAT BOOM

East Contra Costa has a wonderful agricultural history. The area is well remembered for the tremendous fruits and vegetables grown in this fertile soil for more than a century, but today the area's supremacy in grain production has, for the most part, been forgotten. Yet those serene days when fields were immense with tall waving grain, and large vessels loaded with wheat sailed the oceans were as important economically to California as the Gold Rush.

The Spanish, prior to the arrival of American settlers, grew wheat in California on a small scale; it wasn't until the period from about 1868 to 1884 that grain became the dominant crop grown in this region. Production of grain and hay required minimal initial capital outlay, no irrigation, and relatively little labor. These were important considerations, as settlers would occasionally find their land reclaimed by an earlier claimant.

The Point of Timber, Eden Plain, and Lone Tree areas were well suited for cereal cultivation. The soil was fertile and easy to plow and the long dry summers ensured a hardy, healthy crop. Dr. John Marsh planted the first cereal crop in Contra Costa County in 1837 on his Rancho Los Meganos, and by 1882, the entire region was described as having every inch of arable space waving in fields of grain.

Transportation of wheat to market was a monumental task for the early settlers. Three landings were constructed all, connected by canals: Point of Timber at Indian Slough, owned and controlled by local farmers; Iron House, by Fassett & McCauley (this landing was later abandoned and Babbe's Landing took its place); and Marsh Landing, near Antioch. The San Pablo & Tulare Railroads arrived in 1878, offering stations in Byron, Brentwood, and Antioch. Warehouses were built to accommodate the increasing wheat production.

The wheat industry was booming by the 1870's, primarily because of a profitable trade relationship between San Francisco and Liverpool, England. Buyers in England were willing to wait for California wheat to make its long journey because of its exceptional quality. From the late sixties to the turn of the century, two-thirds of the wheat grown in California was shipped to Great Britain. In 1873 alone, $20 million worth of wheat left San Francisco for foreign ports.

Early settlers were faced with many hardships to overcome, especially those provided by Mother Nature. The Great Flood of 1862 recorded 49 inches of rainfall that wrought extreme damage to the fields. During the years 1863 to 1865, a severe drought killed the farmers' crops. In 1867, 1889, and 1895, floods washed away railroad tracks, roads, and crops. During drought years, it was not uncommon for grass fires to sweep over the landscape, destroying everything in their paths.

During the earlier stages of the wheat industry, farmers were not only handicapped by the weather, but by their lack of credit; city banks were reluctant to loan farmers the capital for their crops. Ultimately the Grange was formed, and farmers established their own bank, with the organization's specific object being to buy and sell directly, eliminating the middleman.

In 1889, 46,000 acres of wheat, the golden cereal, waved in the breeze on the slopes of Mount Diablo and in the valleys of Contra Costa County.

Barley was also a profitable crop, requiring the same conditions as wheat but being less susceptible to damaging infestations. Barley could reseed itself for a second or third crop.

The first wheat farmers in the area threshed out a wheat field by very primitive methods, using horses to stomp out the grain, yielding more than fifty bushels to the acre. As years passed, farmers invented different forms of machinery to make their jobs easier and realize a larger production from their fields. Those early inventions allowed vast tracts of land to be cultivated profitably. Plows and harrows, as well as great harvesting and threshing machines, were built in local blacksmith shops. In the late summer and fall, men with horses could be seen moving slowly around their great fields, turning over row after row of soil, filling the air with the smell of freshly plowed earth.

Sullenger Crew on Deer Valley

By 1880, Port Costa was the main trading and wheat shipping point in the county. The waterfront was lined with warehouses and wharves, and by 1882, Port Costa was the busiest wheat shipping point in California. Ships from every nation docked along the Carquinez Straits to load wheat. More than one hundred years later, it is hard to imagine the sleepy village of Port Costa in its heyday.

Wheat reigned as king in Contra Costa until the turn of the century, at which time it was almost entirely replaced by the cultivation of fruit and nut orchards.

Many early families that settled and farmed East Contra Costa on the other side of yesterday have grandchildren and great grandchildren still residing here. Pioneer families like Barkley, Sullenger, Taylor, Richardson, McCabe, Geddes, Morgan, Plumley, Carey, Cakebread, Netherton, Heidorn, Dainty, Hoffman, Preston, Sellers, Prewett, Bonnickson, Cople and Fletcher were instrumental in the development of this region of California and have definitely left footprints in the chapters of our past. Until Next Time….

HISTORY OF FARMING IN EAST CONTRA COSTA

The East Contra Costa area has a wonderful history, but few chapters of our past are as interesting as the evolution of farming in this region of California.

Native Americans living throughout the Delta and foothills of the area did not need to plant or plow the land. Mother Nature supplied an abundance of food: acorns, soap root, sweet clover, and seeds were readily available.

Spanish dons were the first to plant in Contra Costa County. Although they did not farm the land, they did plant the first trees and vines around the adobe houses on their ranchos. The Spanish primarily raised cattle and horses, letting them run wild on the open range to feed off wild hay growing along the waterways.

Dr. John Marsh was the first to actually begin farming the land, in 1837. Using Indian labor he planted a large garden, a vineyard, and an orchard of pears, figs and olives near his home on Marsh Creek Road. He taught the Indians how to plow fields and sow wheat and barley.

By the 1850's thousands of pioneers had traveled to California. Many originally came in search of gold, and ended up planting their roots in the rich soil of Contra Costa. Flour, a staple and necessity of the early settlers, prompted the first plantings of wheat. During those early years, when the wheat was harvested it was taken to San Jose and ground into flour. In later years, mills were established in Lafayette, Pacheco, and Martinez.

Harvesting Grain. The Bordes Ranch - 1908

By 1860, wheat became the chief industry for Contra Costa County. The best wheat farms were located at Point of Timber and Eden Plain. Point of Timber was located on Indian Slough near Byron, and the land around Knightsen was referred to as Eden Plain. Thousands of acres of golden grain were sowed around Brentwood, Byron, and the Lone Tree area. In the late summer and fall, men with their horses could be seen moving slowly around the great fields, turning over row after row of earth, filling the air with the smell of freshly plowed fields.

The first farmers in the area planted their seeds in the fall from a horse-drawn wagon, using a hopper to scatter the grain. The seed lay in the ground all winter while the rains softened the hard soil. With the warmth of spring, the wheat sprouted up, and the hot summer sun turned the grains almost as hard as tiny pebbles. The combination of winter sowing and hot summers created wheat which absorbed more moisture during baking, producing heavier loaves of bread than other wheat.

Mother Nature gave early farmers much wealth. She also took it away. The life of a farmer was filled with constant concern. Would there be enough rain, or so much that fields would flood? Would the sun be so hot as to scorch the crop? After the stalks had grown tall, would the wind blow them over? The life of the farmer was always at the whim and call of Mother Nature.

George Washington Carters Threshing Crew - 1898

In May or June when the golden grain was ready to harvest, a team of horses would push a header in front of them around the field of ripe wheat. The header cut the heads of grain that fell into a wagon driven alongside. The wagon then hauled the hay to a thresher, which separated the wheat from straw and poured it into grain sacks. Men standing nearby sewed the sacks shut and stacked the heavy sacks on wagons for transport.

Teams of eight or ten horses would pull the wagons loaded high with grain along the dusty roads to warehouses to be stored before shipping to market. Fish & Blum, 1878; M. Grunauer, 1880; and Balfour, Guthrie & Co., 1896 were among the original warehouse owners.

Farmers found that transporting their product to market was a monumental task; grain farming was a large industry long before railroads existed in East Contra Costa. The rivers, sloughs, and bay were the only avenues of transportation. Boats were loaded with sacks of grain at Point of Timber Landing or Babbe's Landing and taken to big wharves in Port Costa, where the grain was reloaded onto ocean-going steamers, leaving for destinations all over the world. By 1878, California was producing more wheat than any other state in the nation.

Although wheat was the main crop grown by the first settlers of the Brentwood area, it definitely was not the only crop. Many farmers planted fruit trees, grapes, and vegetable gardens around their homes. In fact, they tried almost everything. In 1878, Samuel and Sara Sellers planted three thousand mulberry trees to harvest the silk produced by the silkworms that inhabited the trees.

Many of the early families that settled and farmed this section of California on the other side of yesterday still reside in the area. The children and grandchildren of pioneer families like Cakebread, Sellers, Dainty, Netherton, Taylor, Richardson, Heidorn, McCabe, and Cople still live in East Contra Costa today. These early pioneers were free-spirited, hard-working men and women who shaped the colorful history of California. Each was unique, and each made a valuable contribution.

Until Next Time....

COAL MINING IN EAST CONTRA COSTA

Discovery of coal in the foothills below Mount Diablo can be traced to the 1840's. A coal deposit, located on Dr. John Marsh's rancho near Brentwood, was found a few miles from Marsh's adobe home.

Sitting on the northeast flank of the mountain, the Mount Diablo Coal Field was the site of the largest coal-mining operation ever in California. The "Coal Rush" was on when, in 1855, William Israel was cleaning a spring that supplied stock water and stumbled onto a coal outcrop. Within ten years, five towns and ten mines sprang up within five miles of the strike. Coal was used, in the 1850's, to power paddlewheel steamers, factories and mining machinery.

Noah Norton developed the Black Diamond Mine, discovered by Francis Somers, in 1859. The towns of Nortonville and Somersville soon followed. Miners and their families came from Wales, Ireland, England, Pennsylvania, and the California gold fields. Italian, German and Chinese merchants opened businesses, and soon after, hotels, saloons, mercantiles, and churches as well as schools appeared.

East of Nortonville, in the Carbondale District, three more towns were founded: Stewartville, Judsonville, and West Harley. Together the five communities were referred to as the String of Pearls. From 1859 to 1906, this area boasted approximately ten thousand residents and seven hundred voters (men over the age of 21).

The towns in the Carbondale District were relatively peaceful communities, made up of God-fearing families. There were active Masons, Redmen, Knights of Pythias and the Emmet Irish Society. Families were raised, people died—life was lived.

Miners (men and boys) worked in over 150 miles of tunnels, using kerosene lanterns to light their way. The conditions under which the miners worked were hard and very dangerous. It was not uncommon for methane gas emitted by the coal to explode. Illness caused by continued exposure to coal dust and moisture, rockfalls and machinery-related accidents were accepted as a way of life for those who worked underground.

Although the coal was not of the highest quality, a good market was found in California, with production shipped primarily to San Francisco, Stockton and Sacramento, because the mineral was a primary industrial energy source at that time.

Coal was mined using a method called room-and-pillar mining. A mining team made up of an experienced miner and a young boy (known as a knobber) often as young as eight years of age would start from a level passage and drive an opening upward into the coal seam. By doing this, they would leave pillars of coal standing in place to help prevent a cave-in. The area left after the coal was removed was known as the room. Miners used picks and shovels to extract the coal and the knobber's job was to slide the loose coal into an ore cart waiting to be taken to the surface.

Three railroads were built in 1866, 1867 and 1878, connecting the mines to harbors in Pittsburg and Antioch. Trains relied on the law of gravity for locomotion, and when the tracks were wet from winter rains, workers would spread sand on them to aid brakemen in slowing the trains down. The return trip was accomplished by donkey locomotives, and later by coal-burning engines built especially for the purpose.

Production of coal in the Carbondale District peaked in the late 1870's and early 1880's. The largest mine in Nortonville, the Black Diamond, was closed in 1885 due to the rise in mining costs and a glut of foreign coal on the market. Nortonville became a ghost town overnight with many of the miners moving on to another coal field in Washington state, while others moved out of the hills to communities on the waterfront or areas like Brentwood or Byron.

Miners not financially able to move to other coal fields continued to work their veins and meet the local demand for coal. By 1902 mining costs, competition from high-quality Washington coal and the advent of oil as an industrial power source drove most of these mines out of business. Coal primarily used by local residents for their homes continued to be extracted from several of the smaller mines at late as 1916. As coal mines closed, the String of Pearls became ghost towns. Many of the people who relocated moved their homes with them—some of those houses are still standing in Byron, Brentwood, Antioch and Pittsburg.

The Carbondale District supplied almost four million tons of coal between 1859 and 1906 valued at more than $20 million. Some still believe that more than seven million metric tons of coal remain in the ground.

Brentwood Coal Mine, located on Concord Avenue, where the Brentwood Gun Club is today, was established in 1867 by Charles Marsh (Dr. John Marsh's son) but due to financial difficulties, the mine was closed the following year. In 1872, Jack Williams, a promoter backed by the Sanford family of New York, purchased the mine. Williams planned to establish a producing coal mine; build a railroad to deep-water frontage on the river at Marsh Landing; and supply a shipping port and manufacturing center. A wharf extending to deep water was built, expensive mining equipment was ordered, houses for employees were built, and several expensive engineers were hired. The mine's coal vein was found to be narrow, deep in the ground and of inferior quality. To further compound Williams' problems, water flowed into the mine shafts, rendering it impossible to mine the ore. Williams eventually dropped out of sight, leaving the Sanford family to assume his debts.

The Carbondale District and the Brentwood Coal Mine have both had a huge impact on this region of California. Many of today's residents are descendants of the early pioneer coal miners that settled in this area during the 1800's, leaving their footprints in the chapters of our past.

The Black Diamond Mines are now part of the Regional Recreation Area and may be reached by driving south on Somersville Road from Highway 4 to the first sharp left curve in the road, where you will see some white gates. Enter through the white gates to the Visitor Center.
Until Next Time….

EARLY LAW ENFORCEMENT

Contra Costa County during the 1850's and '60's acted like a magnet, drawing men from every part of the country. In 1852, the total population of the county was only 2800 people residing in an area of over 730 square miles. It was a time when bargains were sealed with a handshake and a man's word was his bond. This region of California was relatively lawless and sparsely populated, and individuals tended to rely on their own resources to deal with the criminal element. The first residents felt obligated to make their own laws and dispense justice on the spot. Only after California became a state with 27 counties established (including Contra Costa) did we see the beginning of a court system in Contra Costa. The county consisted of many hamlets dotting the countryside; communities like Point of Timber, Martinez, Antioch, San Pablo, Pinole, Pacheco, Clayton and Concord were connected by unpaved roads traveled by horse-drawn vehicles.

John M. Watson became Contra Costa's first judge on March 29, 1850. He presided over the Third Judicial District, which included Contra Costa, Santa Clara, Santa Cruz and Monterey Counties. By mid-1850, F. M. Warmcastle was appointed the county judge for Contra Costa, with Absolom Peak and Edward Guest as associate justices.

The first legal execution in Contra Costa County took place on August 2, 1852, when José Antonio, an Indian, was hung for the murder of Aparicio Morales. Antonio stabbed Morales in the village of Pinole on May 29, 1852, and was duly tried before Judge Hester. He met his fate when hung from the limb of a sycamore tree on the outskirts of Martinez. A barrel was placed on an old cart and Antonio was made to stand on it while the rope was adjusted around his neck, after which the cart was driven away.

The second execution took place shortly thereafter when Henry Monroe was hung for murdering James Gordon on October 2, 1854. Monroe and two companions went to the Gordon home, located two miles from Dr. John Marsh's residence in the eastern section of the county, with the intent of robbery. When Gordon approached the three visitors Monroe shot him. Gordon fled into the darkness, making his way to Marsh's home before dying. The men were traced to San Francisco and ultimately arrested. Monroe was found guilty of the murder and hung from a tree in Martinez near the school building.

Manuel Juarez was the third person executed by the county, in 1867, after being convicted of slaying Mrs. Elizabeth Robinson, a 75-year-old resident of Martinez. Mrs. Robinson was brutally murdered: her body was found on the floor in a rear room of her home clothed in a nightgown, her head, face, arms and hands fearfully gashed along with several stabs wounds in the breast and throat. Near the body a piece of candle and a candlestick were found, leading to the belief that Mrs. Robinson, aroused by a noise of someone entering the house, had risen from her bed to investigate. The community was in shock that such a violent crime could take place. When Juarez was arrested, items taken from Mrs. Robinson's home were found in his possession.

The fourth and last recorded legal hanging took place on January 23, 1874, in the main yard at the county jail in Martinez. Charles Martin died for his crime of being an accomplice in the murder of Valentine Eichler, a Marsh Creek farmer.

Valentine Eichler and his wife, Elizabeth, had a small farm in the Marsh Creek district and employed Charles Martin as a hired hand. Martin and his employer's wife were involved in an affair and decided to murder Mr. Eichler. Martin traveled to Antioch and purchased a quantity of arsenic which Elizabeth mixed with some stewed pumpkin and served for supper, but her husband wouldn't eat it. When the original plan went awry Elizabeth persuaded Martin to lace a bottle of whiskey with the poison and offer her husband a drink. This plan didn't work either. Elizabeth finally tired of waiting for her lover to dispose of her husband and decided to take matters into her own hands by hitting him over the head with an axe. She and Martin then dragged her injured husband into a barn, where Elizabeth finished the job. Elizabeth was found insane and sent to the Stockton State Hospital. Martin, who never actually swung the axe, died swinging from a rope in Martinez.

Tales like these instill a new appreciation for our current judicial system. Until Next Time....

RAILROAD HISTORY

The railroad had a tremendous impact on the history and development of Contra Costa County. Southern Pacific's rails first pushed into Contra Costa in 1877. The parent company, Central Pacific, confined its early efforts to carving a way through the high Sierra and across the plains of Utah and Nevada, forming the first transcontinental railroad. On May 10, 1869, in a telegraph office in Sacramento the telegraph was ticking, "The last rail is laid! The Pacific Railroad is complete." This message signaled the end of the frontier, as the early settlers had known it. Without the aid of bulldozers, steam shovels or pneumatic drills the railroad was built from Omaha, Nebraska to Sacramento (1776 miles of track). Chinese using picks, shovels, two wheel dumpcarts, and wheel barrels did much of the work. The transcontinental was known as the homemade railroad using man and animal power.

Californians were amazed by the prospect of crossing the continent in seven or eight days. They had been accustomed to thinking of transcontinental travel in terms of the snails pace of an ox-drawn wagon or the body-bruising eternity of a stagecoach ride. By May 1869, scheduled trains were running on the new line—one westbound from Omaha and one eastbound from Sacramento—every day.

For the rich, and those afforded the leisure to travel and a taste for adventure, the availability of coast-to-coast service made a tour of the West something of a social necessity. Compared with a European vacation, crossing the United States by rail was not only an adventure but also a bargain. A first-class ticket from the Atlantic Coast via connecting rail lines to Omaha, then on to Sacramento, and completing the trip to San Francisco by steamboat, cost $173. Sleeping-car accommodations added two dollars per night to the fare. An additional four dollars per day entitled passengers to accommodations aboard the weekly ultra-luxurious Pacific Hotel Express, which featured meals served in the dining car, thus sparing passengers the necessity of wolfing down food at track-side restaurants.

On January 9, 1878, wood burners pulled into Contra Costa County over a newly constructed rail between West Berkeley and Martinez. This new rail was part of a project to construct a water level railroad from San Francisco to Sacramento and the San Joaquin Valley, eliminating heavy grades encountered on the canyon route.

By the 1880's the railroad had become the nations most important form of transportation. Wherever railroads went small towns grew into prosperous cities and new towns were founded; wherever railroads failed to go communities that had been bypassed lapsed into somnolence and decay. Point of Timber, for example, had been the primary hub of activity in East Contra Costa County prior to the arrival of the railroad, but after it was bypassed by the tracks it declined and eventually disappeared. The railroad encouraged economic growth by reducing transportation costs, making East Contra Costa more accessible, widening markets for local farmers and raising land values.

The towns we see in East Contra Costa today can all trace their origins back to the railroad. Brentwood and Byron were a direct result of the San Pablo & Tulare Railroad arriving in 1878 and Oakley and Knightsen developed because of the Santa Fe in 1898.

Prior to the arrival of the rails stagecoaches could be seen jouncing along the dusty roadways. Freight wagons were used to move grain to landings along the river where it was transported to ships waiting in Port Costa.

The San Pablo & Tulare Railroad was incorporated on July 19, 1871 by Central Pacific interests to circumvent Altamont Pass with a line from Martinez to Banta. They constructed a 46.51 mile line between 1876 and September 1878. For more than a year there were surveyors with transitmen and chainmen staking out the path. When the planning was completed the really challenging task remained, the backbreaking job of actually installing the rails. The San Pablo and Tulare Railroad Company spent several years building the line between Martinez and Banta, with engineering corps and survey crews pitching their tents along the route. Once the exact route was determined, an engineer on horseback rode the entire line, placing a stake in the ground every two hours. The stake represented where a station would be built, on the theory that if a train broke down it would never be more than one hour from the nearest source of assistance. There were numerous stations established between Martinez and Banta — Martinez, Avon, Port Chicago, Nichols, McAvoy, Shell Point, Pittsburg, Los Medanos, Antioch, Jersey, Newlove, Arbor, Brentwood, Byron, Byron Hot Springs, Herdlynn, Bethany, Tracy and Banta. Sites where some stations appeared became towns; others catered primarily to locals shipping their products to market. Many of the stations were surrounded by yards for livestock, warehouses for grain, and loading docks.

Brentwood Railroad Station - 1909

The San Pablo & Tulare had no rolling stock of their own so the railroad was operated by Central Pacific until April 1885, then by Southern Pacific until May 1888 when San Pablo & Tulare and Southern Pacific consolidated. By 1889 Southern Pacific had continued the line another 56 miles to Los Banos. The 69 miles between Los Banos and Fresno was constructed between 1891 and 1892 giving Southern Pacific a second main line toward Fresno.

The coming of the railroad paved the way for rapid development. Towns that had been little more than villages expanded into townships, and other towns sprouted up. Trains changed the early settler's way of living and the pace of life in the county. Railroad transportation encouraged development of agriculture in the valley regions and industrial development in other areas of the county.

Delighted with the convenience of trains, travelers used them for excursions as well as business travel. One of the popular resorts was the Byron Hot Springs; travelers came from all over the United States by train to relax and restore their energy at the springs.

The building of the railroad through East Contra Costa County triggered a series of events that propelled this part of California from a remote, tranquil district to a region of booming little communities. The railroad truly was the wonder of the times. Until Next Time….

UNION CEMETERY AND BRENTWOOD FUNERAL HOME

Union Cemetery Association was established November 1, 1878 when C. J. Preston, a pioneer of the Point of Timber area donated four acres of land specifically for a cemetery. The Cemetery Membership Board was instituted with George Fellows as president, Matt Berlinger, Alonzo Plumley, Alpheus Richardson, W. T. Grover, Sylvester Wills and Colburn Preston as the first trustees. Prior to the organization of Union Cemetery families buried their loved ones in a plot on their own property or at the Point of Timber Graveyard, on Will's Ranch, at the corner of Marsh Creek Road and Hwy. 4, Will's Ranch was located across the street from Excelsior School and the Grange Hall. And according to Ellen Hosie Ladd some local residents objected to the location as being close to the school. Some of the existing graves on Will's Ranch were exhumed and transported by wagon to the new Union Cemetery which explains why there are grave markers at Union Cemetery dating as early as 1867, eleven years before the cemetery was established. One of these early dated markers was a member of the Veale Family and another was Sarah Lamb whom died in 1868.

Shafer's hearse - 1905

R.M. Jones surveyed and plotted the cemetery grounds in October 1878. According to early deeds a family could purchase a "Family Plot" for the sum of $20 which would accommodate ten to twelve gravesites. In today's dollars one gravesite would costs over $1,100.

Union Cemetery was originally governed by the Cemetery Association. In 1928 the cemetery fell under the California State Health and Safety Code as a non-denominational public cemetery. Today the district is governed by a board of trustees appointed by the Contra Costa County Board of Supervisors. The trustees in 1998 are Jack Byer, Fred Stornetta and JoAnn Mass.

East Contra Costa's history is carved into headstones resting beneath the towering eucalyptus and pine trees of Union Cemetery. Henry Wilkening's (Byrons first resident) plot holds a tall stone marker dated 1836 —1883. Sheriff Richard Rains Veale was laid to rest in 1937 after serving 40 years as Contra Costa County Sheriff. Frances E. Wilder, daughter of Captain and Mrs. George Donner of the Donner Party, one of 47 survivors of the ill fated immigrants that became snowbound in the Sierra

Nevada Mountains in 1846, found her final resting place at Union.

There are many head stones reflecting the lives of children that died prematurely from disease's we no longer fear and a few markers for "old timers" like Marshall Benn who died in 1984 at the age of 106. Union Cemetery shows an abundance of patriots. There is evidence of locals that have served their country as soldiers, sailors, marines and nurses in the Spanish American War, World War 1 and 11, the Korean and Vietnam Wars.

In 1905 George Shafer, son of William and Elizabeth Shafer (East County Pioneers) founded the first undertaking business in Brentwood. George owned and operated Shafer's Livery. He was elected constable in 1888, and also served the community as deputy sheriff and deputy coroner. George and his wife, Martha (Patty) converted their home, a four-room bungalow, built in the 1880's and moved from Nortonville by Jack Norman to the 839 First Street address, into Brentwood's first Funeral Parlor. In 1931 the Shafer's added a large chapel to serve families and friends of grieving families.

Frank Wiseman purchased the Shafer Funeral Home in 1947, but about a year later the business was returned to George Shafer and the business was resold to Roy Bartheld in 1949.

Roy Bartheld was born and raised in Iowa and attended college in North Dakota. He came west to San Francisco in the early 1930's where he worked for a funeral service. He read that the Shafer Funeral Parlor was for sale in a San Francisco newspaper. Although Bartheld lacked the funds to purchase the business he decided to travel to Brentwood and look the area over. He arranged a meeting with George Shafer, and later expressed that "Shafer made me such a deal I just couldn't turn it down. I stole it! I think Shafer just wanted out."

Roy Bartheld changed the name of the business to Bartheld Funeral Service. He renovated the funeral home into a modern facility and operated it until 1969 when he sold to Patrick and Donnalee McHenry.

Bartheld had employed Patrick McHenry at the mortuary, as a part-time employee while McHenry was a student attending Brentwood Elementary and Liberty Union High Schools. After graduating from Liberty, McHenry attended University of Pacific and San Francisco College of Mortuary Science. He returned to Brentwood in 1962 and worked for Bartheld for seven years before purchasing the business. In 1979, a fire in the mortuary necessitated another remodeling of the building.

Patrick & Donnalee McHenry solely owned and operated the business until 1985, Patrick hired Ray Glosser as a second full time Director in preparation for his retirement,

In 1993 McHenry sold the business to the Loewen Group whose offices are located in Covington, Kentucky with an agreement that he remain as manager until his retirement in 1996.

Brentwood Funeral Home, now under the management of Raymond A. Glosser, is still conducting business at 839 First Street, the original location of Shafer's Funeral Parlor, an establishment transcending over 120 years of time. Until Next Time....

PIONEER DOCTORS OF EAST CONTRA COSTA

Of all the perils confronting the early settlers of Contra Costa County, illness was the most dreaded. Almost all families became sadly familiar with cholera, smallpox, typhoid, or pneumonia. There were countless epidemics that arrived without warning, sometimes striking and killing their victims in a single day.

Before 1900, many of the pioneers lived in a state of medical superstition. Many of the conditions were unsanitary; contaminated food, dust-covered belongings, bedbugs, fleas, and flies were a constant aggravation. In the home and school, common drinking cups spread infection, and the poor diets of pioneers frequently brought about scurvy.

Early settlers called the doctor as a last resort. The nearest physician might live miles away, and his fees were far too expensive for many. Before calling the doctor the pioneer wife would try folk medicines she had learned from her mother. For rheumatism, wahoo-root tea; as a physic, slippery elm; for ague, sulfur and molasses; to trigger sweating, snakeroot tea, and to stop bleeding, cobwebs. Oddly enough, for childbirth, one of the most natural of human trials, the pioneer women generally sought a doctor's help. Often, though, weather prevented the doctor's timely arrival, and many children were born with only their fathers in attendance. Whether mother or baby survived was mostly a matter of luck.

Preceding the first doctor's arrival, traveling salesmen peddled their "cures" in the Byron and Brentwood areas. Horse liniments were hailed for humans. A common dose of internal drugs was one for a man and two for a horse. Most tonics were at least 25% alcohol, unsuspectingly consumed by teetotaling pioneer women and given to infants. I remember my grandmother, Cassie Armstrong, telling stories about traveling medicine men that came to my grandparents' ranch as late as 1908.

Many of the first doctors in the West had limited educations. Some held degrees from diploma mills, having only a one-year apprenticeship with an older doctor, and some were self-proclaimed physicians with virtually no training at all.

Unable to make a living by medicine alone, a doctor would often double as a pharmacist or dentist. He acted as nurse and clergyman too; his care was often a mixture of folk remedy, medieval practice, and shrewd improvisation.

The earliest doctor in East Contra Costa, arriving in 1836, was Dr. John Marsh, who doctored the Indians that worked for him, the vaqueros on his rancho, his neighbors and friends.

Dr. Patterson settled near Bethany, an early community east of Byron, and practiced medicine as far away as Antioch for many years in the 1860's. Dr. C.A. Hertell resided in the Point of Timber area about 1869, and Dr. Meyers, a French doctor, performed miracles in the early 1870's. Dr. Charles Connors came to Brentwood in 1886 from Los Angeles, and remained about two years. Dr. H. V. Marsh located in Marsh Creek about 1880, and later moved to Brentwood, where he practiced until his death. Dr. William Marsh arrived in Brentwood in 1893, and practiced for a short time. He was followed by his brother-in-law, Dr. C. A. Bell, who remained for two years. Dr. H. Rosas located in Brentwood in 1900, and practiced for one year. Dr. A. C. Bowerman, Dr. George Wise, and Dr. Gardner all moved to the area and opened practices for short periods.

Dr. James Hammond came to Byron in 1898. In the 1890's and early 1900's Hammond could be seen in his horse-drawn carriage making house calls with his black bag full of medical supplies. He was four feet, eleven inches tall, never weighed over 125 pounds, and always carried a pistol in his belt. He established a rather remarkable record delivering his own children and grandchildren, and at the age of 89 delivered his great-grandson, Doug Hammond. Dr. Hammond (also known as Doc) delivered my father, Oliver Armstrong, and many of my aunts and uncles.

In the 1920's, Dr. Hammond maintained professional offices in Byron, Brentwood, and Oakley. He delivered hundreds of babies in these communities; attended patients during various epidemics; and cared for all the general health needs of hundreds of families in East Contra Costa. Dr. Hammond died at the age of 99, in 1955.

Doctor Frank Cooks Home and Office

Dr. Frank Cook came to Brentwood from San Francisco immediately following the earthquake and fire in 1906. Many of the old-timers remember Dr. Cook's home, located where the Brentwood Post Office is today, on the corner of Dainty and First Streets. Dr. Cook offered the community a two-room medical clinic attached to his home for many years.

The first hospital in Contra Costa County was built in 1881. The Board of Supervisors purchased two lots in Martinez for $825. Three one-story buildings were erected for hospital purposes at a cost to the taxpayers of $3,225. This facility was replaced by a second county hospital in 1910. Until Next Time….

THE ONE-ROOM SCHOOLHOUSE

Education of their children was of primary importance to the first settlers of East Contra Costa. Schoolhouses and places of worship were among the first items addressed. Often the first teacher was a neighbor, and initial classes were held in a pioneer home. Early schools were simple at best, consisting of one or two rooms with few frills. They were heated by a pot-bellied stove, which ensured that students would be either too hot or too cold during the winter months. Sanitation was all but non-existent, with drinking water taken from a common pail. Most early classrooms had a blackboard (usually of slate), a world map, desks nailed to the floor and a "rod" (for the rod was not spared in those days). Children came to school, often a distance of several miles, on foot or on horseback.

Playground equipment consisted of a swing or two hung in a nearby tree and a "sack-base" baseball diamond. Pupils played games such as snap the whip and blind man's bluff.

Vasco School, Established 1890

Most of the first schools had only one room, containing grades one through eight with anywhere from five to fifty youngsters in attendance, all taught by one teacher. School was not compulsory, and many students dropped out by about the third grade. These young people went to work on local farms, or became apprentices to carpenters, blacksmiths, etc., and thus learned a trade.

In order to graduate from grammar school a student had to pass an examination that covered a wide range of topics: written and oral arithmetic, reading, grammar, composition, penmanship, civics, physiology, geography, history, drawing and word analysis. The examination was written by the office of the county superintendent of schools in Martinez and was given at a central school, where all eighth-grade students would assemble for three days of testing under the supervision of an independent examiner. Each examination question was printed on a separate sheet of paper and all answers were written in essay form.

Excelsior School - Byron, Established 1865

Teachers, although respected in the community, were poorly paid and few remained in the profession without another job. Many of the early teachers were very young, and often their knowledge extended little beyond the textbooks they taught from. The earliest textbooks in wide demand from the 1850's to the 1920's were Noah Webster's speller, grammar, and reader. Most classrooms also offered a Bible, hymnal and farmer's almanac as primary resource material.

Male instructors were a rarity. With few career opportunities available for them, many bright young girls would take cram courses (about three months) at schools especially established for the purpose of preparing them to pass a state examination entitling them to a teacher's certificate.

Teachers' salaries varied from one district to another in the early years. In 1895 Brentwood paid their teachers $145 per month, while Byron Hot Springs teachers were receiving $65 per month and Deer Valley district paid $60.

At one time, there were thirteen schools within what is now the Liberty Union High School District. Early records reveal the following four one-room schoolhouses established as early as 1865: Liberty School, located on Marsh Creek Road; Excelsior School, on the corner of Highway 4 and Marsh Creek Road; Eden Plain School, on Eden Plain Road; and Iron House School, on Cypress and Sellers Avenue In 1867, Lone Tree School was established on Lone Tree Road, and Deer Valley School was founded in 1869. Byron Hot Springs School was opened in 1879 and located where the Byron Airport is today, and Brentwood Grammar School was founded the same year. Sand Mound School in Bethel Island was erected in 1880. The town of Byron built their first school in 1886 on the corner of Camino Diablo and Holway. Vasco School was opened in 1890 where the Los Vaqueros Dam is being built today. Live Oak and Jersey Schools were both located in the Oakley area.

Liberty School - Marsh Creek

With the progress of time and the increase of population, the rural one-room schoolhouse disappeared. Small districts began to consolidate and the expanded facilities of larger schools offered much more for the student. The Brentwood Union Elementary District absorbed Deer Valley in 1918 and Liberty in 1944. Byron Hot Springs (1943), Vasco (date unknown) and Excelsior (1946) were absorbed by Byron Union School District. Iron House and Sand Mound joined Oakley School District in 1936.

Whatever its imperfections, the country schoolhouse definitely left footprints in the pages of our past. Their evolved successors are modern structures, well heated and well lit, with multipurpose rooms, libraries, cafeterias, audio-visual equipment, computers, bus service, attractive surroundings and endless extracurricular activities. There is now an emphasis placed on the individual student versus the mass teaching which by necessity was common procedure in the schools of yesterday… and yet I can't help but believe that there is much we could still learn from our great-grandparents' generation.

POINT OF INTEREST:

The *Contra Costa Gazette,* August 1878, published the county school census statistics. According to this article, the total number of children between the ages of five and seventeen living in the county was 3,282 of whom 1,655 were boys and 1,627 were girls. (There were 1,367 children under the age of five.) Approximately two thirds (2,290 children) attended public school during some portion of 1877.

The following East County schools were listed in this census: Briones Valley, 26 students; Deer Valley, 78 students; Eden Plain, 74 students; Excelsior, 110 students; Green Valley, 40 students; Iron House, 62 students; Liberty, 57 students; Lone Tree 55 students. Until Next Time….

*Iron House School
Established 1862*

*Lone Tree School
Established 1867*

*Liberty Union
High School
Built 1908*

*Byron School
Established 1886*

*Eden Plain School
Established 1865*

*Brentwood School
Established 1879*

EDUCATION IN EAST CONTRA COSTA
LIBERTY UNION HIGH SCHOOL

The growth and development of Liberty Union High School is one of the most interesting bits of history in the annals of our area. The splendid structure presently located on Second Street in Brentwood had its beginning in 1902, when the first Liberty High School was established.

As early settlers started filtering into East Contra Costa in the 1850's, a need for education was immediately recognized. The first settlers to arrive in the area taught their children at home, but by the 1860's, one-room schoolhouses began to spring up throughout the region.

The first school in the county was established in Martinez in 1850, consisting of six students from three families. These students gathered in a private home for the first few months, but by the end of the term the enrollment had increased from six to twenty-six students and a second location was required. The first schools in the far eastern end of the county came into existence by the 1860's. First, Iron House, then Point of Timber (later to be known as Excelsior School), and soon there were thirteen districts. Within a few years the Eden Plain, Byron Hot Springs, Deer Valley, Vasco, Marsh Creek (known as the Liberty School), Live Oak, Jersey, Sand Mound, Brentwood, Byron, and Oakley districts had all been established.

These early schools were simple, basic structures without many frills. Often students sat on wooden boxes without desks, or a single desk would be shared by several students. The older students would help teach the younger ones, and the classes were not clearly defined. The buildings were usually cold in the winter and unbelievably hot by late spring. The focal point in the room was the wood stove that sat in the center of the room. Lunch boxes (usually made from old tobacco tins), coats and other necessities were kept in a small anteroom.

Students came from two or three miles away and arrived in carts, on horseback or on foot. On cold days, they wrapped their hands in flour sacks to provide warmth. Chores were required of each student. The boys cared for the horses, chopped and stacked wood, and did much of the general repair work around the building. The girls assisted the teacher and cleaned the classroom. There was no indoor plumbing, and drinking water was kept in a bucket with a dipper.

East Contra Costa County's one-room schoolhouses offered the children of the area the opportunity for an excellent general education, but if they wanted to advance to a secondary level they had to travel to Martinez. The first high school in the county was established there in 1888. This was a two-year high school course under the direction of Miss Clara Wittenmeyer. Students from East County would either board with a family in Martinez or ride the train to and from school. Unfortunately, most families couldn't afford to send their children.

The need for an intermediate school between grammar school and the university was long felt in the Brentwood area before it became a reality. Antioch began organizing a high school district in the late 1890's. Charles Montgomery, then editor of the *Antioch Ledger,* took an active part in developing the local high school facility. His intent was that there be one high school, located in Antioch, to accommodate all the students in East Contra Costa County. The citizens of Brentwood, lead by Robert Dean, refused to get involved. They wanted a high school in Brentwood and would settle for nothing less. By 1902, both communities had their own high school districts. Antioch's was known as Riverview District and Brentwood's as Liberty Union High School District.

In 1902 when Liberty Union High School District was formed, not everyone in East County was enthusiastic about the idea. There were residents that believed ten or twelve years of schooling were unnecessary for the youth of the area and definitely a waste of time and taxpayers' dollars. They argued that there weren't enough children wanting a secondary education to justify establishing our own high school. There were numerous public meetings and debates before the High School District was officially formed.

The citizens decided to have a twelve-member school board to oversee the activities of the high school. These board members, selected from each of the local grammar school districts that would feed into the newly formed high school district, were: Eden Plain, William Shafer; Ironhouse, Oliver C. Wristen; Deer Valley, Andrew Smith; Sandmound, J. J. Eppinger; Brentwood, Hans Bonnickson; Oakley, Charles Horr; Lone Tree, Fred Heidorn; Excelsior, Anderson Allen; Liberty (Marsh Creek), Alfred Humphreys; Hot Springs, Henry Mehrlens; Byron, Fred Holway; and Jersey, Henry McCoy. Hans Bonnickson was elected first board president.

The first matter of importance the newly elected school board dealt with was the selection of a location to hold classes. After much discussion the back rooms of the Brentwood Grammar School were secured and became the first home of Liberty Union High School. The Brentwood Grammar School was located where the Liberty Swimming Pool is located today.

Soon there were two instructors, Professor Wright and Miss Hagmayer, with Wright acting as

Graduating Class of 1906
Effie Chadwick Bonnickson, Roy Heck, Bertha Sanders Biglow,
Hattie Russell, Annie O'Hara, Pearl Grove Sellers and Fern Cummings.

combination teacher/principal, and the school rolls showed eight students.

While students were pleased to have the opportunity to continue their education locally, they were also aware of the shortcomings of their facility. The rooms, once used for storage, were small; the walls were yellowing with age; the floor was uneven; their furniture and learning materials were limited at best. As more and more students began to enroll, space became a major problem. Students were seated around tables, shelves were fastened to the walls, and when all students were in attendance there was no space for aisles. During the rainy season the classrooms were cold and damp, and in the late spring they got unbearably hot. By 1905, the school was terribly overcrowded and everyone agreed that it was time to build a new school.

Liberty Union High School held its first graduation ceremony on June 3, 1905, over ninety years ago. Edith A. Sellers was the only graduate. She was presented with a diploma and a LUHS class pin. By 1906, the number of graduates had increased to seven.

The students at Liberty had the opportunity to earn two different types of diplomas: they could become involved in a two-year or a four-year program. The four-year program offered them a standard diploma that prepared them to enter a university. The two-year, or "commercial" program, offered students training in bookkeeping, typing, commercial arithmetic, spelling, penmanship, and English, preparing them to go directly into the work force.

In 1908, a new Liberty Union High School building was constructed on the Chapman lot (the corner of Maple Avenue and First Street) consisting of four rooms with a basement for laboratory work, at a cost to the taxpayers of $8500. The Brentwood Women's Club hosted a housewarming party for the community to visit and tour the new school. Students provided musical entertainment and county officials, the principal, and the school board president, Hans Bonnickson, delivered several addresses.

On September 14,1918 Liberty Union High School was completely destroyed by fire, starting from chemicals in the school laboratory. The building and annex were well insured, but the loss of books to the pupils was heavy.

A magnificent, modern, well-equipped school was built on Second Street in 1920, at a cost of $93,000. The new Liberty not only offered its students more classrooms, a library, athletic fields, wood and blacksmith shops, but even an auditorium that would seat eight hundred people. The auditorium had a stage 40 feet wide and 27 feet deep and was used not only by the students, but also the community at large.

Liberty Union High School has played a vital role in the history of East Contra Costa County. It has grown and changed enormously over the years. Only one thing has remained constant—our faith in the power of education. Until Next Time....

*Liberty Union High School
Built 1920*

EAST COUNTY CHURCHES

The early settlers of East Contra Costa County relied on their own resources for both the necessities and simple pleasures of life. Byron and Brentwood were not founded until 1878, when the San Pablo & Tulare Railroad laid track through this region of California, and prior to that time Point of Timber was the leading hub of activity. This little hamlet was located where Bay City Building Materials (corner of Highway 4 and Byron Highway) is located today, offering early settlers a small general store, stage depot, post office, cobbler, Grange hall, blacksmith, a one-room schoolhouse and the area's first church.

The first recorded church in the area was the Methodist Episcopal Church, established at Point of Timber in 1868. Prior to the formal organization of this church, early settlers took their religion in infrequent doses, relying on the circuit riders that passed through the area three or four times a year. Circuit riders were preachers that did the Lord's work, preaching on a street corner, in a farmer's barn, around a campfire or under an oak tree on Brushy Peak.

The first settlers of the far eastern section of Contra Costa were isolated from the more developed areas. One of the few comforts they depended on was their religion. In response to the call of circuit-riding preachers, many of them self-ordained, the early settlers and their families would load their wagons with provisions and travel long miles to join camp meetings at some designated location. Brushy Peak was often used as a gathering spot, drawing families from the Altamont, Point of Timber, Eden Plain and Livermore areas. Such a gathering afforded a rare opportunity to meet with distant neighbors, gossip, arrange trades of livestock and perhaps even find a husband or wife.

Byron Congregational Church - 1890

Below are short histories of some of the early churches established in East Contra Costa:

1850, Saint Catherine's Catholic Church: The first church established in Contra Costa County (Martinez). The priest crossed the Carquinez Straits once a month for services until the church was built.

1854, Grace Methodist Episcopal Church: The first Protestant church established in Contra Costa County (Martinez).

1868, Point of Timber Methodist Episcopal Church: The early settlers of East Contra Costa first met to worship in private homes. By 1873 the Grange had built a hall at the corner of Marsh Creek Road and Byron Highway, and the Methodists held services in that facility. In 1887 the Grange organization had relocated to Brentwood, and the Methodists moved the Grange hall south to Byron, to the site where the Methodist church is located today. An ornate steeple and gothic windows were added to the old hall. In 1921 a new church was built.

1868, Eden Plain Methodist Episcopal Church: According to the 1917 *History of Contra Costa County,* there was a church erected at Eden Plain in 1868. It was a small building without a steeple and stood on the southeast quarter of section five. Later it moved to Brentwood, was occupied and used for services for a while, then sold and used first for a lodge room, later as a private residence, and finally destroyed by fire in 1915.

1883, First Congregational Church of Byron: This church was established on Holway Street next to the Byron Grammar School in 1883 and disbanded in 1929. The church and the school had a common well, and the church facility was often used for school functions. When the church closed in 1929 the Byron School purchased the church building and property for $1750.

1907, Oakley, Saint Anthony's Catholic Church: In 1906 James O'Hara donated land for a Catholic Church in Oakley. Prior to 1907 early settlers traveled to Martinez or Antioch to celebrate mass. The first church cost $4000 to build, seated 180 people, and had a bell that originally came from Saint Patrick's Church in Somersville.

1913, Byron Seventh Day Adventist: A handsome church was built on Byron Highway at a cost of $1000 in 1913. Religious services were held each Sabbath at three p.m. Doctor James Hammond was the elder and his wife was treasurer. This church is a private residence today.

1917, Byron, Saint Anne's Catholic Church: St. Anne's was founded as a satellite of Livermore's Saint Michael's. The site where the church was erected was donated by Manuel Pimental. The church's total cost was $5,000. Built of concrete with a seating capacity of 250, it was originally considered a mission. Before St. Anne's was built, locals would travel to Livermore for mass.

1927, Brentwood, Saint Alban's Episcopal Church: Located on the corner of Second Street and Birch Street, the church was dedicated June 22, 1927. St. Alban's is named after a third-century Briton who, when he observed the police coming to arrest a Christian priest who was his house guest, put on the priest's vestments and was duly carried off and executed for being a Christian.

1949, Brentwood, Immaculate of Heart of Mary Catholic Church: This church was dedicated August 1949 with Archbishop John Mitty of San Francisco officiating and Father John Kenny as the first pastor. According to parish records, mass was celebrated at the old Coates Hall from 1901 to 1907. Between 1943 and 1949, the Reverend Neil McCabe conducted mass in the American Legion Hall.

There were other houses of worship, not mentioned here, that served the early residents of East Contra Costa. Each played an important role in the early development of this region of California and each definitely left footprints in our past. Until Next Time....

Christian Church - Brentwood
Members of the Dainty and Howard Families

CATHOLIC CHURCHES OF EAST CONTRA COSTA

Roman Catholics were the first to hold services in Contra Costa County, originally attending mass at a building located in Martinez which had been erected in 1849 as a mercantile establishment. After the Church purchased the building in 1850, Catholics gathered there to attend mass, worship and hold reunions. In 1851, construction began on an adobe building that was never completed, and in 1855, a church was built. This church lasted until 1866, when it was blown down by a gale.

Early settlers of East Contra Costa were primarily men wanting to mold their own destiny. They came from all walks of life. Many left crowded cities in the East or Europe, looking for land and an opportunity to build a new life for themselves and their families. Facing numerous hardships, one of the few comforts they could depend on was their religion. However, settlers of East Contra Costa took their religion in infrequent doses, finding it necessary to travel to attend mass.

Brentwood's Catholic Church of the Immaculate Heart of Mary was dedicated August, 1949, with Archbishop John J. Mitty of San Francisco officiating at the impressive dedication ceremony and Father John J. Kenny as the first pastor.

Settlers of the Brentwood area who wished to attend Catholic services before 1900 found it necessary to travel to Martinez or Antioch. From 1901 to 1907, according to parish records, services were held at the old Coates Hall in Brentwood. Brentwood Catholics worshipped at Saint Anthony's in Oakley or Saint Anne's in Byron until 1943, when the Reverend Neil McCabe began conducting mass in the American Legion Hall in Brentwood.

The lot at Dainty Avenue and First Street had been purchased in 1945, and construction of the new church began November 21, 1948. The architect was Martin Rist and the builder, O. J. Mooney. The church was completed and ready for an informal opening three months before it was officially dedicated.

Adjacent to the church, and similar in architectural design, a rectory was built to house the presiding pastor. The Reverend John J. Kenny was the first pastor to occupy the rectory.

The dedication ceremony consisted of three parts. The outer walls were sprinkled with holy water and the altar blessed, then the inner walls were sprinkled while the choir chanted the Miserere, followed by mass with the Archbishop on a throne decorated for the occasion.

There was a grand attendance at the dedication, including many church notables. Participating in the ceremony were Father Kenny as celebrant of mass, the Reverend Raymond Thomas of Byron as deacon, and the Reverend John Dermody of Walnut Creek as sub-deacon. Assistants to the Archbishop were the Reverend Philip Ryan of Napa, former pastor of Saint Anthony's and Saint Anne's; the Reverend Lawrence Hennessey of Concord; and the Reverend James O'Conner of Stockton. The Reverend William Kitchen of San Francisco was master of ceremonies, assisted by Walter Fleming of Menlo Park. A choir of seminarians from Menlo Park under the direction of the Reverend Joseph Martinelli supplied the music.

Saint Anthony's Catholic Church in Oakley dates back to 1906, when James O'Hara donated land for a church. Prior to 1907, Oakley residents wishing to attend mass traveled to the Antioch parish. By 1907, it had become apparent that a church was necessary in Oakley. Masses were conducted twice a month in a local store, with a pastor from Antioch presiding. On December 4, 1908, Saint Anthony's was completed under the direction of the Reverend Father Peter Alphonse, pastor of the Antioch parish. This church was located on the corner of Fourth and Ruby Streets. Church members completed most of the construction with Joseph Jesse, a local builder, supervising.

The facility cost $4,000 to build, seated 180 people, and had a church bell that originally came from Saint Patrick's Church in Somersville.

The Reverend Eugene Warren was the first resident pastor of Saint Anthony's Parish. During his pastorate, property at O'Hara and Home Streets was purchased to build Oakley's second Catholic church, with construction beginning in 1926. Services were held at this location until 1955, when under the direction of Father Raymond Reali, the church purchased five acres on the corner of O'Hara Street and Cypress Avenue for the present church.

Construction of the new church began in February 1955; the church, hall and rectory were dedicated in December of that same year. In 1968, the church purchased four acres of adjacent land for parking and future development.

Saint Anne's Catholic Church in Byron was founded in 1917, as a satellite of Livermore's Saint Michael's. Prior to the building of Saint Anne's, Byron residents traveled to Livermore to attend mass. In 1916 Manuel Pimental, Frank Cabral, Joseph Santana, A. L. Bovo, Anthony Thomas, Lewis Mead and John Kennedy formed a fund-raising committee that met with Archbishop Edward Hanna in Byron to discuss the possibility of constructing a church in town. Manuel Pimental offered to donate a site for the church and others donated funds to offset the construction costs. The new little church cost $5,000 to build. It was constructed of concrete, with a seating capacity of 250, and was originally considered a Mission (a full-service church without a priest in residence), serving approximately twenty families in the Byron area.

Over one hundred people attended the dedication ceremony with Father McNamara of Livermore conducting the first mass. Numerous notable guests attended the service. Bill and Veronica Sproul arrived in town in their private railroad car and presented the new church with a bell and a beautiful cross for the altar. (Sproul was president of Southern Pacific Railroad.)

For many years mass was only celebrated twice a month at Saint Anne's, with a priest traveling from Livermore to conduct the services. In 1924, according to a letter from the archives of the San Francisco Archdiocese, the congregation requested a Portuguese-speaking priest for Byron, because of the predominance of Portuguese in the parish.

Saint Anne's became a mission of Saint Anthony's, in Oakley, in 1925. By 1947, Saint Anne's was transformed into a parish church with Immaculate Heart of Mary Church in Brentwood as its mission. In March 1975, after serving the community for more that half a century, Saint Anne's held First Confirmation with Bishop Floyd Begin confirming eighteen children. Today mass is still held at St. Anne's on a regular limited schedule; the congregation has outgrown the walls of St. Anne's, but East County residents still take comfort in the "Little Church" on Camino Diablo. Until Next Time....

BUSINESSMEN COME TO EAST COUNTY

Brentwood and Byron are both railroad towns, founded in 1878 when the San Pablo and Tulare Railroad laid tracks through East Contra Costa. Both communities were already prosperous agricultural regions and the railroad encouraged growth by reducing transportation costs, making the area accessible, widening markets for local wheat farmers and dairymen, and raising land values.

By 1882, Brentwood and Byron had both become progressive small towns that offered endless opportunities for merchants and businessmen looking for a location to plant their roots. According to the 1882 edition of *History of Contra Costa County* by Slocum, Brentwood had a population of one hundred residents, three stores, a post office, three saloons, a schoolhouse, a railroad depot, a blacksmith shop, and a warehouse. Byron had sixty fulltime residents, a fine hotel, a post office, one store, three saloons, two blacksmith shops, a warehouse, one harness shop, a railroad depot, and a livery stable.

Byron Hotel

The first settlers of this region of California came to toil the rich soil that the area became famous for. But along with them, or half a step behind, came men and women who proposed to make their livelihood by providing goods and services for the rest of the population. These were the townsmen. The butcher, baker, bootmaker, banker, merchant, saloonkeeper, doctor, barber, blacksmith and many others. These early settlers were a sturdy and resourceful breed equipped with boundless energy.

Henry Wilkening, a young man from Germany, arrived in Byron in 1877 (a year before the railroad started). He built the Byron Hotel, a saloon, and a livery stable. The hotel was simple by today's standards. Each bedroom (there were only four) was furnished with a washstand, bowl and pitcher, chamber pot, chair, bed and smoky kerosene lamp.

Wilkening's Saloon offered patrons a place to linger over a nickel glass of beer, or a shot of whisky or bitters, while conversing with their neighbors or other men passing through the area. Some played checkers, tossed horseshoes, or engaged in a game of billiards. In 1882, a "respectable" woman would never have considered entering the saloon.

The local livery stable offered residents and visitors an establishment to shelter their horses while they attended to business in town. Another service of the livery stable was the rental of a buggy and team to salesmen who wanted to make the rounds of the countryside, land hunters, loan agents, or young men who wanted to treat their girlfriends to a moonlit ride. You could rent a buggy for two dollars a day or four dollars with a driver.

Louis Grunauer was a native of Prussia who in 1878, at the age of twenty-four, moved to Brentwood and built the new town's first general store. Grunauer's Store was the chief focus of Brentwood's commercial life, offering its customers everything from coal to Sunday bonnets. Bacon, hams, luggage and lanterns hung from the ceiling. Dry goods lined one wall, hardware another. The back of the store was filled with clothing and groceries. By the front door, you could find the newly established post office.

The general store carried almost anything the early settlers might crave: sugar and salt, molasses and meat, gunpowder and ammunition, crockery and coal oil. Everyone within walking or riding distance called at Grunauer's Store regularly, hovering over the shelves of goods, loitering amid the deliciously mingled odors and the warmth of the potbellied stove.

No town was complete without a blacksmith, whose services were needed to shoe horses, sharpen plows, repair wagons and perform a multitude of other maintenance tasks for the community and outlying area. Joseph W. Carey constructed a blacksmith shop in Brentwood in 1878. Carey originally had a blacksmith shop near Point of Timber, but when the railroad announced that they were going to build a depot at Brentwood he decided to be on the ground floor of helping to establish this new community.

In 1882, buckboards and farm wagons could be heard clattering along the dusty streets of Byron and Brentwood. Most of the townspeople fetched their water from a windmill-powered well that was located near the general store. The towns had no plumbing or sewers; all the buildings had privies in back.

The introduction of the railroad to East Contra Costa was truly the wonder of the times. It was a time of boom and boomers, linking this region of California to key cities all over the state and triggering the events that propelled a remote, tranquil district into a region of bustling little communities. Until Next Time....

EARLY BANKS OF EAST CONTRA COSTA

We live in a world of ATMs and credit cards, checkbooks and federally backed commercial banks, so it is difficult at best to imagine the world our forefathers lived in. During the horse and buggy days, the streets were dusty in the summer and muddy in the winter. Horse-drawn wagons and carts delivered milk and ice to home customers. General business practices were handled very differently than they are today. There were no banks, no places for early settlers to deposit their money, and consequently, they were very creative in hiding their valuables. Some used a hollow tree to hide their treasures; others used cellars and hollow walls, or buried their money.

The first commercial bank in Contra Costa County was established in 1858 (eight years after California became a state) in the town of Pacheco. At the time, Pacheco was the largest shipping point and business center in the area. William and Henry Hale owned a general store that housed a large iron safe. Preferred customers would place their personal funds and other valuables in the Hales' iron box for safekeeping. As more and more people asked them for the use of their safe, the Hales realized that private

Brentwood Bank - Built 1913

banking could become a part of their business and draw customers to their store. They paid eight percent interest, issued passbooks to depositors, paid checks and withdrawals, and loaned money. The firm began private banking in 1858, and in 1870, incorporated as the Contra Costa Savings and Loan Bank. In 1872 it became the Contra Costa Bank. Finally, in 1893, the bank moved to Martinez and became the Bank of Martinez.

Brentwood: Balfour, Guthrie Company underwrote the Bank of Brentwood Inc. on April 4, 1913, with a capital of $50,000. The new bank opened for business on July 15, 1913, and local residents deposited $22,138 on the first day. The first bank officers were Robert Dean, president; Robert Wallace Jr., vice president; and Lee Durham, cashier. The original directors were Dean, Wallace, Alex Burness, R. F. MacLeod and Frank Luddinghouse. On May 1, 1920, the Bank of Antioch took over the Bank of Brentwood and conducted business as a branch. In 1927 the Bank of America of California absorbed the branch, and the Bank of America National Trust and Savings Association took over in 1930.

Brentwood's first bank was an ornate concrete building on the corner of Oak and First Streets, constructed at a cost of $15,000 for the building, furniture, and equipment. Balfour-Guthrie hired Hercules Logan to act as superintendent in the construction of both the bank and the Brentwood Hotel. Logan had been a contractor in San Francisco when Balfour-Guthrie hired him. He ended up staying in Brentwood and was very active in the early development of the town. The old bank building houses The Brentwood Press today.

Byron: On May 1, 1911, with $50,000 capital, the Bank of Byron was organized. It was a branch of the Bank of Tracy. George Dodge was the first president; William Schmidt, vice president; O. H. Root, secretary; and A. L. Bovo, manager. Local directors were Matt Preston and J. Saxouer. The Bank of Tracy and the Bank of Byron were both sold to Bank of America of California and were absorbed by Bank of America National Trust and Savings Association in 1930.

Byron's Bank was located on Main Street where Byron Bethany Irrigation is today. The original building, built at a cost of $6,000, was considered one of the most modern and safe banking facilities in this region of California. Records indicate the interior fixtures of the building cost more than $2500, a sum considered an enormous amount of money in 1911.

The institution supplied its customers a general commercial, savings and safe deposit business. The bank offered real estate and business loans; savings accounts earning four percent interest; and safe-deposit boxes large enough to hold valuable documents, jewelry, and other valuables rented for two dollars a year.

According to the *Contra Costa Gazette,* the Byron bank was burglarized on January 26, 1919. Robbers got away with $50,000 in currency, liberty bonds, jewelry, and securities stolen from safe-deposit boxes. They burned a hole through the Bessemer steel plates around the combination to the safe-deposit vault.

Oakley: The Bank of Oakley was organized on August 23, 1920, with $25,000 capital. The first officers were James H. Shaw, president; W. H. Hall, vice-president; F. C. Anderson, secretary; and Paul A. Anderson, cashier-treasurer. The first board of directors was O. C. Champlin, James Shaw, E. J. Sinclair, Paul Anderson and W. H. Hall.

By 1922 Oakley Bank had resources of $200,000, and deposits of $150,000. The bank was located on the corner of Main and Third Streets.

The Bank of Oakley was discontinued in 1930 because of a scandal when funds were found to be missing. The local Santa Fe agent and the bank's cashier began speculating in the stock market in the late 1920's with the bank's money. When the stock market crashed in 1929 the bank's money couldn't cover the losses. The cashier committed suicide by putting a gun to his head and the bank closed. Until Next Time....

EAST CONTRA COSTA FLOOD, FIRES AND EARTHQUAKES

The American West acted like a magnet, bringing together early settlers from many different backgrounds in a mixture of nationalities, cultures, and languages. In the 1800's, most Contra Costa residents had encountered incredible hardships traveling to California and faced many difficulties in their daily lives. We often look upon that period as glamorous and full of romantic legend, when in reality it was a hard life. Mother Nature brought prosperous years, but she also brought conditions that plagued the pioneers with disaster.

Floods: Many early settlers established their farms near streams, creeks, and rivers. They built their homes and barns on good farmland where the soil was rich and fertile for planting crops. Then, a winter of heavy, torrential rains would come, darkening the winter skies and causing waterways to overflow their banks, creating landslides which blocked roads, ruining crops, and carrying houses and barns away in the rushing waters.

Records show that between 1849 and 1940 there were eleven major floods in Contra Costa County. (The average annual rainfall during this period for East County was fourteen inches of rain.) The "Great Flood" of 1862 is recorded as the most devastating. In that memorable season, 49 inches of rain fell. On January 4th it began raining and did not let up until January 11th, causing extreme destruction countywide.

Other years recording uncommonly high rainfalls: 1866-67, 34.92 inches; 1867-68, 38.84 inches; and 1889-90, 47.5 inches at Briones Valley. All of these flood years brought devastation to the residents of Contra Costa. Losses in crops, cattle, and property ran into the millions. The 1889 flood left Pacheco Valley under one sheet of water, Concord completely flooded, and the road between Martinez and Port Costa blocked by heavy slides. Brentwood and Byron found themselves isolated from the rest of the county. On January 5, 1895, the county again flooded. Most streets in the county's communities were filled with water that flowed like rivers, washing away railroad tracks and roads.

Earthquakes: California earthquakes have been known to cause the ground to leap, sending out destructive shock waves for hundreds of miles. Long before California became a state, the mission fathers kept journals that recorded the history of this area. The Presidio in San Francisco recorded an earthquake on July 18, 1808, that had at least 21 shocks. A merciless quake shook southern California in September 1812, almost totally destroying Mission San Juan Capistrano and Mission Santa Barbara (33 people were killed in this shock). In 1818, a mission church in Santa Clara was thrown down, and again in 1851, San Francisco buildings shook and windows broke. November 1858 brought a grim shock that damaged most of the buildings in San Jose and in 1865, another severe shock hit San Francisco.

There is little known about how these early quakes affected Contra Costa, but no doubt they were felt here and left their mark. The first earthquake I was able to find information about which affected Contra Costa occurred October 21, 1868 at about 8:00 a.m. Although San Francisco again seems to have been most severely damaged during the 1868 quake, lives of early settlers in this region were definitely touched. The shock extended for several hundred miles along the coast, on what we know today as the Hayward fault. Chimneys crumbled to the ground, walls cracked, and trees were uprooted. John Marsh's stone house was damaged and the courthouse in Martinez sustained grave damage. Many early settlers of East Contra Costa spoke of the earth shaking, trembling, and quaking.

Another awesome force of nature burst out of the Pacific off Humboldt Bay on April 18,

1906, racing along the San Andreas fault at two miles a second, skirting the coastline, demolishing towns and causing at least one steamer to sink. San Francisco received the brunt of this event, but East County also sustained damage.

Fires: According to the *Contra Costa Gazette* on October 5, 1915, a business block in Brentwood burned, causing a loss of $20,000 to the following properties: Tremley's Hardware Store and Peter Olsen's adjoining building, the residences of Frank Golden and Mike Sargent, two barns, plus a tank and tank house owned by the Balfour, Guthrie Company.

In 1903 the first Brentwood Hotel, owned by Louis Grunauer, burned. This blaze was fought by dozens of townspeople running a bucket brigade to battle the flames. The hardware store next door was also destroyed. In 1918 the Liberty Union High School fire started in the school's chemistry lab. This fire destroyed the building, but all students were safely evacuated without any injuries. In 1919, again, a fire swept through the downtown area of Brentwood. This blaze started in Jansse Store, which was located on the south corner of Oak and First Streets. In 1929 Balfour, Guthrie's grain warehouse burned to the ground. In 1946 a fierce fire razed the Shell Oil Company tanks, office, storeroom and loading dock on the corner of Railroad and Dainty Ave. In 1963 the central portion of Liberty Union High School containing the administration offices, library and some classrooms went up in flame. Several students started this fire.

In Byron, a blaze that struck Main Street was reported in the March 5, 1923, *Stockton Record*. Seven business buildings were destroyed, with losses estimated at over $50,000. The fire started in the barber shop, just as Constable Tobe LeGrand walked in: a gasoline water heater took fire. LeGrand grabbed the heater and endeavored to throw it into the street, creating an explosion in which he was badly burned.

The seven buildings that burned included the *Byron Times* (owned by Harry Hammond), barber shop (Tobe LeGrand's), post office, shoe shop (Stanley Cabral's), general merchandise (Alonzo Plumley's), meat market (Ellis Howard's), and Hotel Santos (Jess Santos).

Other Byron fires: In 1884 the Byron Hotel, owned by Henry Wilkenson, burned; in 1901 the Byron Hot Springs hotel and cottages, with twenty rooms, laundry, gas plant and ice plant, were destroyed; in 1902 the business section of town was wiped out—the town's lack of fire-fighting equipment left buildings and the rest of the town at the mercy of the flames; in 1912 the second Byron Hot Springs Hotel and several cottages were destroyed. In 1917 the Byron Hotel, now owned by Fred Holway, was destroyed by fire.

Much of what early settlers built in the 1800's has faded from the scene, destroyed by fire, flood, earthquakes, and time. Much remains as a monument, in memory at least, to the enterprise of our forefathers who showed the way to the generations of today. Until Next Time….

HEADLINES FROM THE CONTRA COSTA GAZETTE

It was not until California was proclaimed a member of the United States that the people of this state were introduced to journalism. Since that beginning, California has seen thousands of newspapers come and go, with each having a definite effect on its town or area. The *Contra Costa Gazette* was such a paper. As the official newspaper of Contra Costa County, the *Gazette*, from its birth in 1858, played a vital role in the history of the county.

The *Gazette* is an important source for research of the early accounts of the area. The following information was gleaned from the front page of early copies of this publication.

October 11, 1859: The first Contra Costa County fair was inaugurated and an excellent exhibit took place in Pacheco. (The present 73-acre County Fairgrounds in Antioch were purchased in 1949.)

May 8, 1869: The May Day Picnic at the grove near the John Marsh stone house last Saturday is said to have been one of the largest and happiest gatherings of the kind that have ever been known in the county. There were from seven hundred to one thousand people present.

September 6, 1890: A devastating fire in Brentwood destroyed Moody & Brewers Blacksmith, Shafer's Livery, and Mr. Humphrey's Printing House.

April 29, 1891: President Harrison's train stopped in Brentwood. He gave a short speech and shook many local residents' hands.

February 24, 1892: E. W. Netherton established the *Contra Costa Herald*, a new eight-page newspaper to be published in Brentwood.

June 7, 1902: As a result of a fire in Byron today, the business section of the town was wiped out. The town not being equipped with fire fighting apparatus was at the mercy of the flames.

December 24, 1914: The new library and reading room at Brentwood will be opened to the public January 5, 1915. Brentwood can claim the distinction of being the first town in the field to put up its own building. Entire credit is due the Library Association which was formed last February, with Mrs. Andrew Bonnickson at its head and an executive committee of earnest and progressive women.

October 5, 1915: A business block of Brentwood was burned, causing a loss of $20,000 to the following property: Tremley's Hardware Store, Peter Olsen's Building adjoining, the residents of Frank Golden, Hercules Logan and M. Sargent, two barns, and the tank and tank house owned by Balfour, Guthrie.

September 14, 1918: Liberty Union High School at Brentwood was completely destroyed by fire, starting from chemicals in the school laboratory. The building and annex were well insured, but the loss of books to the pupils will be heavy.

January 26, 1919: In a Byron Bank robbery, $50,000 in currency, Liberty bonds, jewelry and securities were stolen from 154 safe-deposit boxes. The robbers burned a hole through the Bessemer steel plates around the combination to the safe deposit vault.

January 19, 1924: Rural free mail delivery began at Brentwood, extending to Marsh Creek, Deer Valley and Antioch Road, 25.6 miles. The service includes 115 homes. Will Coates is the temporary carrier.

Journalism in Contra Costa County has seen the passing of the years. From the days of stagecoach travel to the modern age of high-powered automobiles, the newspapers have witnessed our past. The value of the collections of newspapers like the *Contra Costa Gazette* cannot be measured in monetary calculations, for from their fading pages comes the history of this region of California. Until Next Time....

REMEMBER THE WINDMILLS

There was a time when windmills could be seen dotting the countryside throughout East Contra Costa, when early settlers harnessed the wind to irrigate their crops and supply drinking water.

Folks are always asking me where I find information or decide which topic to write about. Well, one day I was talking to my Dad, Oliver Armstrong, about his ability to witch for water, and as he talked about the wells he had witched over the years a story was born.

A water witch is an individual with the ability to locate underground water by mystical vibrations. Dad could walk over a patch of dirt with a forked, Y-shaped willow switch held in both hands and find water. If the tail of the Y began to tug downward, or to bounce or vibrate, Dad would indicate that there was water directly below, and sure enough, there was! I remember once watching him witch using a wire clothes hanger.

Bordes Ranch - Vasco Region

At the turn of the century water could be found throughout East Contra Costa County twenty feet below ground level. Astonishingly, most wells were dug by hand. A pioneer would scoop out dirt, one shovelful at a time, throwing it over his shoulder for as long as he could until the shaft became too deep. He would then rig a windlass and crank the dirt up in buckets. Sometimes the rope would break and a bucketful of earth would hurtle back down the shaft to the man at the bottom. Shallow wells were used for irrigation and livestock, but usually deeper wells were dug to 32 feet for household use, as windmills could not lift water much higher than that.

East Contra Costa has abundant water near the ground surface in most locations, and with winds generally prevailing from the west to northwest, windmills were often used. Rarely would breezes fail for more than a day or two in summer; only during winter's foggy spells were hand pumps required. Many windmills were built locally at blacksmith shops. Moody's Blacksmith in Brentwood and Armstrong's Blacksmith in Byron were both noted for building and repairing mills. Many early settlers purchased their mills from John S. Davis, a resident of Stockton who manufactured windmills for more than twenty years (1858 to 1883), producing an average of sixty mills a year. A mill could be purchased in Stockton and transported to East Contra Costa via the river to Point of Timber or Babbe's Landings.

There were many types of windmills, many with a regulating feature which included a hinged vane set off-center and a spring arrangement to pull the fan out of the direct wind when the velocity reached a point dangerous to the fan. To avoid having the blades blow off during high winds, most mills had a swivel allowing the vane to turn the fan to face toward the wind; others were adjusted by hand.

Early windmills were constructed out of wood, but in 1894 Richard Wilson (resident of French

Camp) introduced the "Hercules Windmill," a metal windmill with steel gears and fans made of galvanized iron.

Many of the first residents in the area constructed their own mills, either for financial reasons or because pre-built mills were not available. This was a tricky business, as the mills needed to be well balanced or they would fly apart in the wind. Often these homemade mills only had four blades.

Windmills were often perched atop a stilt-legged tower, with a platform near the top and a ladder to enable access for repairs. There were several windmills on the ranch were I grew up in the Byron hills. I remember climbing the tower and gazing out upon the great Diablo Valley, spending hours reading on my perch in the sky.

When water was brought to the surface it needed to be stored, and was piped into troughs for livestock, irrigation ditches for crops, and holding tanks for household use. Most tanks were mounted on twenty to thirty-foot towers. The higher the tower, the greater water pressure it delivered. The first tanks were built out of wood, and if left to go empty and dry out they would shrink and leak. It was also unwise to build a tank with knots in the wood, for they would surely shrink and fall out at a most inconvenient time.

You can still find a few tank houses tucked behind older homes in the area. Many early tank houses were simply boarded-up towers with space below the tank for storage. Some tank houses were well finished, two or three-story buildings with the space below converted into a washroom, a pantry or an extra bedroom. Until Next Time….

WOMEN OF EAST CONTRA COSTA

Pioneers arrived in East Contra Costa during the 1850's and 60's with their wagons full of hope which was the one common thread that wove them together with their neighbors. Most had dreams of a better life than they had left behind. Some dreamed of fabulous wealth and others of streets of gold. Many saw the west as a place where they could work hard, grab their fortune, and return home triumphantly to claim a bright future for themselves and family. Others saw it as a place where they would finally own enough rich soil to plow, plant crops, and raise a family.

Of the early settlers it was primarily men who sought freedom from civilization, and women who brought civilization with them. The women were instrumental in the formation of churches, schools, and civic organizations.

As I research early newspaper publications of East Contra Costa during the 1800's, I am amazed at how few names of women appear in the records. A true lady was generally to remain anonymous and silent at home. Her name was to be in the paper three times during her life, when she was born, married, and died (the last time as Mrs. Husband).

Women were subject to laws made without their consent. They were vested with little freedom, and were subject to the will of their husbands. The man of the household had sole custody of any children, decided where the family would live, and owned and controlled any property as well as his earnings which included any money earned by the women of the household.

In researching the chapters of our past, a few women did manage to receive recognition for the parts they played in the development of this region of California.

ELLA JANE FORWARD PEARCE:

Ella Forward was born in 1858 in Tehama County and came to East Contra Costa in the 1880's to teach at Byron Hot Springs School. She boarded with local families of students attending the school and taught at this facility until 1892 when she met and married William J. Pearce.

Between 1888 and 1931 Ella taught at Byron Hot Springs, Iron House, Eden Plain, Knightsen, and Holland Island schools. At the age of seventy-three she was still teaching on Holland Island where she would travel every school day, in good weather and bad, along the levee road crossing the river on the Holland Island Ferry.

After school on May 20,1931 Mrs. Pearce was in route home via the ferry when her car failed to stop after she had driven onto the vessel and plunged into fifteen feet of water. Witnesses said that after the car drove onto the ferry it suddenly jumped ahead and off the end. It was believed that Mrs. Pearce had intended to place her foot on the brake and instead stepped on the gas.

Mrs. Pearce was remembered in several newspaper articles as being sincerely dedicated to the youth of East Contra Costa. In 1930 she recounted her early years in the classroom reflecting on the times when she taught all ages in one room, built the fire, and cleaned the classroom. Most schools had a blackboard, but books provided by parents were usually only a Bible, a hymnal, an almanac, and a dictionary. Mrs. Pearce often used the Contra Costa Gazette or the San Francisco Sun newspapers as teaching tools. During her 43 years of teaching, Mrs. Pearce touched hundreds of lives. Her teaching career played a vital role in bringing the children of our area into the American mainstream.

SARAH C. ABBOTT SELLERS:

Sarah Abbott was born in New York. Her husband, Samuel Sellers, was born in Pennsylvania. In 1850, as newlyweds, they traveled via Cape Horn to San Francisco. The Sellers spent several years mining gold in Mariposa before moving to East Contra Costa in 1860 where they purchased one hundred sixty acres of rich farm land in the Eden Plain District.

Sarah is credited with several very progressive ideas for the times. In 1862 she applied for the formation of the Iron House School District and served as the first women in California to become a school trustee. Sarah and Samuel Seller's daughter Edith was the first graduate of Liberty High School in 1905.

Sarah played a major role in the development of California's silk industry. In 1867 she planted a grove of mulberry trees near her home for the purpose of producing a supply of leaves to feed her silk worms. By 1882 her grove numbered over 3000 healthy trees. Sarah also built a cocoonery near her home that quickly developed a reputation for its scientific management.

According to reports Sarah could hatch as many as 30,000 silkworms from a single ounce of eggs by feeding the worms mulberry leaves four times a day. At the county fair in 1878, Sarah exhibited cocoons and silkworms that attracted much attention from visitors. The Contra Costa Gazette published several articles about Sarah.

Sellers Avenue is named for this pioneer family and is a constant reminder of the impact they had on the early development of this region of California.

MARTHA CANDACE "PATTIE" BAINBRIDGE SHAFER:

Pattie Bainbridge was born in 1871 in Missouri and moved with her family overland to Ripon, California in 1873. She married George H. Shafer when she was seventeen and moved to Brentwood where Shafer operated a livery stable on First Street between Oak and Maple Street.

In 1905 the Shafers established the areas first mortuary which they operated until 1949 when they sold to Alice and Roy Bartheld.

George and Pattie Shafer both became licensed embalmers with Pattie being one of the first women embalmers in California.

The Shafers conducted a modern undertaking and embalming establishment which provided every accommodation and convenience for funerals such as carriages, hearses, pallbearers, ministers and flowers. Funeral arrangements were handled anywhere in the country surrounding Brentwood. Bodies were embalmed for shipment to distant points with caskets and shrouds furnished.

George Shafer was the first mail carrier for Brentwood, Oakley, and Jersey Island areas and for more than forty years served as constable in Brentwood as well as deputy sheriff and deputy coroner. Because of George's responsibilities the business details mostly fell to Pattie who managed both the mortuary and livery stable.

Patty Shafer

Unfortunately we have few records of the first women moving west, most of their stories have been lost with the passing of time. But Ella, Pattie and Sarah each definitely left footprints in the chapters of our past. They are an example of the key roll women played in the development of the Diablo Valley. Until Next Time….

STREET NAME ORIGINS

I'm always being asked questions as to the origin of particular street names in the area. Many were named after pioneer families or early developers of East Contra Costa, and each has it's own tale to tell.

MARSH CREEK ROAD:
Named for Doctor John Marsh, the first American to settle in Contra Costa County. Marsh purchased Rancho Los Medanos from Jose Noriega in 1836.

POINT OF TIMBER ROAD:
Long before the founding of Brentwood or Byron in 1878 the hamlet of Point of Timber was the center of life in the far east county. This small community had a general mercantile, a post office (established November 5,1869), a blacksmith, a stage depot, and a cobbler. Point of Timber Road runs east from Highway 4 at Bay Cities Concrete Plant to Indian Slough. In the 1880's there was a landing and warehouses for grain storage located on the west bank of Indian Slough. Wheat was loaded on barges at the landing, then transported to deep water where it was transferred to larger vessels for transport to Port Costa. The street's name comes from a point of timber that once ran from Mount Diablo toward the river.

SELLERS AVENUE:
This roadway was named for Sarah and Samuel Sellers who settled on a farm in 1860 where the railroad crosses Sellers Avenue today. Sarah is noted in Contra Costa history for planting 3000 mulberry trees and establishing one of the first silk plants in California. She was also responsible for forming the Iron House School District in 1861, and became the first woman school trustee in the state of California.

ARMSTRONG ROAD:
Named for John Samuel Armstrong (*my great grandfather*) who came to the Byron Hot Springs Area in the 1870s. He was instrumental in establishing the Byron Hot Springs School, by donating a corner of his farm as a school site. He served as the first school board president. At one time there were six Armstrong farms located off Armstrong Road (*where the Byron Airport is today*). John Samuel's sons, John, Wesley, Sam, William, and Elwood each farmed a section of land. (*I grew up on one of these farms*).

MINNESOTA AVENUE:
Named for immigrants from Minnesota that settled in this area.

BALFOUR ROAD:
Robert Balfour and Alexander Guthrie came to California in 1869 from Liverpool, England to make their fortune in the new world. They first established Balfour, Guthrie Company in San Francisco as an insurance company. They later expanded their interests and purchased the Marsh Ranch (*12,616 acres*) for $650,000. This company is credited with much of the early development of Brentwood.

LONE TREE WAY:
There was once a one room schoolhouse on this road that had a large old tree in front of it. Joseph Granville Prewett is said to have nailed a sign to the tree naming the road Lone Tree Way.

DAINTY AVENUE:
James and Elizabeth Dainty traveled to California from England in the 1850s. James worked in the coal mines of Nortonville, and later settled in Broines Valley (*near Deer Valley Road*) where he

raised his eight children. William (*James' youngest son*) purchased a parcel of land next to the creek on the outskirts of town. Today the old Dainty house is known as Dainty Center. Dainty Ave was originally named Maple Street.

BIXLER ROAD:
At one time the Santa Fe Railroad stopped at the end of Bixler Road, where it connects with Orwood Road, and picked up milk and cream from the dairies and produce grown locally. The Railroad Company is credited with naming the station Bixler after Louis A. Bixler, a progressive Union Island farmer. Bixler planted eleven hundred acres of milo corn, 850 acres and 310 acres of alfalfa in 1935. For many years there was a railroad crossing sign that bore the Bixler name on this roadway.

EDEN PLAIN ROAD:
William Shafer is credited with naming this road. He settled in the area in 1867 and said this region of California looked like the Garden of Eden.

HOFFMAN LANE:
Ferdinand Hoffman settled in the Byron Area in 1861, purchased 960 acres on which he planted grain. He was instrumental in the promotion of Point of Timber Landing and very active in the Grange and local fraternal organizations.

TAYLOR LANE:
This lane is located at Borden Junction in Byron. Alexander T. Taylor was originally from Canada, coming to California via the Isthmus of Panama in 1866. He purchased 320 acres of rich farmland, which he planted in grain. Taylor was involved in every aspect of the early development of the area. He served on the school board, cemetery board, and was a church deacon. He also held offices in the Grange and local fraternal organizations.

O'HARA AVENUE:
James O'Hara came to California overland in 1857. He purchased hundreds of acres of land in the Oakley area for $5 per acre. He later subdivided the land into 130 parcels. This was the start of Oakley. The road leading to James O'Hara's home became O'Hara Avenue.

VASCO ROAD:
The primary road running between East Contra Costa and Livermore. This road, which has been recently rerouted to the east of the Los Vaqueros Reservoir, took it's name from a group of Basque settlers who lived there in the 1860's and 1870's; the general area became known as "the Vasco".

PAYNE, EUREKA, & CONCORD AVENUES:
These three roadways off of Walnut Blvd. were all named after varieties of walnuts. Some of the first walnut orchards in Brentwood were planted in this area.

SANDMOUND BOULEVARD:
Many years ago Bethel Island was known as Sand Mound because of the mounds of sand there. It later became Stone Tract, then Bethel Tract, and finally Bethel Island. The first school on Bethel Island was named Sand Mound School.

OAKLEY STREETS:
Randolph C. Marsh plotted the streets in the first Oakley subdivision naming the first five streets Main, Acme, Rose, Star, and Home after each of the five letters spelling "MARSH".
Until next time....

DID YOU KNOW?
EAST COUNTY TRIVIA

While researching local history I repeatedly run across bits and pieces of trivia that are noteworthy, but do not necessarily warrant a full column. I attempt to collect these items and occasionally share them with you. DID YOU KNOW?

In 1931 there was a public drinking fountain in front of the Bank of America Building on the corner of Oak and First Street. The fountain was built by the "Best in the West" club, a local social organization founded in 1914 by Mary Reynolds. The fountain was constructed of rocks gathered on the slopes of Mountain Diablo. The plumbing was donated by W.T. McClarren and the masonry work was done by Jack Williams.

Judge Joseph S. Silva was elected supervisor for the 5th district in 1957. Silva had served eighteen years as Judge of the 9th township, three years as director of the fair board, two years as mayor of Brentwood, and six years as Trustee of Brentwood Elementary School.

The Brentwood Methodist Community Church purchased a new electric organ in 1948. Mrs. Vernon Noble became the official organist of the church. The organ was equipped with a reverberation control and a powerful amplifier which when properly used gave what was described as a real pipe organ effect.

The first Apricot Festival was held in Antioch as part of a celebration dedicating the newly built Antioch Bridge in 1926. It wasn't until 1928 that the festival moved to the Brentwood Park. The last Apricot Festival was held in 1936.

In 1955, LUHS's football team was rated the best Class B team in all of Northern California. Scoring a total of 222 points with only 38 points against them. They won seven of eight games played, losing only their first game of the season to Antioch 6-0, and winning all league games. In fact, between 1949–1955 they lost only two league games, and won five championships. Lou Bronzan was acting coach and Jack Ferrill was assistant coach.

R.R. Veale held the office of sheriff in Contra Costa County for forty two years. In 1938 a committee was appointed to design and finance a bronze bust to perpetuate his memory. Upon completion this bronze was placed in the Contra Costa County court house rotunda in Martinez.

Bethel Island flooded in 1927 when a farmer who was installing a floodgate in the levee left the project unattended. During the night a high tide came rushing through the opening washing the levee out and flooding the island.

Dr. Hugh Maiocco established a general medical practice in Brentwood in 1957. He was a native of New York, a graduate of New York University and completed his residency at Contra Costa County Hospital in Martinez. His first office was located on Oak Street and his first patient was Vern Allen.

Snow in Contra Costa County? Yep! A fall of snow blanketed the entire county in 1937. Mount Diablo was capped for almost a week with 15 inches of snow and the Berkeley hills reached depths of five to seven inches. Water pipes froze solid, keeping local plumbers busy replacing burst pipes.

Byron had a Lions Club founded in 1931 with George Anderson acting as the organization's first president. There were 21 charter members. This group was intensely active in all aspects of Byron's development for approximately twenty years.

Enrico Lembi, almond grower, received the appointment of Justice of the Peace for Byron in 1949. He succeeded Mrs. Mildred White, who resigned the position after only three weeks of service. She had been appointed to the position when Hal Lewis resigned due to ill health.

Remember Robert W. Casey? 1 opened my first bank account with Mr. Casey when I was four years old. He became manager of the Brentwood Bank of America in 1944. He joined the bank in 1930 as a bookkeeper at the Antioch branch, later serving in branches in Alturas, Dunsmuir, Loyalton, and Martinez before coming to Brentwood.

The Liberty Union High School baseball field was dedicated "Wallace Field" in July 1937 in honor of Robert Wallace Jr. The first game played on the field was between LeMoine Super Service and the Diablo Club teams.

Brentwood Postmaster R.J. Wallace announced house-to-house mail delivery July 1957.

In 1936 forty eight seniors received their diplomas from Principal E.G. Nash in the high school auditorium. This was the largest graduating class to date. The valedictory was given by Ethel Harrer and the salutatory by Blynn Hannum. An instrumental duet by Mildred and Donald DeMartini completed the program. The speaker for the evening was Edwin A Lee, superintendent of San Francisco schools.

Remember the flood of 1955? In Brentwood, as well as throughout the state, the 1955 Christmas holidays were exceptionally wet. The flooding that took place statewide was considered the worst major disaster in California history since San Francisco's earthquake and fire of 1906.

The Brentwood Fire Department was officially organized in January 1931 with W.C. Watson as Fire Chief. There were twenty-eight charter members. Phone calls reporting fires were handled by the local telephone operator (in the back of W.W. Morgans store) who would sound the fire siren. The first firemen to reach the firehouse would call the operator and learn from her the location of the blaze. The siren was located on the Bank of America Building.

Agriculture was booming in 1938. Shipments for the year from Brentwood, Arbor, Bixler, and Oakley reached a total of 2070 railroad cars. In 1937, there were 2340 cars shipped and in 1936, 1799 cars. In 1938 tomatoes headed the list of shipments, grapes were next, then melons, apricots, peaches, and nectarines.

The magneto phone system in Byron was replaced with dial phones in 1948. A new dial central office was built by Alex Chaim next to his grocery store on Main Street.

"King," a gentle German Shepherd belonging to Douglas Allen of Brentwood, had the distinction of wearing the No. 1 dog license issued under the Contra Costa County dog-licensing ordinance, passed by the Board of Supervisors in response to pleas by stock ranchers because wild dogs were raiding their herds in 1937. License fees were $1.50 for male and $3.00 for females.

ROLLER SKATING

During the late 1800's and early 1900's, roller skating was very popular in the United States, and East Contra Costa County sported its share of rinks.

An American, James Plimpton, invented the modern roller skate in 1863, and by the 1880's, skating rinks were found from coast to coast. A fine pair of skates could be purchased for three to six dollars.

Roller-skating came to Contra Costa County in 1884, with the first rink established in Martinez. The communities of Antioch, Brentwood and Byron were soon to follow. Rinks in big cities of the East were large, elegant places of amusement, offering customers red velvet wallpaper and crystal chandeliers, while for the most part local rinks were converted empty retail stores with the partitions removed.

When the rink was not in a converted retail store, it was usually located in a rented multipurpose building or hall. The Brentwood American Legion Hall was an example. Rinks were generally open on Saturday night and weeknights as well, and some offered afternoon skating. Skate rentals were free, men were charged a 25¢ entry fee and women were admitted at no charge. Originally, spectators were also admitted free of charge but apparently as popularity of the sport grew and spectators became numerous, some rinks imposed a 10¢ charge.

In the 1880's, skating attire was very formal. Men generally wore a coat and tie and often a dress hat or skating cap. Ladies wore a full-length dress of the time, a hat, and often carried a small handkerchief.

As with many other sports, roller-skating threatened participants with injuries from sudden falls, and the local press often reported these events. Most injuries were minor and ordinary, but one accident was spectacular. In 1885, Stevie Cleaves was skating at the Antioch rink, located on the second floor of Marshall's Hall, when he rolled out an open window and fell fifteen feet to the ground. Young Cleaves was knocked unconscious but found to be otherwise unhurt.

At some rinks, musicians played popular tunes of the time for dancing, and the rink owners often offered prizes for the best exhibition by a couple or a single performer. Racing was frequently included in the skating program, but given the small size of local rinks (37 laps to the mile in Antioch) these competitions were rarely valid tests of speed. Instead, the races were often intended to provoke laughter.

Byron and Brentwood rinks both offered masked carnivals as a stimulus for attendance. The practice of dressing in costume and mask seems to have been popular, with participants, and prizes were given for the best costume.

I was unable to locate a lot of information about the first skating rinks in the area. However, according to an article in the February 28, 1885, *Antioch Ledger,* Mr. Van Sant opened a skating rink in Brentwood and formed a "kid's skating club." According to the *Contra Costa Gazette,* Mr. Grunauer managed this rink in March 1886. On March 28, 1885, the *Gazette* announced the opening of a new rink in Byron.

In 1995, I had the opportunity to interview Ellen Hosie Ladd, and she told me a great story about the Byron Skating Rink, which was built by her father, Thomas Hosie, in 1906. Hosie mortgaged his home to secure funds for construction of the rink. It was an unfinished, hip roof building 50 by 100 feet, located on Hosie Lane. The building itself was never finished, but the hardwood floor was made of beautifully matched maple. The rink was open almost every day of the week, with Friday afternoon reserved as a free admission day for Byron and Excelsior School children.

Tom Hosie organized a couple of hockey teams, reserving the rink one night a week for practice or play. Wire cages, big red polo balls and hockey sticks were the equipment. Local residents supplied the enthusiasm. There was also a women's basketball game on skates. They, too, had a special night for practice or games with out-of-town teams.

Thirza Hosie and Jennie Plumley operated a snack bar in one corner of the rink, offering sarsaparilla and homemade baked goods for sale to the skaters and onlookers.

Hosie's rink closed in 1908. The maple floor was removed, and the building used as a hay barn for many years.

Records of the exact locations of skating rinks are limited, but many old-timers have wonderful memories of skating as a child. There was a portable skating rink under a tent in an open field behind Rolando's (today, McCurley Floor Covering) during the 1920's and '30's. In the 1930's Mr. Billingsley operated a skating rink in the American Legion Hall, later moving his enterprise to a building on First Street, where Brentwood Furniture is today. Young residents of Brentwood could also be seen skating in the pavilion at the park, on the sidewalks along Oak Street, and in the concrete foyer of the Brentwood Hotel.

The Rancho, located on Highway 4 between Brentwood and Oakley, also offered a skating facility. This building was used for skating during the week and dances on Saturday night. According to Liberty High School yearbooks from 1908 to 1911 the Oakley Skating Rink, owned by Jesse and Bryner, was open Tuesday and Saturday evenings. Until Next Time....

EAST CONTRA COSTA HISTORICAL SOCIETY

The story of East Contra Costa begins with the Yokuts and Miwok Indians that lived in the shadow of Mount Diablo ages before white men set foot on the shores of the western world. Later came the Spanish explorers, trappers, soldiers, missionaries, gold seekers, cattlemen, wheat farmers, coal miners, sheepherders and merchants. Together they tell the story of this region of California.

The East Contra Costa County Historical Society was founded in 1970. According to the *Brentwood News,* over sixty local residents attended an organizational meeting at the Liberty Union High School cafeteria on April 30 of that year. At this meeting the following slate of officers was elected: Walter Sharafanovich, president; Edna Hill, first vice-president; Charles Bohakle, second vice-president; Gwen Richart, secretary; and Fabian Richart, treasurer. The board of directors consisted of Lou Bronzan, Charles Weeks, Mary Jane Barnes, and Mrs. Agnes Bonde. At that first meeting the group accepted and adopted a constitution and bylaws, and they also set goals for the organization. It was agreed that one of the group's primary goals would be to restore and preserve the home of Doctor John Marsh, on Marsh Creek Road.

The East Contra Costa County Historical Society is dedicated to collecting, documenting, interpreting and preserving our vast and varied past. However, saving memories is of little value unless they are shared. Today, the ECCHS has a wonderful museum where the public can see an example of what life was like on the other side of yesterday.

The organization was established sixteen years before the members' dream of having their own museum became a reality. The society's first attempt to establish a museum arose in 1984 when Mel Gill offered the organization the old Allen house. The main condition Gill attached to his gift was that it would need to be moved from its location on Second Street (across from the city park). The Historical Society's first choice of where to move the house was into the city park, but there was so much opposition to that idea that the society gave it up. In July 1985, a fire gutted the Allen house and the prospect of establishing a local museum looked dim.

Joel Noia offered the society the old Noia house in Oakley, but the Society discovered that it too would need to be moved, and at that time the funds were not available to do the job.

In 1986, the Nail family offered the society a large historic home built in 1878 and 1.3 acres of land belonging to James Nail. John R. Byer, an early pioneer in Brentwood, originally owned the house and sold it to James Nail in 1922. The downstairs of the house contains a living room, parlor, kitchen, bedroom, and two bathrooms. Upstairs there are four bedrooms, two on either side of the hallway. And unlike the first two prospects, this building could remain on the property.

The Nail house has been restored to the splendor that the Nail family, and the Byer family before them, must have enjoyed. With primarily volunteer labor, the Historical Society has wallpapered, painted, rewired, dug a new well, widened the driveway and created a large aggregate parking area, planted trees and shrubs, installed a drip irrigation system, erected a pole barn and many more improvements.

The Nail house not only provides a showcase of photographs and artifacts, but also protects precious records and research materials. The society has collected and restored numerous pieces of old farm equipment, wagons, and early tools.

The East Contra Costa Historical Society Museum is located at 3890 Sellers Ave. It is open on the first Saturday and third Sunday of each month, April through September, and is also open by appointment. The museum offers information about all the communities of East Contra Costa. The four bedrooms upstairs are dedicated to Byron/Discovery Bay, Knightsen, Oakley and Bethel Island, and the downstairs represents Brentwood.

Walter Sharafanovich was the Historical Society's first president, elected in April 1970. He was followed by Bob Gromm 1971–1978; Barbara Bonnickson 1978–1983; Lois Kelly 1983–1986; Rose Pierce 1986–1988; Janeth Estes Gessler 1988–1990; Carolyn Sherfy 1990–1992; Carol Slatten 1992–1994; Mike Ambrosino 1994–1995; Fred Stornetta 1995–1996; Carolyn Sherfy 1997–98; Patrick McHenry 1998–99 and Kathy Leighton 1999-2000.

For information about the East Contra Costa Historical Society phone the museum at (925) 634-8651 or write the society at P.O. Box 202, Brentwood. The organization holds quarterly dinner meetings, with speakers on varied topics of interest to the society. They also publish a wonderful history newsletter, the "Los Meganos," four times a year. Support through membership dues, contributions, memorials, and donations enables the Historical Society to maintain the Nail House and improve the facility.

Nail House with Family Members

Those who settled this area in the 1850's lived lives very different from ours today. It is rewarding to look back to the other side of yesterday occasionally and reflect on what life was like for our forefathers. The East Contra Costa Historical Society works toward a better understanding of our past, providing us with information that serves us well in the building of our future. History is not only the past, but also rests in the present. The story goes on and continues to be told. Until Next Time….

BRENTWOOD

BRENTWOOD TIMELINE

1500 —1800.....Native Americans roamed this region of California.
1772.....Spanish explorer, Captain Pedro Fages, discovered this region of California.
1835.....The Spanish land grant, Los Meganos was deeded to Don Jose Noriega.
1837.....Doctor John Marsh purchased the Los Meganos Rancho.
1841.....The first immigrants, the Bidwell Party, arrive at John Marsh's home on Marsh Creek Road.
1865.....The Liberty School, a one room grammar school, was established on Marsh Creek Road. This school eventually merged with Brentwood Union School District.
1867.....The Brentwood Coal Mine was established.
1867.....The Lone Tree School was established. This school merged with Brentwood in 1959.
1869.....The Deer Valley School was established. This school merged with Brentwood in 1918
1874.....Louis Grunauer and Joseph F. Carey established the first businesses in Brentwood. Grunauer a mercantile, and Carey a blacksmith shop.
1876.....Brentwoods first saloon was established by E. Bacigalupi.
1878.....The San Pablo & Tulare Railroad comes through town.
1878.....The Brentwood Post Office was established with Clarence Esterbrook as the first postmaster.
1879.....The Brentwood School was established. This was a one-room schoolhouse, however it wasn't until 1887 that official school registers were kept by the school district.
1879.....The Union Cemetery was established on four acres donated by Colburn Preston.
1881.....The first map was filed for Brentwood as a township.
1882.....Brentwood boasted of having one hundred residents.
1884.....The Brentwood Hotel was built by Louis Grunauer. This building burned November 29,1903.
1885.....The Methodist Episcopal Church established.
1886.....Doctor H.V. Mott was appointed postmaster.
1887.....Brentwood Grammar School District built a large two room addition onto their existing school.
1888.....The Sanford Family donated land for the Brentwood City Park. This site was known as Brentwood Grove until 1935 when a Park Council was established. In 1946 a park district was formed with Karl Abbott, Grace Nunn, and John Bernard as trustees.
1889.....The First Christian Church was dedicated.
1890.....Brentwood was the largest shipping point for grains between New Orleans and San Francisco.
1890.....There was a devastating fire in town. Moody & Brewers Blacksmith, Shafer's Livery, and Mr. Humphrey's Printing House burned.
1891.....President Harrison's train stopped in Brentwood. He gave a short speech and shook many local residents hand.
1892.....The Brentwood Courier, Brentwoods first newspaper, was established.
1897.....Fred Eachus established the Brentwood News. He later sold his plant to E. W. Netherton who started the Brentwood Enterprise.
1900.....Robert Wallace was elected Justice of the Peace.
1901.....The Brentwood Women's Club was organized with Henriette Stone as president.
1901.....Liberty High School was established with classes held in the grammar school storeroom.
1901.....The first Brentwood Library was established as part of the Liberty High School.
1902.....E. W. Netherton established the Contra Costa Herald, a new eight page newspaper being published in Brentwood.

1902.....The Brentwood Masonic Lodge 345 organized with Will Jerrisleu as first Grand Master.
1903.....The Brentwood Hotel burned to the ground.
1905.....Liberty Union High Schools first graduation. Edith A. Sellers was the only graduate.
1905.....Brentwoods first high school is built on the corner of First Street and Maple Street.
1908.....Brentwood School had 111 students enrolled.
1910.....Balfour, Guthrie and Company purchased the Marsh Ranch (12,616 acres) for $650,000.
1912.....There was a scarlet fever epidemic in the Brentwood area which closed the schools for several weeks.
1913.....Balfour, Guthrie and Company built the Brentwood Hotel on same site as the first Brentwood Hotel had been built at the corner of Oak Street and Railroad Avenue.
1913.....The Bank of Brentwood was built. The bank was absorbed by Bank of California in 1927 and later taken over by Bank of America in 1930.
1913.....Balfour, Guthrie and Company maps the town and sub-divides farm land.
1915.....The Brentwood Public Library and reading room opened. Credit is given to the Library Association with Mrs. Andrew Bonnickson as president.
1915.....Oak Street was paved.
1915.....Fire hits Brentwood burning several businesses on First Street. Lost to the flames were Tremley's Hardware, Peter Olsen's Building; the residences of Hercules Logan, Frank Golden, and M. Sargent, two barns, and the tank and tank house owned by Balfour, Guthrie and Company.
1917.....Ninety four young men from Brentwood signed the roll for the draft (World War I).
1917.....Erastus Granville Nash became principal of Liberty Union High School, a position he held for twenty nine and a half years.
1918.....Liberty Union High School burned from a fire started in the Chemistry lab.
1919.....Roy Frerich's Post 202, American Legion was established.
1919.....Fire swept through downtown Brentwood. The fire started in Jansse Store, which was located on the corner of Oak Street and First Street.
1919.....Dudley D. Watson settled in Brentwood. He became one of the biggest property managers, Realtors, and farmers in the area.
1920.....Sam Hill purchased the Brentwood News from H. W. Bessac.
1920.....A new Liberty Union High School was built on Second Street costing $93,000.
1922.....The first orchards were planted in Brentwood area.
1923.....The new Brentwood Elementary School was built on Second Street.
1924.....The American Legion Hall was built on the corner of Maple and Second Street.
1924.....The Gregory Brothers Nursery acquired acreage for seedling and experimental trees for fruits and nuts.
1924.....Rural free mail delivery began in Brentwood extending to Marsh Creek, Deer Valley and Antioch Road. The service included 115 homes.
1925.....William T. Kirkman Jr. came to Brentwood from Fresno and purchased 1600 acres. He planted many of the first fruit trees in the area.
1926.....The first Apricot Festival was held.
1926.....H. P. Garin came to Brentwood and leased 600 acres. By 1935 Garin controlled more than 30,000 acres in the state.
1926.....By an overwhelming vote, the residents of Brentwood established the first Contra Costa water district to serve the town with a domestic water supply. A $20,000 bond was posted to purchase existing equipment, install complete fire protection, and develop new wells for local supply. This was the first district in Contra Costa County under the county water

district act.

1926.....East Contra Costa Irrigation District was established. The new district consolidated Lone Tree, Knightsen, and Brentwood Irrigation Companies.

1927.....Saint Albans Episcopal Church was founded.

1928.....The Brentwood Fire Department organized with Clyde Watson as the first fire chief.

1928.....The Union Cemetery District was formed. Prior to this time the cemetery was governed by the Union Cemetery Association.

1929.....The Brentwood Lion's Club was established with Dean Watson as the first president.

1929.....H. P. Garin Company had three packing sheds and twenty two cottages for employees. The Garin Company shipped 794 carloads of fruits and vegetables, and used the first refrigerated railroad cars.

1930.....Charles Barkley was elected constable, a position he held for thirty years.

1930.....Balfour, Guthrie and Company had the state's largest dry-yard and packing shed. They had more than 600 employees.

1931.....Edgar Allen purchased the Brentwood News from Sam Hill.

1931.....Dr. Catherine Holden moved the Brentwood Hospital to the second floor of the O.K. Garage building on Oak Street.

1932.....The Diablo Valley Post, Veterans of Foreign Wars was organized in Brentwood.

1932.....The Brentwood School closed for several weeks because of a measles epidemic.

1934.....The Apricot Harvest Strike hit Brentwood. It was estimated that 1,000 to 1,500 more pickers than needed came to Brentwood seeking employment.

1940.....Brentwood School had an enrollment of 417 students.

1940.....Mary P. Allen was librarian at the Brentwood Library.

1943.....Brentwood Irrigated Farms (Balfour, Guthrie) sold their holdings (2,250 acres) to Tom Peppers of Mentone, California.

1947.....The Edna Hill School site was purchased. This school was first known as Brentwood Primary School and renamed Edna Hill in 1955.

1948.....Brentwood incorporates. John Lane is the town's first mayor.

1948.....The Brentwood Police and Planning Departments were organized.

1948.....The Brentwood Order of Rainbow Girls was instituted.

1949.....The Brentwood Rotary Club was established with Clyde Olney as the first president.

1949.....The Immaculate Heart of Mary Catholic Church was built on First Street.

1949.....Oliver Danielson was appointed mayor.

1950.....Joseph Silva was appointed mayor.

1952.....The Brentwood Chamber of Commerce was organized with Ben Peterson as president.

1952.....Everett LeMoine was appointed mayor.

1953.....The first Lion's Carnique was held. This annual event was the Lion's primary fund raiser until 1977.

1954.....Wesley Curtis was appointed mayor.

1955.....Liberty Union High School was rated the best Class B football team in all northern California. Scoring 222 points and only 38 points against them. They won seven of eight games played, losing only their first game of the season to Antioch 6-0, and winning all league games. In fact, between 1949 - 1955 the team lost only two league games, and won five championships. Lou Bronzan was acting coach and Jack Ferrill was assistant coach.

1956.....William "Pete" Gibson was appointed mayor.

1957.....Postmaster Robert J. Wallace announced house-to-house mail delivery.

1958.....Clifford Avery was appointed mayor.

1960.....Art Christensen was appointed mayor.
1960.....Hugh Armstrong was elected constable.
1962.....The Brentwood City Hall was built on Third Street.
1962.....The Brentwood Gun Club was founded with Charles Cogswell as the first president.
1963.....The central portion of Liberty Union High School containing the administration offices, library, some classrooms, and school entrance burned.
1963.....The Brentwood Health Center was established in the old Barkley home next to City Hall on Third Street.
1964.....George Nunn was appointed mayor.
1967.....The Post Office was built on the corner of Dainty Avenue and First Street.
1967.....The Brentwood Hotel was torn down to make way for a new service station.
1969.....The Garin School was built on First Street. This school is named for H.P. Garin.
1968.....Alan Jensen was appointed mayor.
1970.....The East Contra Costa Historical Society was founded. Walter Sharafanowich was the first president.
1970.....The Soroptimist International of East Contra Costa was organized with Kay Davis as president.
1970.....George Gamble was appointed mayor.
1971.....The last passenger train passed through Brentwood. The tracks continued to be used for freight runs.
1972.....Charles B. Weeks Sr. was selected Brentwood's first Citizen of the Year.
1976.....Joe Cunningham was appointed mayor.
1978.....Bruce Ghiselli was appointed mayor.
1978.....The Brentwood Library was built on Third Street.
1980.....The Southern Pacific train depot was demolished.
1980.....Barbara Guise was appointed mayor.
1980.....Brentwood's first Harvest Festival was held in the City Park.
1982.....Roger Moore was appointed mayor.
1984.....Nathan Fisher elected mayor. He was Brentwood's first elected mayor.
1986.....Catherine Palmer was elected mayor.
1986.....The Nail Family donated a large historic home on Sellers Avenue to the East Contra Costa Historic Society for a museum.
1990.....Art Gonzales was elected mayor.
1992.....Brentwood's first Cornfest was held in the Brentwood City Park with Kathy Leighton and U'Geni as chairmen.
1994.....Bill Hill was elected mayor.
1996.....John Morrill was elected mayor.
1999.....Quintin Kidd was elected mayor.

CITIZENS OF THE YEAR:

In 1972 Charles B. Weeks was selected Brentwoods first Citizen of the Year.
1973, Harry A. Geyser,MD; 1974,Genevieve C. Preston; 1975, Homer L. Beasley; 1976, Frank M. Stonebarger; 1977, Arthur C. Christensen; 1978, Rose Pierce; 1979, Charles W. Cogswell; 1980. Barbara Bonnickson; 1981, Warren Wristen; 1982, Marge, Curtis; 1983, Acey "Buck" Cardiff; 1984, Barbara Guise; 1985, Edie Harmon; 1986, Jeanne and Jack Adams; 1987, Catherine F. Palmer; 1988, Lois M. Kelley; 1989, Hoyle Beasley; 1990, Lenora Roehm; 1991, David Blumen; 1992, John Slatten; 1993, Bob Selders; 1994, Dewey DeMartini; 1995, Eunice Castoro; 1996, Bill Putman; 1997, John Becerra; 1998, Richard Allen; 1999, Bertha Ruiz, and 2000, Gilbert Dominguiz.

JOSEPH F. CAREY
&
SOLOMAN DAVIS

Our past is filled with many fascinating stories of hard working adventurous pioneers responsible for shaping this region of California. By the 1860's numerous wheat farmers had settled in the Brentwood area, aware the closest towns were Antioch and Point of Timber. The town of Brentwood was not founded until 1878.

Joseph F. Carey is credited with being one of Brentwood's first residents and businessmen. Carey, a native of Amsterdam, New York was born September 17, 1833. When a child his family resettled in Wisconsin where they tilled the land in a small farm community with few schools. Consequently, Joseph's opportunity for a formal education was limited. However, before leaving his family and moving west in 1853 he did manage to receive a common school education.

Joseph and his younger brother, Levy Carey, decided to seek their fortunes in the gold fields of California. The two young men crossed the plains via ox drawn wagon arriving in Salt Lake City in August and found themselves mining for gold in El Dorado County, California by October of the same year. They remained in El Dorado mining for several years hoping to strike it rich, but by 1857 Joseph had given up on mining and became engaged in the milling business serving local farmers and miners.

Joseph met Mary A. Steel and was married on November 10, 1861. In the fall of 1862 Joseph traveled to the Brentwood area to acquire land under the Homestead Act Laws with plans to have his wife join him. His plans to establish a store front and develop a home for his family were altered in 1863

Carey & Davis Blacksmith

when Mary died of consumption. Following his wife's death Joseph abandoned his original idea and went to Washoe County, Nevada where he remained for several years.

In 1865 Joseph returned to the Brentwood area, this time with farming in mind. He met Laura Ann Welsh, a native of Illinois and they were married in February of 1866 with the union producing five children. Joseph began practicing the blacksmith trade from his farm, mending wagon wheels and working on farm equipment for his neighbors.

By 1874 Joseph had decided to form a partnership with Solomon Paul Davis and establish a profitable blacksmith and repair shop under the firm name of Carey & Davis. This was to be the second recorded business in Brentwood, the first was a general store erected by Louis Gruneaur. By 1878, when the railroad came through, Brentwood was developing into quite a busy little town with several established businesses to its credit. By 1882 there were three saloons, three stores, a blacksmith shop, a school, a railroad depot, the Fish and Blum warehouse, and more than 100 residents.

Soloman P. Davis was born in Missouri in 1843 and came overland with his family when he was ten. They traveled across trackless plains, rugged mountains, and waterless deserts. It was a journey that could not be undertaken until spring, when the grass and foliage were tall enough to sustain the oxen and pack animals. It took the Davis family five months and ten days to arrive in California where they settled in the Clayton area.

Soloman Davis had an interesting history before settling in Brentwood. As a young boy he was employed by Captain Steingrant, to manage and care for government horses pastured at the base of Mt. Diablo. He later resided in Pacheco, Mariposa, and Markleeville. When he was sixteen he became an apprentice to the blacksmith's trade. In 1867, Davis married Louisa Jane Moore and settled at Point of Timber where he began a blacksmith shop.

There are always men like Carey and Davis who pave the way so those who follow may reap the reward, whether it be the formation of a nation, establishment of a state, or building of a new town. These settlers had to survive the rigors of the overland trek to a new wilderness as well as survive the daily hardships of pioneer life upon their arrival.

The strength, courage and endurance our forefathers needed to settle this land and reap the bounty are reflected in the chapters of Brentwood's history. Until Next Time....

THE POST OFFICE

The early settlers of East Contra Costa faced numerous hardships. Mail service did not exist when settlers began to arrive in the late 1840's. Mail sent west usually arrived by ship at the San Francisco post office, where it remained until picked up. Occasionally it would be delivered to John Marsh's rancho. By the time California became a state in 1850, regular stagecoach lines had been set up between San Francisco and San Jose and between San Jose and Sacramento. Coaches began transporting passengers along with three big sacks of letters and one bag of newspapers over rough roads and trails to their destinations.

Pulled by four or six horses, each coach traveled both day and night, stopping at many different stations along the way. East Contra Costa mail was delivered to the Antioch post office. Main stations were forty to fifty miles apart and stops were often made at smaller stations along the way to drop off or pick up mail. In 1850, it could take six to eight months to receive a letter from the East—if it was delivered at all.

The Pony Express was started in April of 1860. Riders for the Pony Express were strong, adventurous young men. My great-grandfather Simon Taylor Barkley rode for the Pony Express during the 1860's in Colorado.

Employing 80 riders, serving 190 stations with over 400 station men, the Pony Express carried mail between St. Joseph, Missouri, and Sacramento, California. Relay stations were spaced every ten miles where the rider received a fresh pony, then raced on to the next station. Each rider was scheduled to ride thirty miles, but sometimes a relief rider would not be at the relay station, so the original rider would continue on until reaching a station where a rested rider waited. Mail was carried to California by the Pony Express for sixteen months. By the mid-1860's the railroad had taken over mail service, and the long wait for news from the East was reduced to a few weeks.

The first post office in the farther reaches of East Contra Costa was established at Point of Timber in 1869. Early settlers of the area, primarily wheat farmers, received mail twice a week from Antioch.

Clarence Esterbrook was appointed the first postmaster of Brentwood in 1878, the same year the railroad was introduced to East Contra Costa. The first post office was located in Louis Grunauer's Mercantile Store on the corner of Oak Street and Highway 4 (where Shanks Chevron is today). In the past 118 years, Brentwood has seen sixteen postmasters and has moved its post office at least ten times. Old newspaper articles refer to several locations, primarily located on Oak Street, although on at least a couple of occasions the post office was moved off Oak. Doctor Motts established a post office in his medical offices on the corner of Dainty and Railroad in the 1880's, and in the 1960's the office was moved to its present location on Dainty and First.

Other locations that housed the postal service were: where Fertado Realty is today; in W. W. Morgan's Store; a building on the corner of First and Oak (this office burned); a building which later was to be Ken's Market; a facility across the alley from the Brentwood Hotel; a building adjoining Irene's Dress Shop and in 1951, a new facility which still houses Irene's today.

In 1951, Mr. and Mrs. Mark Eisele built a new post office and leased the building to the government. This new facility had a third more space to meet the growing demands of the community, giving Brentwood one of the most attractive post office structures of cities comparable in size throughout this part of the state. Evidence of the city's growth was shown by the fact that while the number of lockboxes increased from 480 in the old building to 676 in the new building, all were rented almost immediately, creating the need for a waiting list. The building offered postal workers 2,100 square feet of workspace with an exterior area covered with slab rock.

In 1958, the Brentwood Post Office had a staff of nine employees, two rural routes, and two city carriers, serving a population of approximately 6,400 residents.

The present Brentwood Post Office was built in 1967, on a lot originally occupied by Doctor Cook's home and clinic. This one-story facility with an interior of 4,300 square feet offered postal employees twice the space, with modern equipment and air conditioning.

Brentwood Postmasters: Clarence Esterbrook, 1878; Louis Grunauer, 1880; Doctor Henry Mott, 1886; John Grennen, 1888; James Grennen, 1888; Joseph Carey, 1889; Louis Grunauer, 1890; Alice Benn, 1893; Walkins Morgan, 1897; Charles French, 1915; Minnie Sheddrick, 1917; Carrie Berry, 1921; Charles French, 1922; Richard Wallace, 1936; Dorothy Collins, 1965; Manuel Vilchez, 1970.

DATE POST OFFICES ESTABLISHED

POST OFFICE	ESTABLISHED	DISCONTINUED
Antioch	October 21, 1851	
Bethel Island	August 16, 1946	
Brentwood	September 30, 1878	
Byron	October 30, 1878	
Byron Hot Springs	August 17, 1889 (Moved to Byron)	December 31, 1930
Jersey	April 7, 1879 (Moved to Brentwood)	March 19, 1871
Judsonville	October 24, 1879 (Moved to Antioch)	March 19, 1891
Knightsen	November 22, 1900	
Nortonville	February 2, 1874 (Moved to Somersville)	December 31, 1890
Oakley	October 7, 1898	
Orwood	December 4, 1913 (Moved to Middle River)	November 30, 1921
Point of Timber	November 5, 1869	November 27, 1882
Sand Mound	February 17, 1888 (Moved to Brentwood)	March 31, 1891
Somersville	August 19, 1863 (Moved to Clayton)	November 15, 1910

Until Next Time....

THE MEN WITH THE BADGE

You can't look at the history of Brentwood without noting the fine lawmen that have served the area during the past 145 years. These guardians of law and order held a variety of titles: judge, constable, county sheriff, justice of the peace, police chief and policeman.

Contra Costa became a county in 1850 under the direction of the state legislature. At that time twenty-seven counties were established. Contra Costa was originally comprised of 1500 square miles, but in 1853 it was reduced by one half; the portion that Contra Costa lost became Alameda County.

John M. Watson became Contra Costa's first judge on March 29, 1850. He was judge for the Third Judicial District which included Contra Costa, Santa Clara, Santa Cruz, and Monterey Counties. A few weeks later, the first county judge of Contra Costa, F. M. Warmcastle, took office. The associate justices were Absolom Peak and Edward G. Guest. The first sheriff was Nathaniel Jones.

Judge Wallace

There have been many constables serving East Contra Costa, including Louis Duhnken (1873), A. Miller (1875), Thomas Irvan (1877), and Claus Peers (1881). Two of my uncles served Brentwood as constables from the late 1920's until 1975. Charles Barkley was constable from the late 1920's until he retired in 1960. Uncle Charlie was quite a character, and is remembered warmly by all whose lives he touched. Hugh Armstrong was elected constable for the Brentwood Judicial District in 1960 and served in that capacity and later as deputy marshal until his retirement in 1975.

Early justices of the peace included D. K. Berry (1873), T. D. Uren (1875), H. B. Jewett (1879), R. Shipley (1880), J. W. Carey (1882), and Robert Wallace (1900).

The location of the offices where the justice of the peace, the constable, and the court were housed varied over the years. At one time, there was a justice office where Rich's Drive In is today. The constable's office was behind the fire station, and the court was located across the tracks on

Walnut Boulevard, in the building where the California Custom Art frame shop is doing business today.

Richard R. Veale was county sheriff from 1894 to 1934, followed by John A. Miller.

The Brentwood Police Department was established in 1948 when Brentwood incorporated. The first police station was located in the American Legion building on First Street, along with other city offices. The second station was located on Second Street. In 1962 it was moved to 708 Third Street, where it remained until 1989, when it was again relocated, this time to the corner of Chestnut and Highway 4.

Joe Gomes of Pittsburg is on record as the first Brentwood police chief (1948). Gomes was a Pittsburg policeman and took a ninety-day leave of absence from the Pittsburg department to organize the new Brentwood Police Department. James Patrick Hannratty was later hired by the city council to fill this position. Hannratty had a keen Irish wit, and left footprints in the memories of many of Brentwood's citizens. Arlie H. Worden, remembered for being particularly supportive of local youth groups, followed Hannratty as chief and served in that capacity until 1959. In 1959, Bob Abney was appointed temporary chief and was followed by Edward Weyand. Weyand is credited with updating police equipment, files, and general operating practices. He was acting chief when the department moved to the new Third Street station. Bob Abney was promoted to the position of police chief in 1962. He had served Brentwood for nineteen years as a police officer, and remained as chief until 1967.

The Brentwood Police Department has had numerous officers since it was established. Floyd Ditmars was the first official officer, followed by Tommy Allen, Orvil Reddick, Benny Lindsey, Bob Abney, L. P. Garner, Manuel Quesada, Buddy Sadler, Hoopie Holeman, and Daniel Hargis.

The lawmen mentioned above have definitely left a deep and decisive imprint in our community. Dedicated men like these helped tame this region of California. Prior to 1850, crime was dealt with on the basis of "let the punishment fit the crime." Courts and judges did not exist, and justice was swift and final. Law and order were slow in coming to the West, and people obliged themselves by making their own laws and dispensing justice on the spot. Until Next Time….

BRENTWOOD NEWSPAPERS

For over one hundred years, Brentwood has had a newspaper, in a time that has been one of the most amazing in history. Throughout the 1890's Brentwood was surrounded by thousands of acres of golden wheat. By 1903, the Wright brothers were just succeeding in lifting a heavier-than-air craft off the ground for a few yards, and Henry Ford was preparing to make transportation for the masses possible with his Model T.

The first editions of Brentwood newspapers were coming off the press before there were irrigation systems or orchards in East Contra Costa, and if anyone in Brentwood wanted to go elsewhere, they traveled by train, horse or buggy. The local newspaper played an important role in the lives of Brentwood residents, reporting primarily local gossip, announcements, advertisements and editorials blasting corruption.

The *Contra Costa Herald* was the first newspaper east of Antioch, established in Brentwood in 1891 by Edward W. Netherton. He located his newspaper office in a small cottage on Oak Street between First and Second Streets shortly after a court decision had settled the Marsh Grant litigation and a boom was on in the district. Netherton acted as both printer and writer of his publication. After publishing the paper in Brentwood for about a year, he moved to Santa Cruz, intending to start a paper there.

The *Brentwood Courier,* Brentwood's second newspaper, was born and died in 1892. Unfortunately there was only one edition of the *Courier* printed. The newspaper office burned the day the *Courier* was to hit the street, destroying the printing press and all but one bundle of papers. The few papers that were saved were sold for fifty cents apiece.

Brentwood was without a town newspaper for several years, but in 1896 Reverend Briggs established the *Brentwood Aurora.* Little is known about Briggs' paper.

The *Brentwood Enterprise* was started in 1897 by Fred Eachus and Herman Neubert. Eachus changed the name of his publication to *Brentwood News* in the early 1900s.

In 1914 the *Brentwood News* was owned and edited by J. B. Dixon. Dixon sold his interest to J. J. McCulloch in 1915. From 1916 to 1918 the paper was owned and published by Henry W. Bessac. The newspaper office was located next to the Bank of America building on First Street. Edward Kynoch purchased the paper in 1918 and relocated the newspaper offices to the corner of Chestnut and First Street (where the Centro Mart is located today).

Sam Hill acquired the *Brentwood News* in 1920. He is credited with installing some of the most modern printing equipment (electrically driven) and building the paper's circulation to 650. Hill had very little formal education, having dropped out of school when he was ten years old to work for his hometown newspaper, the *Mountain Messenger* in Downieville. By the time he came to Brentwood he had forty years of newspaper experience. Sam Hill married Edna Heidorn, daughter of a pioneer family, in 1924. It is for Edna Hill, one of Brentwood's teachers, that the Edna Hill School is named.

Editor/publisher Hill was not only colorful in his writing but also very controversial. According to several old timers Hill often wrote editorials that were not considered politically correct by some of the leaders of the community. There are very few copies of the *Brentwood News* published by Sam Hill left, because in 1931, when he sold out to Edgar Allen, the new owner dug a hole behind the newspaper office and burned all the newspapers Sam Hill had produced.

Edgar Allen came to Brentwood in 1931 from the Midwest. He and his wife, Gertrude, purchased the *Brentwood News* and published the hometown weekly for more than 25 years. When

Allen bought the paper it was operated in a small frame building on First Street, where the current Centro Mart is located. In 1940 Allen moved the newspaper to a building on Chestnut. In 1950 Allen built the present *Brentwood News* office at 654 Third Street. One of Allen's most popular columns in the paper was "Over The Back Fence."

Loyal and Janice Bisby of Oakland purchased the paper from Allen in 1955. They operated the paper until 1957, when they sold to Gentry W. Durham. Durham had been city editor of the *Antioch Ledger* for sixteen years prior to moving to Brentwood to become publisher of the *Brentwood News*. In 1965 he sold to John C. Henderson. Durham moved to Sacramento, where he engaged in public relations for state agencies.

Henderson owned the *Brentwood News* for less than a year, selling out to Ernie and Elizabeth Cox in 1966. The Cox family ran the paper until 1969, when they sold out to William H. Brewer. Ernie Cox went to work for the *Oakland Tribune* after leaving Brentwood. Brewer came to Brentwood from Oakland and published the paper until 1971, when he sold to Tom and Samuel Mathews, publishers of the *Tracy Press*. Bob Gromm was managing editor of the paper until 1979, when Lynn Clousing joined forces with the Mathews brothers. In 1986, California Delta Newspapers, owned by Dean Lesher, purchased the *Brentwood News*.

Knight-Ridder Inc. purchased the *Brentwood News* in 1995. In addition to the *Brentwood News* they acquired the *Ledger Dispatch, Contra Costa Times, West County Times, San Ramon Valley Times,* and *Valley Times.*

Harry Green established the *Brentwood Bee* in 1993, a weekly newspaper specializing in local news. This publication prides itself on covering schools, churches, organizations, city hall and local police reports.

Brentwood's newest publication, The Brentwood Press, was established in August 1999 with Rick Lemyre, editor and Jimmy Chamoures, publisher. The Press is a weekly newspaper distributed to every address in Brentwood, Byron and Discovery Bay. The Press truly is a wonderful hometown newspaper, offering East County residents what the early papers of the area offered – local news.

Much of what our forefathers built in East Contra Costa has been erased from the scene by the fate of fire, flood and time. The local newspapers that recorded events as they took place act as a wonderful chronicle of our past. Until Next Time….

BRENTWOOD CITY PARK

Brentwood City Park has been a green spot of community pride for many years. Miss Josephine L. Sanford, gifted the land for the park to the community of Brentwood in 1888, with a provision of the deed requiring the land to be used only as a park. Since the town was not incorporated at that time, the Contra Costa County Board of Supervisors appointed a board of three to administer the park and for many years the property remained undeveloped.

The park, originally referred to as Brentwood Grove, is located on Second Street next to Liberty Union High school. The property became a favorite strolling place for students in the 1920's because of the numerous eucalyptus trees that offered Brentwood residents shade on hot summer days. The park was often used by local youth groups for overnight camp-outs, and children could be seen laughing, running, kicking up and playing in the fragrant eucalyptus leaves.

For a few days in late June the normally quiet park buzzed with activities of the Apricot Festival. The festival, sponsored by the East Contra Costa County Chamber of Commerce, was first held in Antioch, then Oakley the following year, and then moved to Brentwood in 1927. Booths for the event were erected and a stage with a pavilion and dance floor was built.

In 1929, J. W. Williams, a local contractor, constructed a tall welcoming arch in the southwest corner of the park. The arch resembled concrete, but was actually built of wood and finished with plaster in a design typical of the era. It was gray-beige in color, with BRENTWOOD imprinted across the arch. E. R. McClelland of Diablo Electric Company installed electrical utilities, which supplied the park with a myriad of lights.

Brentwood City Park Entrance

During the 1930's the Brentwood Women's Club spent many backbreaking hours planting a strip of lawn along with a row of pyracanthas in an effort to hide the weeds and unsightly litter left by picnickers during the summer harvest season. In 1934, Michael Antonocci, a planning engineer for the city of San Jose, came to Brentwood and consulted with the Women's Club about how to best landscape the park for their purposes.

The improvements installed by the Women's Club gave residents a hint of how beautiful the park could be if the community banded together and created a park district for development of the site. In March of 1935, Mrs. Harold Butcher, Women's Club president, met with the Apricot Festival committee to establish a Brentwood Park Council. This group held numerous meetings discussing how to transform the park from an abandoned, overgrown no-man's land into an attractive and useful recreation center for the entire district

The Brentwood Lions Club soon became involved. Clyde Moores, then president of the Lions Club, appointed a special committee to work on the park project. This committee, headed by W. W. Morgan Jr., consisted of other Lions members: Charles B. Weeks, J. S. O'Meara, George Shafer, Bob Wallace, Millard Diffin, and Arthur Honegger. The committee members, along with other Lions members, were often seen trimming trees, hauling off brush, and building picnic tables.

In April of 1936, the park council presented a petition to the county board of supervisors requesting that a park district be formed using the same boundaries as the local fire district. This would enable the park district to receive funds from taxation for improvement of the grounds. The proposal was placed on the ballot in June 1936, but was defeated by a wide margin of 118 to 81. Blame was placed on the Diablo Valley Grange members who had actively campaigned against the district. Their main complaint was that a definite plan for park improvement had not been presented to the public prior to the election. As the election approached, rumors of spending huge amounts of tax dollars for park improvements and removing all the eucalyptus trees ran wild and could be heard on every corner.

For the following ten years the Brentwood Women's Club, Lions, and American Legion became principal caretakers of the park. In January 1946, Lowell Griffith and Joe Mendez once again spearheaded a petition to attempt the formation of a park district which would permit a small tax for park maintenance and development to be levied. To place the petition on the ballot, they needed 350 signatures of registered voters living within the boundaries of the proposed district. The proposal was placed on the ballot in April 1946, with the townspeople showing an overwhelming sentiment for the formation of a park district. Brentwood residents voted 221 to 15 in favor of the district and elected a board of three to administer it. Elected as trustees were Karl Abbott, with a total of 171 votes; John G. Barnard, with 162 votes; and Mrs. Grace Nunn with 159 votes.

In 1951, the Brentwood city council authorized numerous improvements for the park. The entire site was curbed, walks were added, landscaping was upgraded, and a plaza was constructed at the corner of Oak and Second Street.

Almost every old timer that I have interviewed has wonderful warm memories of Brentwood Park. Many tell stories of the two-day Apricot Festivals that took place at the park in June from 1927 to 1937. Others remember camping out beneath the monstrous eucalyptus trees with their Boy Scout troop, or shooting birds with their first .22-caliber rifle; some reflect on roller skating in the pavilion, or attending dances in the warm summer moonlight. I've even had two Brentwood ladies tell me they became engaged in the park in the 1930's.

The tale of Brentwood Park is demonstrative of the "heart" of this community; residents, and the organizations they belonged to, were not afraid to get involved. Until Next Time….

CITY OF BRENTWOOD PARK TIMELINE

1888.....Brentwood "Block K," located between Second and Third Streets and Oak and Maple Streets, was donated by Miss Josephine Sanford to the community for use as a park.
1890.....The community planted eucalyptus trees in the park. The park became known as "Brentwood Grove."
1927.....The first Apricot Festival held in the park sponsored by the Contra Costa County Chamber of Commerce. The last Apricot Festival was held in 1937.
1928.....Open Air Pavilion built for $3,000. Thirty Brentwood businessmen signed a promissory note at the bank. The note was paid off in 3 years with funds from the Apricot Festival. The pavilion was used for dances under the stars and roller skating.
1929.....Arch with "Brentwood" imprinted on it was built by J.W. Williams and E.R. McClelland. The arch was a tall welcoming arch in the southwest corner of the park. It resembled concrete, but was actually built of wood and finished with plaster, in a design typical of the era.
1930.....San Francisco mayor, James Rolph, was guest of honor at the Apricot Festival. He crowned the Apricot Queen, Marjorie Hannum, of Byron.
1931.....California State Governor James Rolph was the guest of honor and the principal speaker at the Apricot Festival in the park.
1933.....California Lieutenant Governor Frank Merriam, was guest of honor at the Apricot Festival. He crowned the Apricot Queen, Josephine Reichmuth.
1934.....Michael Antonocci, city planner from San Jose, consulted with the Brentwood Women's Club about how to design the park.
1934.....Civil Works Administration ("CWA") workers removed 7 eucalyptus trees on the second street side of the park.
1934.....The Brentwood Women's Club planted a strip of lawn and a row of pyracanthas to hide the weeds and unsightly litter left behind by picnickers in the summer harvest season.
1935.....Lieutenant governor George Hatfield was guest of honor at the Apricot Festival. He crowned Bernice Bunn of Byron as Apricot Queen.
1936.....The Brentwood Lions Club built and installed picnic tables in the park.
1935.....Election held to form a park district. By a vote of 118 to 81 the proposition failed.
1939.....The open air pavilion was demolished. J.O. Brixey from Knightsen purchased the lumber for $187.00
1946.....Joe Mendez and Lowell Griffith co-chaired a joint park committee. They circulated a petition to get the Park District on the ballot. This time residents voted 221 to 15 in favor of the district.
1946.....First park board elected. Karl Abbott (171 votes), John Barnard (162 votes), and Grace Nunn (159 votes)
1949.....New Park District members elected: Mable Jacobsen, Grace Nunn, John Barnard
1949.....Contra Costa County Sheriff's Office supplied prisoners from the Marsh Creek Prisoner Facility to clean the park
1950.....Curbs and sidewalks were installed
1951.....City council authorized the construction of a plaza on the corner of Oak and Second Streets. Grace Nunn elected chairman of the Park Board.

1952.....Lions Club built a brick barbeque pit in the north east corner of the park, next to the playground.
1953.....Mrs. Alex Juett donated $500 to the park for the purchase of playground equipment.
1953.....Lions Club held their first Carnique in the park. The Carnique featured food and game booths, a BBQ, a car raffle, and a firework display. Held on July 4 for 24 years, the Carniques generated between $4,000 and $6,000 annually. These funds were reinvested in the community.
1956.....The Park Board divided the park into plots for local clubs to plant brightly colored flowers. The park was maintained for many years by these organizations.
1961.....Ground breaking for the building to house the park sanitary facilities.
1962.....Brentwood City Hall was built on Third Street across from the park.
1963.....New Park Board members: Grace Nunn, Paul Barnes, Barbara Bonnickson, Floyd Pedersen, and Mable Jacobsen.
1963.....City of Brentwood purchases property next to the new city hall, future home of the community center.
1963.....Brentwood Health Center opened next door to the city on Third Street. The Health Center was in the old Barkley House.
1965.....Sprinkler system installed by volunteer committee, Floyd Pedersen chairman. Improvements installed had a total value of $3,400 but because of donated labor the cost to the Park District was only $1,200.
1966.....A "submarine" was installed in playground as donated by the Brentwood Women's Club. The new piece of playground equipment was designed and built by W.E. Pledger at a cost of $175.
1977.....The Lions Club held the last Carnique in the park.
1978.....A public library built in the park. The new building was part of the Community Center and financed by a federal community development grant. The building was 4,074 sq. ft. and had 27,100 books.
1980.....Brentwood Chamber Of Commerce held their first "Harvest Festival" in the park in August.
1986.....Brentwood Chamber Of Commerce held their first "Art and Wine Festival" in May.
1988.....Brentwood's 40th birthday party held in the park
1989.....Gazebo built. Dick Allen (chairman), Janet Hammond, Misty Hummel, Dave Bluman, Ann Templeton. Landscaping around gazebo done by the "Dig" group.
1990.....Memorial Christmas tree planted in the southwest corner of park. It is dedicated to Bob Metez and Jackie Nebergall, chairmen: Duane Schnittker and Hoyle Beasley.
1992.....First Cornfest held in the park. Kathy Leighton and Geni Murdock were chairmen. Byron Bonnickson was Kernal Korn and Chantelle Leighton was the first Cornfest Queen.
2009.....The last originally planted eucalyptus tree was removed from the park

BRENTWOOD FIRE DEPARTMENT

I found researching the history of the Brentwood Fire Department a challenge at best. I make every effort to tell the history of whatever topic I'm researching as factually as possible. However, history relies on the memories of old-timers—often very selective— as well as old newspaper columns, journals and personal letters (written to reflect an incident as the writer saw it), and early history books.

The Brentwood Fire Department was organized in 1928. Prior to this time, when there was a fire, someone would ring the church bell and every man within hearing distance would respond. Farmers rushed to town from their fields and local businessmen closed their stores. Townspeople would grab a sack and a bucket to be used in the possible firefight ahead. Most fires in the early days were fought with bucket brigades.

Frank Dowell, a local mechanic, and Hercules Logan, a local builder, decided the town needed a better way to fight fires, as in those days Brentwood was surrounded with fields of volatile grain. The two men fixed up an old four-cylinder Star-Durant chassis for fire fighting. This makeshift fire truck lasted for a while, but the chassis gave out and the town found themselves in need of new equipment. This first engine was kept at the Oak Street Garage and Machine Shop (the garage later became LeMoin's OK Garage). When the chassis on the first engine gave out, Everett LeMoin and Clarence Bray took a 1917 Chevrolet touring car, stripped it down, installed a ten-gallon tank for a seat, a basket carrying two 35-gallon chemical tanks, and a one-inch, 110-foot hose. This engine was first kept at the OK Garage and later in the Ford Garage on First Street (where Brentwood Furniture is located today).

The chemical tanks on the fire engine each had a screw cap. A little frame hung down in each cap that held a small lead container filled with sulfuric acid. When the fire fighters got to the fire they turned each tank over, dumping the acid into a soda-and-water solution, thereby creating the pressure necessary to force the water out through the one-inch hose.

The siren on this makeshift fire engine was hand operated: one of the volunteers would crank the siren's handle while the engine made its way over a dirt road to its destination. They always tried to carry extra bottles of acid and packages of soda for recharging the tanks.

The first two fire trucks in Brentwood were privately owned. The first truck by Dowell, then LeMoin, then Roy Griffith, and finally, Frank Lawrence.

By 1927, the townspeople started talking about organizing a real fire district enabling them to collect taxes. By 1928 a committee was in place to actually recruit volunteers and start purchasing fire equipment. Clyde Watson, Jerry O'Meara, Charlie Wells, Everett LeMoin and Harold Anderson were members of that organization committee. Clyde Watson was the first fire chief and Ray Wallace was the second chief. The first goal of the organization was to acquire a better fire engine.

An engine was ordered in 1928, but did not arrive until 1929, because it had to be built. The first Brentwood engine purchased with tax dollars was a 1929 Seagraves and was usually driven by Everett LeMoin or Charlie Cogswell on fire calls. It wasn't until 1949 that the department purchased a 1941 GMC pumper truck.

Some of the Brentwood Fire Department's first volunteers were Harold Anderson, Aud Lawrence, Jerry O'Meara, Charlie Cogswell and others. These dedicated men served on a volunteer basis with absolutely no pay or reimbursement of their personal costs.

The county built the first Brentwood Fire Station in 1930 on First Street, next to the American Legion Hall, to house the town's new fire engine and the old Chevrolet engine that had served the community so well. This building was later moved to the back of the property to be used as the town's courthouse. Justice of the Peace Joe Silva and Constable Charlie Barkley's offices were originally located there. Later

Brentwood volunteer firefighters promote ticket sales to the annual Brentwood Fireman's Ball. Seated: Bob Abney, Chief of Police, City of Brentwood.

the building was used by Judge Blair Rixon and Constable Barkley; and as time passed the building was eventually used by the fire district as an office. Today it is used as offices for the publishers of the *Brentwood Bee*.

For many years the Volunteer Fire Department hosted an annual Firemen's Ball. The first ball was held in 1932. This event was one of the top social events of the year for the community as well as the fire department members.

Receipts from the ball went into a special savings account that was used for the benefit of firemen who had been injured on duty, or were in need of financial aid because of illness or injury.

In 1950 Lowell Griffith was fire chief and the organization had twenty active members. At that time a fireman received $1.50 for answering a call, but only if there was an actual fire. This did not begin to cover the cost of the men's clothing or shoes damaged while fighting fires, and they were also expected to donate at least 76 hours a year in drills.

Brentwood's first volunteer fire fighters would be amazed at the modern equipment East Diablo Fire District has today. We've come a long way from the 35-gallon tanks on the old Chevy touring car. The department today has a 3,000-gallon tender that can provide a running supply of water to fight fires in remote locations and immediate access to the precious liquid from hydrants in town.

It was men like those mentioned in this story that truly took an active part in developing Brentwood in the early years and they have all left footprints in the pages of our past.

FIRES:

1903: The first Brentwood Hotel burned. This fire was fought with dozens of townspeople running a bucket brigade to battle the flames. The hotel and a hardware store next door were both destroyed in the blaze.

1915: An entire business block on the east side of First Street between Oak and Chestnut was leveled.

1918: Liberty Union High School fire started in the chemistry lab. The building was destroyed, but the students were safely evacuated without any injuries.

1919: A fire started in Jansse Store and swept through the downtown portion of Brentwood.

1929: Balfour, Guthrie's grain warehouse. This was the first big fire where Brentwood's "new" fire engine was used. The warehouse burned to the ground but the firemen were able to save the Southern Pacific depot next to it.

1946: A fierce fire razed the Shell Oil Company tanks, office, storeroom and dock on the corner of Railroad and Dainty Avenue.

1963: The central portion of Liberty Union High School burned, including the administration offices, library and some classrooms. Until Next Time....

1915 Fire in Brentwood gave the bucket brigade a workout as it burned, from right Trembley's Hardware Store, Pete Olsen building adjoining, Frank Golder, Hercules Logan and the A. Sargent residences plus the tankhouse. Notice the bucket brigade on the roof near the tank house, on the porch roof and the board walk at the left of the picture.

BRENTWOOD HOTELS

As we look back into the chapters of Brentwood's past, it is interesting to note the town's early hotels. This region of California was famous for its rich soil and the wheat produced by early settlers. Many young families planted their roots in the shadow of Mount Diablo, and as the area became populated, opportunities arose for early merchants to establish businesses.

Louis Grunauer was the first merchant of Brentwood. He built Brentwood Mercantile in 1878, the year the railroad from Antioch to Banta was established, and built the town's first hotel six years later. The first Brentwood Hotel was on the corner of Oak Street and Railroad Avenue (today's Highway 4).

Like so many of the early settlers, Grunauer saw a need and filled it. Brentwood was a busy little village, there were land speculators, drummers (traveling salesmen), railroad men, wheat buyers and young families from the East looking for a community where they could plant their roots and raise their children. Grunauer's hotel offered these weary travelers a place where they could wash off the road dirt and spend a night, enjoying the comfort of a bed and fine food and drink while tending to their business.

The Brentwood Hotel was of frame architecture, a two-story hostelry offering twelve guest rooms, and a decorative balcony where guests could bask quietly in the morning sun. There was a large wooden water trough with several hitching posts for guests' horses near the entry, and a row of locust trees lining the perimeter of the building. The hotel had wide wooden sidewalks on two sides with benches where townspeople could rest and visit with neighbors. The hotel also offered its guests a tavern and dining room.

On November 29, 1903, a young man employed at the hotel was fired by the hotel manager, Frank Brown, for stealing hotel property. Angry with Brown, the boy decided to take revenge by starting a fire in the basement of the hotel, where boxes and old papers were stored. In the middle of the night the Brentwood Hotel burnt to the ground. Fortunately all guests were aroused. Some slid down the posts that supported the upstairs balcony, and others fled, wearing just their nightshirts, into the street.

In 1913, Balfour, Guthrie & Company hired Hercules Logan, a building contractor from San Francisco, to construct the Bank of Brentwood and a second hotel, to be named Hotel Brentwood, on the same site where the original hotel was located. A magnificent, $50,000 hotel offering guests every convenience and service available at the time, it was one of the most modern establishments in this region of California. Balfour-Gutherie located their offices on the main floor of the Hotel. After completing the hotel and bank, Logan decided to settle permanently in Brentwood and over the next four decades built numerous businesses, homes, dairies and ranch houses in the area.

The Hotel Brentwood was a two-story structure, built in a semi-Mission ornamental style of reinforced concrete and steel. It consisted of forty rooms, including three suites, and two courts beautifully arranged for the pleasure and comfort of its guests. The outdoor pergolas and lawns were kept neatly manicured, and guests could often be seen taking tea there on a Sunday afternoon.

The reception room, or lobby, was 35 by 80 feet, with a huge fireplace where great log fires burned in the cool evenings and early mornings. The dining room was 40 by 50, feet offering the community a location for receptions and balls.

Hotel guests were offered luxurious furnishings, fine dining, and spacious private rooms with hot and cold water provided in every room. There were electric call bells, electric lights, telephones, and baths offered as special features of this luxury establishment.

In July 1967, the Brentwood Hotel went down in a cloud of dust. Once the center of Brentwood activity, the hotel was leveled to make way for a new Standard Oil Company service station. Until Next Time....

SWEENEY'S HISTORY

More often than not, one of the first business establishments in an early western town would be the saloon. Saloons functioned as social centers for the community, places where people would gravitate to gather around a potbellied stove and gossip while tipping a nickel beer. Today the potbellied stove has been replaced by central air and heat, with the nickel beer costing a couple dollars. Brentwood still has a saloon that has acted as a gathering place for locals for over one hundred years.

Sweeney's was one of the first businesses established in Brentwood, originally known as Bacigalupe's Bar in the early 1880's. James Torres came to California in 1880 from Genoa, Italy, and settled in East Contra Costa in 1887. In 1888 he became proprietor of Bacigalupe's Bar and operated the saloon until his death in 1917.

When Torres purchased Bacigalupe's Bar in 1888 he renamed the establishment Torres' Saloon & Ice House and built two small buildings out back, one for storing ice and the other as a bath house that offered his customers a bath for 25 cents.

There were hitching posts and a watering trough in front of Torres' Saloon where you could water your horse before enjoying a brew. The building had a covered, wood-plank porch on two sides where shelter could be found from rains during the winter or sun in the summer. You could usually find an amicable poker game inside, and a witty bartender to lend you an ear. According to old-timers, the hitching post and water trough were on the site until the late 1940's.

Behind the Saloon & Ice House on First Street was Cowen's Blacksmith (this later became Grigby's Blacksmith), Shafer's Livery and Liberty Union High School. Brentwood's first high school was built on the corner of First Street and Maple in 1901 where the Legion Hall is located today. By 1913 Brentwood had attracted numerous businesses—across the street from Torres' Saloon were W. W. Morgan's store, Rolando's saloon and the Bank of Brentwood.

History remembers "Jimmie" Torres as a small, humorous man with an infectious smile who was filled with energy and involved with Brentwood's early development. Jimmie owned one of the first bicycles in town and could be seen peddling down the dusty roads throughout East Contra Costa. He was active in campaigning for the county to build a high school in Brentwood; involved in several regional fraternal organizations and social orders; was instrumental in

Jimmie Torres

forming a volunteer fire brigade; served on the Brentwood Businessmen's Committee (a group of local merchants) for many years; was involved in the town's getting electricity and its first paved street; and was a true supporter of several area athletic teams.

In 1913 Torres purchased forty acres located a half mile from Knightsen and planted walnut and orange trees along with potatoes, corn and other vegetables. Although he is primarily remembered as a businessman in Brentwood, he enjoyed his time spent farming the land.

While playing a friendly game of poker with several townsmen in 1917, Jimmie Torres was murdered. The murderer, who was never apprehended, shot through a rear window of the bar, hitting Torres in the back. Many employees that have worked at the tavern since his death are convinced that Jimmie Torres' ghost still resides on the site.

Since 1917 Torres' Saloon has had many proprietors and several facelifts. At one time part of the building had a second floor that housed boarding rooms where salesmen and others passing through town could find a night's lodging. The second floor was burned in the late 1930's and never rebuilt.

Robert Wallace owned most of the businesses on Oak Street for many years and leased the saloon to different businessmen. I was unable to find who operated the business right after Torres' death, but according to several old timers the bar was renamed Diablo Inn and Joe Rolando managed it for a short time during the 1920's. Rolando had come to America in 1891 from Turin, Italy, settling in Michigan before moving west to San Francisco in 1904. In 1913 he came to Brentwood, where he first worked at the Brentwood Hotel, then the Pioneer (a saloon located near where Rich's Drive In is today). Joe Rolando purchased the corner of Oak Street and First Street in 1922 and built the Rolando Club.

By the 1930's, George Murchio and Bert Kiefier operated the Diablo Inn, renaming it the Diablo Club. About 1938 they remodeled the building, changing the establishment from a "bar" to a "night club." A dance floor was added and the building was enlarged.

Between 1945 and 1956 the Diablo Club changed hands numerous times. Sid Hulbun; Archie Reed and Johnny Tipton; Carl Hopper and the Lee brothers; and Tommy Stewart were among the managers. In 1956 Willy Lindsey purchased the bar, and in 1974 Larry Lindsey and Ken Bloodworth took ownership. Roger Sweeney bought the Diablo Club from Lindsey in 1986, renaming it Sweeney's Station Four, and today the business is owned by Patty and Angelo Arminio.

Through several name changes and owners—Bacigalupe's Bar, Torres' Saloon, Diablo Inn, Diablo Club or Sweeney's—the little bar on the corner of Oak and First Streets has played an important role in the history of Brentwood. Businessmen have made deals, sealing their transactions with a few quiet words, a handshake and a drink; birthdays, weddings and wakes have been celebrated within the tavern's walls, and many old-timers remember the bands and dance floor. Over the years residents and folks passing through Brentwood have found a place where they could try their luck at poker or pan. During the twenties, thirties and forties, there were slot machines ready to except a customer's change. For many years there were two active bordellos within a block of the saloon, and at different times during history the tavern has offered a café or restaurant.

During Prohibition, when the sale of alcohol was illegal (1920 to 1932), the bar became a billiard hall, but it is said that booze was still available to customers known by the bartender and that the basement was well stocked. Brentwood is said to have had no shortage of bootleggers.

Sweeney's still offers the residents of Brentwood a place to meet with neighbors over dinner or a cold brew and discuss politics, business transactions and local gossip. I'm sure that if the walls of this historic establishment could talk, endless great tales would be heard.   Until Next Time....

JOHN FLETCHER

I've stumbled onto several great characters while digging through chapters of my family's past. A great great aunt of mine, Olive Barkley, was one of them. Olive was a teacher in East Contra Costa during the 1900's and married into the Fletcher family in 1906. Her father-in-law was John Fletcher, Sr.

John Fletcher was the ninth child of William and Mary Fletcher. He was born on February 7, 1839 in Whitesboro, New York and came to California in 1859 at the age of 20. He worked as a teamster at the Mare Island Naval Shipyard and later as a ranch hand near Vallejo.

In 1862 John was one of the first one hundred Californians to join the war effort by enlisting in the U.S. Army as a member of the California Hundred to fight for the preservation and unity of his country in the Civil War. This brave company played a courageous and active part in the struggle to maintain the Union.

On December 11, 1862 the California Hundred sailed from San Francisco on a three week voyage through the Isthmus of Panama to Readeville, Maine. They became Company A, 2nd Massachusetts Calvary, a unit which participated in 51 engagements.

By 1864 John had earned his Sergeant stripes in Company A. He was also captured at the Battle of Opequen Creek, Virginia that same year and confined to the Confederate Libby Prison for several months. Upon his release on May 21, 1865, John was promoted to 2nd Lieutenant of Company A.. He completed his military career in Virginia on July 20, 1865 and returned to California to engage in farming.

John married Mary Hallman on October 30, 1871. They made their first home on a ranch in the Vallejo area, where they had 6 of a total of thirteen children William, Carolyn, Florence, Belle, Georgia, and Robert. In 1877 the Fletcher family moved to the Chadbourne Ranch in Deer Valley, Contra Costa County where Richard, Mary, Dorothy, Maude, Edna, Anna and John Jr. were born (John Jr. was to marry my great great aunt Olive Barkley). In 1915 the Fletcher family again moved to another ranch on Marsh Creek near Brentwood.

The Fletcher children received their elementary education in a little one room school house on Deer Valley Road. During the 1880's and 1890's, average enrollment of the school was about 25 students. You may recognize their classmates names like Elsworths, Sullengers, (my great great grandmother was a Sullenger), Shellenberger, Van Buren, Diffin, Darby, Saunders, Joslin and Sprawlings that also attended Deer Valley School. Students would graduate at the completion of 8th grade and go on to a central school such as Brentwood to take a final examination. They were tested in every subject presented in the elementary school programs for graduation from Public School.

Deer Valley School was also a social center and gathering place for families of the region serving as a meeting house as well as a place for dances and other school, and social activities, and programs.

John and Mary Fletcher eventually moved back to the Vallejo area for the remainder of their lives but many of their children remained in East Contra Costa. John died in Vallejo in 1927, as the last surviving member of the California Hundred.

Like so many of early settlers John Fletcher definitely left his footprints in the chapters of our past. Until Next Time....

JUDGE ROBERT WALLACE

Robert Wallace Jr. is noted in Brentwood history for serving as justice of the peace for many years and as a prominent figure in local politics. It is impossible while researching the early settlement years of this region not to recognize Wallace as a key player in the development and taming of East Contra Costa.

Robert Wallace Jr. was born in San Francisco on September 28, 1859, the son of Robert and Anne Wallace, both natives of North Shield, England, who had traveled to California in 1856.

Several years before the town of Brentwood was originally founded, Robert Jr. moved with his family to the area at the age of twelve. They originally purchased 160 acres of land south of Brentwood and were among the first wheat producers of the region.

Judge Wallace's office was located in a small building where Rich's Drive In is today. He was elected as justice of the peace in 1903, a position he held for many years. His office acted as headquarters not only for judicial affairs of the area and his business affairs, but also as a place to sell wood, coal, ice and baths, which could be taken at the rear of the office where a tub had been installed. He was instrumental in establishing the Bank of Brentwood, becoming a director, and was also the first insurance salesman of Brentwood, selling Home & Connecticut Hartford Insurance to residents and business owners.

Chapters of Brentwood's history are peppered with Judge Wallace's contributions to the area. Judge Wallace was a gravel-voiced man fond of cigars and derby hats. He was heavily involved in business, church and school matters and many fraternal organizations. He was a charter member of the Masonic Lodge (organized in February 1902), serving as master for five years. He was also active in the Byron Odd Fellows, a member and director of the Point of Timber Cemetery Association and a member of the Contra Costa County Agricultural Association.

Wallace married Alice J. Murphy of Concord and they produced five children. They purchased a beautiful two-story home on Railroad Avenue (today Highway 4) between Dainty Avenue and Pine Street in 1897. This home was the largest in the area for many years and is currently the home of Sue and Steve Fox.

One of Judge and Alice Wallace's sons, Richard, was manager of the Bank of Brentwood for many years, and then became Brentwood's postmaster, a position he held until retirement. Richard Wallace married Minerva Weihe, whose father was station master of the Southern Pacific Station in Byron.

Looking back once again to the other side of yesterday, one cannot help but be impressed by Judge Wallace and the pioneers like him who paved the way for East Contra Costa's development. They saw settling this territory as a challenge, took the challenge, and definitely left footprints in the chapters of our history. Until Next Time....

THE SHAFER FAMILY
BRENTWOODS FIRST UNDERTAKER

Funeral Homes as we know them today didn't appear in East Contra Costa until 1905. Early settlers of the area took care of their own when it came to preparing the bodies of their loved ones. When ice was available the deceased was laid out in an ice coffin to help preserve the corpse.

Final respects to the deceased were usually extended in the parlor of the family home where family and friends would gather. Neighbors provided homemade wreaths and bouquets. When it was time for services, friends and relatives would line their carriages up behind a horse drawn wagon which carried the deceased to a local church or sometimes directly to the cemetery. Family and friends usually sang church hymns at the graveside, and if the departed was a member of a fraternal organization, lodge members often participated in the service.

In 1905 George H. Shafer, the son of William and Elizabeth Shafer, established the first undertaking business in Brentwood. It served the entire east county.

William Shafer was a native of Pennsylvania, coming to California in 1855 via the overland trail. Elizabeth (Pierce) Shafer traveled across the plains by wagon from Ohio with her parents in 1852. Elizabeth and William met and married in 1861.

William was known as one of the early rivermen of the area. He and Elizabeth settled on a farm near Isleton raising vegetables and transporting them down the Sacramento River to coal mines in the foothills near Antioch. In 1867 the young couple relocated to the Eden Plain District (at the corner of what today is known as Sellers Ave. and Delta Road). William Shafer is credited with naming this area near Knightsen, Eden Plain. Elizabeth reflected on the area many years after her arrival, saying, "The wild oats grew in profusion, and wild cattle and horses roamed at will over the vast domain; wild flowers of every hue and variety grew upon the hillsides and in the valleys." William and Elizabeth eventually farmed 900 acres in the area and had five children, Adrian, George, Mable, Winifred, and Hannah.

George Shafer grew up on his parents farm and attended Eden Plain school. At age sixteen he went to Stockton and entered a normal school and business college. After graduating he worked for C. A. Hardware & Implement Co. for several years. He returned to East Contra Costa County where he purchased a livery business from P. J. Moody in Brentwood and successfully operated the livery for twenty five years. George bought, sold, and traded horses as well as teams and livestock. He outfitted land buyers, sightseers, traveling men, and hunting and pleasure parties providing horses and buggies, teams and vehicles, and any kind of equipment requested. Each outfit, on request, was provided with a competent driver familiar with the countryside. As a sideline, George bought and sold hay and grain.

George met and married Martha Bainbridge, a native of Missouri, in 1888. He was elected constable of the area that same year holding the office for more than forty years. He also served as deputy sheriff and deputy coroner. George and Martha had a son named Earl in 1890. Earl received a local education and became a partner in Shafer & Son Funeral Parlor. Earl Shafer died in 1944.

George became a licensed embalmer at age 39 and engaged in the undertaking business. In 1910 the Byron Times described his business as follows: "Mr Shafer conducts a modern undertaking business and embalming establishment, providing every accommodation and convenience for funerals, such as carriages, hearse, pallbearers, minister and flowers. Funeral arrangements are handled anywhere in the country surrounding Brentwood, bodies are embalmed for shipment to distant points, caskets and shrouds are furnished, all in a quiet and decorous manner." The Shafers funeral parlor consisted of a four room house located on First Street. In 1934 a new funeral parlor was built.

Looking West on Oak Street - 1913

George retired from the undertaking business in 1949 selling the business to Roy Bartheld.

The Shafer's were both very active in fraternal organizations. George was a member of Masons, Odd Fellows, Eastern Star, Native Sons, Pyramid of Scots, Florence Knight Rebekahs, the Foresters, Brentwood Lions (of which he was a charter member) and the Diablo Valley Grange. He held fifty year pins with the Masons and the Eastern Star and served as president of the East Contra Costa Chamber of Commerce.

The Shafer family played an active role in the development of East Contra Costa. William was one of the first settlers in this region of California, and his son George was one of the first businessmen when Brentwood was little more than a village.Until Next Time....

CAKEBREAD
PIONEER COALMINER - WHEAT FARMER

As we look at East Contra Costa's history, on the other side of yesterday we find wonderful stories of adventurous, enthusiastic young men and women that came here and turned the wilderness into thriving little hamlets and towns. This region of California grew and prospered with these pioneer families who saw California as a virtually inexhaustible repository of open living space. The state offered room to stretch for a better life, and rich earth available to anyone sufficiently daring and hardworking to claim and use it.

There were several ways to reach California from the East in the 1850's, with each route having its good and bad points. The safest way was via Cape Horn (the southern tip of South America), a 17,000-mile trip that cost approximately $150. The voyage took five to six months in close quarters, with few stops for replenishment of food and water supplies. Passengers experienced long days of boredom with a diet of salted meat and dried bread. It was the first voyage for most passengers, and they became seasick as the ship was tossed about by the waves and the winds of an occasional storm.

Robert Cakebread, at 19 years of age, was lured to California by the warm yellow glow of gold dust he had heard about. He brought his 17-year-old wife, Martha Smith Cakebread, to California from Bloxham, Oxfordshire, England, via Cape Horn in 1857. After reaching the San Francisco harbor they immediately set out for the Tuolumne gold fields, where they spent nine unsuccessful years attempting to mine their fortune.

In 1866, they moved to Somersville (south of Antioch), where Robert found employment in the coal mines. Conditions in the mine

Cakebread trucks loading alfalfa hay into Southern Pacific Railroad Cars

where Robert and his co-workers labored were hard and dangerous; it was not uncommon for methane gas emitted by the coal to explode. Illness from continued exposure to coal dust and moisture and injuries from falling rock and machinery-related accidents were accepted as a way of life in the industry. Robert worked in the coal mines for nearly nine years.

In 1874, in partnership with Thomas Vivian, Robert purchased 480 acres of land near Judsonville as a way out of the mines. He and Thomas raised sheep on their holdings, marketing the lambs throughout the Carbondale District. By 1879, East Contra Costa County was booming. The railroad had arrived in 1878, and the communities of Byron and Brentwood were experiencing their first stages of development. Robert sold his holdings to Vivian and purchased 320 acres of hilly land about two miles south of the John Marsh Stone House on Marsh Creek Road and moved his family to the new acreage.

The acreage was covered with timber (primarily oak), and there was a good market for fuel wood to power steamboats along the rivers. Robert cleared the hillsides, transporting endless cords of wood to Point of Timber Landing, where they were purchased by ship captains.

After the land was cleared of trees, Robert planted his acreage with wheat and other grains, and within a few years he had saved enough money to lease an additional one thousand acres near the Stone House, on which he also planted grain. Robert scratched the soil without benefit of tractor or electricity from sunup to sundown, 365 days a year. During the late summer and fall he could be seen with his horses and plow turning over row after row of rich, fertile earth. Once the soil was tilled he would hitch up his team and wagon and use a hopper to scatter seed over the freshly turned fields. The seed was left to lie on the ground all winter. After the rain softened the hard soil, the wheat would sprout in the spring and early summer and was soon ready to harvest.

By 1891, Robert was reaping the rewards of his efforts and was able to purchase land in Antioch to build a new family home as well as an additional 160 acres on Lone Tree Way, where he planted almonds and grain.

Of Robert and Martha Cakebread's fifteen children, only eight survived to adulthood: Mary Ann (married William Chick); John (married Lena Guest); Elizabeth (married Fredrick Wickham); William (married Henrietta Schwendel); James (married Anna Smith); Robert Jr. (married Alfaretta Lincoln); Charles (married Odel Powell); and Mattie (married Sam Morgan).

Robert and Martha valued a proper education for their children and saw that the children attended school first in Somersville and later, Liberty School, a one-room schoolhouse located on Marsh Creek Road. Robert (and later his son William) served as trustees to this facility, and three generations of Cakebreads were present on the Liberty School roll. Robert and Martha were diligent members of their community; they were active church members, they were involved in school matters, and they were active with the Odd Fellows Lodge. Robert Cakebread died in Antioch in 1912 at the age of 74, and Martha died in Los Angeles two years later.

The tale of the Cakebread family is representative of many families of the time. They came to this rugged wilderness, carved out a life, raised their families, and cleared the way for generations to follow. Until Next Time….

JAMES BALL DAINTY

East Contra Costa grew and prospered because of early settlers laboring behind the scenes, men whose names are interwoven and identified with development of this region of California. Many of these pioneers saw California as a virtually inexhaustible reservoir for new living space with room for a family to stretch for a better life. The rich earth was free to anyone sufficiently hardworking and daring enough to claim and use it. James and Elizabeth Dainty are a good example of pioneer spirit at its best.

James Ball Dainty, born June 21, 1834, and Elizabeth Harriet Whitehouse, born September 5, 1833, in Dudley, Worcestershire, England, were married at the parish church in the parish of Sedgley, county of Stafford, England, on June 13, 1853. This pioneer couple and two infant daughters traveled by ship to the New World. They first sailed as far as Australia, where they remained for several years before continuing to California. While residing in Australia the Daintys had a third child that died and was buried there.

According to Zelma Dainty Beaman, James and Elizabeth's granddaughter, the young couple first settled in Pittsburg, California. James obtained a job as a miner in the Nortonville coal mines. He had never mined before, and although he disliked mining he continued for many years before becoming a wheat farmer.

One Sunday afternoon the young couple, having decided to picnic in the foothills, packed a lunch and hiked across the hills to a location where they relaxed under an oak tree overlooking Briones Valley. Both were so taken with the scenic little valley that they decided to apply for a land grant. On January 8, 1875, they received a 160-acre U.S. land grant signed by Ulysses S. Grant. The Daintys built a small house and a barn, and made numerous other improvements to the property. James continued to travel across the hills to the Nortonville mines each day. The Dainty children attended school, first in Nortonville, then later at Liberty Grammar School on Marsh Creek Road.

I had an opportunity to visit the original Dainty homestead in Briones Valley, where evidence of this pioneer family is still very apparent, a few months ago. The small farmhouse James and Elizabeth built over a hundred years ago remains nestled between the rolling green hills of this peaceful valley. The wooden porch has shifted off a rock foundation that once held it in place, and the house itself looks a little forlorn. There is an old barn and the remnants of wooden corrals. I saw parts of an old windmill that no doubt once hummed in the night breeze, and I couldn't help but wonder what life must have been like for this family in the 1870's.

Elizabeth and James had eight children: Sophia Hannah (married Harrison Welsh); Isabella Ball (married Holland Elsworth); James (fate unknown); Samuel (died as a child in Australia); William Mark (married Ella Nicholson); Elizabeth Harriett (married Andrew G. Diffin); and two children that were born in England and died before the family moved to California. Many of Elizabeth and James Dainty's descendants still reside in East Contra Costa. Names like McHenry, Benn, Geddes, Andrieu and Moody are but a few.

James did not begin farming full time until his children were old enough to help with chores. Then he raised cattle and grew wheat and barley. Depending on Mother Nature for their crops' development, he and his family planted wheat on the rolling hills surrounding his farm. Wheat did not require intensive cultivation and was a relatively easy crop to raise and harvest.

The Daintys did most of their shopping and banking and received their mail in Nortonville until 1878, when Brentwood was established.

In 1891, William Dainty (the youngest son) purchased property bordering his father's ranch by obtaining financing from the bank in Nortonville, as Brentwood did not have banking facilities at the time. William married Ella Nicholson, a young girl from Morgan Territory, on December 11, 1889. They had four children: Leonard (married Marge Helm); Esther (married Jack Moody); Zelma (married Foster Beaman); and Wilma (married Carleton Seabury).

Ray Wallace driving William Daintys' running grader

William and Ella Dainty felt strongly that their children should receive a proper education. The children attended grade school at a little one-room schoolhouse on Marsh Creek (Liberty School), but the nearest high school was in Brentwood, too far for the children to travel daily, so the family relocated to town. They purchased thirty acres of unimproved land on the outskirts of Brentwood in 1908, and rented a small house near town so the children could attend high school. In 1917 they built a beautiful rock home, surrounded with magnificent gardens, that was a showplace in Brentwood for many years.

Brentwood's first streets were all named after trees: Pine, Maple, Oak, Chestnut, Birch, Elm and Fir. Maple Street was changed to Dainty Avenue because William and Ella Dainty had a ranch on the west side of town. Dainty Center Preschool is now at the same location. The stone house William Dainty built and lived in with his family for many years still stands on the school grounds. After his death, his daughter Esther and her husband, Jack Moody, lived in the old stone house. Barbara and Oliver Armstrong (my parents) purchased the house in the late 1960's and later sold it to Cookie and Shawn Guinn, the present owners.

The history of East Contra Costa is rich with wonderful stories of young idealistic pioneers like the Daintys who came west to build a new life for themselves and their families. It is impossible not to be impressed with the hardships they overcame, the "can do" attitude they displayed, and the determined outlook they held about their lives. They depended on each other and were quick to extend themselves to their neighbors. This pioneer family has definitely left footprints in the chapters of our past. Until Next Time....

ROBERT GARWOOD DEAN
PIONEER ENTREPRENEUR

As I thumb through the chapters of Brentwood's past I find wonderful stories of adventurous, enthusiastic, young men that came to East Contra Costa and turned the wilderness into a thriving community. Many came for a time, then moved on to plant their roots in fertile soil elsewhere. Among those who came and helped settle this region of California was Robert Garwood Dean.

Dean was a key player in all aspects of Brentwood's early development. He was a wheat farmer; a businessman; a politician; a banker; and instrumental in the establishment of Liberty High School.

Born in 1832, of Quaker parentage, Dean was orphaned when sixteen, and thrown upon his own resources for survival. He was working as a clerk when he heard about the gold in California and decided to come west to seek his fortune. On July 4, 1849, he boarded the schooner *Francisco*, bound for the California gold fields. This little vessel only carried four passengers besides himself, and the trip was not uneventful. The party encountered a terrible storm on the coast of Brazil that damaged the foremast and forced the vessel to seek refuge in the port of Santa Cathrini, about three hundred miles below Rio de Janeiro, where they remained for six weeks awaiting repairs. The *Francisco*, its crew and passengers arrived in San Francisco on January 21, 1850, almost seven months after leaving New York.

Dean, now eighteen years old, immediately headed for the Mother Lode and built a log cabin at Bear Valley, intending to wait out the winter and work the gulches by early spring. His plans were changed when Indians in the area stole his mules and supplies. Feeling fortunate to escape with his life, Dean joined Major Birney and his company and found himself a part of what would later be known as the Mariposa War. For his services, Dean received a government land warrant and four dollars a day from the state.

Robert Dean's uncle, Seneca Dean, was living in the Stockton area; he owned a general store and was justice of the peace. Robert decided to delay digging for gold and work for his uncle for a short time, but he found the life of a storekeeper not to his liking and was soon off on his next adventure. Having grown to love the out-of-doors, he traveled into the Delta region, "just for a hunt," and found the Delta plentiful with wildlife. In later years he spoke of the huge elk, antelope, mustangs and the grizzly bear he encountered. His hunting trip was to last almost two years, and in 1853 he wandered through Contra Costa County and the spot that was to become his home a few years later.

Between 1854 and 1859, Dean returned to the mines, working on the Merced and Tuolumne Rivers; he followed the rush to British Columbia, where he worked for the Hudson Bay Company; and finally returned to California, where he worked again with his uncle, who had asked him to join in a stock-raising venture. Seneca Dean planned to have his nephew take a hundred head of horse from California, drive them to Salt Lake, and exchange them for the footsore and worn-out cattle of the emigrants. Robert Dean arrived in Carson Valley late in the fall of 1859, much too late to drive the horses on to Salt Lake until spring. As luck would have it, the winter of 1859 was one of the worst the area had seen; cattle in the valley froze to death and horses that survived fell away to skeletons.

Meantime, discovery of the great silver mines hit, and Dean abandoned his trip to Salt Lake. He decided to open a store (hoping to get rich) to accommodate prospectors who would be arriving in the spring in search of silver. He knew that supplies, tools and lodging would be in demand, and if he could beat the rush he couldn't help but profit. At the age of 27, Dean put on a pair of Norwegian skis and, with a pack on his back, climbed the east ridge of the Sierra, camping on fifteen feet of compacted snow. From there he worked his way down into the valley, where there were only three feet of snow. Here he rolled pine saplings together, dug an opening in the snow-covered earth and started construction of a building. Later he built a two-story hotel on this site and sold it to a man from Sacramento.

Dean next moved to Douglas County, Nevada, where he taught school for three years and then managed a grocery store. By 1870, he again felt a need for a change of scene. Over the years he had never forgotten his hunting trip through the Delta. He returned to East Contra Costa and settled on Marsh Creek, where he became a successful wheat farmer. Robert Dean's characteristic enthusiasm would not allow him to simply farm, and he began buying grain. He shipped the grain to Port Costa and on to other markets. In 1880, he and several others built warehouses in Byron and Brentwood, which they later sold to Fish & Blum for a respectable profit.

Robert Dean was united in marriage with Jerusha H. Martin in 1864. Jerusha was a native of Vermont and came to California via the Isthmus of Panama in 1860 with her parents. By 1883, Dean had become an agent for Balfour, Guthrie & Co., and he retained that position until 1912, when he became president of the Bank of Brentwood.

Brentwood was founded in 1878 and very little business transpired in the city during its first four decades that Dean was not involved in. He definitely left footprints in our past. Men like Robert Garwood Dean saw the impossible and accomplished it. They are the foundation of America.
Until Next Time....

THE PREWETTS PIONEER FAMILY

*Prewett Ranch
Corner of Deer Valley & Lone Tree Way*

There are always those who pave the way that those who follow may reap the reward, whether it be the formation of a nation, the establishment of a state or the building of a new town. As I research the chapters of East Contra Costa's past I am ever amazed by the personalities that came west to carve out a new life for themselves and their families.

In the 1880's East Contra Costa was just starting to develop. California was a remote island, cut off from the civilized world of the East by hundreds of miles of broiling desert, dry plains and rugged mountains—yet there were free-spirited, adventurous young men that came and planted their roots in the fertile soil of the Delta. Joseph Granville Prewett was such a man.

Joseph Granville Prewett and his son Edward A. H. (Pappy) Prewett, his grandson Edward A. Prewett, and his great-granddaughter Jo Prewett Tennant have all left footprints in the chapters of our past and continue to be an active part of the development of the area. It is families like the Prewetts, that have lived in this region of California for more than 100 years, and played a key role in the development of East Contra Costa.

Joseph G. Prewett was born in Kinmundy, Illinois, in 1861. He moved, with his parents, to Missouri in 1869, where he received his formal education. At the age of 23 Joseph traveled to California and settled in East Contra Costa, near Antioch, on Deere Valley Road. In 1909 he purchased a section of land (640 acres) on Lone Tree Way for $22,000. Joseph was united in marriage with Ellen O'Brien, Patrick O'Brien's daughter, in 1889 and they had three sons: Edward, 1891; Raymond, 1897; and Harold, 1904.

Joseph farmed the land and raised stock. He played an active role in his community, serving on the school board for both Lone Tree Grammar School and Liberty Union High School for many years He was a director on the board and vice-president at First National Bank in Antioch. He was president of both the Oakley and Brentwood Horse Breeders Associations; president of Antioch Warehouse Association; president of the Lone Tree Telephone Company; and actively involved in all aspects of the development of East Contra Costa in the early 1900's.

Edward A. H.(Pappy) Prewett followed his father's example, dedicating his life to his family and the community. Pappy Prewett attended Judsonville School (off Empire Mines Road), Iron House School (near Knightsen), Lone Tree School and Riverview High School in Antioch. He was a sergeant in the Army Motor Transport Corps during World War I. After the war, in 1919, he married Emmy Gieseler, who had traveled from Milwaukee to work in Antioch. They had two children, Edward and Virginia (Dallas).

Pappy and Emmy purchased the Brentwood Grammar School building that was located where Liberty Union High School is today, and tore it down to salvage the lumber. With the lumber from the school they built a home on Lone Tree Way, near the Southern Pacific railroad tracks. Next to their home they built the Arbor Inn, a combination gas station, restaurant and grocery store. Across the street from the Prewett's home and business, where Valley Oak Nursery is today, there was a railroad shipping station.

In 1926, Pappy Prewett and many of his neighbors organized the Lone Tree Shipping Association because they needed a facility to ship their own products. By 1932 there were 35 farmers in the association. They had built two large buildings, complete with scales, and a spur of the Southern Pacific tracks. The association went out of business sixteen years after it was started, in 1942.

Prewett was active in the formation of Lone Tree Irrigation District, and he was one of the early farmers that helped pioneer the transition from dry farming to the irrigated orchard farming this area became famous for.

He was a charter member of the Antioch American Legion and the Brentwood Rotary Club. He served as an officer in both organizations. He also was a life member of the Delta Memorial Hospital Foundation, president of the Lone Tree Farm Bureau and active in many farm-oriented organizations.

Pappy Prewett actively farmed until his eighties, growing primarily almonds, walnuts and apricots.

Pappy's son, Ed Prewett, also grew up on the Prewett ranch. He has lived his whole life within a mile of where his grandfather settled 112 years ago, attending Lone Tree Grammar School, Liberty Union High School and UC Berkeley. In 1943 Ed entered the Army, and when the U.S. invaded Europe he was sent to the Ardennes Mountains in Belgium, where he fought in the Battle of the Bulge.

After World War II Ed returned to college. On a caravan to Death Valley he met Mary Alice (Reddie) Yelland and married her a short time later. Ed and Reddie had three children: Yvonne, Jo and Edward.

Ed went to Connecticut to study insurance and opened his own insurance agency when he returned to California. In 1948, Ed formed a partnership with Fred Abbott and eventually had offices in Brentwood, Antioch and Concord.

In later years Ed was a financial consultant, stockbroker, accountant, and a farmer.

Ed and Reddie Prewett are retired today, enjoying their family, traveling, the stock market, Rotary Club, church and community activities.

Ed and Reddie's daughter Jo Prewett Tennant was also raised on the Prewett ranch, and like her forefathers is actively involved in her community. Jo attended Brentwood schools, graduating from Liberty before becoming a student at Humboldt State, where she majored in physical education. She transferred to the University of Montana in 1971, graduating with honors in 1973.

After graduation Jo returned to Brentwood, planning to stay only temporarily while she decided what she wanted to do with her newly earned degree. She took a part-time position with the Delta Recreation Department, which soon turned into a full-time supervisory position.

In 1976 Jo married Gerald Tennant, a descendant of a local pioneer family in the Byron area. The Tennants have two sons, Jason and Tuck, and live in Byron on a farm where Jo is secretary and bookkeeper for the family business, Houston Orchard Company.

Jo has served as director for the Delta Community Center and is an active member of the Republican Women's Organization, a PTA member and a school volunteer. Since 1989, she has been a Byron School District trustee.

The pioneer families like the Prewetts laid the foundation that this region of California is built on. The threads of their effort are woven throughout the chapters of our past and they definitely have made a valuable contribution to us all.

Much of the information presented here about the Prewett Family was gleaned from a report written by Jason Tennant about his roots. Jason is fifth generation East Contra Costa. Thank you Jason! Until Next Time....

JEREMIAH MORGAN

Jeremiah Morgan was born in the Cherokee Nation, on the banks of the Tennessee River in Alabama on June 8, 1818. His father was killed in a battle in the Mexican American War in 1846. Jeremiah married Sarah Ellis in February of 1834 at Wright County, Missouri. He lived in Alabama, Illinois, Missouri, Texas, Wisconsin and Iowa before moving west to California in 1849.

Jeremiah and several other Iowa farmers had heard of the fortunes being mined in the California gold fields. In March of 1849 he left his family in Iowa and, with six companions, set out for the Pacific Coast with the intention of returning in the spring with pockets full of gold. The seven men outfitted a wagon with ox teams and set out to cross the trackless plains, rugged mountains and waterless deserts. The men survived the rigors of the overland trek and arrived at Bidwell's Bar_ on the Feather River in August, six months and one day after leaving their farms.

Jeremiah mined for gold until September 1850, but found that he could earn more money killing game near the American River and selling it to the miners. On October 5, 1850, he sailed from San Francisco via Panama for Iowa, and returned to his family and the farm.

Although Jeremiah returned to Iowa, he found he could not forget the rich soil and wonderful climate he'd experienced in California. In 1853 he once again undertook the overland journey to the Golden State, this time accompanied by his family. For the trip he purchased a large wagon and filled it with the supplies they would need to establish a new home in the West.

The Morgans originally settled in the Ygnacio Valley, where they built a small cabin. While bear hunting in 1856 on Mount Diablo, Jeremiah discovered the tract of land which would later be known as Morgan Territory. He claimed and fenced 10,000 acres; however, after a survey Jeremiah's holdings were cut down to 2,400 acres. The family moved onto the land in 1857 and built a home, barn and several outbuildings from lumber Jeremiah hauled from the Santa Cruz Mountains with his eight yoke of oxen.

Sarah and Jeremiah Morgan had sixteen children, only six of whom survived: William, Elizabeth, Joseph, Benjamin, Isaac and Josephine. Sarah died in 1869 and Jeremiah married Louisa Coan (from Clayton) that same year. This second union produced one child, Jesse.

Jeremiah Morgan could neither read nor write, but he was an exceptional businessman and a key player in the early development of Contra Costa County. He raised cattle on his Morgan Territory holdings, had four acres in Pacheco and ten acres in Concord, where he raised carp, two artesian wells, nine lots in the town of Concord and a slaughterhouse.

In 1858, Morgan Territory School was established, with William Ellis as the first teacher. This one-room school was attended by Jeremiah's children, along with children of other early settlers of the area. Alonzo Plumley, John Weber, Solomon Perkins, Samuel Foster, Francis Gibson and their families had also settled in the shadow of Mount Diablo.

When Jeremiah first settled Morgan Territory, he found a hunter's paradise. In later years he told great stories of hunting elk and mountain lion, and killing 46 bears in one year. It was a time when not a fence or a house could be seen, only groves of oaks, wild alfilaria and wildlife in abundance. Deer, antelope, beaver, coyote, fox and wildcats were common, and the streams were filled with a huge selection of fish. Most of Jeremiah Morgan's land is developed today. Morgan Territory Road is lined by small ranchettes with oversized homes, luxury barns and swimming pools. Jeremiah Morgan died January 23, 1906. I wonder if Jeremiah would recognize the grassy slopes where he planted his roots and raised his family? Until next time....

W. A. Davis
Brentwood's First Drug Store

William A. Davis was born in Pennsylvania, April 25, 1859. At the age of two, he traveled overland with his parents to Calaveras County, California, where they resided until 1868. His parents then moved and resettled in Nortonville, Contra Costa County. William attended grade school in Nortonville and after graduation entered the Pacific Business College of San Francisco, graduating from that institution in 1877.

On completion of his education, William returned to Nortonville and accepted employment with W. W. Dodge's general store as a salesman. He remained there a total of four years. In 1881 he moved to Somersville, and became a partner with Mr. Hughes in a general merchandise business, under the name of Davis & Hughes.

In 1887, at the age of 28, William Davis sold his interest in the store in Nortonville and moved to Brentwood, where he established a new general merchandise store on Oak Street. The original store consisted of one small room, but within a few years he enlarged his facility to three rooms. By 1897, the W. A. Davis Company consisted of three departments: one for groceries and drugs, a second for clothing and dry goods, and a third for hardware.

William Davis' store was well known throughout East Contra Costa for its well-selected line of drug and pharmaceutical preparations. The hottest selling items stocking his shelves were patent medicines, which, if labels were to be believed, could handle just about any and every complaint. One concoction gladly promised to cure thirty different disorders, including "nervous debility caused by the indiscretions of youth." Mostly the remedies relied on a heavy lacing of alcohol to work their proclaimed wonders. Hostetter's Stomach Bitters, for instance, soothed indigestion with a formula packing a 50-proof wallop.

Local residents could purchase not only the medicines they needed, but also a fine assortment of perfumes, scented soaps, lotions, face creams, tooth powders, brushes and other toiletries. Davis also carried a fine line of magazines and periodicals. The corner of his drug department was filled with literature of all kinds: adventure, detective, love, romance, glamour and educational, and current copies of the *Contra Costa Gazette*, which was published in Martinez.

The town of Brentwood was, in 1897, a growing community with a population of six hundred, located in the center of the most prolific wheat-growing district in California. For miles in all directions, as far as the eye could see, were mammoth fields of wheat. During harvest season hundreds of men would gather in town from all parts of the country. There were three general stores, a well-kept hotel, blacksmith shops, livery stable, cobbler, railroad station, taverns, several fine warehouses and more.

On rainy days, buckboards and farm wagons would clatter along Oak Street spraying mud on pedestrians. William Davis constructed boardwalks in front of his store so customers could escape the thick dust in summer and the slushy potholes of the unpaved street during the winter months. Local residents would often gather in front of Davis' to visit with their neighbors.

William Davis is representative of many early businessmen of the time. He came to California in 1861 in an ox-drawn wagon from the East, eventually settling in Brentwood, and definitely leaving footprints in the chapters of our past. Davis was a broad-minded, public-spirited man as well as a successful merchant, and was often quoted in early publications promoting Brentwood and the surrounding area. Until Next Time….

BARKLEY HISTORY

A few years ago I decided to research family history for my grandchildren with the intent of writing a short story about their ancestors. My plan was to spend a few days talking to other family members and compile what information I could find. However, as most things in life, it wasn't that easy. For each question I'd find another answer which would lead to another question. Who were my great great grandparents? Why did they come to America? How did they endure the hardships they must have faced?

As I began researching my roots, I found myself fascinated by the variety of characters I'd discovered. Many of my forefathers were men and women that underwent inconceivable hardships to fulfill their destinies. Tracing their histories has been like putting together an extraordinary puzzle, one piece at a time. I am fortunate in that the Barkleys (*my mother's family*) have resided in Contra Costa County since the 1850's and consequently records are easily accessible. I was well hooked on genealogy before having to do any long distant research. I was further blessed with Great Aunt Alice Barkley, who had compiled a box of family notes and memorabilia in the 1940's. She had interviewed my great grandfather and kept wonderful records of family stories. Then there was Aunt Enid Crosslin who had saved a suitcase full of family treasures (*birth announcements, wedding invitations, newspaper clippings, etc.*) that her children had given me. What started out as a short term project will no doubt be a part of my life forever.

My Grandchildren will be able to trace branches of their family tree back more than 130 years (*seven generations*) in Byron's and Brentwood's history, but the story doesn't stop there. I've traced my mother's family, the Barkleys, back to Scotland. Robert Barclay (*the spelling of the name was changed later*) was born in Gordonstown Morayshire, Scotland in 1648. He was a writer, a Quaker Preacher, and very outspoken for his time. Robert befriended George Fox, the founder of the Quaker Religion and William Penn, a fellow Quaker, and was jailed with them for their religious beliefs. When they were released from prison William Penn decided to found a colony (*Pennsylvania*) in the new world where his fellow Quakers could settle and practice their religion. Robert Barclay traveled throughout England, Holland, Germany and the Netherlands teaching and preaching.

Robert Barclay's son, Isaac Barclay, was born in West Scotland in 1694. Little is known about Isaac's life. We do know that he followed in his father's footsteps and was a dedicated Quaker Preacher and known as a strict disciplinarian.

Isaac Barclay's son, Lazarus Thomas Barclay was born in England in 1740. When Lazarus was sixteen his father placed him with a cobbler to learn the trade of shoemaking. He hated working with leather so he ran away and took passage on a war ship, the Augusta, bound for Canada. He joined the military serving under the British General James Wolf and fought in the battle of Quebec in 1760. He remained in the military for a few years, and upon his discharge ventured to the New World settling in West Virginia where he became a farmer. Lazarus changed the spelling of his name from Barclay to Barkley hoping to prevent his father from finding him.

Lazarus Barkley's son, Robert Lazarus Barkley, was born in West Virginia in 1773. He was the first white child born in Green Brier County. He received a common school education as good as the colonies provided at that time. At 37 years old (*1810*) Robert, his wife Hanna, and their six children (*ranging in age from 1 year to 14 years*) moved to Bath County Kentucky on horseback leaving most of their worldly possessions behind. In 1824 they again pulled up roots and moved further west to Lawrence County, Indiana where they farmed.

Robert Lazarus Barkley's son, James Barkley, was born in West Virginia in 1801 and received his common school education in Kentucky. In 1841 James, his wife Mary Ann (*pregnant at the time*) and seven children ranging in age from eleven months to fifteen years, traveled by wagon to a new homestead in Iowa where they planted their roots. MaryAnn had ten children, she died when her youngest child, Simon, was six months old. James married Amelia Drumm in 1848, and fathered six more children. The town of Lisbon, Iowa is built on the Barkley Homestead. James Barkley is credited with being its founder.

James Barkley's son, Simon Taylor Barkley was born in Iowa in 1847. He was raised on his parent's farm, receiving his formal education in a one room school house. At the age of nineteen *(1866)* Simon saddled up his mount and headed for the Rocky Mountains where he spent the next few years attempting several different jobs. Two of his brothers had moved west during the gold rush and settled in California. Simon decided to come west and see what the area could offer a young man.

After arriving in Brentwood, Simon met and married Sarah Sullenger. Sarah was born in Napa and was raised on her family homestead on Deer Valley Road west of Brentwood. Their marriage was the second recorded marriage in Brentwood. The newlyweds made their home on a 160 acre homestead on Vasco Road raising 12 children. Simon farmed most of his land, and Sarah sold eggs and milk in town.

The Barkley's were among the pioneers who witnessed and contributed to the development of the Diablo Valley. They were actively involved in their church, schools, and several social organizations. The Barkley name appears as charter members in the local Masonic Lodge, Odd Fellows, and Legion Auxiliary.

Although Simon and Sarah themselves were not highly educated, they recognized the importance of a good education for their seven sons and five daughters. All twelve Barkley children graduated from Liberty Union High School. Five of the Barkley boys went on to graduate from U. C. Berkeley. Two of them became engineers, one an attorney, and two were school administrators.

All of the Barkley children have left their mark on Contra Costa County's history. George became the County attorney; Joe was head engineer for the Broadway tunnel and instrumental in building the Panama Canal as well as Buchanan Field. He also served as the county surveyor for many years. Anna (Pendry) was a writer for the Antioch Ledger. Robert was involved in the construction of the East Contra Costa Irrigation System. Charlie was Constable of Brentwood for more than 30 years. Hank was an engineer for Shell Oil in Martinez. Ted and Jim were both school administrators. Emma, Polly and Dorothy*(my grandmother)* were all homemakers and actively involved with their community.

Simon and Sarah were proud to declare themselves staunch Republicans. Simon would boast that he voted for Ulysses S. Grant for President in 1868 and was quick to tell people he never missed a presidential election in his 94 years.

Simon's interest in politics and his love of his country truly became apparent in 1918 when four of the boys joined the service to help American forces drive the Germans out of Belgium. The three remaining brothers registered for the draft. Simon was very proud of his sons, and often said it was an honor to send his sons to fight for freedom. All four boys saw action and all returned home to Brentwood safely.

The original Barkley homestead is now owned by the Cowell Foundation and will no doubt eventually be developed. As I drive along Old Vasco Road and gaze out toward the bluff where my forefathers tilled the land and struggled to raise their families I am amazed at the hardships they overcame. The houses they built, the fields they planted,and the swimming holes they created have all been given back to the earth. I am convinced their pioneer spirit still lays over this valley and hopefully will continue to shine through my grandchildren and one day their children. Until next time....

SIMON TAYLOR BARKLEY

The American West is often looked upon as glamorous and full of romantic legends. The reality is that the pioneers lived a hard life. It was the Eastern journalist, novelist, and sketch artist that gave the harsh frontier life an aura of colorful adventuresome fantasy. The early settlers of Brentwood were a mixed breed. There were miners who had left the gold fields carrying disappointment instead of fortunes. There were farmers, soldiers, clerks, lawyers, and young adventurers. Each brought with him his own dreams of a better life, and each had a phenomenal tale to tell. Simon Taylor Barkley, my great grandfather, was such a man.

Simon was born February 10, 1847, the son of James and MaryAnn Barkley of Lisbon, Iowa. His father had been born in Bath County, Virginia and had traveled with his family (a wife and seven children ranging in age from 6 months to 15 years) west to Iowa in 1841 via covered wagon. Upon arrival in Iowa, James homesteaded 160 acres which he farmed. James and MaryAnn were to have a total of ten children.

Simon Taylor Barkley

MaryAnn died of influenza when their youngest child (Simon) was six months old. James married a second time having six more children with this union.

Three of James Barkley's sons eventually traveled west and settled in California. James Robert Barkley Jr. traveled by ox-cart to California in 1852, mined for gold, and ultimately settled in Fresno. Lazarus came west by covered wagon in 1853. He spent several years in the gold country before settling in East Contra Costa County on a quarter section of land now known as the town of Knightsen. James and Lazarus sent an endless stream of letters to their family in Iowa describing California and praising the mild climate, healthful conditions, and the deep fertile soil. Simon decided to venture west to visit his brothers and see California for himself in 1876.

Prior to traveling to California, Simon spent several years as an adventurer. He first left his father's Iowa farm when he was nineteen trekking to Colorado where he resided for several years. One of his first jobs was carrrying mail fifty miles from Denver to Post Rockport via horseback. He later worked as a clerk in a mercantile, a lumberjack in the Rockies, and a ranchhand on a ranch near Greeley. Between 1869 and 1875 Simon made three or four trips between Iowa and Colorado unsure as to which area he wanted to settle permanently. In 1876 he headed west to visit his borther Lazarus.

Lazarus had settled on a government grant in the Eden Plain area in 1862 and established one of the first farms in that region. In 1883 Lazarus sold 110 acres to George W. Knight, the founder of Knightsen, and eventually moved to French Camp.

In 1877, shortly after arriving in California, Simon obtained a job with a crew of men sent into the virgin forests of Washington State to cut extra long timbers for construction of the ferry, "Salono". The Salono was being built by the Southern Pacific Company at Port Costa. It was the largest ferry built during the late 1800's. Simon's job was to spot trees suitable for the ferries construction and assist in cutting them down.

Simon met Sara Ella Sullenger at a dinner dance held at the Grange hall in 1878. Sara's family had settled in Deer Valley in 1864 where her father was a wheat farmer. Sara and Simon were united in marriage on December 30, 1880 by Judge Wallace in Brentwood. Their union was the second recorded marriage in Brentwood township.

In 1881 Simon and Sara established a 160 acre farm near Kellogg Creek in the Vasco region. The Vasco was a rugged unforgiving land where the wind blew fiercely, oaks and chaparral grew wild, and the water was laden with large deposits of alkali. Simon had 40 improved acres planted in wheat, four horses, two milk cows, eight calves, a few head of sheep, hogs, and miscellaneous poultry. Their home was a one story, single-wall, three bedroom, wood house which was papered with burlap. The house had been moved to the Vasco from the town of Nortonville. Brisk winds would sail through cracks in the boards of the house and blow the burlap loose. On cold winter nights Sara would warm bricks in the wood burning stove and place them at the foot of the children's beds. Their furniture was simple including a large homemade dining table and iron beds. The farm included a large barn, a grainery, a tack room, a chicken house, a wooden corral, a windmill, and an outhouse behind the residence. Simon and Sara were fairly successful farming this hilly ground.

Simon and Sara had twelve children, seven boys and five girls. Their lives were typical of the times. The children were expected to gather eggs, milk cows, churn butter, fill the horse trough with buckets of water from the creek, repair fences, and numerous other daily chores. They worked hard and played hard. My grandmother would tell stories of swimming in the creek, picnics with the Odd Fellows at the old Stone House, playing for hours with a rag doll that her mother had made, and an endless list of practical jokes she and her siblings played on each other. It was not uncommon for the Grueninger children who lived on the neighboring farm to visit.

The Barkley's lived a simple life by today's standards. They worked from sunup to sunset eking out a living. Simon would hitch up the spring wagon and venture into Brentwood at least once a week to collect the mail and supplies or have something repaired at Moody's Blacksmith Shop. They were active members of the Odd Fellows and attended monthly meetings in Byron.

Simon raised farm animals for home butchering, and Sara canned fruits and vegetables that Simon purchased in town. Water on the Vasco was in limited supply and not of great quality, so the family never raised much of a home garden. They did manage to grow a few plants for daily use. Sara was proud of her chicken house and the beautiful hens she raised. She carried on a brisk trade with the Byron Hot Springs selling the luxury resort eggs at six cents a dozen including delivery.

The Barkley's are remembered as good-hearted and fun loving. They frequently hosted gatherings which included family, friends, and neighbors. These festivities provided the perfect opportunity for locals to congregate. The men spoke of politics, the women brought their best preserves to share, and the young people spent hours wading and swimming in Kellogg Creek. In the early spring of each year the Barkley boys would dam the creek creating a wonderful swimming hole near the bluff behind their house.

Simon and Sara loved their farm in the hills, but they also recognized the importance of a proper education for their children. The Barkley children attended Marsh Creek School, a one room school house two miles from the farm. They went to school on foot, horseback, or took the family wagon. As the Barkley children reached their teen years, the family moved into town to enable the children to attend high school in Brentwood to further their education. George Barkley, Simon and Sara's oldest child, graduated from Liberty with the third graduating class. All twelve Barkley children graduated from Liberty, and five of the sons went on to college.

James, George, Joe, Hank, Charlie, Robert, Ted and Simon Barkley

The Barkleys purchased land behind Brentwood Grove (known today as the Brentwood Park) and moved their home from the Vasco onto the parcel of property where the Brentwood Community Center is located today.

Simon found employment as a mail carrier for the post office. One of his jobs was to pick up the mail in a hand pulled cart daily at the railroad depot and deliver it to the post office on Oak Street.

Simon outlived Sara by eleven years and died in 1941 at the age of ninety four. The Barkley home was occupied by Anna (Barkley) and Orra Pendry until their deaths at which time the property was sold to the City of Brentwood in 1964.

I'm extremely proud of my heritage. It was my great grandfather, and early settlers like him who wove the fabric from which the great state of California is created. Until Next Time....

WALTER HINEBAUGH'S MEMORIES

In the interest of history, I spend a lot of time researching at the County Library in Pleasant Hill, the Contra Costa County History Center, the California Room at the new San Francisco Library, the Office of the Brentwood News, and regional museums. I love interviewing old timers and generally scrounge information from anywhere I can find it. Not long ago I stumbled across an article written by Gertrude Hagy for the Contra Costa Gazette during the early 1930's and found it so interesting that I would like to take this opportunity to share it with you.

Walter Hinebaugh arrived in the Brentwood area several years before the town was founded. He and his wife, Nellie Barkley Hinebaugh, lived on the corner of First Street and Chestnut for many years. Their home still stands today and is occupied as a residence. The Hinebaughs were extremely active in local fraternal organizations, schools, and the Methodist Church.

Following is the article as written by Gertrude Hage in the early 1930's with notations in parenthesis only to identify current buildings in town.

"Walter Hinebaugh, one of the first residents of Brentwood, remembers when there was no Brentwood. Mrs. Nellie Hinebaugh remembers when the railroad was being built in 1877, and it was not until 1879 that Brentwood came into being, the veteran resident recalls. In the spring of 1879 Louis Grunauer and his brother built the first general store, with a whiskey shop in the basement, on the site of the present Brentwood Hotel.(*Oak Street and Railroad Avenue*).

Joe Carey then built a blacksmith shop next to the present LeMoine home on Oak and Second Streets(*across from the Brentwood Park*). Louis Bacagallupi built a saloon on the corner where the Pioneer (*Rich's Drive In today*) now stands across from the Brentwood Hotel. He had to have someone else buy the lot for him, as no one would sell him a lot for a saloon.

Louis Bacagallupi Saloon - 1880's
Brentwoods 1st Tavern

John Carey, brother of Joe, was the first justice of the peace and built houses opposite the present Legion Hall.

Early autograph albums in the possession of Mrs. Hinebaugh show the names of early settlers with fancy writing and sentimental verse in the manner of the times. The date 1880 is conspicuous.

Mrs. Hinebaugh's parents (*Mr. & Mrs. Lazarus Barkley*) came to Knightsen in 1862 and obtained a government grant of land in what was then Eden Plain. Her father came from Iowa and her mother from Indiana.

Walter Hinebaugh came in 1876 from Indiana to work for A. C. Wristen on Marsh Creek. The Hinebaughs were married in the L. G. Barkley home in Knightsen and celebrated their fiftieth anniversary in August 1933. They were married by Rev. E. A. Winning in the house where she was born.

Many of the early homes were hauled on mountain wagons by 24 horse teams from Stewartsville, Summersville, and other little towns of the old abandoned coal mining communities. Houses could be bought cheaper there, costing about $40 or $50. They were hauled down the five or six miles lashed to the teams by chains on an "A" frame, often literally being pulled out of the hillside onto the frame. Sometimes a number of these were added together to make a larger house, making the ceilings and floors at different levels."

In a 1947 Brentwood News interview, Nellie Hinebaugh revealed memories of the area as it was in her childhood. She recalled a time when there were only two houses between the Barkley Ranch (*the town of Knightsen today*) and Antioch. The Barkley children attended school at Eden Plain, some of their playmates were Richard Rains Veale who later became sheriff of Contra Costa County for 40 years, George Shafer the first undertaker in Brentwood, and the Heidorn children.(*Edna Hill School is named for Edna Heidorn Hill*)

According to Nellie, the young people of her day had just as much fun as those of today. They rode horseback through the chaparral and oak groves, danced at the ranch houses to violin and organ music, and made long trips to Antioch to do the family shopping.

She said there was wildlife everywhere, and the Barkley family often ate game for dinner. The early settlers had endless hardships to overcome. Floods were a menace, Marsh Creek in its natural state did not offer any drainage or diversion ditches to keep the creek from overflowing and going on an annual rampage of its own.

Researching the history of East Contra Costa has become quite a hobby for me. Whenever I think I know exactly what happened other information surfaces that contradicts the previous information I've collected. Walter Hinebaughs memories are a good example of this. I was under the impression that the first saloon in town was where Sweenys is today, and the first blacksmith shop was on First Street, not Second. I also was sure Joe and John Carey were the same person, not brothers.

In my research I try to take every effort to make my columns as factual as possible . However, history relies on old timers memories (often very selective); old newspapers, journals, and personal letters (written to reflect the incident as the writer saw it); early Contra Costa History books, and my own family folklore as I remember it. Such as the fact that Nellie Hinebaugh was the daughter of my great great uncle Lazarus Grimes Barkley which would make her my ——— cousin????

History is not only the past, but also rests in the present. The story goes on and continues to be told. Until Next Time....

COATES HALL
COLONEL ROBERT COATES

If you remember Coates Hall, you are definitely an old timer! While researching the other side of yesterday I continually find references made to events that took place at Coates Hall, so a few weeks ago I decided to make the rounds and ask a few of our older residents if they could enlighten me. I knew there had to be the makings of a story—and there were!

Coates Hall was a direct result of the Masonic Lodge forming a chapter in Brentwood in 1902. The first Masonic meetings were held in private homes, but by 1904, the membership needed a permanent meeting place. Will Jerrisleu (the organization's first Grand Master) announced at a meeting that he thought Colonel Robert Coates, a fellow Mason, might be persuaded to build a two-story hall on a lot he owned in town. The lot was located on Railroad Avenue (Highway 4 today) between Oak and Chestnut Streets. Jerrisleu approached Coates with the proposition and he agreed to the terms if the organization would sign a five-year lease agreeing to pay twenty dollars per month for the facility. The ground floor became Brentwood's social center, the scene of graduations, dances, community meetings, dramatic productions and weddings. The second floor, with its own entrance via stairs at the rear of the building, was for the Masons. The Masonic Lodge used the hall until 1920 when they constructed a new building on the corner of Oak and Second Street. (Cap's today).

After the Masons moved to their new facility the Diffin family purchased Coates Hall and remodeled the upper level into a boarding house, offering fourteen rooms that could be rented by the day, week or month, with the ground floor utilized as a restaurant. In 1942 Pete Prelli purchased the building from the Diffins and opened Prelli's Italian Restaurant. Leo Martin bought the site from Prelli in 1966; he opened the Mexicolindo Restaurant downstairs and rented the upper rooms.

Coates Hall has numerous stories to tell. At one point in the 1920's the Brentwood School burned and students met at this site for several months. Rumor also has it that the hall was a "house of ill fame" and gambling hall at one time. When Coates Hall was demolished in 1980 it belonged to Jesse Valle and Cresencio Ramirez.

Who was Coates? Well, Colonel Robert Coates was a native of Maine born in 1826. At the age of 23, he traveled to San Francisco via Cape Horn, hoping to get rich in the gold fields. He secured a claim at Boones Bar, on the Feather River, where he succeeded in making a small fortune.

Learning that there was a great demand for pork in the Hawaiian Islands, Coates and a companion decided to buy a shipload of hogs for transport to the islands. Unfortunately, about halfway to their destination the hogs were taken ill and died. The young men, having invested all their money in the livestock, were now penniless and signed on as able seamen to continue their voyage. For more than a year they worked as sailors, visiting the South Sea islands and Central and South America in their travels before returning to San Francisco in 1851.

Coates returned to his claim at Boones Bar and was again successful. At this point he decided to return to Maine and spend some time with family and friends. He purchased a farm, engaged in the lumber business, and became involved with a ship-building firm. In March 1852, Robert Coates married Juliet Fisher, the granddaughter of a well-known colonial family. To this union there were two children, Juliette and Margaret.

At the beginning of the Civil War when the call for troops was made, Robert responded. He is credited with helping organize Company A, 15th Regiment, Maine Volunteer Infantry, having been selected as sergeant. His military record was outstanding, and he was promoted rapidly for bravery; at the end of the conflict he returned home with the rank of colonel. During his service he was wounded many times, with one ball shattering his left hand, another plowing a furrow through his scalp, and a third shattering his ankle.

After the war Coates returned to California with his family. In 1867, he ventured to Boones Bar but discovered he had lost all rights to his claims, and finally settled in the Brentwood area. Coates had a 160-acre soldier's grant that he used to acquire his first holding, and he later purchased an additional 480 connecting acres at the junction of Bixler Road and Orwood.

Juliet Coates died in 1878, the year the railroad came to East Contra Costa. Robert was remarried in 1880, to Elizabeth Madigan. Between 1880 and 1915, Coates found himself involved in numerous business ventures. He engaged in the cattle business, farming, and general merchandising business with Henry Brewer in Antioch. Robert Coates died in 1915 while still an active member of the community.

In researching the history of the area's pioneers I am ever amazed by characters like Robert Coates. I am reminded of something B. C. Forbes said: "History has demonstrated that the most notable winners usually encountered heartbreaking obstacles before they triumphed. They won because they refused to become discouraged by their defeats!" Until Next Time….

BALFOUR, GUTHRIE & COMPANY

The Balfour, Guthrie Company is credited with much of Brentwood's early development and with revolutionizing this region of Contra Costa County. Robert Balfour was 25, and Alexander Guthrie 24, when they arrived in San Francisco in 1869. They had traveled from Liverpool, England, to seek their fortunes in the New World. A third partner of the company, Robert Forman, elected to stay behind in Liverpool and handle the company's affairs on that end, which resulted in the omission of his name from the firm's official title: Balfour, Guthrie & Company, Limited.

These three well-educated young men came from moderately wealthy families and were backed by an established mercantile house, Balfour, Williamson & Co. of London. Balfour and Guthrie originally started an insurance firm, offering policies covering crops and mortgages and extending credit for agricultural endeavors. Even as early as 1869, it seemed certain that California would become one of the world's great business and industrial centers.

Robert Balfour and Alexander Guthrie began probing all of northern California in search of other business opportunities. In their research of various investment possibilities, they were impressed with the large grain fields of East Contra Costa. Their fondness for Guinness ale, a British product made from barley malt, resulted in their decision to export vast quantities of grain to England.

In 1882 they established large grain warehouses with accompanying wharfes at Port Costa and within a year they had purchased warehouses in Byron and Brentwood as well as throughout the San Joaquin Valley. At the time California was the largest wheat producing state in the country. By the early 1900's they had become the largest grain buyers in the world. All the while they continued to dabble in financing farmers, assuring themselves of a constant supply of barley and other grains for exportation.

On May 6, 1910, the *Byron Times* reported: "One of the largest land deals in the history of California, and one of tremendous importance to Brentwood and Byron, as well as all of East Contra Costa, was closed last Friday, when the great Marsh Ranch was sold to Balfour, Guthrie Investment Company of San Francisco." According to the *Times* article, the transaction included the sale of approximately 12,616 acres of land for $650,000, for speculation and development.

Balfour, Guthrie crew picking and packing apricots in the Brentwood area in the 1920's

Balfour, Guthrie and Company began this development by building a great canal system through the heart of what is known as Diablo Valley, and began growing fruit, vegetables, melons and nuts. Later, the Brentwood Irrigation District was formed. Stock was sold, a share per acre, launching the area as one of the leading agricultural regions in the state. Balfour, Guthrie and Company literally built the town of Brentwood. They were responsible for the city's water and sewer systems, paved many of the streets, instituted the telephone system, and built the Brentwood Hotel and Bank of Brentwood. They also built a large two story mansion, complete with grounds designed by the same man who designed Golden Gate Park, to house the Balfour, Guthrie superintendent. This home was the Brentwood Hospital in 1930.

Balfour, Guthrie and Company subdivided much of their holdings by offering 98 tracts, or lots ranging from 5 to 34 acres, for sale at $300 an acre, with all of the lots to receive water from the irrigation system. Balfour and Guthrie were noted for their marketing skills; they advertised their property around the world and employed special trains to bring eager buyers to Brentwood. Their prospective buyers were wined and dined at the Brentwood Hotel.

Once the irrigation system of canals and pumps was in operation, Balfour, Guthrie and Company used the name of Brentwood Irrigated Farms for their farming operations. They became one of the world's greatest producers of dried apricots and would often have as many as 30,000 trays of apricots at a time drying in the sun. During a season's peak harvest period, the company would employ close to 1500 workers to pick and pack the fruit on their Contra Costa farms, with 625 women and girls in the cutting sheds alone.

Peaches, nectarines, apricots, plums, pears and many other types of fruit and nuts were planted. Orchards belonging to Balfour, Guthrie and Company could be found from Brentwood to Marsh Creek. Row crops such as sugar beets, tomatoes, melons and cucumbers were planted in the unused soil between newly planted fruit trees until the trees began producing. The company also ventured into other enterprises: they raised horses, sheep and hogs, and ran a dairy on Walnut Boulevard.

The Balfour Irrigated Farms packing shed was located on Walnut Boulevard in Brentwood near where the Lions Club hall is today. This facility was a city block long and emitted a constant buzz of activity. In 1937, the company built a cooling plant in the shed designed to be the most modern and efficient fruit handling system in the country.

The company provided living compounds for their employees. BG Camp was built just south of Brentwood and consisted of 54 cottages and many tents. The camp offered electricity, community kitchens, mess halls, showers with hot water, modern latrines and pure running water from a deep well on the property, and natural gas was available for heating and cooking. They even erected a nursery complete with attendant nurses to accommodate 150 children while their mothers worked in the cutting sheds.

According to a *Brentwood News* article dated July 1, 1955, Balfour, Guthrie Co. sold Brentwood Irrigated Farms (approximately 2,250 acres) to Tom Peppers of Mentone, California, in 1943. Pepper's estate sold it in 1955 for a figure in excess of $1,497,577 to Abbott Kinney Co. and M. Philip Davis and Thomas Davis.

The Davis brothers, attorneys in Stockton, sold off their portion of the farms piece by piece, selling the last of their holdings in this area in the early 1970's.

Although the names of Balfour and Guthrie are found throughout the history of this region of California, both young men ultimately chose to return to their native England to end their years. Alexander Guthrie left first, and Robert Balfour followed to Liverpool after residing in San Francisco for 24 years.

Balfour, Guthrie and Company began the most important horticultural movement ever identified with rural California and definitely left footprints in the chapters of the history of East Contra Costa. Until Next Time....

HERCULES LOGAN BRENTWOOD CONTRACTOR

Chapters of Brentwoods' history are filled with colorful characters but few are as interesting as Hercules Logan. Throughout East County there are still many buildings standing that Logan designed and built as one of the regions first building contractors.

Hercules Logan was born April 26, 1875, a native of Scotland and the son of John and Christina Logan. He left Scotland at 28 years of age for America. He settled in New York, and in 1904 came west to visit his brother, Adolph, who had settled in Humboldt County during the 1890's.

Having learned the carpentry and building trade in Scotland, Hercules found employment in Eureka helping build the Eureka City Hall, a building which is still in use today. Following the work he moved to San Francisco and worked on the German Hospital and several large buildings on Angel Island. Hercules soon developed a reputation in the building industry for his outstanding carpentry skills especially on large projects.

Hercules Logan married Ethel Jane Brangwin, a native of England on July 10, 1900. The couple had five children, three sons and two daughters.

When the devastating earthquake of 1906 struck San Francisco men with Logans knowledge and expertise of building were in great demand, and he was immediately retained to construct Healds' Business College in the New San Francisco.

Brentwood Hotel under construction - 1913

In 1912 Logan was hired by Balfour, Guthrie & Company to build the Brentwood Hotel (at a cost of more than $40,000) and the Bank of Brentwood. Construction of the Hotel began in 1913. It was located on the corner of Oak Street and Hwy 4. It would be a two story structure of reinforced concrete and steel of a semi-mission ornamental style. There were to be 40 rooms including three suites; two courts for the pleasure and comfort of guests with outdoor pergoias and lawns surrounding the building. The lobby was 35 x 80 feet with a huge fireplace and seating area. The main dining room was to be 40 x 50 feet and was used for receptions as well as dining by local residents of Brentwood. Hot and cold water, electricity, and telephones which were still considered a novelty in 1913 were provided the guests. The first manager of the hotel was Mr. A.C. Reynolds. In 1967 the Brentwood Hotel, once the center of activity was leveled making way for a service station.

Brentwood's first bank was an ornate concrete building on the corner of Oak and First Streets. It was constructed at a cost of $15,000 for the building, furniture, and equipment. The Bank of Brentwood, underwritten by Balfour, Guthrie & Company, opened for business on July 15, 1913. Local residents deposited $22,138 on the first day. The first bank officers were Robert G. Dean, president; Robert Wallace Jr., vice president; and Lee Durham, cashier.

Logan decided to settle permanently in Brentwood. He became known as a full service contractor and would not only build you a house but would also draw up the plans, furnish materials, and personally finance the entire transaction. Many early residents of Brentwood made their mortgage payments directly to Logan. Over the next three or four decades, Hercules built numerous homes, stores, dairies, and ranch houses.

Logan was a pioneer who could find a need and fill it. He eventually built the Logan Building on First Street (next to where East Contra Costa Irrigation District Offices are today) to house his business office as well as a plumbing and electrical shop. From his new offices Logan would contract to install irrigation lines, bore wells using a power system to a depth of 500 feet as well as contract for electrical installations and repair.

In the early 1920's Logan became the distributing agent in the Brentwood territory for the Fairbanks Moore Company, one of the largest machinery manufacturing concerns in the world. In 1922 he was selling one and a half horsepower engines for $50.00.

Logan was also involved in the farming and dairy industries. He had 42 acres of land in walnuts and figs and had a 20 acre section of land devoted to a dairy. He was president of the Chamber of Commerce in 1922 and, for many years, a key player in the development of the town of Brentwood.

It is men like Hercules Logan that have formed the foundation of Brentwood and were instrumental in development of early businesses which have definitely left footprints in the history of this region of California. Until Next Time....

OSCAR STARR
INVENTOR

The Los Vaqueros Reservoir is located nine miles south of Brentwood, where cattle and sheep once grazed beneath oak trees in this magnificent valley. There is 100,000 acre feet of water storage contained behind a 192-foot earth dam built by Contra Costa Water District. The water is piped from Old River into a valley that was home to thousands of California Indians for centuries before the white men came and settled this region.

The Vasco area has endless tales to tell: stories of Indians gathering acorns for the winter; cowboys branding herds of steers; bandits hiding in caves nestled in the foothills; and sheepherders tending their flocks; but one of the most interesting anecdotes is that of Oscar Starr.

Oscar Starr was born in San Francisco in 1885. As a young man he worked for Union Iron Works, a manufacturer of steam engines and boats, and later he worked with Gorham Engineering Company in Alameda, where the first gas-propelled engine with a turbine pump was built. By the early 1900's he was known as an astute inventor, and in 1910 he and Bill Gorham are credited with fabricating a new type of aircraft (a two-cylinder radial airplane engine). They sold this engine to Stanley Hillar, father of the Helicopter name of today.

Starr was next hired by the Holt Manufacturing Company in Stockton to produce a gasoline engine for their early Holt Caterpillars, track-laying tractors originally developed by Holt.

Best Gas Tractor Company, another pioneer tractor firm located in San Leandro, hired Starr away from Holt. Over the next few years Starr bounced back and forth between these two companies, accepting employment with whoever offered him the highest wage. At one time, while working for Best, he is said to have earned a higher salary than the company president.

In 1925 Holt and Best decided to merge and become the Caterpillar Tractor Company. Starr became a director and vice-president of the newly formed company, as head of all research activities.

Oscar Starr purchased 7,883 acres in the Vasco territory in 1935 from the Mary Crocker estate. His main residence was located near Mission San Jose, but he used his Vasco holdings to test and further develop his tractors and other inventions.

The Starr compound could be seen for many years from the "old" Vasco Road, surrounded by a cluster of oak, pepper and eucalyptus trees with an eight-foot-high adobe fence. The site always looked mystical from the road. Starr built two Spanish-style houses, a machine shop, shed, silo, bunkhouse, chicken coop, barns and miscellaneous other outbuildings. He installed a modern generating plant and a-state-of-the-art water system which included several redwood water tanks at various locations around the ranch to accommodate the facility. The grounds were landscaped with hand-cut sandstone patios, fruit trees and a large vegetable garden. Starr and his wife, Hazel, would visit the ranch often to relax and allow Oscar an opportunity to work in his shop.

The machine shop was the primary site for Starr to secretly test engines and other inventions. He is said to have perfected at least two Caterpillar engines in this shop. Neighbors remembered seeing Starr test his tractors in the fields near the shop.

Oscar Starr was considered a "gentleman farmer." He retained a foreman and several hired hands to oversee the ranch. They raised hay and grain and bred horses, sheep and about five hundred head of good Hereford breeding stock.

My grandfather, John James Armstrong, had a ranch near the Starr holdings and purchased 320 acres from Oscar Starr in the late 1930's.

Starr sold his ranch in 1948 to Edith Ordway, a wealthy San Franciscan with a tale of her own to tell. Mrs. Ordway is remembered as an eccentric woman who could out-drink and out-fight most of the local cowboys.

The Oscar Starr compound is now under approximately 170 feet of water. The beautiful valley where history was made in the 1930's has become a breeding place for schools of fish, a water source for over 400,000 customers (not a one from the far East County, where the reservoir is located), and offer more than 20,000 acres of watershed area where natural resources will be protected. Ain't progress grand? Until Next Time....

HENRY COWELL FAMILY

Henry Cowell and his decedents have definitely left footprints in the history of Contra Costa County. In the mid 1850's Henry Cowell and his brother, John, traveled to California from Massachusetts to make their fortune in the gold fields. They eventually established a drayage and storage company making deliveries throughout the Mother Lode and Stockton areas.

Devastating fires swept throughout California towns during the 1800s requiring the need to rebuild and creating a market for concrete and mortar of which lime is a key ingredient. Until a source of local limestone was found, all lime was shipped to California from the East Coast making the product very expensive. While John Cowell worked for Albion P. Jordon and Isaac E. Davis, who were credited with accidentally discovering limestone in the Mount Diablo area, the brothers became interested in processing lime.

John Cowell purchased an interest in a Santa Cruz lime works owned and operated by Jordon and Davis. In 1865, Henry Cowell bought out Jordon's share of the company and moved to Santa Cruz. The business thrived and by 1888 Henry was the sole owner. John had returned to Massachusetts in 1860 because of failing health, and Davis had died. Thus, Henry established the Henry Cowell Lime and Concrete Company.

Henry Cowell married Harriet Carpenter, his Massachusetts sweetheart, in 1854. They had three sons and three daughters, Roland (1857-1858) Ernest V. (1858-1911) Isabella (1858-1950) Samuel H. (1861 - 1955) Sarah (1863 -1903) and Helen (1866 - 1932). Ernest was the only one to marry. However the marriage did not produce any children.

By Henry Cowell's death, in 1903, his estate included real estate holdings from Washington State to San Luis Obispo. He owned schooners and steamers, cement plants, cattle ranches, and property in fourteen California counties. Henry's two sons, Ernest and Samuel, inherited the family business. Ernest managed the firm until his death in 1911. In his will he carried out several family interests and concerns that had been established by his father's philanthropy, contributing to many causes throughout California such as education, health, and employee welfare.

Lester Cakebread - 1913

Samuel (better known as Harry) Cowell took over and ran the business when his brother died. Harry is well remembered as a conservationist. While in control of the family business, he purchased thousands of acres of grazing land and established Hereford cattle and horse breeding farms. In addition, he worked hard to preserve California's natural beauty. Cowell Beach along the Santa Cruz waterfront and the Henry Cowell Redwood State Park in Felton are among these. The Cowell family was instrumental in establishing medical centers at major universities and colleges including UC Berkeley, University of Pacific, Stanford, and Mills College.

Harry died in 1955 at the age of 93 leaving no heirs. His bequest created the S. H. Cowell Foundation, a charitable foundation designed to carry on the philanthropy practiced by his family during their lifetimes. In 1993 the foundation was valued at approximately $135 million. Since it's inception, the S.H. Cowell foundation has awarded grants in excess of $100 million to hundreds of programs and projects throughout Northern California.

In 1924, the Cowell Portland Cement Company purchased the John Marsh Ranch. This location was important to the Cowells because of it's rich silica sand which was mined on the property and could be used at the company's cement plant in the town of Cowell, adjacent to Clayton.

Since Cowell's purchase of the Marsh Ranch, portions of the property have been taken for public purposes, including powerline easements, underground gas pipes, the Marsh Creek flood control dam and reservoir, PG&E natural gas compression station, and the Los Vaqueros Reservoir and water transfer pipeline. In addition, Contra Costa will require additional land for the State Route 4 bypass.

The S.H.Cowell Foundation donated Doctor John Marsh's Stone house located on Marsh Creek Road near Brentwood and four surrounding acres to Contra Costa County in 1960. In 1981 ownership of the Marsh House along with an additional ten acres was transferred to the State of California Department of Parks and Recreation. The S.H. Cowell Foundation has also financially supported many projects for local schools, donated substantially to the addition to the Brentwood Library, and have shown their generosity repeatedly throughout East Contra Costa.

In 1986 the Cowell foundation began seeking a General Plan Amendment and various approvals for a Master Planned Community on the remaining 4277 acres. After fourteen years of trying, their efforts were unsuccessful. Today the Marsh Ranch remains essentially unimproved. Until Next Time....

APRICOT FESTIVAL

Festivals are not new to the community of Brentwood. The Brentwood Park has an extraordinary history of community events, among them the Apricot Festivals of the twenties and thirties. The Lions Club Carniques in the fifties, sixties and seventies, the Harvest, and Art & Wine Festivals of the eighties, and the Cornfest of today's era all have noteworthy tales to tell. Each of these events required an unbelievable amount of community participation, and offered residents of East Contra Costa an opportunity to gather.

The first Diablo Valley Apricot Festival was combined with the opening of the American Toll Bridge Company's Antioch Bridge in 1926. In the beginning, the Apricot Festival was little more than a sideline to the bridge dedication. J. S. O'Meara of Brentwood proposed that a committee consider recognition of the apricot industry as an up-and-coming enterprise of East County. At the time the orchards were young, with few people knowing how many apricot trees were actually planted in the district. The East Contra Costa Chamber of Commerce met at the Antioch city hall to plan the celebration.

The second festival was held in Oakley, with emphasis placed on the growing importance of Diablo Valley as an apricot-producing district. The third festival and all succeeding Apricot Festivals were held in Brentwood Park, which at the time was a grove of eucalyptus trees offering an ideal setting for the celebration. Each year the event drew thousands of visitors from all over the Bay Area. Some of the distinguished guests included Governors James Rolph, Clement C. Young and Frank E. Merriam.

From 1928 to 1937, the East Contra Costa Chamber of Commerce sponsored the Apricot Festival and for three days in late June of each year Brentwood Park, originally referred to as Brentwood Grove, would come alive with activity as residents prepared for the festival. Professional carnival vendors, local businessmen and women, farmers and children could be seen setting up for the celebration. Stands were erected, a stage constructed, a horseshoe pit built, and the park was groomed to welcome thousands of expected guests.

A committee was organized by the Chamber of Commerce comprised of a general chairman, secretary/treasurer and manager to oversee the event. Events requiring committee chairmen included the parade, queen contest, sports, publicity, fruit booths, dance, carnival and more.

During the first celebration, held in Brentwood in 1928, a train chartered especially for the Apricot Festival came from Richmond, California, carrying the Richmond Maennerchors, a well-known men's chorus, to perform. The train was decorated for the event and offered low rates for passengers anxious to attend the festival from all over the Bay Area.

On Friday evening, opening day of the festival, the Liberty High School band would march into the crowded park escorting the queen, Miss Apricot, with her attendants to the open air pavilion for coronation ceremonies. The Queen's Coronation Ball followed at the American Legion Hall.

On Saturday night, the Liberty High School band put on a concert in the park. Men were lured to demonstrations of "fast boxing" and wrestling and women could be found discussing recipes at food booths displaying dishes prepared with local apricots. The Brentwood Women's Club sponsored an apricot pie contest each year that always had between fifty to one hundred entries.

Sunday activities included the annual parade featuring bands, floats from all parts of the county, baseball games at the LUHS field, a festival luncheon at the Legion Hall, a baby show, and numerous other activities. A professional carnival came to town and children would be heard laughing as they rode on the merry-go-round. Young men could be seen attempting to win prizes for their sweethearts at the baseball toss.

Over the years improvements were added to Brentwood Park as a result of the festival. In 1929, J. W. Williams, a local contractor, constructed a tall welcoming arch in the southwest corner of the park. The arch resembled concrete, but was actually built of wood and finished with plaster, in a design typical of the era. It was gray-beige in color, with BRENTWOOD imprinted across the arch. E. R. McClelland of Diablo Electric installed electrical utilities, which supported the park with lights, and a pavilion with an open-air dance floor was built.

As years passed the festival grew in scope. By the mid-1930's the Apricot Festival ranked as one of the outstanding events in the state, drawing visitors from far and wide. Most of the old timers I interview have wonderful, warm memories of their time spent at the festival.

By 1934 the Chamber of Commerce was experiencing difficulties finding members to chair the many different committees necessary for the success of the Apricot Festival. To insure a sufficient quantity of choice fruit for the festival, it was necessary to schedule the event during the time when apricots were at their peak. A farmer's harvest for the entire year took place during these few weeks in late June and July when he processed his crop and transported the fruit to market; contributing time to the festival was a sacrifice that could cost a farmer serious loss of income.

During the 1936 festival, Ray Wallace, Judge Wallace's son, was struck from behind with a blackjack by thugs from Pittsburg. He was taken to Dameron Hospital in Stockton, where he lay unconscious for several days. Ray showed signs of improvement and regained consciousness for brief intervals, allowing friends and family to believe he would recover. On July 10, 1936, Ray Wallace took a turn for the worse and died from his injuries. Wallace, born and raised in Brentwood, was only 44 years old. He had been very active in the community, as chief of Brentwood's volunteer fire department and an active member of the Masons, Lions, and other civic organizations.

Wallace's death affected the entire town, and by 1937 when the festival committee met to discuss the upcoming Apricot Festival, the Chamber of Commerce decided to withdraw as sponsor. Officially, the committee announced that opposition from growers was the principal reason they declined to carry on the event. Many said the celebration had grown to a point where it was out of hand, difficult to manage, and the incident the previous year convinced committee members to rethink their involvement in the event. Until Next Time....

H. P. GARIN COMPANY

There are many interesting characters reflected in the chapters of Brentwoods past, men that were instrumental in the development of this region of California. Henry P. Garin was such a man and was known as one of the most progressive men ever to be identified with the agricultural and horticultural development of East Contra Costa County.

Born in Berkeley, California in 1880, Garin moved at the age of seven to Hayward with his father. His father farmed and shipped produce throughout the Bay Area. Henry entered the vegetable growing and shipping business for himself when he was twenty three. He established himself as one of the best known shippers of fruits and vegetables in our country as well as gaining a reputation internationally.

In 1923 Garin arrived in Brentwood and leased land for farming. In 1929 he purchased 600 acres and leased an additional 600 acres. In that year 794 carloads of vegetables were shipped from the Garin holding. Although Garin never actually lived in Brentwood he and his wife, Elsie, were frequent visitors to the area and had many friends there. Originally maintaining his business headquarters in San Francisco, he relocated the business in 1937 to Salinas retaining operations in Brentwood, Firebaugh, and the Imperial Valley.

By 1935 Garin had operations all over the state, with more than 7000 acres planted in the Brentwood area producing cauliflower, cabbage, lettuce, peppers, peas, tomatoes, and other vegetables.

The H.P. Garin Company owned several packing sheds and a storage yard in the Brentwood area. The main shed was located near where Safeway is today. Another was located on Walnut Blvd. near the site where the Lions Club building is today. The company also operated the R.L. Sanford packing sheds and the D.D. Watson warehouse at Bixler Station along the Santa Fe Railroad.

During the depression, in 1933, the H.P.Garin Company was forced into receivership with an indebtedness of more than half a million dollars. Henry Garin himself was named receiver, a tribute to the high regard in which he was held, and a step which was unique in that era for a business filing insolvency. He could have paid his creditors a fraction on the dollar, but insisted on full payment to all creditors despite the difficult conditions. By 1941 the company was back on a firm financial basis.

By the mid 1940s Henry Garin owned and operated more than 30,000 acres in California and Arizona. The H.P. Garin Company became one of the largest concerns of it's kind in California. .

The H.P.Garin Company was very progressive. In 1936 they installed the first Teletype in Diablo Valley. The Teletype, operating over special telephone circuits, typed out messages giving the company an accurate record of interoffice business. Garin also installed Teletypes in his other field offices throughout the state.

Henry Garin maintained a private plane which he used for transportation to keep in touch with his widespread operations and was often seen landing in a field west of Brentwood. Henry had three sons, Henry Jr., Robert, and William. He also had a daughter, Elsie Jane. Henry P. Garin died January 16, 1947, at the age of 67 of a heart condition.

The H.P. Garin Company was involved in all aspects of Brentwood for more than thirty years. They were a primary employer in the area with 1500 to 2000 employees on the companies payroll at the peak of the season in 1935. Many "old timers" remember working in the packing sheds or the fields.

Henry Garin created a widespread agricultural empire growing a huge variety of fruits and vegetables. Besides crops in the Brentwood area Garin grew celery near Walnut Grove, asparagus and sugar beets on Bouldin Island and Grand Island, carrots and onions near Stockton and Tracy, onions and garlic in Hollister and Gilroy, and lettuce, peas, parsley, tomatoes, cantaloupes and watermelon in El Centro.

Walter G. Norris was manager of Garin's Brentwood operations for many years. The Garin School, located at the end of First Street, was built in 1969 on property once farmed by the H.P. Garin Company. Until Next Time....

CIVIC, FRATERNAL AND FARM ORGANIZATIONS IN THE 1930'S

By the 1930's, Brentwood and the surrounding area had become a prominent agricultural center, and life here had changed greatly. It was an era when neighbors depended on each other; when the homecoming parade on Oak Street was a major community event and the Apricot Festival was the summer's highlight, and Mrs. Krumland motoring to Stockton was a news item. In 1997, there is a lot of talk about volunteerism and discussion of mandatory community service. It's hard to believe that the early improvements to Brentwood Park, the first school breakfast program, benches around town, school field trips, our local fire protection, and hundreds of other projects which affected the daily lives of residents were donated freely by willing volunteers—without government intervention. Local doctors and dentists visited schools annually to participate in a health fair, and the Lions Club sponsored a vision screening open to the entire community free of charge. The streets of Brentwood were even cleaned by volunteers. Fred Abbott started a youth group, Hi-Y, that met early in the morning before school and cleaned the public streets.

The foundation of East Contra Costa was built by volunteers and the area was noted for having a large number of civic, fraternal and farm organizations in the 1930's, all of which took an active interest in the district's welfare.

Both Brentwood and Oakley offered women's clubs that were affiliated with state club federations. Brentwood's women's group was organized in 1901 and Oakley's in 1913, and Byron founded a library club in 1923. These three women's organizations were instrumental in the development of the library system in East County and spearheaded many other projects for the betterment of their communities.

Byron and Brentwood both had Lions Clubs (founded in 1929 and 1932) that were actively involved in many worthwhile projects to improve their hometowns. Roy Frerich Post, American Legion (established in 1919 after World War I), was one of the outstanding veteran groups in the county and today has a boundless list of achievements to its credit.

Native Daughters Play - 1940's
Vivian Graham, Edith Davis, Bertha Sattler
Bella Morchio, Clara Dal Porto and Helen Wristen

Each year the Post would present medals to the leaders of the eighth-grade graduating classes in the district, the awards being based upon scholarship, character, and evidence of leadership.

Boy Scout troops were active in both Byron and Brentwood. Weir Fetters was the Brentwood scoutmaster, and M. E. Rogers was Byron scoutmaster. There were also Campfire groups for girls in both Brentwood and Knightsen.

The East Contra Costa Chamber of Commerce, with directors representing the four towns in the district, was active during the depression era, serving as a means of contact for Diablo Valley with the state at large in matters of civic interest.

The Best in the West club was active in Brentwood, organizing and dedicating their time to social activities and community projects.

East Contra Costa also offered residents numerous fraternal organizations. The Masons (organized in 1902) and Eastern Star met in Brentwood; the Odd Fellows (organized in 1887) and Rebekahs (1902), and Native Sons (1891) and Daughters (1911) would meet in Byron.

Byron and Oakley had the IDES Men's Portuguese Lodge (instituted in 1911) and Byron offered an SPRSI Women's Portuguese Lodge, UPEC Men's Portuguese Lodge (1920) and Woodmen of the World #486. Oakley had the Pocahontas and Red Men Lodge.

With the primary industry of Contra Costa being agriculture, the area's farm group membership had ample access to reliable information relating to farming, as well as social opportunities, through the Farm Centers, the Grange, Home Department and 4-H.

The Knightsen and Lone Tree Farm Centers were subsidiaries of the Contra Costa Farm Bureau. Monthly meetings offered speakers on interesting subjects and member discussions of current events, local problems, and changes in the communities. The Diablo Valley Grange (organized at Point of Timber in 1873) met regularly in Brentwood and offered an active program for their members as well as a home economics division, which offered demonstrations in cookery, canning and needlework.

The 4-H Clubs conducted an active learning program for the girls and boys. Girls learned sewing and cooking and practiced other home projects, while boys principally raised livestock and learned about horticulture. Members displayed their 4-H projects at the county fair, winning recognition and ribbons for their handiwork. Many club members also attended 4-H camp in the Sierra each summer, where they interacted with nature and had the opportunity meet and become acquainted with other young people from all parts of California.

Liberty Union High School offered a Future Farmers of America chapter, made up primarily of young men who planned to make agriculture their life's work. FFA members actively participated in regional and state competitions.

There have been many changes in East Contra Costa over the years. Fraternal organizations like the Odd Fellows and Masons have disbanded through time and along with the clubs we have lost some of the glue that bound the community together. The brotherhood and sense of community which these groups and their members offered as they gave freely of themselves, are slowly becoming another chapter of our history. Until Next Time....

ROBERT FREDERICK
MAJOR GENERAL

Doctor Marcus W. Frederick purchased property south of Brentwood in 1930 and resided in Diablo Valley until his death in 1938. Frederick was born in New York City; spent much of his youth in Nevada; received his education in Europe; and then attended Harvard, where he was personal friends with classmate William Randolph Hearst. After graduating from Harvard he returned to Europe to study medicine at Leipzig and became an eye, ear and nose specialist with an active practice on Post Street, San Francisco.

Frederick's ranch was located approximately one mile south of Brentwood, where the highway turns from paralleling the railroad right of way. For many years this site was referred to as "Frederick's Corner." In the early days the road made a sharp "L" turn, and in the 1950's the corner was widened and made into a long, sweeping curve.

Doctor Frederick is remembered as a brilliant man with wide and varied interests who loved his ranch near Brentwood. He was a master of several foreign languages, an accomplished musician, an avid reader and spent endless hours grooming his prized walnut grove.

Several months before Doctor Frederick's death, he wrote a letter for his wife, Pauline, to be opened after his departure, requesting that his remains be cremated and the ashes scattered over his walnut grove. His wishes were complied with.

After Doctor Frederick's death, his wife moved to Oakland, but she continued to oversee the management of the ranch for many years.

Doctor Frederick had two children, a daughter, Marcia, and a son, Robert. Robert became a famous general during his military service in World War II.

Robert attended high school in San Francisco, transferring to a military academy in Virginia to complete his senior year. He continued his education at West Point, where he earned the rank of cadet captain, graduating in 1928, the youngest in his class. Upon graduation from West Point he started his tour of duty for the U.S. Army.

World War II was the most destructive conflict in modern human history. Hitler's forces invaded and blitzed through Poland, precipitating a declaration of war by Britain and France on Germany. More than sixteen million men and women served in the armed forces. When it was over the tragic count was nearly 300,000 U.S. battle deaths and more than 670,000 wounded, totals three times greater than World War I.

General Frederick earned his first star at the age of 31. He was the youngest ground forces general to serve in World War II. He was commander of the Sixth Army and head of the First Special Forces, and is remembered for his involvement in the Devil's Brigade. In later years he acted as a technical advisor on a film produced about the Devil's Brigade. During his military service Frederick was wounded nine times, making him the most wounded general in modern military history. As a result of his service he was highly decorated, earning nine purple hearts.

Major General Frederick retired from the military in 1952 with a brilliant war record, which included commanding the first airborne task force to land in southern France. Following the war he served as commandant officer at the Fort Monmouth, Virginia, artillery school and commanding general at Fort Ord.

After retirement he moved to Brentwood and devoted his time to operating the family walnut ranch. General & Mrs. Frederick had purchased a home in Palo Alto and built a second residence at the ranch in Brentwood, intending to split their time between the two residences. Many old-timers remember that the general enjoyed patronizing local taverns regularly, usually sitting quietly at the end of the bar observing other patrons. While living in the Brentwood area, Frederick was an active member of the Diamond Walnut Growers Association.

In February of 1955 Frederick was involved in an accident when the pickup he was driving went out of control and crashed into a tree on Railroad Avenue (Highway 4 today). A witness said it appeared he was trying to roll up the window on the passenger side of the cab when he lost control. He suffered a fractured arm and leg and head injuries, and was paralyzed on his left side. Frederick was taken to Pittsburg Community Hospital, where he was cared for until he was transferred to Letterman Hospital at the San Francisco Presidio.

The general had been a divisional commander under Eisenhower during the war and they had become personal friends. Eisenhower (then president) called Letterman Hospital to check on Frederick's condition. General Frederick's daughter has several letters the President wrote to her father while he was recuperating.

Frederick was released from the hospital and returned to Palo Alto, where he was confined to bed for many months. As a result of the accident he had to learn to walk and talk again, but eventually recovered. Frederick never returned to Brentwood to live, although he did oversee the management of the ranch until he sold it to Vic Castello in 1968.

Major General Frederick died of heart failure in 1970 at the age of 63 and was buried in National Cemetery at the Presidio in San Francisco.

While researching the history of East Contra Costa I am continually amazed at the variety of interesting characters I find. Major General Robert Frederick definitely left footprints in our past. Until Next Time....

BRENTWOOD INCORPORATES

The year 1948, when Brentwood incorporated, was a very busy year. The United States thwarted a Russian blockade of Berlin by an airlift of supplies and food. Israel was declared a state. The world's largest telescope was dedicated at Mount Palomar. Harry Truman pulled a spectacular upset victory for president defeating Thomas A. Dewey. The Metropolitan Opera was televised for the first time. And the Kinsey Report, The Sexual Behavior of the Human Male, was released causing a sensation across the country.

Prince Charles of Great Britain, Al Gore, Richard Simmons, Jeremy Irons, and Barbara Mandrell were born in 1948. The average yearly income in America was $3,000. A T-bone steak cost 59 cents a pound, coffee 58 cents a pound, a tube of toothpaste cost 41 cents, and for an Oldsmobile automobile you would pay $2,078.

The town of Brentwood was founded in 1878 when the San Pablo & Tulare Railroad came through East Contra Costa. Seventy years later it became the first incorporated city in the far east county. The group that spearheaded the effort to incorporate was the Brentwood Improvement Association. Officers of the association were Dr. William Painter, president; Oliver Danielson, secretary; E. J. Spiering, vice-president; and Robert Casey, treasurer. Residents of Brentwood were dissatisfied with the way Contra Costa County was running the community. They were looking for better police protection, cleaner streets, elimination of slums and fire and health hazards; and increasing the attractiveness of the town.

In October 1947 the Brentwood Improvement Association started a campaign to sign up the necessary number of property owners representing twenty-five percent of the assessed valuation within the proposed boundaries. These signatures, in the form of a petition, were presented to the the County board of supervisors in Martinez. Within two weeks, forty percent of the property owners had signed.

On January 15, 1948, the residents of Brentwood went to the polls in record-breaking numbers voting three to one to incorporate as a city. The *Brentwood News* reported the vote was 337 in favor of incorporation and 118 against. At the time, Brentwood had a population of 1,729.

Brentwood incorporated February 19, 1948, with Jack Lane acting as the first mayor, although he only served for six months. He was followed by Oliver Danielson who served for three and a half years. Brentwood's first city council was made up of John Dyer, Bob Jansse, Oliver Danielson, and Adolph Boltzen.

Jack Lane owned the Delta Theater; John Dyer, with partner Jim Hannum, owned and operated Western Auto on Oak Street; Bob Jansse owned Jansse & O'Meara Grocery Store (located where Brentwood Liquor is today); Oliver Danielson had a jewelry store on First Street (where Castle Bridal Shop is today); and Adolph Boltzen worked for Garin Company.

Joseph Gomes Jr. of the the Pittsburg Police Department was appointed acting police chief on a ninety-day leave of absence from Pittsburg in order to organize the new Brentwood Police Department. James Patrick Hannratty was later hired to fill this position and Floyd Ditmars was employed as a patrolman. The city purchased its first police car, a red 1948 Ford, in June 1948 from Brentwood Motors at a cost to the city of $90 a month.

The new council named George Wedgwood as city clerk, a position he held for sixteen years. He was succeeded by Bill Stanton in 1964. Blair Rixon accepted the position of city judge, with Robert Blewett as the first city attorney. Other local officials were: Charles Barkley, constable; E. J. Spiering, fire chief (he was also principal of Brentwood Elementary School); Grace Nunn, chairman of the park board; and Richard Wallace, postmaster.

Shortly after incorporating, the council appointed Brentwood's first Planning Commission with Harold Anderson as chairman. The rest of the board consisted of Mrs. Charles French, Tinsman Craig, Marion Phillips, and Andrew Bonnickson. William F. Sykes was named building inspector.

The city received its first revenue from fines in February 1948, when Judge Blair Rixon assessed a $25 fine on a young man for reckless driving near the high school.

The first city offices were housed on the second floor of the Veterans Hall and were open six days a week from nine in the morning to one o'clock in the afternoon. The offices remained in that location until 1951, when City Hall was moved to a building at the corner of Second and Oak Streets. The present facility was not occupied until May 1, 1963.

The city's budget in 1948 was $28,550. The 1999 budget will top $9 million. City records show the community's first assessed valuation was $700,000. The first entrepreneurs to hold City of Brentwood business licenses were: 1)Diablo Club, Sid Hulbun, proprietor (Sweeney's today). 2) Pioneer Ice Cream Parlor, Carl Hopper and Archie Reed, owners (located where where Rich's Drive Inn is today). 3) Al's Restaurant, Al Smith, owner. 4) Hotel Brentwood, Tony Continente, proprietor (located where the Chevron Station is today); and 5) Rolando Inn, John Rolando, owner (located where Not Only Baja is today). Until Next Time….

BRENTWOOD MAYORS:	Lane, John	1948 - 1949
	Danielson, Oliver	1949 - 1950
	Silva, Joseph	1950 - 1952
	LeMoine, Everett	1952 - 1954
	Curtis, Wesley	1954 - 1956
	Gibson, Pete	1956 - 1958
	Avery, Clifford	1958 - 1960
	Christiansen, Art	1960 - 1964
	Nunn, George	1964 - 1968
	Jensen, Alan	1968 - 1970
	Gamble, George	1970 - 1976
	Cunningham, Joe	1976 - 1978
	Ghiselli, Bruce	1980 - 1982
	Guise, Barbara	1982 - 1984
	Moore, Roger	1984 - 1986
	Fisher, Nathan	1986 - 1990
	Palmer, Catherine	1990 - 1992
	Gonzales, Art	1992 - 1994
	Hill, Bill	1994 - 1996
	Morrill, John	1996 - 1998
	Kidd, Quintin	1998 - 2000
	McPoland, Mike	2000 - 2001
BRENTWOOD CITY MANAGERS:	Wedgewood, George	1948 - 1964
	Stanton, Bill	1964 - 1972
	Poertner, Eugene	1972 - 1977
	Buell, James	1977 - 1980
	Gill, Harry	1980 - 1988
	Russell, Don	1988 - 1993
	Corey, Jay	1994 - 1997
	Elam, Jonathan	1998 - Current

BRENTWOOD INCORPORATES—PART II

Happy Birthday Brentwood! Brentwood was founded in 1878 when the San Pablo & Tulare railroad came through East Contra Costa and seventy years later became the first incorporated city in the far east county. The group that spearheaded the effort to incorporate was the Brentwood Improvement Association. Officers of the association were Dr. William Painter. president; Oliver Danielson, secretary; E.J. Spiering, vice president; and Robert Casey, treasurer. Residents of Brentwood were dissatisfied with the way Contra Costa County was running the community. They were looking for better police protection, cleaner streets, elimination of slums and fire and health hazards, and increasing the attractiveness of the town.

In October 1947 the Brentwood Improvement Association started a campaign to sign up the necessary property owners, representing 25% of the assessed valuation within the proposed boundaries. These signatures, in the form of a petition, were presented to the Board of Supervisors in Martinez. Within two weeks 40% of the property owners had signed.

January 15, 1948 the residents of Brentwood went to the polls in record-breaking numbers voting 3 to 1 to incorporate as a city. The Brentwood News reported the vote was 337 in favor of incorporation and 118 against. Brentwood had a population of 1,729 residents in 1948.

Brentwood incorporated February 19, 1948, with Jack Lane acting as the first mayor, although he only served for six months and was followed by Oliver Danielson, who served for 3½ years. Brentwood's first City Council was made up of John Oyer, Bob Jansse, Oliver Danielson, and Adolph Boltzen. Jack Lane owned the Delta Theater; John Oyer, with partner Jim Hannum, owned and operated Western Auto on Oak Street; Bob Jansse owned Jansse & O'Meara Grocery Store (located where Brentwood Liquor is today); Oliver Danielson had a jewelry store on First Street (where Castle Bridal Shop is today); and Adolph Boltzen worked for Garin Co.

Joseph Gomes, Jr of the Pittsburg Police Department was appointed acting police chief on a ninety-day leave of absence from Pittsburg in order to organize the new Brentwood Police Department. James Patrick Hannratty was later hired to fill this position. Floyd Ditmars was employed as a police officer. The city purchased its first police car, a red 1948 Ford, in June 1948 from Brentwood Motors, costing the city $90 a month.

The new council named George Wedgwood as city clerk, a position he held for sixteen years, being succeeded by Bill Stanton in 1964. Blair Rixon accepted the position of city judge. Robert Blewett was the first city attorney. Other local officials were: Charles Barkley, constable; E.J. Spiering, fire chief (he was also principal of Brentwood Elementary School); Grace Nunn, Chairman of Park Board, and Richard Wallace, postmaster.

Shortly after incorporating the council appointed Brentwood's first Planning Commission. Harold Anderson, chairman and a board consisting of Mrs. Charles French, Tinsman Craig, Marion Phillips and Andrew Bonnickson. William F. Sykes was named building inspector. The city got its first revenue from fines in February 1948 when Judge Blair Rixon assessed a $25 fine on a young man for reckless driving near the Liberty Union High School. The first city offices were housed on the second floor in the Veterans Hall and remained in that location until 1951 when City Hall was moved to a building at the corner of Second and Oak Streets. The present facility was not occupied until May 1, 1963. The first city offices were open six days a week from 9 a.m. to 1 p.m.

In 1948 the city budget was $28,550.00. The 2019 city budget was in excess of $62,647,000.00 according to the "The City of Brentwood Comprehensive Financial Report: Fiscal Year Ended June 30, 2020." The community's first assessed valuation in 1948 was $700,000. In 2019 the assessed value and estimated actual value of taxable property was $9,969,529,190.00 according to the same Financial Report. That is almost $10 billion dollars in assessment value including residential, commercial, industrial and other property. It excludes tax-exempt properties. Wow, how we have grown!

City records show the first businesses to hold a City of Brentwood business license as: 1) Diablo Club, Sid Hulbun, proprietor (Sweeney's today), 2) Pioneer Ice Cream Parlor, Carl Hopper and Archie Reed, owner (located where Rich's Drive Inn is today), 3) Al's Restaurant, Al Smith, owner, 4) Hotel Brentwood, Tony Continente, proprietor (located where Shank's Chevron is today) and 5) Rolando Inn, John Rolando, owner (located where McCurley's Floor Covering is today).

BRENTWOOD 1951
A CITY ON THE MOVE

As I research the history of Brentwood, some years stand out more than others as eventful windows of time. 1951 was such a year! Brentwood had been incorporated for three years; the young, energetic leaders of the community were busy developing a city they could be proud of. A new Brentwood Post Office was built; the city park was enhanced; city streets and drainage problems were addressed; farming was our leading industry; and the Liberty Lions football team won the league championship.

Brentwood's first post office was established September 30, 1878, with Clarence R. Esterbrook as postmaster. The first post office was located in Louis Grunauer's Store. (By 1951, it had been in nine different locations with numerous postmasters: eight different sites on Oak Street and a location on the corner of Dainty and Railroad.) Some of the early postmasters were: Joseph W. Carey, Louis Grunauer, Mr. Claghorn, Mr. Grennan, Dr. Mott, Mr. Lieber, Mrs. Ida Morgan, Mrs. Minnie Sheddrick, Mrs. J. J. Berry, Charles French, Richard Wallace and Lawrence F. O'Brien.

On Labor Day weekend, 1951, the post office staff moved into a new facility, built by Mr. & Mrs. Mark Eisele and leased to the government. The new building offered Brentwood a third more space to meet the growing demands of the community. The city's growth was evidenced by the fact that although the number of lockboxes was increased from 480 in the old building to 676 in the new, all were rented almost immediately, creating a waiting list. The present post office, on the corner of Dainty Avenue and First Street, was not built until 1967.

Brentwood's first city hall was located in the American Legion Hall in 1948. By 1951, the city offices were moved to Second Street, near Oak, into a building that provided the community with a good-sized court and council room, a separate room for the city clerk, and an adjoining office for the justice of the peace.

Although Brentwood City Park had been the center of activity in town for many years the city council authorized numerous improvements to the site in 1951. The entire park was curbed, walks were added, landscaping was upgraded, and a plaza was constructed at the Oak and Second Street corner.

Street improvements were another progressive step that the city fathers engaged in. Walnut Boulevard, Dainty Avenue, and Sycamore Drive were surfaced and a plan was developed to improve First, Second and Third Streets.

Receipts from city sales taxes were sufficient to begin addressing the city's drainage problems. In 1951, plans to install storm sewers and prepare the community for possible flooding were put into action along with steps to adopt a civil defense program.

Brentwood service clubs were active in 1951. William D. Dickey was president of the newly formed Rotary Club, and Hugh Armstrong was president of the Lions Club. The Lions gave their traditional Halloween Party and football dinner. It was not until 1953 that the famous Lions Club 4th of July Carnique was established.

Prior to 1951, Brentwood businessmen had established the Brentwood Improvement Association. This organization was instrumental in Brentwood's incorporation efforts during the late 1940's, but by 1951, the group decided to reorganize and form a Brentwood Chamber of Commerce. At that time, a committee of five, Ben Petersen, Ray Scoggin, Bill Dickey, Oliver Danielson and Richard Wallace, was appointed to lay the foundation of the new organization. The first official Chamber meeting was held in 1952, with Ben Peterson serving as president.

Efforts to establish a mosquito abatement district in the eastern end of the county finally bore fruit, through the persistent work of a group headed by Cleveland Von Konsky and Ray Graf.

1951 was a good year for fruit growers and farmers. The area shipped out 1,755 railroad cars of fruit and vegetables. This figure does not reflect hundreds of truckloads of cherries, figs and other products transported to market by truck. There were 991 rail car loads of tomatoes, more than all other products combined. Next came honeydews, 271 cars, with peaches third with 210 cars. Apricot billings totaled 191 cars; plums, 14 cars; nectarines, 29 cars; corn, 5 cars; pears, 6 cars; grapes, 9 cars; and mixed fruit, 29 cars. Point of interest: field workers were paid 20¢ per fifty-pound lug for round tomatoes and 24¢ a fifty-pound lug for pear tomatoes.

Brentwood mourned the passing of a number of longtime residents: Mrs. Dora Heidorn, Allan Monroe, Bert Bancroft, Ed Olsen, F. P. Milet, Hazel Rodriques, Jacob Winger, Mrs. Charles Petersen, Chester Armstrong, Omer Morris, Bill McGillvray, and Mrs. Del Sargentis all left their marks in the chapters of Brentwood's history.

Under the direction of Coach Lou Bronzan, the Liberty Football Team played undefeated and won its league championship. The baseball team, also coached by Bronzan, shared the league title with Livermore. Until Next Time….

1951 CITY OFFICIALS

Mayor	Joe S. Silva
Councilmen	Adolph Boltzen
	Bill Stanford
	Ted Wells
	Mr. Ruetenik/replaced by Ray Graf midyear
City Clerk	George Wedgewood
Chief of Police	James Hanratty
Constable	Charlie Barkley
City Judge	Blair Rixon
Fire Chief	E. J. Spiering
Chairman of Park Board	Grace Nunn
Postmaster	Lawrence O'Brien

BRENTWOOD WOMEN'S CLUB

The Brentwood Women's Club has been an active part of Brentwood's history for at least 96 years and probably longer. As I researched the history of this organization it was interesting to find that the group has changed its name several times over the years, but has always had the best interests of Brentwood at heart, and has definitely played a vital role in this community's past.

The club was instrumental in founding the first Brentwood Reading Room, in 1902. They paid for and installed the town's first street signs in 1904; raised funds to finance streetlights on Oak Street in 1906; and gave a housewarming for the new high school in 1906. They built a small library in 1915; sent special packages from home to our boys in Europe during World War I, and helped earn money for the fire engine fund in 1918. The members established the Brentwood Library on Second Street in 1922 and participated in Brentwood's Annual Apricot Festival during the 1920's and '30's. They planted a strip of lawn and a row of pyracanthas in the Brentwood park in 1932, and have constantly supported local schools and youth groups, leaving footprints in the chapters of our past.

According to early club records, on October 12, 1901, a group of ladies from Brentwood and the outlying areas met at the home of Mrs. Sarah Ivory to talk over the idea of forming a club for the advancement and improvement of Brentwood. Mrs. Ivory's husband, M. B. Ivory, was at one time sheriff of Contra Costa County and they lived in the John Marsh Stone House for many years. It was decided to form the Brentwood Women's Club, with Mrs. Henrietta Stone as president. Each member was charged a 25-cent initiation fee and one dollar annual dues (which could be paid quarterly). One of the first projects the group undertook was finding a location in town where they could open a reading room. A committee was appointed to take charge of locating books, papers and magazines that could be used to start the facility. Early records show that the ladies had a clubhouse, but I was unable to find its exact location, although I know it was on property owned by Robert Dean (the first president of the Bank of Brentwood, in 1913).

In 1907, for some unknown reason, the members of the Brentwood Women's Club decided to rename the organization "Los Meganos" (meaning sand hills). The reorganized group met twice monthly at the Masonic Hall for a rental fee of two dollars a month.

In 1910, the club again changed its name. The Brentwood Library Association was founded, with Mrs. Andrew Bonnickson as president. The group decided to dedicate themselves to establishing a better-equipped reading room and eventually a library for the community. By the end of 1914 the ladies had saved enough money in their Library Building Fund to pay Herk Logan (the contractor that built the bank building and the Brentwood Hotel in 1913) $400 to build a 16 by 20-foot structure with electric lights. This building was located on the corner of Third and Oak Streets, on a lot that had been "loaned" to the Library Association by Balfour, Guthrie Company, and was completed in March 1915. The club recorded paying $6.60 for three years' insurance on the building. In 1919, Balfour, Guthrie Co. gave the ladies notice that the lot was listed for sale and the library building would have to be moved.

The ladies of the Library Association were at a loss as to what to do. They approached Mrs. Sanford, whose family had donated the land for the Brentwood park, and asked if they might place the library in the park. Mr. Sanford refused to allow this, but he did donate one hundred dollars and a lot on Second Street to be used for a library.

On September 14, 1918, a fire that started from chemicals in the school laboratory destroyed Liberty Union High School. A new school was built on Second Street (its present location) and the school board decided to dispose of the old school site and buildings. The Brentwood Library Association purchased the LUHS Domestic Science Building for $765 and moved it to the lot donated by

Sanford. The building wasn't actually moved to the new site until April 1922.

With the Brentwood Library in its new spacious home, the Brentwood Library Association spent the next few years collecting books for the library and landscaping the grounds around the building. Mrs. Gregory of the Gregory Nurseries donated several trees to be planted in 1926.

The Brentwood Library Association changed their name for the fourth time in 1931, when they once again became the Brentwood Women's Club. The decision was made to dissolve the association, making way for a women's organization with a broader field of activity. In 1933, the Women's Club deeded the building at 648 Second Street to the county, with the understanding that they would still use the facility for their meetings. (The present Brentwood Library, next to City Hall, was built in 1979.)

Mrs. Charles A. French, wife of Brentwood's postmaster, was the organization's president during World War I. During the war years, the association was involved in the Red Cross, working for the war effort.

Mrs. Robert Wallace Jr., wife of the justice of the peace, served as president for two terms, during the period when the organization raised enough funds to purchase and move the building that was used as the Brentwood library for 57 years.

When Mrs. E. G. Nash, wife of the high school principal, was president, the club did a production of "The Whole Town's Talking" to earn money for the purchase of library books. During the term of Mrs. Carra Cook (Dr. Cook's wife), the club was involved in numerous fundraisers for improvements to the Brentwood park. The ladies of the Women's Club were key players in the design of the park, and for many years maintained a garden area.

The Brentwood Women's Club continues to work for the improvement of their community. They have sponsored hundreds of fundraisers over the years. The club has had bake sales, fashion shows, box luncheons, drama productions, quilting bees, raffles, cooking contests, and an endless list of other activities to enrich Brentwood. The organization has offered the women of Brentwood an opportunity to socialize with their neighbors and to truly make a difference in the community they live in. I'm proud to say that I have been a member of the Brentwood Women's Club since the early 1970's. Until Next Time….

BRENTWOOD MASONIC LODGE

Masonic Hall - Built 1920

The Brentwood Masonic Lodge #345 was organized February, 1902 and chartered October, 1902. The group played an active role in the development of Brentwood until 1989 when they disbanded and joined the Antioch Chapter.

The Masonic Lodge started in California about the same time as statehood. Most early records of the California Masons were lost in a fire resulting from the San Francisco earthquake in 1906. These records were stored at the Grand Lodge when the building was completely destroyed during the quake. The organization is presently in the process of collecting early records from lodges throughout the state to recreate this early history. They are hoping to have this project completed by 2000 for their 150th anniversary.

In 1901 Will Jerrisleu, a Jewish gentleman from Southern California, arrived in Brentwood. He traveled to the area in his horse and buggy for the sole purpose of establishing a Masonic Lodge in this region of Contra Costa County. Will had found the Masons in Southern California to be prejudiced and decided to move north and form a new group.

Upon arriving in town Will found lodging at the Brentwood Hotel and decided to become acquainted with local residents. One of the first men Will met was George Shafer, the local undertaker. George seemed interested in becoming involved in Will's project and agreed to introduce Will to local farmers and businessmen.

Will and George spent the next few days visiting with community leaders they thought might be interested in being on the ground floor of establishing a local Masonic Lodge. They met with Has Bonnickson, a local wheat farmer and the first president of the Liberty High School Board; Byron Grigsby, a local businessman owner of a Blacksmith Shop on First Street; Robert Wallace, Justice of the Peace; Alan Monroe, a local carpenter; Herk Logan, the contractor that built the Brentwood Hotel, and others.

Candidates for the organizations membership were invited to attend a general meeting where it was decided to proceed with the formation of a local lodge. Will Jerrisleu was the first Grand Master and there were thirteen charter members. The first meetings were held in private homes. By 1904 the membership had grown and they began looking for a permanent meeting place.

Jerrisleu approached Colonel Robert Coates, a member of the Antioch Masonic Lodge, about constructing a facility on a lot he owned in Brentwood. The lot was located on Railroad Avenue (Highway 4 today) between Oak and Chestnut. Coates agreed to build a two-story building if the Masons would commit to a five-year lease. The buildings lower floor was designed as a hall that Coates could rent for community events and the upper floor was to be used by the Masons. The access to the upper floor was via stairs that were built outside the building. The Masons agreed to pay a monthly rental fee of $20.

The ground floor of the building became Brentwoods social center. It was the scene of graduations, dances, community meetings, dramatic productions, and weddings for many years. The upper level became the Masonic Temple. Coates Hall was used until 1920 when the Masons built a new building on the corner of Second Street and Oak Streets.

In order to construct their new building the lodge had to obtain a $20,000 loan from the Bank of Brentwood, which was co-signed by Judge Robert Wallace, O.C. Prewett and W. J. Shoemaker. During the depression the Masons were as pinched for funds as everyone else. Many members couldn't pay their dues and consequently the lodge developed financial problems with the bank threatened to foreclose on their loan. Judge Wallace met with a committee from the bank and convinced them that there really wasn't a market for the building. The bank decided to work with the Masons and the mortgage was eventually paid in full.

When the Brentwood Masons were first organized they didn't have a set meeting night. They met on the Friday before the full moon each month.

I was unable to find a complete list of past Grand Masters of the lodge, but I did locate about a dozen: O.C. Prewet, 1909; Austin W. Collins, 1912; P.F. Bucholtz, 1917; Alex Burness, 1919; Bob Wallace, 1920; C.H. Noyes, 1922; M.O. Diffin, 1923; A. E. Williamson, 1925; Julian Wagenet, 1928 (also in 1942,1943 & 1944); W. M. Reynolds, 1930; Adolph Boltzen, 1932; and G. A. Howard, 1934.

A number of other organizations are related to the Masons. A women's group, the Order of the Eastern Star, was formed in Brentwood in 1922. The Masonic Lodge also sponsored Rainbow Girls, an organization for young women in the 1940s. The Eastern Star disbanded in 1993 and the Rainbow Girls in the early 1980's.

The Masonic Lodge is one of the oldest and largest fraternal organizations in the world. The organization is dedicated to the ideals of charity, equality, morality, and service to God. Masons donate millions of dollars each year to charitable projects including hospitals, homes for widows, orphans, and the aged; relief for people in distress; and scholarships. The organization has millions of members worldwide including more than two and one-half million in the United States.

The Masons evolved from the builders' guilds of England and Scotland. On June 14, 1717, four lodges in London convened and formed the first Masonic Grand Lodge. As a nonsectarian and nonpolitical association, it appealed to a wide membership that increased and spread to other parts of the world.

Fourteen Presidents of the United States have been Masons, from George Washington to Gerald R. Ford. Nine signers of the Declaration of Independence and 13 signers of the Constitution of the United States were Masons. Other famous people that were active Masons include: Wolfgang Amadeus Mozart, Robert Burns, Will Rogers, Henry Ford, Charles A. Lindberge, Douglas MacArthur, John Wayne, Norman Vincent Peale, and Edwin E. Aldrin, Jr. Until Next Time....

AMERICAN LEGION HAS A LONG HISTORY

The American Legion has played an active part in Brentwood's history over the last 81 years. Roy E. Frerich, Post 202, was founded in 1919 at the end of World War I. Charter Members of the Post were: W. H. Anderson, Robert R. Barkley, Roy L. Barber, F. S. Cook, MD., Cedrie DePledge, F. M. Donaldson, Clarence Elsworth, Charles D. Forbes, Herbert E. Estes, Everett LeMoine, William Murphy, A.F. Mansfield, L.E. Planchon, A. J. Porter, Ernest A. Regill, Walter E. Swift, Frank Shellenberger, R. J. Wallace, W. E. Wooley and Orville C. Wristen. W.E. Wooley was the first post commander.

Ed Grueninger - 1918

Melvin LeRoy Frerichs was born and raised in Byron, he attended Byron school and graduated from Liberty Union High School. Roy, as he was known to all the townspeople, was an accomplished athlete and a leader of his peers. He could be seen riding one of the first cut-down sports cars of the area (equipped with a motorcycle engine) along the dusty back roads of East County.

Melvin LeRoy Frerichs was assigned to Company A, 316th Engineers, 91st Division during World War I. He was the first war casualty from our area and died on October 6th, 1918.

Roy's father John L. Frerichs, arrived in Byron in 1898 and established a saloon on Main Street which in later years housed the Byron Post Office and today is the Byron Saloon. Mr. Frerich was an avid sports fan and instrumental in obtaining and maintaining sports fields in the area. He sponsored many teams, and his saloon became Byron's baseball headquarters where teams would meet after a practice session to discuss the evenings game.

Recognized as an all around sportsman, Mr. Frerichs exhibited his love of fishing and hunting by decorating the saloon with animal heads and antlers. Also an automobile enthusiast, he was one of the first East County residents to own a fine 1913 Chalmer's.

Thirteen Legion Halls were built in Contra Costa County during the 1920's. Brentwood Legion Hall was constructed in 1924. It was funded by a state bond with the monies turned over to the county to administer. The Brentwood Hall was built by the George H. Field Company of Antioch for $16,860. The American Legion has maintained the hall since it was built and has had numerous managers through the years, Fred Merit, Vern Currier, Jim Timms, John Becerra and Johnny Johnson, to mention a few. These men were responsible for renting and maintaining the building.

After completion of the hall members decided an additional meeting room would be needed. According to Janeth Estes Gessler several of the charter members had excavated a basement creating additional space where members held meetings and socialized. This room had a pool table, card tables, and a well worn piano that could tell great tales of war stories shared among members over the years.

The walls of the Legion Hall basement are covered with American flags, plaques, certificates, photos, and wonderful military memorabilia dating back to World War I. Copies of the Bill of Rights and the instrument of Surrender, dated September 2, 1945, signed in Tokyo Bay, Japan may be found proudly hung where they have no doubt been on display for decades. Upon entering this room I could not help feeling the sense of pride these men, both past and present, carry to be an American. It made me proud to know that some of my forefathers were among those listed on the rolls. Past Post Commanders include my husband Bill and my Uncles Orra Pendry and Robert Barkley.

The upstairs over the stage is a meeting room where the Legions Auxiliary met for years. The room has had many uses through the years. It was used to store supplies after World War II, rented for several years and was finally remodeled in 1987. It is now a meeting room for the Diablo Valley Post of Veterans of Foreign Wars, which formed in 1932.

The American Legion Hall has seen many different uses through the years which have all played an important role in Brentwoods History. During the 1920's and 30's the Peterson family ran a Movie Theater in the hall prior to building the Delta Theater in 1938. And Mr. Billingsley used the hall for a skating rink. In 1948, after incorporation, Brentwood's newly named city clerk, police chief, city attorney, and patrol officer shared the area over the stage for a few months. When Liberty Union High School was partially burned down the hall was used for classrooms from 1963 to 1965. I remember attending Mrs. Barnes English class in the hall during my senior year of high school. More than sixty Firemen's Balls have been held in the hall by the Volunteer Fire Department. On election day you will find Brentwoods citizens entering the hall to cast their ballots. In 1978 the county temporarily converted the hall into an evacuation center for flood victims from Holland Tract. The hall has also been host to dance recitals, school plays, Rotary Trade Club dinners, scout meetings, Christmas pageants, weddings and receptions, as well as numerous other community gatherings.

The American Legion covers a wide field of endeavors, and since it began has served the Community of Brentwood in an unbelievable number of ways. They have been particularly active in education, youth activities, feeding the needy, and have extended a helpful hand to the community for more than eighty years. They have sponsored Boy's State, scholarships, citizenship awards to eighth grade graduates, youth athletic teams, Boy Scouts, 4-H and F.F.A. projects, band uniforms for Edna Hill Band, and much more.

After World War II the Legion began a holiday food box program. In 1994 they supplied a Thanksgiving grocery box to over 600 area families, distributed more than 500 pounds of rice and 2000 pounds of potatoes to the needy. The Legion actively assists the local Meals on Wheels and Community Chest as well as several local Churches.

Founded at a caucus of American Expeditionary Force members in Paris, France after World War I the American Legion was formally incorporated by act of Congress on September 16th, 1919 and has dedicated itself to veterans, community, and national interests since. Membership in the Legion was limited to American soldiers, sailors, marines, and nurses who had served on active duty during World War I until 1942 when the charter was amended to include World War II veterans. The charter has also been amended in 1950 to include Korean War Veterans, in 1966 for Veterans of Vietnam and again in 1991 to include Persian Gulf Veterans. In 1990 Veterans of actions in Grenada, Lebanon, and Panama became eligible for membership. The Legion is the largest Veterans organization in the United States with approximately 16,000 local posts today.

The American Legion has left many footprints in the chapters of Brentwood's past and continues to play a vital part in our community today. In closing I'd like to take this opportunity to thank the veterans for all they have contributed to Brentwood and AMERICA!! Until next time....

LIONS CLUB

Many service clubs were established in Contra Costa County in the 1920's. Organizations like the Lions, the Elks, Rotary, Kiwanis, and various chambers of commerce were established by local businessmen to advance the interests of local business and work for charitable causes within their community.

The Lions Club International was founded in Chicago in 1917 and today ranks as the world's largest humanitarian service organization. There are 1.4 million members in 180 countries and geographic areas.

Dean Watson, a prominent real estate and insurance man, and primary organizer with encouragement from Johnny Miller, established the Brentwood Lions Club in 1929. Miller was an active California Lions member and approached Watson about starting a Brentwood Lions Club. Miller, a Richmond resident, later became Contra Costa County sheriff. Watson served as the organization's first president and Charles French served as secretary for eleven years.

The Lions Club has played an active role in the development of Brentwood and outlying areas, working with the Park Council to develop land donated by the Stanford Family which is now the city park. Other early activities included sponsoring Christmas and Halloween parties for local children; making Christmas baskets for needy families; and honoring the Liberty Union High School football players at an annual dinner. In 1933, the Lions purchased new football uniforms for the team, and it is reported that the team was called the Liberty Lions after the Lions Club.

Other early projects included organizing a drive in 1939 to form the Brentwood Sanitation District, in a joint effort with the American Legion to promote a state-of-the-art sewer system for the community. The Brentwood Lions also joined in with the national organization to back a campaign to provide the blind with white canes.

In the past 67 years the Lions have donated several hundred thousand dollars to Brentwood, collected and purchased hundreds of pairs of eyeglasses for children, and financed and supported vision correction for numerous children. They have supported 4-H entries in the county fair, supplied playground equipment, picnic tables, restrooms and landscaping for the Brentwood park, and involved themselves in many of the community's worthy projects.

Brentwood Lions have supported the youth of the area, the schools, the library, the scouts, and the volunteer fire department. They have held Easter egg hunts, Halloween parties and Christmas parties for the local youth, purchased band uniforms and athletic uniforms, placed benches in the city park, and an endless list of other contributions to our community.

Few old timers can think of the Lions without remembering the wonderful Fourth of July Carnique held in the eucalyptus-covered Brentwood Park for many years. The name Carnique originated from the words carnival and barbecue. The event, which started at the Legion Hall, was moved to the city park in 1953 when Art Honegger was president and Ken Dwelley was chairman. This event was the Lions' primary fundraiser until 1977.

The Carnique featured food booths, game booths, a car raffle and entertainment. The day's activities were capped off by a fireworks display ignited by Jack Adams. Over the years, the Carnique generated between $4,000 and $6,000 annually. These funds enabled the Lions to contribute to an endless list of service projects for our community.

Early meeting places for the Lions included the Methodist Church, American Legion Hall, Rolando Inn, Borden Junction, the Continental Hotel, and the barn on the Maggiore Ranch. In 1971, the organization built the existing Lions Club community building on Walnut Boulevard, and it has been used for meetings, dances, political gatherings, wedding receptions, a polling place, and innumerable other purposes since then.

The Brentwood Lions Club has left many footprints in the chapters of Brentwood's history. The club continues to support community functions as well as the Brown Bag and Food Pantry programs, East Contra Costa County Historical Society and the Nail House, a local yearly Smith Ranch Jamboree for Handicapped Children, and an annual fresh vegetable U-Pick Day for the blind at Dwelley's Ranch. The Lions remain a vital part of our community today.

CHARTER MEMBERS IN 1929: Dean Watson and Johnny Miller were among the charter members. Others were: George K. Anderson (a farmer in the Byron area), William H. Anderson (a farmer), A. Sidney Ashe, Dr. I. R. Bailey (dentist), J. G. Barnard, George Beed (farmer), Fred Bushby, B. J. Callaghan (local educator), R. B. Crawford, Andrew Davis Jr. (farmer), R. I. Dinney, Charles A. French (Brentwood postmaster and insurance), Roy Griffith (Chevrolet dealer), Byron Grisby (manager of Los Nogalas Housing Project), Sam Hill (editor of *Brentwood News*), Warren Hilliard (agriculture teacher, Liberty Union High School), H. Jansse (merchant), Bert Kiefier (saloon owner), F. A. Lawrence, Hercules Logan (builder), E. R. McClelland, Walter Moffatt Sr. (insurance), Clyde Moores (druggist), W. W. Morgan Sr. (general store owner), W. W. Morgan Jr., E. G. Nash (principal of Liberty Union High School), J. S. O'Meara (owner of local grocery store), S. N. Parsons, Mott Preston (employed at Shafer's Funeral Home), Dr. W. A. Pulver, Stanley E. Ramos, Joseph Rolando (saloon owner), George Shafer (funeral director), C. M. Shoemaker, F. H. VonderAhe (educator), and Charles Weeks Sr. (manager of the Balfour, Guthrie farming operations). The original initiation fee was ten dollars. Until Next Time….

ROTARY

Nineteen members of the Brentwood, Byron, and Oakley communities took final steps to organize a Rotary Club in Brentwood as a unit of Rotary International, world wide service organization in April 1949. They were the sixth Rotary Club to organize in Contra Costa County. Antioch, Martinez, Walnut Creek, Pittsburg, and Concord had active groups already established.

The first Rotary officers were Clyde C. Olney as president, William D. Dickey as secretary, and Richard J Wallace as treasurer. Brentwood was represented by Fred Abbott (local insurance agent) Anders C. Anderson (manager of Brentwood Lumber) Wilfred H. Carpenter (farmer—almond and walnut broker) Clair B. Cheseldine (owner of Brentwood Hardware) William Dickey, James DeFermery Jr. (farmer, Lone Tree area) Mark E. Eisele, William E. Jones, Douglas S. Lewis(farmer—manager of East Contra Costa Irrigation) Robert C. McMillian (banker) Stanley E. Nunn (farmer and chairman of LUHS school board) Delos G. Sargentina (manager of Standard Oil distribution yard in Byron) Frank H. VonderAhe (Liberty High School Principal) and Richard J Wallace (manager of Bank of America and later as postmaster). Charter members representing Oakley were Elmer E. Espercia, Clyde C. Olney, Edward (Pappy) Prewett (almond, walnut, and apricot grower and president of the Lone Tree Farm Bureau), Frank R. Shellenberger (farmer, Neroly Road). Fabin Richart (farmer, school board member, and served on the Byron Bethany Irrigation board) represented Byron.

The night the club was officially formed there was a dinner hosting more than 200 guests. District Governor, Al Tisch, presented President Clyde Olney with the clubs charter. The Liberty Union High School band, under the direction of Vernon Noble, started the program with the "Star Spangle Banner". Other musical numbers included a violin solo by Nancy Sad of Oakley accompanied by Margaret Gehinger of Concord and songs by Connie Magbuhos. Henry Spiess, from the Antioch club, acted as master of ceremonies.

Oak Street, Brentwood

In 1949, when Brentwood Rotary was founded, Rotary International had 6,796 clubs with a membership of 327,000 business and professional men in 80 countries and geographic regions.

The Brentwood Rotary has been extremely active in the development of Brentwood for more than fifty years. This organization has contributed an unbelievable amount of time, energy and money to East Contra Costa. Thank you, Rotarians. Until Next Time….

BRENTWOOD CLUBS

It's impossible to research the history of Brentwood without realizing that local civic groups contributed an unbelievable amount of energy to the town's evolution. Listed below are a few of the organizations that definitely left their footprints in the chapters of our past.

American Legion: Roy Frerich Post #202 was founded at the end of World War I in 1919, with twenty charter members, and was named after the first WWI casualty from East Contra Costa, Melvin Leroy Frerich. The Legion Hall was constructed on the corner of Maple and First Streets in 1924. This hall has been used as a skating rink; movie theater; Brentwood's first city offices; the Volunteer Firemen's Ball for over sixty years; classrooms, after Liberty High School burnt in 1963; school plays; Boy Scout meetings; wedding receptions; and many other community functions. The American Legion has supported an immeasurable list of projects for the betterment of Brentwood.

Brentwood Women's Club: This group organized on October 12, 1901, with Mrs. Henrietta Stone as the first president. The organization has played a major roll in the development of Brentwood for almost a century. Women's Club members were involved in the development of Brentwood Park; the conception of a free library; the building of a high school in East Contra Costa; held fund-raisers to purchase special equipment for the volunteer fire department; and installed the first street signs in town, to name just a few of their projects that enriched Brentwood.

Chamber of Commerce: The Brentwood Chamber of Commerce as we know it today was formally organized May 22, 1952. The forerunner to this organization was the Brentwood Business Association, which had been active for many years. The 1952 Chamber president was Ben Peterson and the board members were Bob Casey, Bob Wallace, Oliver Danielson, and Rex Griffith. The Chamber has spearheaded numerous projects to advance the community. They purchased the first Christmas decorations; placed refuse containers in the park and at key locations throughout town; and published maps and a promotional pamphlet for Brentwood. The Chamber also installed the "Welcome" signs at the edge of town and organized the Art & Wine Festivals, the Harvest Festival and the Cornfest, as well as being actively involved in the general development of Brentwood.

E.C.H.O. Club: The East County Humanitarian Organization was created when the local chapter of Kappa Beta Sorority disbanded. The first president of the organization was Sheila Adams and their primary purpose was community service. Through the years, this group has been involved in various community events. One of their main projects has always been support of La Paloma High School, having donated supplies and scholarships to the school for many years. E.C.H.O. reorganized a few years ago and today they are known as the East Valley Service Club.

4-H Club: I'm not sure exactly when the Brentwood 4-H Club organized, but the first club in the county was established in Martinez in 1929, and there are records of the Brentwood Club being active by 1934. 4-H was originally a Home Economics and Agriculture Club, but over the years it has evolved into a much more multifaceted organization. Today the group offers instruction in crafts, horticulture, photography, sewing, cooking, and much more.

Grange: The National Grange organization was founded in 1867 in the East for the purpose of helping farm families cope with the loneliness of farm life, but by the early 1870's the group had become quite political. The group participated in addressing farmers' water problems; helped construct local landings on the rivers to assist farmers in transporting products to market; lobbied for their membership in Sacramento; and offered members a gathering place to receive beneficial information about farming. The local Grange originally organized in 1873 at Point of Timber with Robert Dean serving as first master, and moved to Brentwood in 1887. Very little happened in the Brentwood district between 1870 and 1940 of which Grange was not a part.

Lions Club: Brentwood Lions Club International was established in 1929 with 34 charter members. Dean Watson, a local insurance man and real estate agent, was the club's primary organizer and first president. This organization was heavily involved in the evolution of Brentwood. For many years the Lions sponsored Christmas and Halloween parties for local children; made holiday food baskets for needy families; were actively involved in promoting the improvement of Brentwood Park and the town's sewer system. The Lions also sponsored an annual Fourth of July Carnique in Brentwood Park for 24 years and a great deal more. They purchased football uniforms for the Liberty Union High School football team in 1933, and it is reported that from that date forward the team was known as the Liberty Lions.

Masonic Lodge: Lodge #345 was organized in February 1902 with thirteen charter members. Will Jerrisleu served as the first Grand Master. The first meetings were held in private homes. Robert Coates later built a two-story building (Coates Hall) on Railroad Avenue and the Masons agreed to rent the upper floor for at least five years for their meetings. In 1924 they built the Masonic Temple (today this building is Cap's Restaurant) at a cost of $20,000. The Eastern Star and Rainbow Girls also used this facility. Due to declining membership the Brentwood Lodge has joined with the Antioch Lodge in recent years.

Rotary: The Rotary Club of Brentwood received its charter with nineteen members in June 1949. The first officers were Clyde Olney, president; William Dickey, secretary; and Richard Wallace, treasurer. The Rotary has played an active role in all aspects of the development of Brentwood for almost half a century. The Rotary selects its membership on a basis of one active member from each recognized business and profession in the community. They have been heavily involved with our schools, volunteer fire department, health care, community food pantry, and much more.

Soroptimist: Soroptimist International of East Contra Costa County was chartered on May 11, 1970, as part of Founder Region, Soroptimist International of the Americas, Inc. The first president was Kay Davis. This organization has been very active in many local projects. One of their first projects was to spearhead the construction of new dressing rooms at the Liberty Union High School swimming pool. They were also instrumental in the purchase of the "Jaws of Life" for the fire department, installing public benches throughout Brentwood, and many other appreciated projects. One of the primary things the Soroptimists have accomplished in the community is encouraging women to become more involved in local politics. Today we see women serving on the city council, planning commission and various local boards.

Brentwood Gun Club: Charles Cogswell, the club's first president, founded Brentwood Gun Club in 1962. Some of the charter members were Cogswell, Vern Allen, Leroy Hartwig, Walt Swicegood, Cotton Bloodworth, Les Maggori, John Carlisle, and Les McClelland. The Gun Club clubhouse and shooting range, on Concord Ave, were originally the location of the Brentwood City dumps, owned by the county. The county wanted to sell the property because rats were breeding there. The Gun Club purchased the site, three acres, for $130. The club immediately invested $2500 grading, leveling and adding landfill to the site. The Concord Ave. site has served the organization well for more than 35 years, but as housing tracts develop in the area it appears they will soon have to relocate. Until Next Time....

BYRON

BYRON TIMELINE

1500—1800.....Indians roamed this region of California.

1772.....The spanish explorer, Captain Pedro Fages, discovered the area. Fages was the first person to record a description of this region of California.

1837.....John Marsh purchases Jose Noriega Rancho in Northern California.

1841.....The Bidwell, Bartleson Party, the first immigrant wagon train to come west, arrives at John Marsh's home. Marsh's home was 1 1/2 miles west of Byron.

1850.....California becomes a state.

1853.....The first wheat is planted in the Point of Timber region.

1850s, 1860s & 1870s.....Point of Timber was a thriving community in the area. The village had a stage coach stop, post office, general store, Grange hall, school, blacksmith, and more.

1861.....Doctor Patterson resided at Point of Timber.

1862.....There was a severe flood at Point of Timber.

1862.....Orange Risdon purchased 160 acres where the Byron Hot Springs is.

1865.....The Excelsior School was built at Point of Timber and moved to a site on Marsh Creek Road in 1868. The Excelsior School united with Byron School District in 1946.

1865.....Colburn Preston and Alpheus Richardson both settled in the area and grew wheat.

1867.....George Cople arrived in Byron region from Switzerland. He was a wheat farmer.

1867.....The Methodist Episcopal Church built a parsonage at Point of Timber.

1868.....Alexander T. Taylor and Thomas McCabe came to area and became wheat farmers.

1868.....The Excelsior school moved to the corner of Marsh Creek Road and Highway 4. The first Excelsior was a two room school house. This school was replaced with the present building in 1906. Today the Excelsior School is a private home.

1870.....The course of Kellogg Creek was established. Prior to this time the creek ran wild. To confine the water the local settlers used horses and a Fresno scraper to redesign the direction of water flowed. Kellogg Creek was named after a man by the name of Kellogg who was hung from a tree near the creek. He was a cattle thief.

1872.....Joseph P. McCabe was appointed postmaster at Point of Timber.

1872.....Isadore Lipman purchased the mercantile at Point of Timber from Wolfe, Kahn & Co.

1873.....Contra Costa County was apportioned into supervisorial districts. Point of Timber was part of 5th District. Point of Timber and Antioch combined had 390 votes.

1873.....The Grange of the Patrons of Husbandry was established at Point of Timber. This group was an outgrowth of the Point of Timber Farmers Protective Club.

1876.....John Samuel Armstrong settled in the Byron foothills near the Byron Hot Springs.

1877.....Matt Berlington planted the first alfalfa in the area.

1878.....Colburn Preston donated four acres of land for the Union Cemetery. It is one of the oldest cemeteries in the county.

1878.....The San Pablo & Tulare Railroad installed tracks from Martinez to Banta. Byron was founded.

1878.....Henry Wilkening erected the first house in town which was his family home and also used as a hotel. He was appointed Byrons first postmaster.

1878.....Clas Peers opened one of the first taverns in Byron. Fish & Blum built a grain warehouse and Fabian & Levinsky opened a general mercantile store.

1879.....Byron Hot Springs School established on a corner of John Samuel Armstrongs ranch. The school united with Byron District in 1943.
1879.....The International Order of Good Templars (IOGT) was organized with eighteen charter members.
1882.....The trees along Byron Highway were planted from Borden Junction to town. The first trees were planted by a San Francisco commission merchant, whose family home and farm were located where the Byron school is today. He planted the first 1/8 mile of locust trees. Mr. A. Richardson Sr. planted the next 1/2 mile. Mr. M. Burlington planted 1/8 mile on Byron Highway and 1/2 mile of locust and cypress on Highway 4 on the road leading to Point of Timber. Mr. C. Preston planted 1/2 mile of mixed eucalyptus and locust.
1883.....The Point of Timber Landing Company was established.
1883.....A cholera epidemic hit the area.
1883.....The Byron Brass Band was organized.
1883.....The 1st Congregational Church was established. It disbanded in 1929.
1884.....Alex Fortheringham was the first local farmer to ship hay to Los Angeles.
1885.....Fred Holway built Byrons second hotel.
1886.....The Byron Hot Springs School was established. This first school burned in 1902.
1886.....The Byron School was built on Camino Diablo and Holway. This school was abandoned in 1951 when the new Byron School was built on Byron Highway.
1896.....The first Byron fire department was organized. The department had littleor no equipment beyond buckets and a make-shift wagon to carry supplies to the site of the blaze. The population of Byron was 300.
1887.....V.J. Engle started the first lumber yard on property he purchased from Fred Holway. The Byron Odd Fellows Lodge 335 was organized the same year with the first meeting held in the Engle Lumber Yard on Main Street. The organization had five charter members and Fred Rahmedorff was Noble Grand.
1889.....The Byron Florence Knight Rebekah Lodge 264 organized and was first known as the Grace Darling Lodge.
1891.....The Byron Parlor 170 of the Native Sons of the Golden West was organized.
1898.....Doctor James Hammond started his medical practice in Byron.
1902.....Most of the downtown business district was wiped out by wind-swept flames.
1902.....The Byron train wreck happened. It was one of the most disastrous train wrecks in California history. Twenty seven passengers were killed when the Owl Limited and the Stockton Flyer collided.
1903.....New Byron School was built.
1906.....The first edition of the Byron Times newspaper, a weekly publication was distributed. The final edition was published in 1938.
1906.....Thomas Hosie built the Byron roller skating rink.
1907.....Byron was damaged by the "Great Flood". There was twenty five inches of rainfall recorded.
1909.....Henry Krumland was elected Justice of the Peace, a position he held for more than thirty years.
1911.....The Native Daughters of the Golden West 193 was instituted at Byron with Mrs. Harry Hammond elected president.
1911.....The Portuguese lodge, I.D.E.S was organized.
1911.....The Bank of Byron organized with capital of $50,000. It operated as a branch of the Bank of Tracy.

1912.....Construction started on the Shell Oil Pumping Station. It was built on 13 acres near where Unimin is located today. Operations started in 1914.
1912.....Byron had two hundred and twenty one registered voters who were all men, since women did not have the right to vote.
1913.....Byron got electricity.
1913.....The Seventh-Day Adventist church was organized. Doctor James Hammond was elder and his wife was treasurer.
1914.....Local farmers, ranchers, and landowners established the Byron Bethany Irrigation Company. The first water flowed in 1917.
1915.....Construction was started on the Standard Oil Pumping Station located on Marsh Creek Road.
1917.....One hundred and thirty young men from Byron signed the roll for the draft. (WW1).
1917.....Union Oil purchased property from A.N. Thomas at the end of Main Street to establish a fuel distribution yard.
1917.....The Byron Hotel, owned by Fred Holway, burned.
1917.....Saint Ann's Catholic Church was founded.
1919.....Construction of a concrete highway to Stockton was started. This roadway was known as Borden Highway.
1919.....The Byron Bank was robbed. $50,000 in currency, liberty bonds, jewelry, and securities were stolen from one hundred fifty four safe deposit boxes.
1923.....There was a devastating fire on Main Street. Seven business buildings were destroyed with losses estimated at $50,000.
1923.....The first Byron Library is housed in the Byron Times Building with Maude Jacoby as the first librarian.
1924.....Borden Highway was completed traversing the entire length of Contra Costa County, offering the residents of Byron an easy route to Stockton.
1924.....Hoof and mouth plague befell stockmen and dairymen in the Byron area.
1924.....Charlie Peterson opened a moving picture theater in the Odd Fellows Hall.
1927.....Vasco Road was rerouted creating a short cut from Stockton to Oakland via Byron.
1928.....The Byron Library moved to new building on Main Street. Renny Plumley and Stanley Cabral, local businessmen, donated the land for the building.
1929.....A Formal Volunteer Fire Department was organized. A splendid $2500 chemical engine was purchased.
1929.....The Byron Library Club was donated land by Stanley Cabral and Renny Plumley to establish a community library on Main Street. The first Library Club Trustees were Laura Krumland, Anna Lewis, L.M. Reynolds, and Glen Van Horn.
1931.....The Byron Lions Club gets a charter with George Anderson serving as the organization's first president. There were twenty one charter members.
1939.....Vasco School lapsed and Vasco students attended Byron School.
1940.....Beth Weihe was librarian for the Byron Library.
1940.....School enrollment: Byron, 65 students; Excelsior, 67 students; Hot Springs, 8 students.
1940.....Fal Lewis served as Justice of the Peace.
1948.....The magneto phone system in Byron was replaced with dial phones. Alex Chaim built a new dial central office next to his grocery store on Main Street.
1949.....Enrico Lembi, almond grower, was appointed as Justice of the Peace for Byron. He succeeded Mrs. Mildred White, who resigned the position after only three weeks of

service. She had been appointed to the position when Fal Lewis resigned due to ill health.
1951.....A new Byron School was built on Byron Hwy.
1956.....Byron flooded.
1959.....Lois Ricioli became librarian at Byron Library. She retired when the library was closed in 1978.
1959.....The Byron Fire Station was built on the end of Holway. The forty by seventy-eight foot concrete block building cost $32,483 to construct. The property was donated to the fire district by Mr. and Mrs. Louis Souza.
1959.....John Maggi purchased one hundred and twenty four acres from Wesley Armstrong for a small private airport. Maggi sold to Contra Costa County in 1973 for a public airport.
1964.....Byron Court was consolidated with Brentwood by the Board of Supervisors.
1966.....The Clifton Court Forebay was established.
1969.....Nick Papadakos was appointed Byron Fire Chief.
1981.....A Southern Pacific freight train derailed and spewed massive iron coils, rails, and train parts on Main Street.
1982.....Byron held its first Byron Rail Faire, sponsored by the Chamber of Commerce, with Marge Miguel as chairman.
1987.....A Southern Pacific caboose was given to the Byron Chamber of Commerce and moved to a permanent site at the end of Main Street.
1989.....Eight railroad cars hauling butane gas derailed near Byron.
1990.....April 23... The Byron Advisory Council was established.
1993.....Construction began for the Byron Airport. The Byron Airport was dedicated on October 8, 1994.
1994.....April 19...Byron Municipal Advisory Council (MAC) was established replacing the Byron Advisory Council.
1994.....The Los Vaqueros Dam and Reservoir project started. The project was completed in 1997.
1999.....The Byron MAC completed the Byron General Plan.
Until Next Time....

EARLY BYRON HISTORY
FOUNDED 1878

It is hard for us to imagine what the Byron area looked like on the other side of yesterday. The story begins with Native Americans that lived throughout the Delta region. It continues with Spanish explorers, early rancheros and vaqueros tending their cattle, and the trappers, mountain men and wilderness wanderers that ventured West.

Hundreds of years ago, Yokuts Indians roamed this region of California. They lived in crude huts of brush along the waterways and in caves near what is now Vasco Road. The Indians lived off the land, searching for food obtainable from roots, acorns and other nuts, seeds, and wild clover as well as a plentiful supply of salmon, waterfowl, antelope and deer. Treats were scrounged from the ground during root gathering. A type of flatworm was used in acorn flatbread for shortening and earthworms and grasshoppers were considered a delicacy.

As a young person, I went on many family outings to the Vasco Caves, where an endless supply of Indian artifacts could be found. It was not unusual to come home with a pocketful of arrowheads, or even an occasional grinding stone. The caves are located about a mile southwest of a ranch where my great-grandfather, John Samuel Armstrong, settled in the mid-1800's.

Like most California Indians, the Yokuts wore little clothing; women wore skirts made of bark fiber, tule or deerskin, and the men were usually naked, though sometimes they wore a deerskin breechcloth. The Yokuts were a peaceful people, and unfortunately ill prepared for the white man. Disease, a declining birth rate, high infant mortality and warfare cut into the tribe's population. In 1833, a cholera epidemic further decimated the people, and by 1900, the state's Indian population had dropped from 150,000 to less than 16,000.

The Spanish were the first white men to discover the Byron area. In 1772, a group of Spanish soldiers led by Captain Fages and Fray Crespi explored Mount Diablo and the surrounding area. Over sixty years passed before the region was deeded to Don Jose Noriega in 1835. In 1836 Doctor John Marsh purchased a ten-by-twelve mile parcel (17,000 acres) from Noriega for $500, about three cents an acre.

At that time, oaks grew so tall that wild cattle and antelope could trail beneath them in a countryside abundant with wildlife. Elk, deer, antelope and bear grazed throughout the region, along with wild mustangs and spotted cattle originally introduced to the area by Mission fathers.

John Marsh's rancho extended from Mount Diablo to the San Joaquin River. He is credited with soliciting immigration to California from the East. Wishing to see California become part of the United States, Marsh wrote glowing letters of the area's attributes and attractions to friends back east. These letters were widely published in newspapers and directly influential in encouraging pioneers to cross the Sierra Nevada to the San Joaquin Valley.

Today, as we see railroads, highways, and planes overhead, attempting to visualize rolling hills covered with groves of oak trees and luxuriant growths of perennial grasses and wildflowers is difficult at best. But this is what the first immigrants saw in 1841, when the Bidwell-Bartleson wagon train arrived at the Marsh Rancho, and began the settling of California as we know it today.

Stock raising was a principal part of life here during the 1840's and '50's. This region of California offered miles and miles of good pastureland, with natural springs and cool streams in the foothills of Mount Diablo, allowing cattle to grow fat on wild oats, clover and alfilaria. For many years, the whole territory operated under a free-range system, until wheat farmers began settling in the region. Roaming livestock became a threat to vulnerable crops, and by the 1860's barbed wire had been introduced to fence rangeland.

Point of Timber played a large part in the history of Byron as an important shipping point for early settlers of the area. Located where Bay Cities Building Materials (on Highway 4) is today, Point of Timber had the area's first post office, school, church, general store, Grange hall and stage stop. A landing for shipping wheat, jointly built by neighboring farmers and known as Point of Timber Landing, offered local wheat growers a facility to ship their products to market.

By the early 1860's, many young families had settled in East Contra Costa to farm the rich soil found here. These families were known as "sky farmers" because they depended on nature for their crops' development. Locally grown wheat was stored in large warehouses near Point of Timber Landing until it could be loaded on schooners or barges headed for Carquinez or Port Costa docks to be transferred onto larger vessels bound for ports all over the world.

Wheat was the chief industry of Contra Costa County in the 1860's. Thousands of acres of the golden grain were sowed in the Byron region. The first farmers planted their seeds in the fall, leaving the seed to lie in the ground all winter while the rains softened the hard soil. With the warmth of spring, the crop of wheat sprouted, and by summer it was ready to harvest.

The town of Byron was actually founded in 1878 when the San Pablo and Tulare Railroad Company (later the Southern Pacific) built a track from Martinez to Banta, creating a direct line from Contra Costa County to the San Joaquin Valley and transcontinental service.

A cobbler named Smith who mended boots and saddles constructed Byron's first building. The first home was built by Fred Wilkening, and in the fall of 1878, a post office was established (Wilkening became the first postmaster). The area drew a mixture of nationalities, cultures and styles, and by the end of 1878, Byron consisted of a hotel, cobbler's shop, saloon, post office and railroad depot.

You can't look at early Byron history without mentioning Byron Hot Springs, a luxurious resort nestled in the foothills two miles southwest of town. The springs were famous for their mineral waters from the time of the California Indians until 1938, when the resort closed. In its heyday, Byron Hot Springs drew people from all over the United States and Europe to bask in the warm sunshine and soak in the healing waters. Doctors would recommend the springs for relief of indigestion, ailments of the stomach and liver, rheumatism and gout. During World War II, the government purchased Byron Hot Springs Resort for use as an interrogation center.

When most of us think of history, we think in terms of great events and famous personalities that have played roles in building the nations of the world. Yet it is clear to me that each of Byron's pioneers left a footprint in our past. Byron's history can be traced from frontier days to modern times; from open range to fenced pastures; from wagon trains to the railroad; from dry farming to irrigated fields; from makeshift and make-do to more convenient, easier ways of life.

Unfortunately many of Byron's landmarks are falling to time each year, as fire, development and "progress" take their toll. The wonderful brick *Byron Times* building of my childhood has been replaced with a modern convenience store. There is nothing left of the Byron Hot Springs resort except a shell of the once luxurious hotel; many of the beautiful oak trees of the Vasco region now lie under the Los Vaqueros Reservoir, and so it goes. Until Next Time....

HOW BYRON GOT ITS NAME

Byron had its beginning in 1878, when the Tulare and San Pablo Railroad (now Southern Pacific) began to run trains through the area and established a rail station. There are several plausible theories of how the town got its name.

According to my grandfather, John J. Armstrong, the original name was "By run." Locations for railroad stations were determined by the distance a horse and buggy could travel in 2 to 2½ hours, This calculated span between stations was called a "by run." Thus, Byron was named.

The early settlers of the area were anxious to see the establishment of the railroad, and saw the railroad as the answer to the monumental task they had been faced with in getting their crop to market. These early settlers purchased the land where the railroad sits today and donated much of it to the railroad for their right-of-way.

The town of Byron grew around the new railroad station. Henry Wilkening built the first house, a family home, but later it was to be Byron's first hotel. The second building was from the Iron House area and Claus Peers named it Peers' Tavern. This tavern became the only place for people passing through to stop, but was also a gathering place for the locals.

In the fall of 1878 a Post Office was added and Wilkening became the first postmaster. A large warehouse was also built that year. Fish and Blum built a warehouse that was used to store the wheat that was to be exported from the area via trains. The necessity for supplies and goods led to the erection of Fabian and Levinsky's general store by 1879

Within a few short years, Byron had attracted a blacksmith, a cobbler, a meat market and numerous other establishments to service the early settlers. It seemed that when a need became apparent someone came to town and filled it

The farm families in the area were a God-loving people and religion played an important part in their lives and in the history of Byron. The Congregational Church was the first church erected. My great grandfather, John Samuel Armstrong, and his family were charter members. My father Oliver Armstrong and his father John J. Armstrong were both baptized in this church.

The church and the activities it offered were a very important part of the Armstrong's lives, as I am sure it was to many of their neighbors. John Samuel and Mary Ann Armstrong had a homestead in the Byron foothills near the Byron Hot Springs in the mid 1960s. They worked hard on those rolling hills to establish a home for themselves and their ten children. They were dry farmers. John Samuel planted wheat and barley and depended on deep plowing and summer farrowing for the success of his crops.

The Armstrong land was located several miles away from where Byron was established, but they seldom missed attending church on Sunday. (John was a trustee on the church board.) They would load their neighbors. My grandfather would tell stories of trips to church on the back of the wagon during spring rains or days when they would leave the ranch with blue skies and sunshine overhead only to have a storm move in before they returned home.

Prior to the establishment of the church the Armstrong children were taught scripture around the dining room table on Sunday morning. The new church not only gave them and their neighbors a place to meet, but also new activities that made up a large part of their social life. Often after attending Sunday services the Armstrongs would gather with the Krumlands, Richardsons, or Middletons for a picnic. My grandfather had many fond memories of the families' Sunday trips to town.

At one time Byron had five churches: Congregational, Methodist, Episcopalian, Seventh Day Adventist, and Catholic. The Methodist was built in 1897 and later rebuilt and enlarged in 1920. The Catholic Church was dedicated in 1917 at a cost of $5,000, with the seating capacity of 250.

I am continually amazed at how many things we take for granted in 1992. As I research my roots I can't help but be impressed what hearty stock I come from. I find that my own life is conveniently too busy for me to jump into my car and drive two minutes (with heat or air as needed) to attend church on a regular basis. The hardships that our forefathers endured, I am sure, also created a bond within their family units that we somehow have lost in the name of progress.

HENRY WILKENING
BYRON FOUNDER

Henry Wilkening was born in Hanover, Germany on November 28, 1835. At the age of sixteen he traveled to the new world arriving in New York on August 20, 1852. He resided there for several years employed as a clerk at a grocery store.

Throughout the 1850's journalists portrayed the west as a wonderland of opportunity and sunshine. Henry heard endless stories about the gold fields of California and, like many young men of the day, was inclined to believe the positive stories about California and discount the derogatory accounts of blood thirsty Indians, drought, disaster, and endless misfortunes that could hit immigrants moving west. In 1854, at the age of nineteen, Henry boarded the schooner, North Star, bound for California arriving in San Francisco two months later.

For the next ten years Henry mined the gold fields on the Yuba River moving from camp to camp. In 1864 Henry gave up his quest for gold and moved to the village of Antioch where he resided for six months and became a member of the volunteer fire department before returning to New York with the intention of making his permanent home in the east.

After living in New York for a year Henry heard that huge gold deposits had been discovered in Placer County, and he once again headed for the Pacific Coast via Panama. For the second time gold dust had lured Henry to the mines where he spent the next seven years seeking his fortune.

Downtown Byron - 1914

In 1874 he decided to leave the gold fields and move to Point of Timber in Contra Costa County. There he built the Red House, a road house on the route from Antioch to Banta. The village of Point of Timber had been established in the early 1860's. It offered early East Contra Costa settlers the James A. Salts Store, a cobbler, a livery, a stage stop, and several homes. The Point of Timber Post Office was established November 1869. The early settlers in this region were primarily wheat farmers.

Henry's establishment offered lodging, a restaurant, and a saloon to customers traveling to the area on the Wright Brothers Stageline which ran from Antioch or Banta. The Red House catered primarily to sportsmen who came to the area to hunt ducks and geese on the Delta. The Point of Timber region was known for its immense flocks of geese and ducks, large coveys of white and gray pelicans, cranes, and other water birds which nested along the river in the vast marsh lands. The foothills were densely timbered and game was abundant. Elk and deer were common and an occasional grizzly gave the spice of danger to a hunter. The bark of a coyote, now seldom heard, was incessant through the night.

Henry placed advertisements in the San Francisco Sun to promote his business encouraging hunters to board a Southern Pacific train bound for Antioch where they would connect with a stage continuing on to Point of Timber. At Point of Timber fresh horses would be picked up before the stage continued on to Banta. East Contra Costa offered the hunting experience of a lifetime. Henry would outfit the sportsmen for their hunt and act as a personal guide.

By 1877 the San Pablo & Tulare Railroad began constructing a railroad line from Antioch to Banta. Henry grasped the opportunity to jump in on the ground floor of founding a new railroad town in the area. The Red House supplied lodging for railroad employees and land speculators who knew the value of the land would increase with arrival of the rails. Henry learned where the railroad planned to locate their station and purchased the site. The town of Byron was established there in 1878.

Henry built the first hotel, a saloon, and a livery-stable at Byron. The town grew very quickly and Henry was appointed Byron's first Post Master on October 30, 1878. Southern Pacific purchased the railroad from San Pablo & Tulare, built a depot, and hired Mr. Consadine as Byron's first agent. Claus Peers moved a building to Byron from the Iron House area He converted it into a tavern which was the forerunner to the Wild Idol Inn. The necessity for merchandise led to construction of the first general store in 1879. It was erected by Fabian and Levinsky. Fish and Blum built a warehouse for grain storage.

Henry married Annie Percy, a native of Somersetshire, England, on October 14,1876. Annie and Henry had one son in 1880 who was named after the newly founded town.

Wilkening, a man so instrumental in the early development of Byron died February 19, 1883 and is buried at Union Cemetery. He came to California with dreams of fabulous wealth from the streams of the Mother Lode, and although he never filled his pockets with gold, he definitely left his mark on the pages of East Contra Costa County history. Until Next Time....

WILD IDOL

The Wild Idol Saloon on Main Street in Byron was destroyed by fire this week (April 1997), so it seems like a good time to reflect on the interesting early history of this landmark establishment. This saloon has acted as the heart of Byron for 114 years and could no doubt tell great tales if the walls could talk.

Byron, like many western towns, began to grow and prosper after the arrival of the railroad in 1878. Henry Wilkening, a native of Hanover, Germany, was Byron's first official resident and postmaster, having purchased property in town during 1877. He built a home, which he also used as a boarding house, along with a livery stable and Byron's first saloon. In time Byron grew and Wilkening's establishments were flanked by shops catering to specialized needs: a cobbler, a mercantile store and a meat market were among other businesses. Wilkening died February 19, 1883, of pneumonia, after which his saloon was sold to Claus Peers.

Claus Peers re-named the establishment Claus Peers Saloon in 1883 and remained proprietor for 27 years. Located on Byron's Main Street, the saloon functioned as the social center for the community. People congregated there to exchange gossip around the potbellied stove. Peers operated a relatively sedate place, where patrons lingered long over a nickel glass of beer discussing politics and issues of the day. Old copies of the *Contra Costa Gazette* refer to improvements that Peers made to his business, and the paper published advertisements about the fine line of wine, liquor, and cigars that he carried.

Claus Peers was noted for his gambling and suffered heavy losses on the horses in 1910. He was about to lose his saloon when Jess Santos offered to buy it in 1910. Santos was a native of Madeira Island, near the Azores, and came to Byron from Turlock, where he also owned a saloon. The new Santos Saloon was frequented by businessmen and farmers alike. Businessmen made deals at Santos Saloon, sealing their transaction with a few quiet words and a handshake over a drink. The bar offered liquid refreshments for fifteen cents and an honest game of cards for anyone willing to pull up a chair. Santos had several businesses in town and expanded his saloon, adding the nine-room Santos Hotel to the same site.

There were three saloons in Byron during the early 1900's: Holway's, Fredich's and Santos'. During prohibition (1920 to 1932), all three taverns remained opened

Claus Peer's Saloon

as billiard halls. Rumor has it that a regular patron could purchase bootleg whiskey by the drink if the bartender knew him. Local law enforcement was aware of the illegal transactions, but tended to look the other way; word has it that Constable LeGrand and Judge Krumland were two of the tavern's best customers.

Pearl and Louis Crist purchased the Santos Saloon in the 1940's. Crist enjoyed the dog races and decided to rename his business the Wild Idol Inn after one of his favorite race dogs. Crist owned the Wild Idol for more than thirty years, and since his ownership there have been half a dozen proprietors.

The chapters of the Wild Idol's past are filled with numerous interesting tales. The Saloon burnt and was rebuilt after the 1923 Byron fire, which destroyed most of Main Street. In the 1970's the bartender, his wife and a customer were murdered during a robbery of the saloon. When a Southern Pacific train derailed on Main Street in 1981, one of the steel coils the train was transporting rolled within a few feet of the front door.

The Wild Idol and its predecessors have seen weddings and wakes, reunions, birthdays and anniversaries along with endless other community events. The establishment has sponsored youth athletic teams, purchased local 4-H livestock at the county fair, contributed to the schools and churches, and played a vital role in the development of Byron. There are stories of local cowboys riding their horses into the tavern and young ladies dancing on the bar. Most locals had their first adult beverage at the Wild Idol.

In the 1960's I received my first traffic ticket, which required that I appear in court. At that time the court was located next to the Wild Idol. As it turned out, my case was the only one on the court docket for that day. Instead of opening court just for me, the judge heard my case in the saloon, using a shot glass as a gavel. I remember receiving a lecture about the perils of speeding and a Shirley Temple. The Judge Stan Pereira would often tend bar if the owner had other business to attend to.

Byron grew and prospered because of early businessmen like Wilkening, Peers, and Santos, men whose names are interwoven with the history and development of this region of California. Until Next Time….

EARLY MERCANTILE STORES

The large supermarkets of today, with seemingly endless items available, are wonderful, but they evolved from an older way of merchandising. Byron was founded in 1878, and by 1880 the first general store was opened by Moritz Grunauer. In the 1890's a second general store, Plumley's Mercantile, was added to the list of businesses lining Byron's Main Street.

These early stores were small by today's standards, but crammed full of everything the early settlers of the area needed. Main Street was little more than a dusty dirt field with hitching posts where customers could hitch their horses, and enough room for wagons with teams to turn around. Wood sidewalks were attached to the fronts of the buildings with benches that offered passersby a perfect place to sit and gossip.

Louis Grunauer General Merchandise Store
Notice the painted sign on the side
"Pioneer Cash Store"

Grunauer's or Plumley's offered their customers everything from coal oil to calico. To step inside either store was to enter a self-contained world of muted sounds and odd odors. The rich aromas of plug tobacco, fresh-ground coffee and leather boots, saddles and belts mingled throughout the store.

On one side of the store stood a counter for grocery items, and on the other side were shelves piled high with dry goods. Hardware filled the back of the store. From the rafters hung hams, slabs of side meat and pots and pans, along with bridles and bits for horses. Throughout the store, placed wherever they would fit, you could find barrels, kegs and bins of everything from nails to sauerkraut and pickles. Fifty-gallon barrels of vinegar and coal oil rested on their sides on a special rack, their spigots allowing customers to fill their own cans or jugs.

Leaning against the counter were opened sacks of potatoes, the tops rolled down for convenience in weighing out the customer's order. Merchandise was weighed on a crude balance scale and poured into brown paper bags, then tied with a piece of string. Each bin had it's own scoop to convey the rice, beans or sugar into a bag. The world of instant cake mixes and store-packaged goods was still a dream of the future.

Farmers' wives (like my grandmother and great-grandmother) from outlying area found a visit to Grunauer's or Plumley's a rare opportunity to visit with other women. Male customers spent many a rainy day seated around the potbellied stove. Some of the customers were farmers in town for a day with their wives, and some were townsmen who dropped by to discuss politics, the weather and gossip.

The general store served Byron's residents in many ways, including that of a banker. When a customer's funds were low, as they usually were until seasonal crops could be sold at market, the store often extended credit. Grunauer and Plumley were both known to accept farm products instead of cash for settlement of a bill and would barter goods for goods. A customer might pay off his account in butter, eggs, meat or tallow, or a client might pay for his purchases in services such as wood chopping or hauling.

These early general stores and the men that ran them were key players in the early history of Byron. The first telephone, post office, judge's quarters, and the first library were each connected to one of these stores in Byron's early years.

Moritz Grunauer was born in Germany in 1852 and traveled to America with his parents as a young man, originally settling in the Tracy area, where his uncle owned a mercantile. In this store Moritz received his business training before coming to Byron in 1880 and opening his own store. In 1882, he erected Byron's first warehouse for wheat storage. This building burnt down in 1916 and was replaced with a modern corrugated iron warehouse.

Moritz married Miss R. Frank, a native of San Francisco, in 1888 and they had one child, Jeanette Byron Grunauer.

By the early 1900's Grunauer had two partners in his Byron Mercantile Company store, Al Copland and Frank Rogers. For many years the Byron post office was located in the store, with Mr. Copland as postmaster. In 1914 Alex Chaim, Grunauer's nephew, went to work as a bookkeeper and buyer for the firm . (He later became the sole owner of the business.) Mr. Grunauer not only ran his businesses, but was also very involved in all aspects of what was happening in Byron. He served on the Byron school board for many years, was active in the Odd Fellows Lodge, and was an active promoter of Byron.

Lorenzo Plumley, whose father, Alonzo Plumley, had settled in the Byron area in 1864, established Plumley's Mercantile in the 1890's. Lorenzo, known to the townspeople as Renny, married Elizabeth Livingston in 1894. They had three children, Rodney, Blanche and Grant.

Plumley's Store was destroyed in the 1923 Byron fire along with seven other businesses as the fire swept down Main Street. The financial loss was estimated at more than $50,000. Renny Plumley estimated his losses as more than $15,000 worth of inventory and stock, with insurance coverage of $8,000.

Plumley constructed a new general merchandise store in 1923. The new building was bigger than its forerunner. It was constructed of concrete, in the Mission style, built for permanence, and with plenty of room for more merchandise than the original building. It was a big double building, with an adjoining room leased to the government for a post office. For the first time, Byron had a first-class post office, with lockboxes, ornamental wire partitions, etc..

In the rear of the post office, Plumley built office space to be used as the judicial chambers of Justice Henry G. Krumland. Many cases were settled in this little courtroom in the 1920's and 1930's.

I'd like to take this opportunity to thank Oliver Armstrong (my dad), Jesse Santos, Ellen Hosie, Micki Moore, Vera Thomas and other old timers that have shared their memories of Byron on the other side of yesterday with me. It is the wonderful stories that they have told me that allow us to take this special peek into a window of our past.
Until next time…

LOUIS AND MORITZ GRUNAUER EARLY BUSINESSMEN

Early settlers of East Contra Costa were a hardy breed with a desire to mold their own destiny. They were from Europe and the eastern United States arriving in California with few material possessions but most brought a wagon full of hopes and dreams for a better life than they had left behind.

Chapters of Brentwood's and Byron's past are peppered with the name Grunauer, a family that was present from the very beginning of both communities. Louis Grunauer was a pioneer merchant in Brentwood. Born a native of Prussia in 1854, Louis emigrated to the United States in 1868 at the age of fourteen. Upon his arrival in California he settled in Amador County where he worked as a clerk in a mercantile store. A year later he moved to San Joaquin (Tracy) where he acquired a clerks job in a relatives store and remained there for eight years. In September 1878, at the age of 24, he moved to Brentwood where he built a store and hotel. Grunauer's Mercantile was the first business in Brentwood. And Louis Grunauer was appointed one of the towns first postmasters.

The Grunauer Store offered early settlers a full line of dry goods, groceries, hardware, and drugs. Prior to 1878 settlers traveled to Antioch or Point of Timber to purchase supplies. By 1900 Grunauer had two partners in his store, L. Kroner and H. W. Heidorn.

Grunauer built the first Brentwood Hotel in 1884 on the corner of Highway 4 and Oak Street. This hotel was a two story structure offering twelve guest rooms and a decorative balcony where guests could bask quietly in the morning sun. The hotel had wide wooden sidewalks on two sides and a row of locust trees lining the perimeter of the building. The first Brentwood Hotel was destroyed by fire in 1903.

Moritz Grunauer (I think a second cousin to Louis) was born in Germany in 1852. He came to America as a lad with his parents originally settling in the Tracy area where his uncle owned a mercantile store. In this store Moritz received his business training. He came to Byron in 1880 to establish his own store, the Byron Mercantile Company. He dealt extensively in dry goods, groceries, boots and shoes, hats, hardware, paints, oils, sporting goods, and ammunition. Byron Mercantile became the headquarters for most of the early ranchers, farmers, and residents of the foothill and island sections of east Contra Costa. The Byron Post Office was conveniently located in Moritz Grunauer's store for many years. In 1882, Moritz erected Byron's first warehouse for wheat storage.

Moritz married Miss R. Frank in 1888, a native of San Francisco. They had one daughter, Jeanette Byron Grunauer. By 1900 Moritz was well established. He took two partners, Al Copland and Frank Rogers, into his mercantile business. This allowed him to devote most his time to his other business interests. By 1915 Moritz Grunauer was the largest individual hay and grain operator as well as warehouseman in the Byron area. He bought and sold in railroad car loads and whole ranch lots, handling his business through personal selling and through distribution systems in San Francisco and other market points. Orders to any part of the world were shipped out of Byron, although most of the products shipped were to San Francisco, Seattle, Portland, and Los Angeles. As early as 1878 California was producing more wheat than any other state in the nation. Moritz often advanced money to local farmers for hay and grain and furnished warehouse facilities where they could store

their product until they could sell for the best price at market.
He also owned four hundred and eighty acres of land which he farmed for many years.

Alex Chaim, Moritz Grunauer's nephew, began working for his uncle at the mercantile in 1914 and eventually became sole owner of the store. As a young girl, in the 1950s, I remember popping into Chaim's Market for an ice cold soda or an ice cream bar.

Downtown Byron - 1915

Moritz was a key player in East Contra Costa County for more than 45 years. He handled the marketing end of the areas crop production and was heavily involved in all aspects of the areas development. He was a staunch supporter of building a local irrigation system and very dedicated to many other community projects. He served on the local school board for many years, and was active in several local fraternal organizations, and a constant promoter of Byron.

The Grunauer family has indeed left their mark on the pages of our past. Both Louis and Moritz Grunauer were pioneer merchants, as was their uncle Mr. A. Grunauer of Tracy before them. This family was instrumental in the development of Brentwood, Byron, and Tracy. The Grunauer name is found on school and church boards, irrigation board offices, fraternal organizations, and numerous other projects designed to encourage business in this region of California.

Until Next Time….

BYRON HOT SPRINGS SCHOOL

The history of the land is the spirit of its people. As I seek out stories of yesteryear, I am ever amazed at the many strengths that become visible to me, and I am impressed by the dedication of early settlers. The Byron Hot Springs School and the many other one-room schoolhouses established throughout East County are a good example of what this strength and dedication could accomplish.

Education in the Byron area was not always as we know it now. Today, we see a system packaged into an organized, nine-month school year or year-round school, with classes taught by credentialed teachers in modern, well-built facilities.

In early schools, students from various grades were educated in one room. Of course, these first schools did not have any plumbing or electricity. The building used lanterns for light, a wood stove for warmth, and an outhouse in the back.

Students arrived at school by various means of transportation. Some walked; some rode a horse; others would come by buggy or wagon. These early students definitely saw getting an education as a privilege. There were hardships for both students and educators to overcome.

The first school established in the region was the Excelsior School, built in 1865, located at the junction of Marsh Creek Road and Byron Highway, opening with a student body of 26.

More than twenty years later, in 1886, the Byron Hot Springs School District was formed to serve farmers of the area and their children. My great-grandfather, John Samuel Armstrong, donated the land and served as chairman of the first board of trustees. The original school was located on Armstrong Road, where the Byron Airport is today.

John Samuel and Mary Ann Armstrong had ten children, seven sons and three daughters, and were concerned about their children's education as were many of their neighbors with large families. At the time, all their children were being taught at home or sent to relatives living in larger communities to receive proper schooling. By 1886, the families decided it was time for the children in the region to receive a formal education within their own community.

As luck would have it, in November of 1886 the Point of Timber Grange decided to sell their hall, which would suit the needs of the newly formed school district. The Byron Hot Springs trustees offered the Grange $900 for the building, which would be moved to a new site. The Grange rejected their offer, and after discussion, conceded to sell for $1000, which would include moving the building (on skids) to the new site along with miscellaneous pieces of furniture, lamps, etc. The contract was signed by J. S. Armstrong, W. K. Doherty and R. G. Houston for the school district and J. S. Netherton, A. Richardson and V. Taylor of the Grange.

Each of the families living in the newly formed school district contributed funds to help establish the school. They organized dances, picnics, and box socials to raise monies for the purchase of books and additional furniture for the school.

Drinking water was carried for several years from the Armstrong ranch, which adjoined the schoolyard. Pupils were responsible for the janitorial work, with boys taking turns tending the potbellied stove and girls keeping the chalkboards clean. In order for the school to function as planned, each person needed to be involved and carry his share of the workload.

Students amused themselves with such games as marbles, jump rope, spinning wooden tops and blind man's bluff. Although the children were allowed to have their playtime, it was always very clear why they were at school. Each day, students would dedicate at least an hour to handwriting, followed by time spent studying arithmetic, spelling, reading, and geography. Students and their parents took education very seriously.

Some of the early teachers at Byron Hot Springs School were Miss Sherbian, Miss Gennasee, Miss Andrews and Miss Johnson. By 1893, the school had an enrollment of 48 students with grades one through twelve taught by one teacher.

When my grandfather, John J. Armstrong, and his siblings attended the Byron Hot Springs School, there wasn't a computer lab, tennis court, or stage with a terrific sound system on which to perform. What they did have was a desire to learn with parents and teachers who recognized the value of an education. As I look at the many problems our education system has today, I again have to ask myself if we have truly made progress. Perhaps we could learn something from our forefathers.

The first school actually built in Byron was constructed on the corner of Camino Diablo and Holway Road around 1890. The Byron Union School, located on Byron Highway, was built and dedicated in 1951. I attended this school in the 1950's, and it is still in operation today.

Other schools that were dealing with the area's educational needs in the 1800's were Vasco Grant School, located on Vasco Road; Liberty Marsh Creek School, located on Marsh Creek Road; and Deer Valley School, located on Deer Valley Road. Each of these schools has its own wonderful tale to tell. Until Next Time....

Byron Hot Sprints District School, in 1890, maybe 93.
Gentlemen to left is John Samuel Armstrong.

DOCTOR JAMES HAMMOND
PIONEER PHYSICIAN

Of all the dangers confronting early settlers in California, illness was dreaded the most. Our courageous forefathers were tragically familiar with smallpox, cholera, diphtheria, and typhoid. Epidemics would appear without warning striking quickly and sometimes claiming its victims in a single day.

Living conditions of the pioneers were often unhealthy. Privies and dirt floored cabins were a breeding place for germs. Dust-covered belongings, bedbugs, fleas, and flies contributed to unsanitary conditions. Water supplies were often tainted, and the practice of sharing common drinking cups at home and school spread infection. Contaminated food and a poor diet frequently caused scurvy.

The community of Byron was indeed blessed when Doctor James Hammond moved to town and opened a medical practice which lasted 57 years.

James William Hammond was born in Sheboygan, Rock County, Wisconsin in 1856, the eldest of five children born to Emily and William Hammond. William was a scout for Kit Carson and made four trips west before deciding to move his family to California in 1860. During his association with Carson, William ventured into a great wilderness of snow capped mountains, high green valleys, great rivers, and burning deserts, experiencing conditions of almost inconceivable hardship and danger.

James was only four years old when he traveled across the plains by covered wagon with his parents to settle in Napa. William opened a shop as a gunsmith, mechanic and cabinet maker. He and Emily became active in Napa's development.

James was a professional gambler until he was thirty four. He often told his grandson and his friends stories about his life as a gambler claiming to have played faro with Wyatt Earp and Doc Holliday. He reminisced that Earp had considerable expertise with firearms and few qualms about using them. Doc Holliday was a dentist by trade and a gambler by choice. He also told a story about playing cards with Joaquin Murietta once and being very careful to lose.

In the early 1890's, James enrolled in medical school at St. Helena's Sanitarium. While attending school he met a nursing student, Ida Hiserman, a native of Salinas, California. Ida and James were married in 1894, and had two sons, William and Mervyn.

Ida was very religious, and when James met her he gave up his wild

Dr. James William Hammond
This is the way he made his house calls in Contra Costa County

ways. He became the recognized leader of the Seventh-day Adventist Church and colony of the region. He was the founder and builder of the cozy little Adventist Church which was built on what today is Byron Hwy, near Camino Diablo.

Doctor and Ida Hammond settled in Byron in 1898 opening a medical practice in their home. The Doctor was a small man never weighing over 125 pounds and a strict vegetarian. He always carried a pistol on his belt, and with his black bag full of medicine made house calls in a buggy behind a fast-stepping trotter. The dedicated doctor answered the needs of the ill and injured often traveling muddy roads, fighting winter storms, and overflowing streams. His patients lived in the Vasco section, Marsh Creek district, Morgan Territory, the Alameda foothills, and out into the Delta of San Joaquin County. By the 1920's the good doctor retired his horse and buggy and could be seen moving around the district in his Studebaker Six automobile.

During the 1920s Doctor Hammond maintained professional offices in Byron, Brentwood, and Oakley. He delivered hundreds of babies and established a rather remarkable record by delivering his own children, his grandchildren, and at the age of 89 his great grandson, Douglas Hammond. My father, Oliver Armstrong was also delivered by Doc Hammond as well as most of my aunts and uncles.

Because of the great distance between rural patients and the general shortage of ready money, the good doctor often accepted a chicken, a sack of grain or a home baked pie for his fee. Consequently, he died penniless.

I've never interviewed a Byron "old timer" who didn't have a wonderful story about the "Doc". According to his grandson, Everett Hammond, "The Doc never sent a bill in his life and never charged anyone who couldn't afford it. He'd deliver a baby and take a dozen eggs as payment." He is cited for his refinement and congenial manners.

Doctor Hammond was a member of the San Francisco Society of the College of Physicians & Surgeons and was affiliated with the Morton Hospital in San Francisco. He was the medical examiner for several fraternal insurance and social organizations and the resident doctor for Southern Pacific of Byron. He was an active member of the State Medical Society and the National Medical Association.

Doctor Hammond's younger brother, Harry, came to Byron in 1906 after the San Francisco earthquake. He established the Byron Times, a weekly newspaper serving Byron for 35 years. Historians still find the Times a silent witness of the areas early history.

Doctor James Hammond practiced medicine until the age of ninety five. He died in 1958, at the age of ninety eight. He is remembered as a compassionate country doctor, a pillar of the community, and definitely left footprints in the chapters of our past. Until Next Time....

JUDGE HENRY G. KRUMLAND

Henry Krumland lived his entire life in East Contra Costa County, leaving many footprints in the chapters of our history. Henry was born on his family's farm in Byron on February 9, 1880, the son of George and Johanna (Dohrs) Krumland. His father migrated to America in 1848 from Oldenberg, Germany, first settling in the East and in 1850 moving west to California via Cape Horn. George Krumland mined the gold fields for more than ten years before moving to Byron, where he found employment on ranches. George later leased land, on which he engaged in farming and stock raising, eventually purchasing the land and establishing his roots deep in the fertile soil.

Henry's mother, Johanna, was a native of Maryland. Johanna and George Krumland raised eleven children in the Byron area and assumed an active part in the early development of this community. George and Johanna's children included Henry (never married); Edward (married Laura Hansen); Herman (married Grace Bunn); Alvina (married Frank Kennerly); Lena (married Louis Stinmetz); Anna (married Mr. Retting); and Diana (married James Middleton). Emily and several other children died very young. The Krumlands' children were educated in the Byron public school and the family was actively involved in the Congregational church and local fraternal organizations. Many of George and Johanna's descendants still reside in East County today.

Henry left the area to attend high school, as a secondary school education was not offered in the district. After high school he enrolled in a business course and returned to Byron in 1907, entering the employment of Lorenzo Plumley at Plumley's Mercantile. Henry worked for Plumley for many years, eventually managing the store and, in 1928, leasing the store from Plumley.

In 1909, Henry was elected justice of the peace for Byron Township, an office he held for more than thirty years, being re-elected to office term after term, usually without opposition. The judge's office was located in the back of Plumley's store. Many local cases were heard and satisfied before Judge Krumland. The *Byron Times* newspaper reviewed all cases brought before the court.

According to Mae Fisher Purcell in her 1940 book, *History of Contra Costa County,* "Township #14 includes Byron, Byron Hot Springs, Point of Timber, Herdlyn and other farming districts. Its area is 76 square miles, or 48,640 acres. It has a population of 1492 and registration of 500. There are 275 homes, two churches and three schools with an enrollment of 140. There are 131 farms with a valuation of $4,867,288. Township officers are: H. G. Krumland, justice of the peace, and J. S. Kelso, constable."

In 1939, Contra Costa had seventeen townships in an area of 714 square miles with an estimated population of 100,000. Each township varied in size as well as topography, and each had a justice court with a presiding justice of the peace and a constable who was the peace officer for the courts' individual needs. These two officers maintained, administered and enforced peace and order. The justice court conducted traffic violations and civil cases involving $300 or less, and misdemeanors with penalties of fines up to $500, as well as preliminary felony trials. Jail terms of up to six months also fell within the justice court's jurisdiction. Justices of the peace also performed most local marriages.

Henry Krumland was a leader in fraternal circles; he held offices in the Byron Lodge #335 of the

Odd Fellows, Native Sons of the Golden West, Order of the Rebekahs and the Brentwood Lodge of Masons. He was a frequent delegate attending state conventions of these orders, and became well known throughout California.

As justice of the peace, notary public, manager of the local mercantile, and leader of numerous fraternal organizations, Henry was involved in most of what went on in the area. Although he never claimed to be a lawyer, over the years he acquired an excellent understanding of the law, and many local residents came to rely on his advice in legal matters.

I never interview an old timer without hearing Judge Krumland's name mentioned; everyone has a story about "the Judge." He is remembered by locals as a light-hearted fellow who enjoyed the taverns on Main Street and was willing to extend a helping hand to his friends and neighbors, while always holding the community's best interests at heart.

Byron and other communities in the region grew and prospered because of early settlers. The names of men like Henry Krumland and his father before him, the names of primarily honest, upright, God-fearing men of good heart and courage, are identified and interwoven with the development of this region of California. Until Next Time....

FRED M. HOLWAY

Byron was founded in 1878 when the San Pablo and Tulare Railroad came through the area. During Byrons first year building and businesses boomed with a cobbler shop, post office, grain warehouse, railroad station, hotel, and tavern as well as several other businesses. Many of Byron's early businessmen were very young unmarried adventurers who came to settle on the ground floor of a new town in its infancy.

Fred Holway was one of the first residents in Byron. He arrived during the spring of 1878 a few months before rails for the new train tracks were to be laid. Fred was to watch Byron grow from a village surrounded with oaks to a prominent small town during his next 68 years as an active part of the community.

Born in Somersetshire, England on May 12, 1856 Fred came to the United States in 1871 at the age of fifteen settling in Chicago, Illinois for several years. He attended school in Chicago; moved on to Denver, Colorado for a short time; and finally to California in 1875.

At the age of nineteen Fred was working in San Francisco driving horsecars before there were electric street or cable cars. He celebrated his twenty first birthday while living in Antioch. The following year he relocated to Point of Timber where the stage coach stopped between Antioch and Banta.

Holway purchased land where Byron is located today. His first enterprise was to establish a Livery Stable catering primarily to home seekers, land buyers, and investors coming to research land values

Holway Saloon - 1915

in the area. Later, advertising in San Francisco papers, he encouraged hunters to travel to Byron by train and hunt the foothills at the base of Mount Diablo for wild game. Holway offered an outfitting service for hunting parties. He supplied hunters with a guide, camp gear, horses and wagons which would take them into the Marsh Creek and Morgan Territory canyons in search of elk, deer, mountain lion, and bear which were all abundant in the 1880's.

In 1883 Fred Holway met and married Emma Luhrsen, the daughter of a pioneering family from Tracy. After building a family home on the corners of Camino Diablo and Holway (named for the family) Fred and Emma proceeded to produce a large family of ten children, three boys and seven girls. All of the Holway children attended Byron Schools which were located across the street from their home. Later as they grew older they rode the train into Brentwood to attend high school. Of the children, Eva married Lee Acrey, Percy worked for Southern Pacific in Napa, Raymond managed the Holway Livery Stable, Herman worked for Southern Pacific in Byron, Viola married Roy Renner, Geraldine married Harry Strang, Irean married Herman Messer, Martha married Chip Hall, Elvira never married, and Aurora died before her first birthday.

Byrons first hotel was built by Henry Wilkening. It burned down in 1884. Fred Holway rebuilt the hotel in 1885. It burned again in 1917 and was never replaced.

Old timers best remember Fred Holway for his Holway Saloon which was located on Main Street near where the Post Office is today. The saloon was a primary gathering place for locals to discuss politics and county affairs. John Samuel Armstrong and Simon Barkley, my great grandfathers were probably two of his best clients.

During the 1920's two momentous events took place, women finally were allowed the right to vote, and prohibition became the Law of the Land. The national prohibition of liquor was widely ignored during its thirteen year span. The Holway Saloon remained open for clients to play billiards and drink soft drinks publicly, although rumor has it there was never a shortage of bootlegged booze available in the back room

Holway acquired extensive property holdings in the area. He not only owned a hotel, livery stable, and a saloon but also sold fire insurance as well as being very involved in the local fraternal organizations. He was a charter member of Byron Odd Fellows Lodge and served as treasurer for many years.

Holway was instrumental in organizing the annual Odd Fellows Picnic, Barbecue, and Ball which took place every spring from 1880 until the 1920's. The event was held in Marsh Creek Canyon near the John Marsh House. Amusements for the day would be foot races, egg toss, and other games. Every year a tug of war was held between married and single men from opposite sides of the creek. The Byron Band, made up of nineteen local musicians, furnished music throughout the event and in the evening played for the Grand Ball at the Odd Fellows Hall in Byron.

Fred Holway died October 18, 1946 at the age of ninety with his wife, Emma preceding him in death at the age of forty in 1912.

As I research Byrons history, I am once again amazed at the drive our forefathers had. I also have found that the foundation that men like Fred Holway laid for us yesterday enables us to progress into tomorrow. Until Next Time....

ALONZO PLUMLEY

There are always those that pave the way and set the seeds for crops that future generations will reap. Alonzo Plumley was among the early settlers of Byron leaving large footprints in our history.

Alonzo was born in New York in 1830, moving on to Canada with his parents as a child. At seventeen years of age, he moved to Cook County, Illinois, finding employment in several different occupations. At 23 he met and married Julia Chilson, a native of Massachusetts.

In 1853 Alonzo and his young bride traveled overland via the emigrant trail by wagon, arriving at Volcano, California, in August, some five months after their departure. From Volcano the couple came directly to Contra Costa County, first settling in Ygnacio Valley for a short time and then moving to Morgan Territory, where they purchased land from Jeremiah Morgan.

During the fall of 1864 (fourteen years before Byron was founded), Alonzo purchased 160 acres one mile north of Byron and engaged in general farming and stock raising. Alonzo was active in the layout and grading of the first roads in the Byron section.

Lorenzo "Renny" Plumley

Alonzo and Julia had a total of twelve children and were heavily involved in church, school and all matters that were of concern to the community. Many of their children stayed in the area, following in their father's footsteps as active citizens of the town they grew up in.

Alonzo was instrumental in the construction of the first church in the area. The Methodist Episcopal Church was built in 1867 at Point of Timber with Alonzo serving on the church board for many years.

Point of Timber was the first organized community in East Contra Costa, approximately 25 years before Byron was founded in 1878. Alonzo and other early pioneers organized the Point of Timber Farmers Protective Club in the 1860's. Alonzo was also a charter member of the Point of Timber Grange, organized in 1873.

In 1879, when the Union Cemetery Association was formed, Alonzo was appointed as one of five trustees to oversee the cemetery. He served on the board for many years.

The Plumley name is connected to almost every major event that took place in the Byron area from 1860 to 1935. Alonzo was in part responsible for the splendid irrigation project that was so important in the development of the area's agriculture. Byron-Bethany Irrigation Company was formed in 1914, with the district being established in December of 1919. Three of Alonzo Plumley's children were original stockholders in the district.

Lorenzo Plumley, Alonzo's son, opened Plumley's Mercantile in 1899 on Main Street. I remember my grandmother Cassie Armstrong reminiscing about Plumley's. She always said, "If Plumley's didn't have it we probably didn't need it!" The store stocked grocery items, sewing notions, tools, hardware, clothing and much, much more. Gramma always said that Plumley's had a homey feeling that you were aware of as soon as you entered. Over the years two fires endeavored to put Plumley's out of business, but Lorenzo would always order new stock and open up again.

Customers of Plumley's Store came into Byron from all the surrounding sections to purchase their goods and supplies and post their mail at the post office inside the store.

The store also housed the offices of Judge Henry Krumland, justice of the peace of Byron Township for many years. Judge Krumland would hold trials in the back office of Plumley's and was retained by Lorenzo to oversee the operations of the mercantile.

*Gentleman standing along side of carriage is E.A. Byer.
Byer Road in Byron is named for this family.*

Pioneer families like the Plumleys carved a life out of the undeveloped wilderness. They coped with solitude and failure, back-breaking labor and the hazards of grappling with nature when they first arrived in California. Alonzo Plumley is one of the first settlers definitely leaving incredible footprints in Byron's history. Until Next Time....

BYRON TRAIN WRECK

When California became a state in 1850, the notion that someone in New York would one day be able to buy a ticket and ride the rails to the Pacific Coast must have seemed as remote as the fantasies of Jules Verne. But in 1862, Congress passed a law authorizing two railroads, the Central Pacific Railroad and Union Pacific Railroad, to build lines from Sacramento and Omaha, respectively, to complete the transcontinental railway. The government pledged to give the railroad companies free rights-of-way. For each mile of completed track, the railroad would be granted land on either side of the tracks in ten-square-mile sections, alternating with sections reserved for the public. They would also receive $16,000 (in the form of loans or bonds) for every mile of track laid in the plains, and more for track laid in the mountains.

On May 10, 1869, some six hundred spectators gathered at Promontory Point, Utah, to watch the last spike be driven. The transcontinental railroad was complete, linking the Atlantic and Pacific coasts. It now took seven days to cross the continent.

The railroad had a tremendous impact on the Byron area. In fact, Byron owes its origin to the railroad. In 1878, San Pablo and Tulare Railroad installed a short line to connect Martinez to Banta. At that time Brentwood, Byron, Bethany, and Tracy were established. Prior to the coming of the railroad, the early settlers of the area depended on stagecoaches (which they boarded at Point of Timber) and old sailboats (which were boarded at Point of Timber Landing or Babbes Landing) as their primary source of transportation. With the railroad complete the locals had affordable passage as well as a swift, safe way to send their product to market. Between Port Costa and Byron as many as fifteen trains passed daily.

By 1880, the San Pablo and Tulare Railroad Company sold to Southern Pacific; Byron was growing; and for the first time East Contra Costa County was easily accessible to "outsiders." Warehouses to store wheat, corrals to hold livestock before shipping to market and other businesses began to spring up. Byron became noted for its mineral springs, which were rated among the best in the United States. Thousands came to the Byron Hot Springs from all over the world; Byron was definitely a community on the move.

Life was much easier for the early settlers with the railroad completed. By the turn of the century, 5,751 miles of track crisscrossed the state. For ten cents, a young person in Byron could ride the train into Brentwood to attend classes at the newly formed Liberty High School (1901) and people of modest means could travel for business and pleasure excursions to urban centers. Land speculators arrived by train to examine the rich, fertile lands of the area, and many settled here. Many of the early homes in the area are constructed from lumber delivered via the rails.

While the popularity of rail travel was on the rise, safety concerns were very visible. Sensational accounts of collisions due to mechanical failure or human error were common front-page fare in California newspapers. On the evening of Saturday, December 20, 1902, shortly after seven o'clock, one of the most disastrous train wrecks in California history occurred in Byron.

The Owl Limited, which was bound for Los Angeles, was one of Southern Pacific's most modern trains. It offered double drawing room/sleeping cars, a diner and a day coach to accommodate weary shoppers, businessmen, and students bound for Christmas reunions in the Fresno area. The Owl left Oakland about 5:00 p.m., speeding past Richmond, Port Costa, Martinez and Antioch, heading for the San Joaquin Valley. Shortly after passing the Brentwood Station the train's engineer, Lewis Kerr, noticed a leaking tube in the boiler of the Owl's locomotive. Steam escaping into the flue threatened to extinguish the boiler's fire. The train labored to a standstill just as it reached Byron, twenty minutes behind schedule.

Kerr immediately instructed the conductor, Mr. Dolan, to send a brakeman to the rear of the train to flag the approaching Stockton Flyer. The Flyer, a commuter train, had been delayed in Port Costa, its only stop between Oakland and Tracy, and was running a half-hour behind schedule. In order to regain lost time, engineer James McGuire pushed his train faster than usual. By the time McGuire saw the red warning lights set out by the Owl's brakeman, it was too late to stop his speeding locomotive. McGuire rammed the throttle closed, choking off the steam and air, then sounded a warning blast before colliding with the Owl.

The Flyer's giant locomotive ran through the Owl's rear coach like a knife cutting cheese, traveling another six feet into the diner car. The roof of the wrecked car rested on the boiler like a huge umbrella, the sides and seats hanging on either side, with men, women, and children pinned between. The impact killed 27 passengers and injured many more. Many of the surviving passengers were hurled to the front of the coach upon impact, to be crushed between masses of debris and burned by the clouds of scalding steam pouring out of the shattered boiler of the Flyer.

Byron residents rushed to the scene to render help. They built light-giving fires along the tracks and tended to the injured and dying. Doctor Bird, a physician from Byron Hot Springs Resort, quickly arrived at the scene accompanied by Doctor Davidson and a trained nurse, both guests of the resort. The Byron Methodist Church and Byron Hotel became temporary hospitals; the Odd Fellows Hall was set up as a temporary morgue.

Meanwhile, a wrecking train was dispatched from Oakland with a crew of medical and rescue workers. In the hours before the rescue team arrived, the residents of Byron offered first aid to the mangled, bruised and burned victims. Townsmen, with the aid of axes and saws, made their way into the wreckage, carrying out the injured. Tobe LeGrand, constable of Byron, was seen clambering over the tangled mound of iron and steel carrying a child to safety.

Many Byron residents opened their homes to uninjured passengers while they waited for relief to arrive from Oakland. As I have interviewed the old timers in the Byron area I have heard many wonderful stories about how the town pulled together and reached out to the victims of this grim accident.

The Byron train wreck was not the only railroad accident that occurred in 1902 and 1903. Resources indicate that between June 1902 and June 1903, 1,059 people were killed in train wrecks and 10,864 were injured. Since 1902, Byron has experienced two more train-related accidents. On July 4, 1981, shortly before 6:00 p.m., 24 cars of a 52-car Southern Pacific freight train transporting steel coils from the U.S. Steel Plant in Geneva, Utah, via Pittsburg derailed, sending steel coils weighing 20,000 pounds each rolling along Main Street.

The Byron Volunteer Fire Department was immediately on site, under the direction of Fire Chief Nick Papadakos, with their pumper, tanker, power wagon and a crew of men. Brentwood Fire Department sent three rigs to the scene and the Knightsen Fire Department sent a power wagon.

Fortunately there were no injuries. Several coils rolled onto the street, hitting parked cars and crushing everything in their way, creating a dark cloud of dust which rose fifty feet in the air. Railroad cars were piled on top of each other, and others were lying sideways on the torn-up track, with bent and twisted rails sticking out of the wreckage. Five grass fires were started from the derailment. The wreckage cleanup, completed by Southern Pacific and U.S. Steel, took almost a week, drawing hundreds of sightseers to the area to photograph the mangled cars. Investigators discovered a broken axle that caused a wheel to fall off; final damages exceeded $400,000.

September 13, 1989 brought yet another train-related accident to Byron. A broken wheel on a Southern Pacific freight train with 33 cars caused eight cars hauling butane gas to derail. Again the Byron Fire Department responded, scrambling to roust and evacuate residents from their homes at 3:30 A.M. as a fog-like cloud of flammable gas escaped from a leaking tanker car. Fortunately, injuries were avoided; had an explosion occurred, an underground fuel line following the tracks could have ignited as well. The school was closed and more than three hundred students were granted a holiday. Until Next Time....

THE BYRON TIMES

The Byron Times, a weekly newspaper serving Byron for 35 years, was established by Harry Hammond. It's first edition was printed on July 20, 1906. Hammond published the small weekly newspaper that would claim national fame and before its demise was responsible for many of the county's civic undertakings. Historians still find the Times to be a silent witness to the history of the area.

Home of the Byron Times, one of the handsomest country newspaper buildings in the west.

Harry Hammond had come to Byron after the San Francisco earthquake to join his brother, Doctor James Hammond, who was practicing medicine in the area. For more than 20 years Harry had worked as a proofreader for a newspaper in San Francisco.

The Byron Times offered something for everyone. The women's page featured fashion news, recipes, and usually some hints on child rearing. International and national news items were relegated to the inside pages. There was a farmers corner with weekly tips on crop and animal raising.

Harry Hammond's newspaper was filled with a mixture of editorial comments and news. So mixed were the two, it often became difficult to separate them. By August 1907 circulation had climbed to 700 readers. The Times developed a reputation for sensationalism, although there was a sober side which was often reflected in the obituaries. "Our hearts have been much saddened at receiving tiding of the death of our much beloved friend Mrs. F.D. Sweetser....She peacefully passed to the life beyond leaving many friends to mourn her loss."

In addition, the Times carried the usual notices such as, "Mrs. J. J. Armstrong traveled to San Francisco on Sunday to visit her sister, returning to Byron Tuesday on the afternoon train."

The reader was informed about who was sick, who had company from out of town, or who just bought a prize bull at the stock auction. Anything and everything Hammond heard around town might appear in the next edition.

Photographs began appearing in advertising by the end of 1907 and circulation had reached over 800. No pictures appeared in the news columns until Hammond's marriage in April 1908. The paper's first front page photograph ran in the April 10, 1908 issue. It was a one column studio portrait of Hammond's bride, the former Margaret Thompson, of Robert's Island.

In the middle of the paper's second year, Hammond announced "watch the letters, they spell out a word." What he meant was that a very stylized letter would begin the first word of each column and when all the stylized letters were put together they spelled out a word. In the case of Hammond's wedding announcement, the letters spelled "HONEY."

By August 28, 1908 the paper had reached a circulation total of 1,000 in 10 towns which included subscribers from Byron, Brentwood, Antioch, and Stockton. In that same year he began his unflagging battle against prohibition, a proposition he said, "attacks the fundamental principles of government. It is the duty of our independent press to uphold these principles no matter what the cost." Prohibition became the law of the land in 1921, and the liquor loving Hammond wrote, "Prohibition is here. It is the law of the land. It is not now debatable. It is our duty to uphold that law." But he was also on hand to rejoice when prohibition was repealed.

Harry Hammond

The Christmas edition of 1909 had a six color front page illustration of Santa Flying over a small village in an airplane packed with toys, while snow flurries fell. That edition ran 20 pages and was the most ambitious undertaking attempted by Hammond to that date. Over 1,700 copies of that edition were printed. On the inside, in addition to the regular Christmas features, were pieces of Christmas fiction including Dickens "Christmas Carol."

The big news in January 1910 was the appearance of a motion picture in Byron. Hammond wrote, "The motion pictures were without exception highest class. The outstanding feature was their clarity when thrown on canvas. There was no flickering." That same month circulation nudged its way up to 1,250.

At the end of its fourth year, the paper boasted a circulation of 1,530 covering 14 towns from Richmond to Newman and the front page was expanded to seven columns. In 1910, Hammond also published the papers first " Booster Edition". This was a semiannual magazine featuring stories about Byron and the Delta's progress and history. Fourteen editions would appear during Hammonds stewardship of the Times. There are copies of these remarkable publications at the County Library in Pleasant Hill. The Byron Booster Editions are a valuable historical record of the great Delta stretching from Stockton to the Oakland hills giving a description of agriculture, horticulture, animal husbandry, industry, culture, community, and political affairs.

Hammond loved a good cause to fight for. A great example of this was his stand on the State's Fishing License Law in 1913. He denounced the license proposal as an "infamous measure, an abridgment of the people's natural rights." The measure was passed and Hammond accepted it, but only after it became law. By 1917 the circulation had climbed to 8,000 with readers from as far away as

Honolulu.

For all its flamboyance and hoopla, the Byron Times had a severe side as was illustrated repeatedly over the years. In 1920, the papers editorial said, "The cigarette is definitely worse than whiskey. It causes tuberculosis. Cigarette smoking young men are not found in the best positions. They are not even wanted. The cigarette habit among the boys of America and an efficient nation do not go together." The paper had a policy against accepting cigarette advertising that lasted throughout Hammond's publishing career.

A devastating fire swept through much of downtown Byron one windy night in March 1923, destroying the newspaper office and many other Byron businesses. The Byron Times arose from the ashes and was published in Antioch until September 1923 when the new building in Byron was completed. That building cost Hammond more than $20,000 and was a landmark for Byron for many years. (located on the corner of Camino Diablo and Highway 4)

Harry Hammond's political ambitions began when he became close personal friends with James Rolph, mayor of San Francisco. When Rolph ran for governor of California, Hammond took a very active role in his election. In 1931 Governor Rolph appointed Harry Hammond to the position of State Printer, a position that paid $25,000 a year. As State Printer, Harry fought to have the State printing plant actually print everything the state required, including school books. This endeavor saved the state millions of dollars.

When Hammond moved to Sacramento to assume his state employment, his son, Harry Jr., took over the editorial duties for the Times. But the elder Hammond remained the publisher of the paper and directed policy from Sacramento.

In 1932 young Harry Hammond (age 30) was returning to Byron from Tracy on a foggy night and his car crashed into the rear of a slow moving truck and he was killed. Harry Hammond Sr. was devastated and much of his interest in the Byron Times died with his son.

On October 7, 1938 an announcement appeared on the front page of the Times announcing its sale to Sam Cross Jr., formerly of Berkeley. After 32 years of promoting Byron, Hammond had retired. He played a huge role in the development of the area. With his pen he helped build the highway from Byron to Stockton, thwarted powerful railroads, found lost dogs for heart broken children, unseated politicians, and generally fought tooth and nail for any cause he believed to be right.

Sam Cross suspended the publication of the Byron Times in October 1939. The Times was a one man newspaper. With Hammond gone there seemed to be no reason to read the Times. Cross found that Hammond was an impossible act to follow.

The value of the collection of newspapers and "Booster Editions" of the Byron Times cannot be measured in monetary calculations, for from these fading pages comes the history of this area.

You can't research East Contra Costa history without repeatedly running across Harry Hammonds influence. Hammond, for his boasting spirit and enthusiasm, must be considered one of the outstanding men of journalism in any history of Contra Costa County. Perhaps Harry didn't realize it at the time, but before his publishing career ended he was responsible for much of the growth in this region of California. He truly was a one man 'Chamber of Commerce'.
Until Next Time....

BYRON IN 1912

As the holiday season approaches, I find myself drifting back to Christmases past and wondering what a shopping trip to Byron would have been like in 1912.

When my great-grandfather, John Samuel Armstrong, settled in East Contra Costa the town of Byron did not exist. What would become known as Byron was at the time acres of dry grain farming with huge wheat fields, vast cattle ranges and a few settlers carving out a life in a new land.

By the time my grandfather, John J. Armstrong, was born in 1878 the railroad had arrived and the town of Byron had also been born. Byron was little more than a hamlet when John was a boy, but by 1912 it had developed into as peaceful and well-regulated a little town as could be found anywhere in the United States. The march of civilization had reached Byron, with its churches, schools and businesses, a population of over four hundred and community of more than three thousand surrounding it. Byron was larger than Brentwood, Oakley or Knightsen.

By 1912 Byron had electric lights, the modern convenience of the telegraph, transportation, telephones and many thriving businesses. I'm sure that a trip to town for holiday shopping must have been quite an adventure for John Armstrong and his wife, Cassie.

I marvel at what Byron must have looked like in 1912. There were three saloons, four churches, a mercantile store, a butcher shop, a hotel, bank and railroad station, two blacksmith shops, an ice cream parlor, a cafe, two livery stables, a newspaper, a school, the Odd Fellows Hall, a park on Main Street and much more. Looking at Byron today, it is difficult to imagine the busy hub of activity that thrived here so many years ago.

Byron about 1913

On coming to town Cassie must have stopped at Plumley's Merchandise, a state-of-the-art general merchandise store supplying groceries, table delicacies, glassware, light hardware, dry goods, notions and almost anything else a customer may have needed. Plumley's Store also housed the post office and Henry Krumland's office of the justice of the peace.

Cassie may have purchased ribbon for a special Christmas gift or extra herbs and spices for favorite holiday recipes. Plumley's was also a gathering place for many of the locals, and Cassie may have found occasion to stop and chat with Bella Morchio, Clara Houston, or Bertha Richardson. While Cassie was shopping and visiting, John very well may have visited with Mr. A. N. Thomas to discuss the price of spring lambs at market in San Francisco, or he may have wandered on down the street to Franke's Blacksmith and Horse Shoeing to have a steel rim stretched or shrank to fit his wagon wheel. Franke's also sold farm equipment, wagons and buggies, and John may have taken time to dream of some new item he hoped to purchase at a later date.

Cassie then may have ventured into Charlie Holman's butcher shop for some fresh fish or C. C. Pratt's bakery to purchase some burnt-sugar cookies. John perhaps would have slipped into Tobe LeGrand's barber shop, treating himself to a professional cut and catching up on the local gossip—of which Tobe LeGrand was well informed, having been elected as constable of Byron in 1896, a position he held for more than thirty years.

Next Cassie and John, after attending to their own chores and necessities, may have attended choir practice at the Congregational Church to prepare for the upcoming Christmas services. Some families probably represented at the church were the Middletons, Heisers, Krumlands, Kelsos and other Armstrongs. After choir practice the Armstrongs may have proceeded to lunch at Jess Santos' Byron Hotel with friends, after which the men would slip into Claus Peers' Saloon for a cold brew, leaving the wives gathered at the hotel exchanging Christmas recipes.

John J. and Cassie Armstrong-1908

By late afternoon Cassie and John had probably stopped by the Bank of Byron, a subsidiary of the Bank of Tracy, attending to current business before heading back to the ranch after a long day of filling all their last-minute holiday needs.

Christmas was an occasion for celebration. The Armstrongs and neighbors busied themselves preparing for this special religious holiday many weeks in advance. It was a time for family and friends to gather for a festive dinner. The season would fill the kitchen with the aromas of freshly baked cookies, breads, brandied fruits, and of course a huge tom turkey which Cassie had grain fed for months.

I cannot help but think, as we see this special holiday become more and more commercial each year in the name of progress, that we have lost much of the true meaning of Christmas. In 1912, most gifts exchanged were candy cane cookies, rich fruit and nut cakes prettily packaged or fruit packed in a glass jar tied with colorful bows.

Young people would spend hours cutting out snowflakes, making paper chains, pulling taffy and listening to their elders tell stories. Christmas morning would not bring elaborate train sets, new bicycles or Nintendo sets neatly placed under the tree as today, but my guess would be that the children found wonderful, warm memories which they could carry throughout their lives!
Until Next Time....

BYRON FUEL INDUSTRY

In the early years of Byron the fuel industry came and helped develop this region of California leaving only a page in a history book marking its passing. I first got interested in the local fuel industry while doing research for a story about the number of jobs available locally for a young person in 1920 compared to today. I was amazed to find the impact that the fuel industry had on many residents. While interviewing old timers, I repeatedly was told stories about family members and friends that had worked at one time for one of the local pumping stations or distribution yards. Although many miles from an oil well in the 1920s, Contra Costa County was definitely a great oil refining center.

Contra Costa County had four oil refineries. The Union Oil Company established their refinery at Oleum in 1895. The Standard Oil Company built a refinery at Richmond in 1902. By 1913 the Associated Oil refinery was built in Avon. And the following year Shell Oil's facility was established in Martinez.

By the 1920s there were three fuel pumping stations and three fuel distribution centers in Byron. The oil that flowed via the pipelines that traveled through the Byron area was delivered to one of the refineries and eventually refined into gasoline, motor oil, lubricants, fuel oil, road oil, asphalt, and other valuable products.

The Shell Oil facility, Meganos Station was located on thirteen acres in the foothills between Byron and Vasco purchased from Bella and Steve Morchio in 1911. The station actually started operations in 1914. A twenty mule team and wagon moved necessary tanks, pipe, and heavy equipment needed to construct the plant. Construction materials were delivered to Byron Main Street via Southern Pacific and transported to the Shell site. Shell installed an eight inch steel pipeline from Bakersfield to Martinez.

Installing a pipeline from Bakersfield to Martinez would be a monumental task with todays technology and modern equipment, and an undertaking I can't imagine doing eighty years ago with the resources available at that time. Pipe was transported by wagon. There was a huge water wagon holding one thousand gallons of the precious liquid needed to settle the pipe into the native ground.

The Standard Oil pumping plant, McCabes Station was constructed in 1915. The plant was located on Marsh Creek Road near the railroad. This site was originally settled by the McCabe family in the 1860's.

The Standard Oil pipeline followed the Southern Pacific railroad rather than going through the foothills as the Shell Oil pipeline did. The primary purpose of the pumping station was heating the oil so it could be transported to the next station and eventually to the oil refinery in Richmond.

McCabes Station had housing on site for employees, as did the other pumping stations in the area. Several of these homes still stand on the site today. Across the street from the station there was a sand plant built by Silica Sand Company to process sand and load it on rail cars to be delivered to the glass factory and to U.S. Steel.

The Associated Oil pumping plant, Tidewater Station was built on Byron Hot Springs Road near the railroad. This station also had employee housing on location. The Associated Oil pipeline was installed from Gustin to Byron and eventually to Avon again following the railroad.

The Tidewater Station closed in the 1950s. Today there are several commercial businesses on this site, and the new Byron Airport is less than a mile away.

Byron also had three fuel distribution centers where bulk oil products were stored and could be purchased by local farmers. Union Oil, Signal Oil, and Standard Oil all had yards. The Union Oil yard was located at the southern end of Main Street, where a trucking company is located today. This site was purchased by A.N. Thomas in 1916. Thomas was a sheepman, arriving in the Byron area in the 1890s. Thomas' daughter-in-law, Vera Thomas, still resides in the house next to the old Union Oil yard.

1913 - Main Street, Byron
8" steel pipe being delivered to Shell Oil Plant

The Union Oil yard had a spur from Southern Pacific where bulk oil was loaded and unloaded. In the 1920's there were warehouses, bulk storage tanks, and loading ramps on this location. Oil was delivered by railroad tankers and pumped into holding tanks. The Union Oil Yard had several managers, Glen Bridgeford and Warren Geddes were the first, later, Hub Anderson, then, Harry Spidel, and finally, Everett LeMoine.

The Standard Oil yard was about a half mile east of Byron next to the railroad tracks. The first manager of this yard was Thomas White. In later years, Dell Sargentina, and then, Mr. Hudson were to manage the yard. In 1920 the company advertised in the Byron Times that the Standard Oil Distributing System in Byron supplied Brentwood, Oakley, Knightsen, Palm and Orwood Tracts, Woodward Island, Byron and Byron Tract, and Clifton and Coney. They also claimed, "The investment here represents an outlay of $10,000 and shows the importance of this section." By the late 1920s this distribution yard was known as Pearl Oil Yard.

The Standard Oil warehouse had BYRON painted on the roof in large bold letters that could be easily seen from the road as you approached town.

The Signal Oil yard was located on Camino Diablo, midway between the Byron Times Building and the town dump. This site was known as Mohawk Yard for a time prior to becoming the Signal facility. The Signal Oil Yard was established by Anthony Thomas and Ernie Sequeira. Sequeira later bought out his partner's interest in the business. He then sold to Warren Martin in the early 1940s.

The oil pumping stations and distribution centers were a real asset to Byron residents. The pumping stations offered employment for many local residents. Men were employed to install pipelines, work at the plants, drive truck, or any one of dozens of jobs. Residents could buy gasoline, kerosene, oil, and other petroleum products at the distribution centers.

Unfortunately there is also a down side to what the fuel industry brought to our community. Some of the sites where these businesses were located have tainted soil contaminated by petroleum products. Pipelines leaked, tankers spilled, and oil containers overflowed. As the area develops I fear we will be hearing much more about the fuel industry and its impact on Byron.
Until Next Time....

BYRON-BETHANY IRRIGATION COMPANY

In January 1914, local farmers, ranchers and landowners of the Byron area gathered at a public meeting to discuss the need for an irrigation system. The Byron-Bethany Irrigation Company was formed. Officers were elected, and it was decided that ten thousand acres would be irrigated.

The Byron-Bethany Irrigation Company became a reality with the original investment of $100,000. Ten thousand shares of stock were sold to local investors for ten dollars per share. No water was sold to anyone who was not a shareholder in the company; landowners desiring water had to own stock in the organization and become workers and boosters. Stock ownership entitled the landowner to irrigation water in proportion to his certificate holdings.

The first officers of the company were: Volney Taylor, president; Charles Petersen, vice-president; R. R. Houston, secretary; and William Saxouer, treasurer. These officers, along with J. A. Modin, engineer and manager, Charlie Cople, J. D. Rosa, W. P. Peterson, and A. Alexson as directors, ran the organization.

J. A. Modin is credited with being the man who originally aroused local enthusiasm for irrigation. Modin felt the contour of the land was ideal for the project, and investigation showed him that Italian Slough, the channel running from Old River, offered an abundance of water. By July 1914, the surveying and engineering of the project had been completed and the work on the slough had begun.

Water was diverted from Italian Slough through a great intake canal dug at tide level for a distance of about a mile, connecting with the main station. At this point the water was pumped into the main canal at an elevation of some 45 feet and on into two branches, one moving water toward Byron, and the other toward Bethany. On the Byron branch there was a relift to 56 feet. On the Bethany branch there were two relift stations, one at a 70-foot level and the other at 120 feet. Separate pumps were used for each lift, distributing the water through a system of laterals.

Farmers and landowners contributed the majority of the work themselves, building a system that supplied abundant water to the Byron-Bethany section. The men behind the project realized water was a necessity if this region of California was going to grow and prosper. Results of their efforts were immediately evident, with thousands of fertile acres producing a wealth of crops for the men who had taken the initiative to purchase stock in the company.

Alfalfa production was one of the most successful crops grown in the Byron area. With the use of irrigation, a landowner could get five crops in one year; farmers had trouble justifying using their land for producing only one crop of grain every two years when they could instead produce alfalfa.

The Byron-Bethany Irrigation Company was definitely a "people's company" owned, built and managed by the landowners, but in 1919 it was proposed that the company be included in an irrigation district to be worked out and voted on by the people according to the Wright and Bridgeford Act. On December 8,1919, the voters of Byron voted to approve the Byron-Bethany Irrigation District by a vote of 173 for to 14 against the proposal.

On May 10, 1920, six years after the district's establishment, the Byron-Bethany Irrigation Company disposed of its entire holdings to the Byron-Bethany Irrigation District for a flat price of $265,000. R. R. Houston was elected the district's first president; A. F. Donaldson, secretary; Fred Tibbetts, engineer; and B. H. Grove, manager.

"Farming made easy and profitable" was the slogan of the new Byron-Bethany Irrigation District. Many changes have taken place with B.B.I.D. in the past 75 years. The pre-1914 point of diversion was altered in 1964 from Old River to the intake channel on the state aqueduct off Clifton Court Forebay. The district has two major pumping operations. One set of pumps was on the north side and the other set was on the south side of the intake channel, with a total capacity of 210 cubic feet per second.

The district applied for a small projects loan in 1964, amounting to $1,765,000 for a rehabilitation program, with priority being given to the construction of twenty miles of underground drainage lines. The purpose of the tile lines was to help lower the water table throughout the district. The project consisted of seven east-west lines placed about one mile apart, starting at Point of Timber Road and extending to a point just south of the town of Byron.

The Byron-Bethany Irrigation District covers an irregularly shaped tract extending north and south along the west side of the San Joaquin River Delta. The junction point of three counties lies within the district: 61% of B.B.I.D. is in Contra Costa, 22% in Alameda, and 17% in San Joaquin.

The district provides water for agricultural crops of varying types. Their network includes an estimated 27 miles of canals and 22 miles of pipeline, totaling 49 miles in three counties. Drainage facilities include 13 miles of ditches and 22 miles of tile drains, totaling 35 miles of drainage facilities. Of the estimated range of forty to fifty thousand acre feet diverted annually within the district, an estimated eight to ten percent is returned to the Delta by way of transmission through the district's drainage network.

The irrigation system began as a farmers' proposition, an immense enterprise planned, handled and built to success by ranchers and landowners who realized the great value of water to this fertile section of Contra Costa County. The men behind the scenes, men whose names are interwoven with and identified with the development of the Byron area, have definitely left their footprints in the chapters of our past. Until Next Time….

BYRON-DISCOVERY BAY FIRE PROTECTION DISTRICT TIMELINE

1884.....Byron's first hotel owned by Henry Wilkerson burned down.
1896.....The first Byron Volunteer Fire Brigade was organized. It had little or no equipment and a make-shift wagon to carry supplies to the site of a blaze. Population of Byron was 300.
1901.....July 25—The Byron Hot Springs Hotel (built in 1886), several cottages, laundry, gas plant, and ice plant were destroyed by fire.
1902.....June 7—Most of the downtown business district of Byron was destroyed by wind-swept flames.
1902.....Byron Fire Department assisted in the aftermath of a train wreck.
1912.....The second Byron Hot Springs Hotel was destroyed by fire.
1915.....According to information recorded on Sanborn Map Company, Byron Volunteer Fire Department included a Fire Chief and 24 unpaid volunteers, a GMC combo hook, ladder and chemical engine with three 40-gallon chemical tanks, three 400-foot chemical hoses, a Barton "U"-34 pump capacity and other various size hoses. The fire alarm was a siren on a garage; the water was derived from domestic wells. Population in Byron was listed as 350.
1917.....The second Byron Hotel, owned by Fred Holway, burned to the ground (it was never replaced).
1923.....March 5—A devastating fire started in Manuel Roderick's barbershop on Main Street, Byron, destroyed seven business buildings (every wooden structure) for a loss estimated

The Byron Hot Springs Hotel built in 1902 tragically burns to the ground in 1912. No one was injured but there was inadequate fire protection at the Springs to save this classic Reid Brothers, architects, *structure.*

to be $50,000. The buildings razed included Santos Saloon (a precursor of the Wild Idol Saloon) and the *Byron Times* newspaper office (causing the *Byron Times* to be published in Antioch for six months until a new building was completed). Without a fire brigade and source of water there was no saving the structures. This fire caused the town to begin to organize a fire department.

1929.....The formal Byron Volunteer Fire Department was established. A $2,500 chemical engine with three 40-gallon chemical tanks and 400 feet of hose was purchased. The Commissioners met at the Highway 4 Garage (and later moved to the Byron Bethany Irrigation District offices).

1937.....Byron Fire Department hosted its first Fireman's Ball.

1938.....Byron Volunteer Fire Department purchased a brand new engine built by J. E. Van Pelt of Oakdale and mounted it on a General Motors chassis. Fire Chief was Tom White; volunteers included Jesse Baker, Arthur Howard, M. W. Reynolds, Constable Jack Kelso, Jesse Santos, Judge Henry Krumland, Frank Rogers, and Herman Messer.

1957.....September—Byron Volunteer Fire Department obtained new oxygenated smoke masks as resuscitator equipment. They had recently purchased their third fire engine, a 1,500-gallon tank pump. Fire Chief was Dick Rodrigues, Assistant Fire Chief was Stanley Pereira; A.M. (Gus) French was one of the commissioners and volunteers included Oliver Armstrong, Henry Ricioli, Mike Granados, Nick Papadakos, Elmer Armstrong, Sam Howard, Everett Hammond, and James Hannum. There were a total of 20 volunteers in the department.

1959.....October 19—The Byron Fire Station was built at the east end of Holway Street. It was a 40 foot x 78 foot concrete-block building that cost $32,483 to construct. The property for the station was donated to the fire district by Louis Souza. The station had room for three engines, an office, recreation-meeting room, kitchen, and bathroom as well as an outdoor patio.

1969.....June—Nick Papadakos was appointed Byron Fire Chief. He replaced Stanley Pereira.

1969.....October—Byron Fire Protection District had four fire engines: a 1964 International with 4-wheel drive and 1,000 gallons per minute capacity, a 1955 GMC tanker with a 1,500 gallon pump, a 1947 Dodge with 400 gallon capacity, and a 1937 GMC which also had a 400 gallon capacity. Byron Fire Commissioners were: A.M. (Gus) French, Sal Lopez, Jeff Hoell, Oliver Armstrong, and Fred Stometta. The volunteers included: Fire Chief Nick Papadakos, Assistant Fire Chief Leroy French, Elmer Armstrong, Stanley Pereira, Leo Thomas, Henry Ricioli, Clarence Lucas, Sal Lopez, Oliver Armstrong, Lawrence Sani, Jim DeBorba, Don Giusti, Keith Redenbaugh, Richard Gonzales, Bob Tucker, Emil Laredo, Greg Reed, David Armstrong, Homer Johnson, Dick Regelman, and Radio Dispatcher Jean Rodrigues.

1969.....October—Byron Fire Department, Brentwood Fire Department, Marsh Creek Fire Department, California Forestry Service, and twenty inmates from the Contra Costa County Rehabilitation Center fought for seven hours to extinguish a blaze on Vasco Road that destroyed 2,500 acres of permanent pasture. It was the largest hill fire in the area since 1944.

1982.....April 12—County Board of Supervisors transferred $25,989 from a construction fund for the Discovery Bay Fire Station into a fund for maintenance allowing the Byron Fire Protection District to purchase a third fire truck to be housed in Discovery Bay.

1983.....July 2—Byron Fire Department held the first annual Cyclathon to raise money for new equipment for their rescue van. The Cyclathon succeeded in raising $1,600.

1983.....September 22—the Gambetta farmhouse, 102 years old, burned down. It was located near Kellogg Creek and Discovery Point in Discovery Bay. The Discovery Bay volunteers responded to the house fire and another blaze of discarded building material simultaneously.

1984.....February 26—Virginia Goldsby and Mary Branscum joined as female volunteers of the Byron Fire Department. They were two of thirty-nine volunteer firefighters that staffed two fire stations in the Byron Fire Protection District which covered 60 square miles from Balfour Road south to the Contra Costa-Alameda County line. Fire Commissioners were Chairman Fred Stornetta, Charles Fuss, Bill Scanlin, Stanley Pereira, and Melvin Abreu. The Byron Station was located on Holway Drive and a second station was in Discovery Bay. Fire Chief was Nick Papadakos and Homer Johnson served as Assistant Fire Chief.

1984.....July 4—Fire caused by an electrical cord gutted a home on Hosie Avenue, Byron, causing $32,000 worth of damage. Byron Fire Department battled the wind-aided blaze and prevented damage to nearby homes.

1986.....December 18—President of the Byron Fire Protection District Commissioners for the past year, Stanley Pereira, died. He had been a member of the fire department since the 1950s. Other members of the Fire Commissioners were Howard Patton and Jack Rademacher.

1988.....April 19—Byron Fire Department held its 51st Annual Fireman's Ball. The event was the department's only fund raiser that allowed it to buy needed equipment and to purchase fruit and candy to give out to the area's children at Christmas.

1989.....Byron Fire Station provided blood pressure checks for citizens and registering for cardiopulmonary resuscitation classes.

1989.....September 13—a Southern Pacific 33-car freight train had eight of its cars derail which was caused by a broken wheel. The cars were carrying butane gas. The Byron Volunteer Fire Department immediately responded and evacuated near-by residents due to the cloud of flammable gas escaping from one of the leaking tanker cars.

1970.....Secretary for the Byron Fire Protection District Commissioners was Judy Johnson.

1971.....March 8—Byron Fire Department with assistance from Brentwood Fire Department extinguished the blaze that destroyed the Pyron Crosslin home on Vasco Road. Thanks to an alert Good Samaritan who spotted flames on the roof, Pyron and Enid Crosslin, and his aged uncle were able to escape the flames.

1976....Discovery Bay Volunteer Fire Department (a branch of the Byron Fire Protection District) was formed. Mark Drummond was the organizer and trainer of volunteers. Greg Peterson replaced Drummond later. A first-aid station and rescue equipment station was built by a few volunteers.

1979.....February—Discovery Bay Property Owners Association obtained 800 signatures to form an assessment district so that a firehouse could be built.

1979.....June 22—Byron Fire Department (4 trucks) with the assistance of Brentwood Fire Department (3 trucks) doused a fire of a 70-year-old home located on Byron Highway that left the Jack Tillery family of four homeless.

1979.....December—The Byron Fire Department had 142 calls in the calendar year—70 calls were for medical assistance and 72 were fire related.

1980.....June—The Byron Fire Protection District added a second station in Discovery Bay. It was equipped with one engine and a rescue unit was added shortly after the opening. The Fire Commissioners were: Chairman Fred Stornetta, Ed Franke, Charles Fuss, Stanley Pereira, and Bill Scanlin. Firefighters for the Discovery Bay unit included: Greg Peterson, Bob

McDonald, Bob Anderson, Bernie Reitz, Dick Zarro, Ed Calvin, Les Jones, Ed Pastor, Jerry Mann and William Rose.

1980.....August—Byron Fire Station was equipped with one Class A pumper, one power wagon, and two tankers (Discovery Bay also had one pumper). The District was rated by the Insurance Service Office (ISO) as "8" for the residential area of Byron, "9" for the commercial district (due to the lack of fire hydrants on Main Street), and "7" for Discovery Bay.

1981.....Judy Johnson was the first female firefighter to serve in the Byron Fire Department.

1981.....July 4—the Southern Pacific 52-car train carrying heavy steel coils derailed sending 20,000 pound coils onto Main Street. Byron Volunteer Fire Department was immediately on site with their pumper, tanker, power wagon, and volunteers to correct the hazard. Five grass fires were started from the derailment. Brentwood and Knightsen Volunteer Fire Departments assisted Byron.

1991.....November 7—The Byron Fire Protection District merged with the Brentwood Fire Protection District to form the East Diablo Fire District. Citizens of Byron and Discovery Bay fought the merger but a petition failed to gather enough signatures to stop the action.

1991.....December 31—Nick Papadakos retired as Byron Fire Chief.

1995.....August—East Diablo Fire Protection District joined San Ramon, Livermore, and Pleasanton Fire Departments in fighting a 640-acre grassland fire on the Howden Wind Farms property east of Vasco Road that threatened scores of windmills.

1995.....October 3—Quick response by East Diablo Fire Department volunteers saved a local resident's barn.

1997.....April—the famous Wild Idol Inn on Main Street, Byron was destroyed by a fire (it had been rebuilt after the 1923 fire).

2000.....October 20—Fire ravaged the Odd Fellows Hall on Main Street, Byron. The Hall was currently under renovation and due to reopen in November as a restaurant and bar called Blazing Saddles. The building was an historical structure originally built in the 1880s.

2002.....A new fire station was opened on Bixler Road. It was paid for by developer fees.

2002.....November—East Diablo Fire Protection District merged with Bethel Island Fire District and Oakley/Knightsen Fire District to become East Contra Costa Fire Protection District.

THE BYRON FIRE OF 1923

After the Byron-Bethany Irrigation Company was established in 1914, with local farmers reaping the benefits of easily accessible water for their crops, Byron became a flourishing little community that offered endless advantages to its residents. By the early 1920's, it was surrounded by rich agricultural, fruit and dairy industries. Orchards produced apricots, peaches, plums, Kadota figs, cherries, nectarines, almonds and walnuts. Large and small dairies could be seen peppered throughout the surrounding area, with the town of Byron as the main milk and cream shipping station. Southern Pacific railway transported the dairymen's products from Byron station to creamery plants in Holt, Tracy, Oakland and San Francisco.

Byron was, however, as were most small towns of the day, vulnerable to the threat of unpredictable disasters.

On March 5, 1923, seven buildings on Main Street were destroyed by fire: the Santos Hotel, Restaurant and Pool Hall, owned by Jess Santos; *Byron Times* offices, owned by Harry Hammond; Plumley's General Store and Post Office; Rodrick's barber shop; a shoe shop in a building owned by Stanley Cabral; and Ellis Howard's butcher shop were all lost in the blaze.

The fire started in Manuel Rodrick's barber shop when two young men who were horsing around accidentally knocked over a gasoline heater. Constable A. J. (Tobe) LeGrand happened to be entering the shop at the time of the incident; he grabbed the heater and endeavored to throw it into the street. The heater exploded, immediately engulfing LeGrand in flames, burning him seriously. A bystander used his own coat to smother the flames consuming LeGrand's clothing.

The Tracy and Brentwood fire departments responded to calls for assistance. Practically every resident of Byron turned out to fight the blaze, helping the fire departments and a crew of fifty men from Southern Pacific. SP sent for two water-tank cars from Oakland to quell the blaze that was threatening to destroy the entire town.

The *Byron Times* newspaper plant, owned by Harry Hammond, was destroyed, with only a few items being saved. Hammond's roll-top desk, the subscription list and current accounts of his publication survived the fire, but the files, fixtures, press and type were destroyed with the greatest loss being the statistics and data which had required years to accumulate. Determined not to miss a single issue of his paper, Hammond printed the *Times* in Antioch until his own facility was rebuilt.

The Byron Post Office building was lost but all the mail and some of the equipment were saved. The Santos Hotel, whose twenty rooms comprised Byron's chief hostelry, was totally ravaged.

The estimated monetary loss from the blaze was set at $50,000 to $80,000. Plumley's estimated loss was $15,000, Santos' damages were more than $13,000, and Cabral's loss was over $7,000. Most of the businesses were insured.

Within a few days of the fire, Byron townsmen could be seen clearing their lots and preparing to rebuild their lives. By the summer of 1924, you would never have known the town had been reduced to ashes and rubble just a few short months earlier.

The *Byron Times* erected a beautiful $20,000 brick printing and publishing house on the main highway with several fine rental spaces. J. B. Baker opened a modern drug store and the Community Library Club established a facility offering residents a free library. L.G. Plumley built a combination structure with three big rooms on Main Street. The center section housed Plumley's Mercantile, one side was leased to the government for the Byron Post Office, and the other side was rented to Byron-Bethany Irrigation District. Judge Krumland's office was also located in this building. Jess Santos rebuilt next to Plumley's, offering the community a new billiard hall, a barber shop, and a shoe store operated by Antonio Pies.

Pacific Gas and Electric Company improved the street lighting system and installed 250-candlepower and 100-candlepower electric lights at the moderate cost of $600 per year.

Other businesses of Byron in 1924 included a meat market equipped with refrigeration apparatus (Ellis Howard, proprietor); a branch of the American Bank; Byron Clothing Co. run by Joseph Blaustien; Good Lumber Co.; Chaim's General Store; Perry's Garage; Fleming's Restaurant;

Cakebread Trucking; Reynolds' Highway Garage; and Wightman's Studebaker Agency. Three churches provided for the community's religious needs. Three grammar schools, Byron, Excelsior and Byron Hot Springs, furnished an excellent education for youth of the region along with a modern high school in Brentwood which offered bus service for student transportation.

A large hall owned by the Odd Fellows was the meeting place for several fraternal orders and was also used for dances and other district gatherings. In 1924 this hall also offered a moving-picture center where Charles Peterson showed the latest and best pictures.

One of the worst disasters early townsmen faced was the threat of fire. Unfortunately, early fire departments were restricted because of inadequate equipment and insufficient access to water. It was not uncommon for entire towns to be left in ashes after an accidental fire.

According to an article in the *Contra Costa Gazette* on June 7, 1902, "The business district in Byron was wiped out. The town, lacking fire-fighting apparatus, left the buildings at the mercy of the flames."

Until Next Time....

SILICA SAND

The silica sand industry has a long and interesting history in East Contra Costa County. Sandstone beds crop out northeast of Mount Diablo in a mile-wide belt extending from Concord to Byron, a distance of over twenty miles. Suitable material is present in a white sandstone that ranges in thickness from 75 to 400 feet. This sand is used primarily for making glass and molding. Although the silica sand found in Contra Costa County is less pure than the sands mined in Illinois and Missouri, it is one of the principal sources of supply for the glass industry in the state. Approximately 80% of the silica mined in California is used for glassmaking products. Non-glass uses include foundry sand, plaster sand, sandblasting sand, stucco sand, silica flour for abrasives and filter sand.

During the 1920's the Columbia Steel Company mined sand on the Longwell Ranch, near Walnut Boulevard and Camino Diablo in the Byron area, for foundry use.

The Silica Company of California first reported sand production in 1929 from a sand mine located near the Stone House on Marsh Creek Road, three and a half miles southwest of Brentwood. Marvin Greathouse was president of the firm at that time. At this location the sandstone bed crops out in low rolling foothills along the western edge of the San Joaquin River Delta area. The sand was removed through underground workings. Adits were driven southeastward along the strike of the beds and a system of room-and-pillar stopes was carried upward almost to the surface.

In 1934, the Silica Company of California operations were moved about one mile southeastward to the north pit of the Longwell Ranch, where a similar system of mining was done. These workings extended southeastward along the strike for about half a mile to the property line of the ranch. In

Silica Sand Company - 1936

1938, operations were transferred to the south pit of the Longwell Ranch, which was an open cut operation. Mining began at the north end and was extended southeastward along the strike.

An extensive sand plant was built in 1931 near the Southern Pacific Railroad on Marsh Creek Road. Here the crude sand was processed and a low-iron glass sand was prepared. After the oversized material was screened out of it, the sand was washed and classified to remove the fines. Chemical leaching was done to reduce the iron content. The finished product was suitable for use in glassmaking, and in the manufacture of silicate of soda. Three grades of foundry sand were also prepared from the washed and screened sand, as follows: #1 Foundry, fine sand for gray iron work; #2 Foundry, minus 20-mesh plus 80-mesh for standard steel molding; #3 Foundry, minus 10-mesh plus 40-mesh (coarse) for steel breather sand.

The sand plant on Marsh Creek Road across from the Standard Oil Pumping Station (known as McCabe's Station) consisted of a heavy-timbered seven-story classifier and washing plant. A well was dug with a heavy flow of water tapped at a depth of eighty foot. For conservation purposes, the water was stored in a large pond. There was also an office building and several outbuildings on the site. The Silica Company also built a 1,100-foot railroad spur tapping the main Southern Pacific track, which as early as 1931 was shipping five carloads of processed sand daily.

Silica Sand Company of California employed about 40 men in 1931. The number of employees increased to 57 in 1936, and declined to 32 in 1940, with operations ceasing in August 1942, when the plant was removed and the company liquidated.

I seldom interview an old timer from the Byron area without hearing a story about the Silica Sand Mines. Many of the locals were employed at this facility, and there were several deaths at the mine due to cave-ins or accidents. In January 1941, Andrew R. Anderson, night foreman at the plant, plunged into the hopper and met death by suffocation. Apparently he lost his balance while working. Near the place where he fell into the hopper was a safety belt which Anderson had obviously failed to strap on. Anderson was 56 years old, born in Byron, and had been foreman of the plant for ten years. Dr. Harry Geyser of Brentwood was summoned to the plant and pronounced him dead.

After the closure of the Silica Company of California in 1941 the sand industry laid dormant for over a decade in East Contra Costa. In the 1960's, Santos Pit was operating on Camino Diablo, near Byron. In the 1970's, Wedron Silica, a company from Monterey, acquired this pit and constructed a plant. Wedron sold the facility to Martin Marietta in the early 1980's and Unimin Corporation purchased the pit and plant in 1983.

Currently, large amounts of glass sand are being mined by Unimin Corporation for glass manufacturing firms that produce containers for California's substantial wine and beer industry. Until Next Time....

PIONEER FAMILIES PAVED THE WAY TO BYRON

As I continue my research into Byron's history and the roots of my own family, I am ever amazed at the variety of personalities that chose to settle here in the 1800s. Many of the pioneer families have grand and great grandchildren still residing in the area. Some of those early family names can still be seen on local street signs and businesses.

PLUMLEY: Alonzo Plumley was one of Byron's pioneer merchants when Byron was a little trading hamlet which could only be reached by dirt roads. In March 1853, at the age of 23, Alonzo and his young wife left Illinois by wagon and crossed the plains to California. This pioneer couple like so many others spent six months on the trail before arriving in Volcano, California. They were to purchase 160 acres one mile north of Byron and establish a farm. This location is where they raised their twelve children and became very active in the building of a new community. The Plumleys eventually established a mercantile house that served the residents of the area well. Plumley's Store handled a complete line of groceries and hardware. I remember my grandmother, Cassis Armstrong, telling stories about this store. She used to say "If Plumley's didn't have it, you probably didn't need it!"

HOFFMAN: Ferdinand Hoffman was born in Prussia in 1827 and emigrated to America at the age of 20. He worked as a shoemaker for several years in New York and St. Louis crossing this great nation by wagon to the West. He resided in the State for almost ten years before purchasing

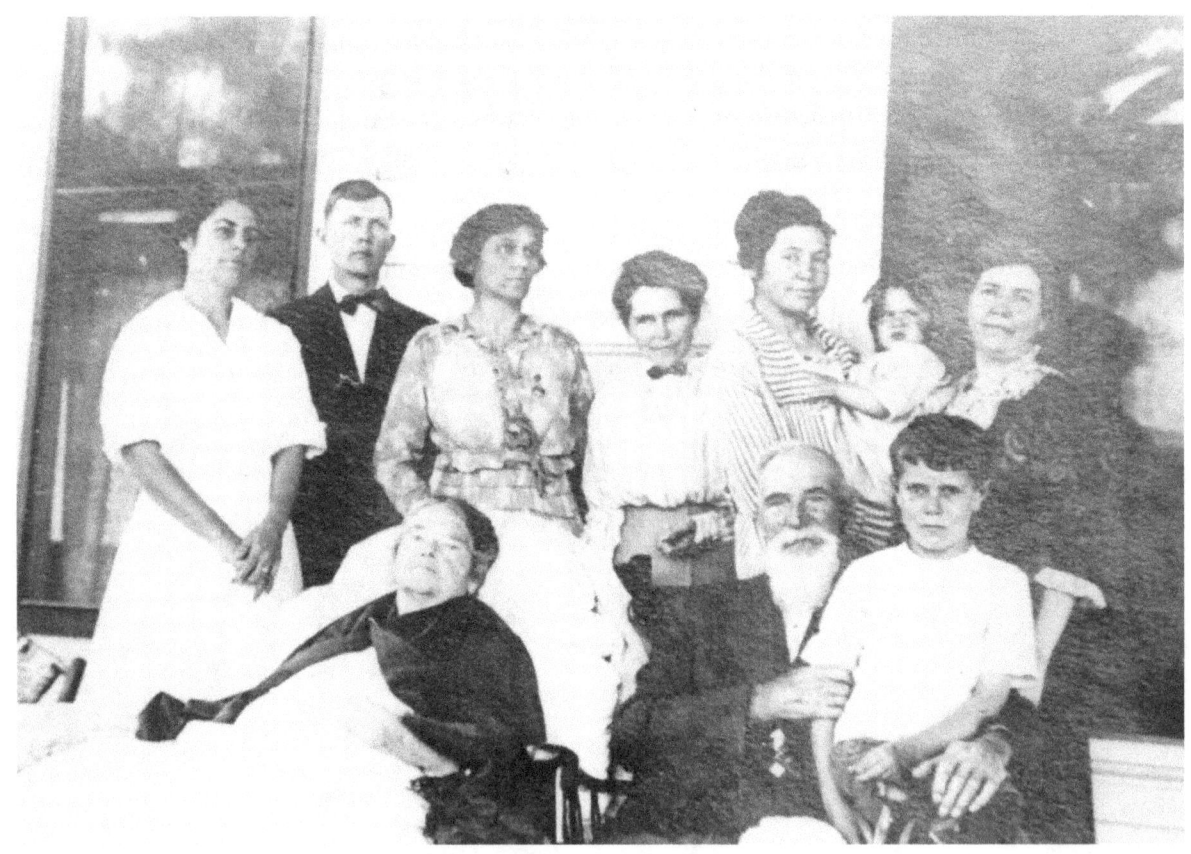

a section of land in 1860 near Byron which he farmed and engaged in the sheep business for many years. Hoffman was very active in forming several local organizations and was involved in the promotion of Point of Timber Landing (located directly across from Discovery Bay) as a shipping point for local wheat farmers to transport their wheat to market. Hoffman Lane was named after this pioneer family.

RICHARDSON: Alpheus Richardson was born in Ohio in 1830 and traveled to California in 1852 at the age of 22. He lived in several locations in California and Oregon before finding his way to the Byron area in 1865. He married Miss A. Taylor, daughter of A.T. Taylor, another pioneer of the area. Alpheus raised wheat in the fertile ground near Point of Timber, and was involved in the construction of Point of Timber Landing. He is remembered by many of the "Old Timers" for 112 miles of gum trees he planted along the roadside near Byron. The Richardson family took an active part in church, school, and local organizations. It is impossible to read Byron history and not be impressed with the impact this family had on the community they settled in.

PRESTON: Colburn Preston was born in Pennsylvania in 1836 and came west in 1864 via the Isthmus of Panama. He and his wife Melissa settled on 320 acres 1/2 mile from Point of Timber where they raised seven children. Colburn was one of the first farmers to grow alfalfa in the area, also growing wheat and raising cattle and hogs. The Prestons were heavily involved in their community. Colburn served as a trustee on Excelsior School and Liberty Union High School Boards and his family donated four acres of land for the first cemetery of the area: Union Cemetery.

WILDER: The history of Byron would not be complete without a mention of Mrs. William R. Wilder. She was the daughter of Captain George Donner of the Famous Donner Party, most of whom perished crossing the Sierra Nevada Range. Mrs. Wilder's husband, a farmer, came to the area in 1865, erected a small home and sent for his family from Sacramento the following year.

The history of Byron is rich with wonderful stories of young idealistic pioneers that came west to build a new life for themselves and families. It is impossible not to be impressed with the hardships they overcame, the "can do" attitude they displayed, and determined outlook they had about their lives. They depended on each other and were quick to extend themselves to their neighbors. Once again I cannot help but believe there is much our generation could learn from our forefathers.

ALEXANDER T. TAYLOR
THE CANADIAN FARMER

As I research the chapters of East Contra Costa County's past I am continually impressed by the characters that settled this region of California—men that grasped the opportunity to mold their own destiny.

Early settlers came to California with a wagon full of hopes and dreams of a better life for themselves and their families. Some dreamed of fabulous wealth from the streams of the Mother Lode, while others saw California as a place where they could plant their roots and build a better life than they had left behind. The rich, fertile soil of East Contra Costa attracted farmers from far and wide. Alexander T. Taylor was such a man.

The Taylor family originated in England, and established themselves in Canada during the early history of European settlement in the Americas. Alexander T. Taylor was born in Canada in 1821, the son of a farmer. When Alexander was nineteen, his father supplied him with two suits of clothes and one dollar, with which he left home to seek his fortune. For the next three years Alexander worked as a farm laborer in Canada, saving his money and attending school to refine his education whenever he could. At the age of 23 he purchased one hundred and twenty acres and began farming his own land. He later sold these holdings and returned to his parents' farm, which he managed for eleven years. The farm was destroyed by fire in 1866 and Alexander decided that rather than rebuild in Canada he would move his family west to California and begin a new life.

Mr. Taylor had married Louisa Bruce, a native of Vermont, in 1844. There were four children from this union: Valeria (1846), Avyette (1848), Volney (1851) and Alexander (1853).

Volney Taylor - 1910

Mr. and Mrs. Taylor and their family left Canada in 1866 and traveled to California via the Isthmus of Panama. They boarded a ship in New York on November 6, 1866, and arrived in San Francisco a month later. During the first two years in California the Taylors settled in Vallejo (Solano County). In September 1868 they came to East Contra Costa (near Point of Timber) and purchased 320 acres of rich farmland.

Taylor Farm was located near where Byron Highway and Highway 4 meet today (Borden Junction). The farm, known locally as the Canadian Farm, had a stream, Kellogg Creek, passing through it, which Taylor used to irrigate his crops. At least 25 grand old oak trees whose branches were said to reach the ground grew in small patches on the property.

Alexander Taylor was actively involved in every aspect of early development in the Point of Timber area. He served on school boards, the cemetery board, numerous fraternal organizations, the Grange and the Methodist Church, and was instrumental in the wheat industry of his day.

Taylor was involved in building Point of Timber Landing and in the introduction of the railroad to this region.

Alexander Taylor died in 1912, one of the most prominent and well-known men in East Contra Costa County.

Alexander Taylor's son Volney Taylor, was to follow his father's lead in the community. Volney came to California with his parents when he was fifteen, having received his basic education in Canada and Vallejo, and graduating from Pacific Business College in San Francisco in 1872.

Volney farmed with his father for many years. The Taylors owned more than eight hundred acres of rich farmland where they grew grain and alfalfa. Volney married twice. His first marriage was to Agnes Andrews, a native of Illinois. To this union was born one son, Everett, who later became a prominent attorney in Martinez. Volney's second marriage was to Carrie Bohmen of Sacramento, and they had one daughter, Beatrice, born in 1905. Beatrice Taylor Cross will be well remembered by locals. She taught sewing classes at Liberty Union High School in Brentwood for many years. I have fond memories of Mrs. Cross' sewing class where I almost wore out a piece of fabric attempting to make an apron.

Volney was one of the founders of the new Byron Methodist Church. He led the campaign to finance the building of the present edifice of worship in 1921.

Byron Methodist Church - 1921

Volney Taylor was one of the most successful farmers and landowners in the area. He was one of the first settlers here to plant alfalfa and he was one of the local farmers that founded the Byron-Bethany Irrigation Company in 1914, serving as the first president of that organization. With the use of irrigation he was able to produce four to five cuttings of alfalfa hay annually.

In 1919, Volney Taylor decided to subdivide some of his property. This was one of the first subdivisions of its kind in East Contra Costa. Acreage he had purchased for $35 an acre sold for $335 an acre. These smaller parcels are located on Taylor Lane.

Taylor was a Royal Arch Mason and a member of the Eastern Star. He was also an active member of the Byron Odd Fellows and was in the Independent Order of Good Templars. He died August 25, 1923. Until Next Time....

ALPHEUS RICHARDSON

Thousands of Americans packed all their possessions into covered wagons and braved treacherous river crossings, dust storms, prairie fires, poorly marked trails, and other dangers to seek land and opportunity in the wilds of California.

At the age of twenty two, Alpheus Richardson traveled overland to California. Alpheus Richardson was born on his father's farm in Marion County, Ohio, on October 3,1830 and died in Contra Costa County on December 12,1915. He received his education in Ohio prior to joining a wagon train in 1852 headed west, in a company under the leadership of Colonel Hollister.

When Alpheus first arrived in California he worked near Marysville. Then he engaged in placer mining for one winter in Placer County. His attempt at mining was unsuccessful. So he decided to try farming which also failed. Then he traveled to Gilroy in Santa Clara County and tried hog raising. In later years he'd tell the story about his hog raising experience, laughing as he told of buying high and selling low. His next move was to Contra Costa County where he farmed wheat and invested in cattle. He did well with his farming for a few years. But in 1863 he was forced to sell his cattle and relocate to Oregon. In 1864 he again tried mining. Alpheus moved to Alpine County hoping to strike it rich in the gold fields, but moved on the following year dead broke.

In 1865, at the age of thirty five, Alpheus Richardson returned to Contra Costa County. He settled near Point of Timber becoming one of the first settlers of the region. He successfully engaged in dry farming wheat and was instrumental in all aspects of the development of the region.

Alpheus married Avyette Taylor, a school teacher and daughter of Alexander T. Taylor who was also an early wheat grower in the Point of Timber region. Taylor had come to California from Canada via the Isthmus of Panama in 1866.

In 1876 (two years before Byron was founded) Alpheus and Avyette took a trip throughout Canada and the Eastern United States and attended the Centennial Exposition in Philadelphia, traveling some 8000 miles. This trip, being considered remarkable for that time, was well covered by the Contra Costa Gazette.

You can't research the early history of East Contra Costa without repeatedly seeing Alpheus Richardson's name. The Point of Timber Grange #14 was organized in 1873 with Alpheus as a charter member and serving as the organization's first Assistant Steward. In 1878 he served as a trustee for the Union Cemetery Board. In the early 1880's he and several other local farmers consolidated and built the Point of Timber Landing in an effort to better deliver their crops to market.

Alpheus was an active member of the Methodist church serving on the church board for many years. The first church services were held in private homes 1868. But after the Grange was organized in 1873, services were held in the Grange Hall at Point of Timber. When Byron was founded in 1878 the church relocated to it's present site on Byron Highway. Alpheus donated a bible for the alter of the new facility.

At one time there were beautiful trees lining both sides of the roadway along Byron Highway from Point of Timber south leading into Byron. Early writings about the area refer to this road as a shaded boulevard covered with a canopy of locust and eucalyptus branches. The first trees were planted by a San Francisco commission merchant who had a home where the present Byron School is located. About 1884 Alpheus Richardson planted an additional half mile of trees along the road on his property line. Richardson's trees were planted from seeds he was given by William Wilder, a resident of Byron. Trees were also planted along the roadside by Matt Burlington, Colburn Preston, and Alpheus Richardson's father in law, Alexander Taylor. Until next time....

McCABE
PIONEER FAMILY

The early settlers of East Contra Costa came from all walks of life. Some were miners that had left the gold fields with disappointment instead of fortunes, some were farmers, soldiers, clerks, lawyers or adventurers. Most were looking for a new chance, an opportunity to begin a new life for themselves and their families. The tale of the McCabe family is representative of many families of the time.

Thomas McCabe was born in Guernsey County, Ohio in 1810. He received his education in Ohio, and when he was eighteen decided to strike out on his own. He engaged in boating on the Ohio River, and afterward on the Wabash River in Indiana, where he worked for two years. At the age of twenty, in 1830, he moved to Illinois, married Maria Peacock, a native of Ohio, and farmed for more than twenty years.

The warm, yellow glow of gold dust lured thousands of eager prospectors to California between 1849 and 1855. In 1850, Thomas decided to move his family west and seek his fortune in the gold fields. On May 8, 1850, the McCabes loaded their wagon and joined a large company of others. Thomas was elected captain of the train and spent the next five months on the trail.

Time was of the essence to pioneers venturing west. They couldn't depart Missouri before the prairie grass was up, in early or mid-May, if they expected their livestock to survive, and the westernmost mountain barriers must be crossed before the snows began to render them impassable in mid-October. This left a mere five months to cover some two thousand miles in an era when fifteen miles was a good day of travel and a rain-swollen river could delay a wagon train for as much as two weeks.

The McCabe train arrived in Placerville, California, in late September of 1850, and Thomas immediately engaged in mining. In 1852 he loaded his wagon and moved his family back to Illinois for a few months, returning again in the spring of 1853.

On the second trip west, McCabe and his family settled at Snow Point, Nevada, and Thomas once again tried his luck, this time mining for six years. In 1859 he moved further west and settled in Solano County for three years; he then ventured to Napa and tried his hand at ranching for five years. Finally, at 57 years of age, he relocated to Point of Timber in 1867 and purchased 160 acres of railroad land that he planted in wheat.

Thomas and Maria McCabe had nine children, Joseph, Henry, George, Edward, Frank, Annie (married George Fellows), Jane (married Thomas Stuart), Mary (married John Fly) and Ella.

The McCabes' eldest son, Joseph, or J. P, as he was known, was 26 when the family moved to Point of Timber. He had received his common-school education in Illinois before moving west with his parents, and later attended three years at the Collegiate School of Napa City. In 1867 J. P. pre-empted* a quarter section of land in the Point of Timber district, on which he planted wheat. By 1878 he had enlarged his holdings to include a half section (320 acres) near the original farm, and a section (640 acres) on Marsh Creek Road.

Long before the town of Byron was founded in 1878, early settlers of the area bought supplies, caught the stage, and received their mail at Point of Timber. J. P. McCabe held the office of postmaster at Point of Timber for seven years, and was one of the most prosperous wheat farmers in the district. He was actively involved in all aspects of East Contra Costa's development for many years.

J. P. McCabe married Maggie Andrew, a native of Illinois, and had two children, Lester Leroy and Rosie Edith.

When the McCabe family moved to Point of Timber in 1867, their son Henry, at only 23 years of age pre-empted a quarter section (120 acres) of land adjoining his parents' farm. Like his father, Thomas, and his older brother, J. P., Henry grew wheat, but he became identified with ranching in the area and is credited with establishing one of the first dairies in East Contra Costa.

When Thomas McCabe died in 1888, Henry purchased his father's farm from his siblings and ranched until he retired in 1914. He disposed of fifteen acres on Marsh Creek Road to the Standard Oil Company, where they installed a pumping station named McCabe Station and he sold three hundred acres to Doctor Frederick of San Francisco.

Henry married Sarah Powell and they had four children, Henry Jr., Clara E., Thomas and Pearl.

In researching the history of East Contra Costa I repeatedly run across the McCabe name. Family members served on the cemetery board, Methodist church, as school trustees, and were members of the Point of Timber Grange. They were charter members of several local fraternal organizations, and heavily involved in every aspect of the evolution of this area. Families like the McCabes paved the way for the communities of Byron and Brentwood.

* Prior to the Homestead Act of 1862, Congress enacted a temporary measure in 1841 referred to as the Pre-emption Act to recognize the squatters' claims to land they settled. Those who had occupied portions of the public domain in advance of government surveys were permitted to buy their land at $1.25 an acre or, if they chose, to sell their pre-emption rights to the highest bidder, who in turn could purchase the land at the minimum rate. Until Next Time....

JOHN SAMUEL ARMSTRONG

Two years before the town of Byron was founded, my great-grandfather, John Samuel Armstrong, settled in the Byron foothills with his wife, Mary Ann. They came to join her parents, Joseph and Rebecca Conner, who in 1869 had settled on land where the Byron airport is now located. Both families originated in Ireland and traveled to Plymouth, Massachusetts in 1859. They settled in Plymouth for a number of years before continuing west to California.

I often wonder what John Samuel Armstrong's thoughts would be if he could experience East Contra Costa today. He would see the thriving towns of Byron, Brentwood, Oakley and Knightsen; the development of all the land, irrigation systems, businesses, churches, schools; a web of highways leading across the countryside; and airplanes landing where he first settled. There would be trains, trucks and planes delivering passengers and cargo from ocean to ocean, daily newspapers offering events of the last few hours, and live television reporting news worldwide, as it happens, thousands of miles from his home.

Byron, prior to the days of the railroad, was a sleepy, languid land isolated from larger settlements in the state. In 1878, completion of the railroad linking Byron with Stockton, Oakland and other cities brought boom and boomers to the village of Byron. During John's lifetime an unbelievable amount of change and progress took place. He witnessed the introduction of the railroad, truly a wonder of the times, and went from controlling a horse-drawn buggy to driving a horseless carriage.

John Samuel Armstrong and Mary Ann Conner Armstrong were both born in Ireland (1843 and 1854). They had ten children, seven sons and three daughters: Sarah (1870), Elizabeth (1871), Rebecca (1873), John (1878, my grandfather), Joseph (1881), Robert (1883), William (1886), Samuel (1889), Elwood (1890) and Wesley (1893).

John S. Armstrong and crew

John Armstrong was a "dry farmer," dependent on the whims of Mother Nature to determine the success or failure of his crops. Perhaps the greatest surprise John would see if he looked at East Contra Costa today would be the elaborate canal system winding its way through the dry fields, irrigating hundreds of acres, transforming the region into an agricultural Garden of Eden. I am sure that as he waged his personal war with Mother Nature he never imagined the possibility of controlling water application to the soil to intensify crop production. The independence from drought and variable seasons which farmers today accept as a way of life would have astonished him.

Farming truly was a family venture. The labor of everyone—father, mother and children—was necessary to ensure the family's survival. Their main crops were wheat, barley and hay. They also had horses, pigs, cows, sheep and chickens to raise and look after. The chores were many, the hours were long, and the work seemed never to end, but there were real benefits as well. Relationships within the Armstrong family were very close, each member of the family learning to rely on another. Younger children were taught to feed the chickens and gather eggs, while the older ones plowed and planted fields, pitched hay, hauled well-water, chopped wood and tended the animals.

John J. Armstrong tilling the soil

A progressive person for his time, John purchased the first Petaluma Hay Press in the Byron area during the 1870's. He used the hay press to tend his own fields as well as the fields of many of his neighbors. Considered a "Custom Bailer", John and the Petaluma could bail a six-wire large hay bale weighing between 250 to 280 pounds. The weight of the bail depended on the weather—the drier the weather, the heavier the bale, as dirt and rocks would be swept up and mixed into the baled hay. The Petaluma was powered by a four-horse sweep with a minimum of seven men needed to pull the press around in a circle. First the hay was cut by a horse-drawn mower. Next a horse-drawn sulky rake would rake the cut hay, then a bunch rake would be used to collect the hay into piles where it was allowed to cure for several weeks until it was ready to bail.

John's first farming experience was using a single-blade plow pulled by the family mule. During his lifetime he saw new farm equipment developed to meet the needs of early settlers. He worked on harvesters that would cut the wheat and dump it into wagons. There were many different types of combines, some drawn by thirty to forty mules, and some powered by steam or fueled by burning straw. The horse-drawn combine was a far cry from the mechanized marvels used today to plow, sow, weed, fertilize and harvest crops.

In 1886, the second school in Byron territory was established on a corner of land where the Byron Airport is today, thus establishing the Byron Hot Springs School District. John Samuel Armstrong donated the land and served as first president of the school board, and was very involved with the development of this facility. The Byron Hot Springs district was active until 1943, when it unified with the Byron School District.

John and Mary Ann recognized the importance of a good education for their children as well as the value of proper spiritual development. John was involved in the founding of the First Congregational Church of Byron in 1883 and served as the church deacon for many years. This handsome but simple church was located on Holway Street, next to were the first Byron School would later be built. The church had a large steeple and bell that could be seen from all over Byron. The first pastor, Reverend Tubs, played a huge role in early settlers' lives by conducting baptisms, funerals and weddings at the little church. This church played an important role in the lives of early settlers until 1929, when it was disbanded.

Although they lived several miles from town, the Armstrongs and Conners seldom missed a church service. Sunday morning the families would all load onto the buckboard wagon and head for Byron rain or shine. On rainy Sundays this was not an easy feat, traveling over mud-trenched roads. I am told my great-grandfather was a real taskmaster with strong feelings about where religion should fit in his family's lives, with no excuse to miss Sunday services!

On rare occasions John would surprise the family with a Sunday picnic on the Delta. After services were over the Armstrongs would travel on to Point of Timber Landing and board Captain Lent's schooner. The good captain loved to spin great tales for the children while floating downriver to a little island where the family would enjoy an afternoon in the sun, swimming, picnicking and reading from the "Good Book"! During the 1890's people's needs were simple; a trip to Disneyland, Great America or the zoo would have never been imagined.

The Odd Fellows Hall, built in 1883, has been the heart of Byron for more than a century. John and Mary Ann were active members of the Odd Fellows Lodge; they and their neighbors attended meetings, wedding receptions, dances and Christmas pageants at the hall long before it was converted into a tavern and restaurant. It would be interesting to see the Armstrongs' reaction to what the building looks like today.

The lives and needs of Byron's early settlers were very different from ours today. I wonder if, with a prophetic eye, my great-grandfather foresaw that the wonderful rolling hills and cozy valleys would give way to unparalleled cultivation and development. What would he think?
Until Next Time....

WILLS FAMILY
MABEL AND EDNA

In researching the history of the East Contra Costa region, I repeatedly find the same names involved in all aspects of the early development of the area—names like Bonnickson, Plumley, Morgan, Augusta, Taylor, Richardson, Armstrong and Wills are beginning to feel like old friends. These names are indelibly written in the chapters of our history.

Sylvester Monroe Wills was a wheat farmer at Point of Timber long before Byron or Brentwood were established. As a young man he crossed the plains in a covered wagon. He homesteaded 160 acres on Marsh Creek Road in the 1860's, planting his roots deep in the rich soil of this region. He built his home (presently owned by June Bunn) and raised his family on this ground. Mrs. Lucretta Roberts Wills, Sylvester's wife, taught school at the Iron House School in Oakley.

Although S. M. Wills was an interesting character and a key player in the early development of the Union Cemetery, Point of Timber Landing, Byron-Bethany Irrigation System and the schools, I am writing today about his daughters, Mabel and Edna.

I remember Mrs. Mabel Harley and Mrs. Edna Bowlin as genteel, soft-spoken older ladies that always had a fresh-baked cookie to offer a visiting child. When I was a young person, they were both well into their nineties, living in a little white house surrounded by a white picket fence on the highway. They had been born on their parents' farm in Byron in the 1800's and I loved hearing their stories of Byron on the other side of yesterday.

They were an extremely busy pair. Mrs. Harley and Mrs. Bowlin were active members of the Methodist church. They painted china as a hobby for many years, and in the 1950's sold the china to earn money for the church fund. In later years they painted china as gifts and even sold pieces to locals. I have several of their tea cups that I treasure.

I wish I had taken a recorder when I visited with Mrs. Harley and Mrs. Bowlin, or at least that I had a better memory. They told tales of trips to Stockton on Captain Lent's schooner; picnics at the old Stone House on Marsh Creek Road; the train wreck in 1902 and the Byron fire in 1923. They remembered traveling by wagon into the foothills with their father to cut down a Christmas tree; picking up the mail at Point of Timber long before the railroad came through East County; and seeing their father relocate the bodies that had been buried at the Point of Timber Cemetery (located on the corner of his farm) to the location where Union Cemetery is today. What a shame it is that in our youth we only listen with one ear.

The Wills Sisters
Mabel (Mrs. Harley),
Jean (Mrs. Haag)
Olive (Mrs. Walter Hoffman)
and Edna (Mrs. Bowlin)

Mrs. Harley and Mrs. Bowlin often told a story about the 1906 San Francisco earthquake. As they told it, the Wills family was playing host to a wedding at their ranch home and all was in readiness for the wedding to be held around noontime on that day. Early in the morning the family home rocked on its foundation, breaking many of the flower arrangements, spilling them out of buckets of water and overturning buckets of cream which had been put aside for the wedding banquet after the nuptial rites. The wedding did take place on schedule, with a few wet spots on the carpet, and the morning excitement was the main topic of conversation.

Mabel and Edna attended grammar school at Excelsior and later boarded with a family in Oakland so they could attend high school. East Contra Costa did not offer any secondary school prior to 1901.

Excelsior School - 1895. Sherman Harley - Principal

Mabel married Sherman Harley, who was principal of Excelsior in the late 1890's and Brentwood Elementary School in 1904, 1905 and 1906. Liberty Union High School had been established in 1901 and was housed in the back rooms of the Brentwood Grammar School, and Mr. Harley was actively involved in the early development of the high school curriculum. In 1907 he transferred to Black Diamond, which later became Pittsburg.

Edna married Ed Bowlin, a railroad man, and lived in Dunsmuir for many years before they retired and returned to Byron.

The Wills family and other early settlers wove the threads that created the tapestry of East Contra Costa County. Until Next Time....

JOHN SMITH NETHERTON
PIONEER

The great emigration into California began in 1841. Many of the pioneers saw California as a virtually inexhaustible repository for land. There was room to stretch for a better life, with rich earth free to anyone who was sufficiently daring and hard working to claim it. A stream of wagons was pouring out of Independence, Missouri, with early settlers heading west, walking beside the covered wagons which held all their worldly possessions. Most were American born and were seeking a new home, determined to find fertile land to plant their roots and raise their families.

Most of the pioneers were trying to escape economic hardship; they were not rich but neither were they without funds. It cost from $700 to $1500 to outfit a family for the trip. The immigrant wagons were sturdy farm vehicles pulled by oxen or mules (horses were unable to endure the long haul) each loaded with 1500 to 2000 pounds of supplies. The wagon was piled high with food, tools, furniture, clothes, and books. The early trails west were simply a pair of parallel wheel ruts traced by the wagons across the sod of the prairies, the rock and the rubble of the mountain passes and the sands of the western deserts. John Smith Netherton crossed the plains in 1848.

John was born in Liberty, Clay County, Missouri, on April 30, 1833. His mother died when he was four, leaving John and his seven siblings. John's father married a women that had nine children of her own. Now, that is a large family! John Smith Netherton came by his name because he was a direct decedent of the famous Captain John Smith, who made the history books as the lover of Pocahontas, the famous Indian Princess.

On May 5, 1848, John Netherton (age 15), in the company of his father and brother, started west in an ox drawn covered wagon. Four months later, on August 23, 1848, they arrived in Hangtown (Placerville), El Dorado County. John spent eight years mining on the American, Cosumnes, and Mokelumne Rivers, before moving to Moraga Valley, Contra Costa County, in 1856 and becoming a rancher.

John married Matilda J. Estes, daughter of Joel and Jane Estes, January 9, 1859, on the banks of Walnut Creek near Lafayette. A few months after their marriage the newlyweds drove a wagon east to see the land in the Marsh Grant. They thought it was so beautiful they decided to move there.

John and Matilda Netherton were one of the first families to settle in the Point of Timber area. They had nine children. Carrie Luella, William Price (became an attorney and banker), Frethias J. (an attorney and became the Arizona State Superintendent of Schools), Edward Wallace (owned and published the Brentwood Enterprise, predecessor of the Brentwood News, and was chief of the sales tax division for the IRS from 1917 to 1922), George E. (a farmer and a businessman in Martinez), Walter E. & Delbert W. (both were ranchers), Elmer E. (killed in an automobile accident), and Clara Belle (died at age 15). The Netherton children all attended the Excelsior School before leaving the area to attend college.

The Point of Timber region was well suited for growing hard winter wheat which was harvested in the summer and shipped great distances from Point of Timber Landing with little deterioration. By 1860, wheat had become the chief industry for Contra Costa County. John Netherton was one of the first early settlers to plant wheat. He planted 180 acres and depended on Mother Nature for his crop's development.

    John with his horses could be seen in the fall moving slowly around his fields, turning over row after row of dirt, filling the air with the smell of freshly plowed earth. He planted his seed from a wagon, using a hopper, which scattered the grain as the horses moved through the field. The seed laid in the ground all winter with the rains softening the hard soil. In the spring the wheat sprouted under the hot summer sun and the grains turned almost as hard a tiny pebbles.

    In May or June, when the golden grain was ready to harvest, a team of horses would push a "header" in front of them around the field of ripe wheat. The "header" cut the heads of grain, which fell into a wagon driven along the side. The grain was then taken to a "thresher" which separated the wheat from the straw and poured it into grain sacks. The sacks were sewn shut and stacked on wagons for transport. Mother Nature gave John Netherton and his neighbors much wealth. She also sometimes took it away. The life of these early settlers was filled with constant concern. Would there be enough rain? Or would there be so much that the fields would flood? Would the sun be so hot that it would scorch the crop? John Smith Netherton was 89 when he died in 1923, his wife Matilda, died in 1913 at the age of 75.

    Early settlers, like the Nethertons, underwent incredible hardships traveling to this region of California. Those that survived the journey west and managed to establish themselves in this new land definitely left footprints in the chapters of our past.

FRANK CABRAL
EARLY SHEEP RANCHER

East Contra Costa was noted for its cattle industry long before early pioneers from the East arrived to settle this part of California. By the late 1800's, sheep could be seen grazing on spring grass as sheepmen moved into the area, populating the Byron foothills with thousands of early lambs destined for market. Before the century's end, sheep rivaled cattle and mining as the West's leading industry. In 1914, more than ten thousand lambs, valued at $3.75 per head, were shipped from Byron to San Francisco markets.

Despite the economic importance and growth of sheep ranching during this era, the subject was largely ignored by the press. Reporters preferred to idealize the cowboy and the wild steers he tended. Sheepherding was not glamorous, and the animals were considered to be stupid and unpredictable, requiring tending both day and night. Sheepherders that ventured west were a sturdy breed from many nations. None were more successful than Frank Cabral, a young Portuguese man that settled in Contra Costa and definitely left his footprints in the chapters of East Contra Costa history.

Frank Nunez Cabral was born in Santa Maria, in the Azores Islands. In 1878, at the age of nine, Frank and his brother stowed away aboard a ship sailing to America, and shortly after their arrival set off for East Contra Costa County. They worked as sheepherders, saving their earnings in the hope that they could eventually lease property and raise their own flock of sheep. From this humble start, Frank worked his way up until he eventually owned or controlled between six and seven thousand acres.

On May 18, 1893, Frank married Mary Pernero-Rogers. The couple had four children: Stanley, Mae, Frank Jr. and Rose Cabral.

Frank Cabral tended his sheep in the Vasco Territory, where he and his family lived in a small cabin until his eldest son, Stanley, was old enough to attend school. Cabral then purchased a home in

Byron for his family. The new home, a wood-framed cabin, was secured to floor joists resting on girders that lay directly on the bare earth. The cabin itself was constructed of board and batten siding with a wooden shingle roof and measured 21 by 12 feet. With his family living comfortably in Byron, Frank often stayed at the "sheep camp" on the Vasco, supervising his crew. Frank would often utilize the Vasco Caves as pens for bonding lambs to a ewe, and onlookers could often see close to a thousand sheep grazing nearby. At his peak, it is said that Cabral ran as many as eight thousand sheep.

Although Frank Cabral did not have a formal education and could not read or write, he was a sharp businessman. He would use a knotted rope to count and it was said that by kicking a sack of wool he could tell how much it weighted as well as its value. Cabral improved his flocks steadily with experimental breeding, always trying to develop a larger strain of sheep and a higher quality of wool.

Late in the spring, after lambing season was over, sheep shearing gangs arrived in Byron on the train from Stockton. Cabral would meet them at the station and take them to the sheep camp, where they would remove the heavy winter coats of the adult sheep. Shearing was sweaty, cumbersome work; a good shearer could handle 100 sheep a day, an expert as many as 150. Once the sheep were shorn, they were dipped in a strong chemical bath to kill ticks, scab mites and other parasites, and then branded. The wool was placed into enormous sacks and tramped tight by a boy standing in the mouth of the sack. The sacks were then transported to the woolen mills near San Francisco.

There are many stories about Frank Cabral's impact on the community of Byron. He was a colorful character who is remembered fondly by old timers. In 1910 he purchased a 40-horsepower Garford Studebaker automobile equipped with electric lights, disappearing middle seats, and sliding side windows that could be opened to the fresh air. The auto held seven passengers, and Frank could be seen touring his neighbors around the area on Sunday afternoons. He was the talk of the town!

As Frank Cabral's sheep business flourished he expanded into other endeavors. In the 1920's and 1930's he raised sheep on the east side of Vasco Road, and cattle on the west; he also grew wheat and barley. In 1926 he purchased one of the first McCormick-Deering tractors for tilling his land. As it turned out, much of the Vasco was too hilly to use the mechanized equipment.

Fraternally, Cabral was affiliated with the I.D.E.S. and the U.P.E.C. Societies and was very active in both of these organizations for many years, often attending meetings in Stockton. He also took a personal interest in matters of development and growth in Byron.

During the depression, Cabral loaned money to many ranchers who had fallen on hard times. Unfortunately, many of these loans were never repaid, and eventually Cabral met with financial problems of his own.

Frank Nunez Cabral managed to rise from the life of a simple sheepherder to the owner of valuable sheep and cattle herds and considerable property. It was men like Cabral that truly conquered the West and built the foundation of this region of California that we all enjoy today.

Until Next Time....

GEORGE COPLE
PIONEER WHEAT FARMER

George Cople was born in Switzerland in 1837. He traveled to America at seventeen years of age, arriving first in New York and then traveling on to Ohio and Illinois, where he spent his first three years in the New World. Hearing about the wonders of California, he signed on with the military in 1857 to drive teams from Leavenworth, Kansas to Utah. The following year he traveled on to Benicia, California, where he found employment working primarily on local farms.

The next few years were spent exploring northern California, seeking a location where he could settle and raise a family. In 1867 George purchased 385 acres near Point of Timber, where he planted wheat.

George Cople married Margaret Eachus on April 17, 1870, in Merced County, and to this union there were three children: Charles (born February 1871); Mary Eva (date of birth unknown); and Ralph (born July 1882).

George Cople became a successful agriculturist and was noted early on for his outstanding garden that provided fresh produce for his family and often enough to share with neighbors. He planted not only shade trees, but also fig, cherry, plum, apple and orange trees around the home he had built for his family, and was well known throughout the region for his remarkable garden and orchards.

The Cople farm was fenced and divided into convenient fields. When the railroad came through this region of California in 1878 track was laid about two hundred yards from the Cople property, creating a perfect location for both home and business.

In the 1860's and '70's, wheat was the chief industry in Contra Costa County, with thousands of acres of grain planted in East Contra Costa. During the late summer and fall months, men could be seen moving slowly around Cople's fields, turning row after row of earth and filling the air with the smell of freshly plowed fields. George Cople and his neighbors planted seed in the fall from a horse-pulled wagon using a hopper that scattered the grain seed. The seed rested on the ground, with winter rains softening the hard soil; with the warmth of spring the wheat sprouted and grew to maturity.

In May or June, when the golden grain was ready to harvest, George would hook up his team of horses and prepare to harvest his crop. The mature grain was placed in sacks, loaded on wagons and transferred to Point of Timber Landing, where it was then transported by schooner to Port Costa. From the big wharves at Port Costa, the grain was transferred onto ocean-going steamers headed for destinations all over the world. At one time Point of Timber was the liveliest shipping point between Stockton and San Francisco.

According to an article I found in the *Contra Costa Gazette* dated July 28, 1883, there were 1,500 acres at Point of Timber planted in grain. Cople's 200-acre farm produced 840 pounds of grain per acre.

George Cople was a public-spirited individual and helped lay the foundation for East County. His name is found in early church, school and organization records, and he was also active in the Odd Fellows and the Grange lodges. When Cople arrived in this region of California, much of the area was vast cattle range. He and other hardy settlers did all in their power to create a law-abiding community, as well as accumulate fortunes for themselves.

The Cople children received their formal education at the Excelsior School, with Charles Cople, George's oldest son, attending a business course at the San Jose Business College. After completing his studies Charles returned to his father's farm, where he became engrossed in agricultural and horticultural pursuits.

For many years Charles had listened to his father speak of his annual concerns regarding water supply. Early farmers were always at the mercy of Mother Nature for the much-needed water for their crops. The question was always the same: would there be enough rain, or so much rain that the fields would flood?

In 1909, George and Charles Cople decided to try an agricultural experiment that would control the irrigation for fifteen acres of alfalfa they would plant on a high spot of their farm. Water was pumped from Kellogg Creek to their crop. They knew that if they could bring water to this location economically it would open huge areas to farming and hundreds of acres of alfalfa could be planted.

The experiments proved successful and during the first year four cuttings of alfalfa were harvested. Although his neighbors held little faith in Cople's original experiment, they soon decided to follow suit and placed their own pumps in the creek, which resulted in Kellogg Creek being almost pumped dry. It didn't take long for farmers in the area to organize an irrigation system and district, with Kellogg Creek as the nucleus.

Wedding of Charles Cople to Elsie Johnson

Charles Cople was instrumental in the organization of the Byron-Bethany Irrigation Company and served on the first board of directors. With the arrival of irrigation, farmers were no longer at Mother Nature's mercy. The ability to transport water economically to higher land brought about the cultivation of fruit, nuts and row crops.

The tale of the Cople family is representative of many of the families of the time. They came to East Contra Costa, planted their roots, sweated and prospered, leaving footprints in the chapters of our past. Until Next Time....

BYRON GRIEVES THE LOSS OF AN "OLD TIMER"
LEO THOMAS

It was a sad day in Byron last month when friends and relatives of Leo Joseph Thomas learned of his death after a long illness (January 1994). Leo, the oldest surviving member of one of Byron's pioneer families, died at the age of 88 years. The eldest son of Anthony and Louise Thomas, Leo was delivered in Byron in 1905 by Doctor J. Hammond at his parent's home.

Leo's father, Anthony Thomas, was a native of Portugal and traveled to California during the late 1880s. He was a well-respected resident of Byron primarily involved in the sheep raising business. When Anthony Thomas first settled in the Byron Region he had operated a sheep camp with his cousin Stanley Cabral in the Brushy Peak area. Sheep were often put to pasture following the harvest of the great grain crops when leftover stubble would furnish rich and healthy food for the animals. In 1912 there were from 15,000 to 20,000 sheep in the Byron Territory with ewes valued at about $5 per head on average and bucks valued according to pedigree and stock quality. With their extensive sheep herds Thomas and Cabral shipped lambs and wool to market in San Francisco.

Anthony definitely left his footprints in Byron's history. His name can be found throughout old editions of the famous *Byron Times* with articles of his involvement in the Byron Volunteer Fire Department and several fraternal organizations. Around 1915 he built the Byron Skating Rink (in partnership with Tom Hosie) and also had a home on Camino Diablo and a ranch/dairy on Bixler Road. The Thomases were actively involved in the establishment of Saint Anne's Church located on Camino Diablo in June 1917. Anthony and Louise Thomas had six sons, including two sets of twins. All were born and raised in Byron. The sons attended one-room schoolhouses at the Byron and Excelsior School Districts.

Leo Thomas lived in the same house where he was born all of his life—though he would make it very clear he had spent 8 years living on the Thomas ranch on Bixler Road.

Leo and Veronica "Vera" Duarte Thomas were married in 1929 sixty-three years ago when Byron was in its heyday. When Leo and Vera set up housekeeping on the Camino Diablo property, Byron had a Baker's drug Store, ice cream parlor, *The Byron Times*, a railroad station with four trains daily, 3 barbershops, 2 beauty shops, a Blacksmith, 2 general stores, a butcher shop, 3 saloons as well as numerous other businesses. As a young couple, Leo and Vera would spend weekends enjoying the pleasures of The Byron Hot Springs Resort.

For more than 35 years Leo was an auto mechanic originally working for J.T. Lucas in his garage on the Main Street of Byron. Later Leo established (Borden Junction) Garage which he operated for many years before relocating the business next to his home on Camino Diablo.

Although Leo's primary profession was as a mechanic he also had a dairy, a chicken business, honeybee business, owned sheep and cattle, and was active in the community. Leo was a 35-year volunteer fireman, a member of the Fireman's Association Club of East County, Luso-American Fraternal Federation 51 of Byron, Sociedad da Irmandade do Divino Espirito Santo, or Society of the Divine Holy Spirit ("I.D.E.S.") Lodge #96 of Byron, the Fraternal Order of the Eagles, Aerie Lodge 785 of Antioch as well as a member of St. Anne's Church.

Leo is survived by his wife Vera, his son Leo Thomas Jr., his brother Tony Thomas of Marysville, and two grandchildren. Leo is definitely well missed. He has left footprints on many hearts in the Byron area.

CASSIE HARPER ARMSTRONG

One day last week I was feeling exceptionally frustrated because there just weren't enough hours in the day to do all the things that needed to be done. The laundry was piled high, and there just didn't seem to be enough time to load the automatic washer; the belt on the vacuum was broken and I hadn't stopped to pick up a new one; and once again I had been remiss in taking something out of the freezer for dinner. Then, I stopped for a moment and reflected on what my grandmother, Cassie Harper Armstrong, would have thought of my dilemma, and I could almost hear her nervous laugh and see the amusement in her sparkling eyes.

Cassie and Rachael Harper - 1904

I was named after my father's mother, Catherine Rebecca Harper Armstrong, and have always felt a special bond with her. I've often been told that I resemble her and carry many of her characteristics.

Cassie was born in Castlederg, County Tyrone, Ireland, on March 25, 1887. One of eleven children born to Catherine and Hugh Harper, she loved school and upon graduation from the eighth grade planned to attend a finishing school and become a teacher. Before starting her formal training as a teacher she was presented with an opportunity to come to America. Her older sister, Rachael Harper, had been offered a job in California as a nanny and housekeeper for an Irish family that had moved to the New World several years earlier. Cassie, at sixteen, was not quite sure she was ready to leave home, but her parents did not wish to let Rachael travel abroad alone. So the Harper girls left Ireland in 1903 with a few personal belongings and hearts filled with the hopes and dreams of an opportunity to mold their own destinies in a new land.

Boarding a ship destined for New York, they spent the next eleven days bouncing over the waves of the Atlantic Ocean. I remember my grandmother telling great stories about her voyage. She told of seeing icebergs from the deck of the ship and of being deathly ill from seasickness. In New York the girls boarded a train heading west, traveling overland for eight days, and finally arrived in San Francisco. Cassie often reflected on how amazed she and her sister were by the vastness of this new land, having never traveled beyond the boundaries of County Tyrone. They now passed cities, villages, farmland, plains and endless miles of desert, crossed raging rivers and rugged mountain ranges, all the while observing wildlife that they never new existed grazing alongside the rails .

The early years in California were filled with great adventure for two daring young Irish girls. Cassie obtained employment with the telephone company and Rachael was retained as a housekeeper. I can remember my grandmother telling stories of living in San Francisco, and later Berkeley, as a single woman.

In 1908, Cassie met and married John James Armstrong, a rancher from Byron. They exchanged vows on the Armstrong ranch, a location where John's parents, John Samuel and Mary Ann Armstrong, had settled in the 1870's. The newlyweds established their first, and only, home on a ranch bordering his parents' property. By 1915, four of John's brothers had also acquired properties near the original homestead. These ranches were all located along Armstrong Road, where the Byron Airport is located today.

Cassie and John had six children. Tom, born 1910, married Eleanor Iverson; Lausten, born 1911, married Helen Russell; Hugh, born 1914, married Loretta Smith; my father, Oliver, born 1916, married Barbara Fortson; Catherine, born 1918, died as an infant; and Josephine, born 1925, married Vern Allen.

In the early 1900's the position of housewife and mother was no small task. Cassie not only had her "women's work" to do, but also cows to milk and chickens to feed, along with many other outside chores. As her children grew many of these tasks fell to them, but her role in the family still included mother, wife, nurse, cook, doctor, comforter, teacher and farm laborer.

Cassie cooked on a wood stove until 1946 (38 years), when the ranchhouse was wired with electricity. Her days started early and ended late. She would awaken early to heat up the kitchen with the wood stove long before anyone else in the house stirred. Eight loaves of bread were baked twice a week, and during harvest time she would prepare meals for twenty to thirty hungry men. She spent long hours over her wood stove cooking and canning without plumbing or electricity. Without the advantage of refrigeration, when John butchered a hog or lamb most of the meat would have to be cured, cooked or canned. The remainder that was not eaten immediately would be hung in the well, the coolest place on the ranch.

Laundry day brought out the washtub and scrub board, and in bad weather lines were strung over the cook stove to dry the family's clothing. In 1940, Cassie was surprised with a gas-powered washing machine, and the washday duties were moved out of the kitchen into a new washhouse out back. (I have fond memories of playing in the washhouse as a kid.)

Farming in the early 1900's was truly a family venture, demanding the participation of the entire family and occasionally a hired hand. The Armstrongs' main crops were wheat, barley and oats and there were also horses, cows, pigs, sheep, turkeys, geese and chickens to raise. The chores were many and the hours were long.

The social life of a farmer, his wife and children was limited at best. Most of the Armstrongs' neighbors were relatives and they routinely gathered for potluck dinners or an outing at Brushy Peak. Cassie frequented functions at the Byron Hot Springs School, church teas, an occasional whist party, lodge meetings at the Odd Fellows Hall in Byron, and services at Byron's Congregational church. Generally, once a year John would surprise Cassie with a train trip to San Francisco for a visit with family and friends.

Cassie and John would trek into town twice a month to purchase supplies. These trips were usually scheduled to include necessary family business (voting, doctor's visits, etc.). Their principal stop was usually Plumley's Store, Byron's answer to one-stop shopping. Cassie could find clothing, shoes, fabric and notions, a complete line of groceries, hardware, pots and pans, crockery and much, much more there.

In the early years, the Armstrongs traveled the dusty dirt roads over the hills into town in their cart or spring wagon, but in 1918 they purchased a Studebaker surrey with fringe on top. Cassie was thrilled to have such stylish transportation. After the surrey had served the Armstrongs well for years, it began to show its wear, and one day Cassie decided to spruce it up a little. She used black shoe polish to renew the leather. The polish had an oil base, and halfway to church on Sunday morning the surrey looked like a big dirt clod. It wasn't until the late 1920's that John bought an automobile. His sons drove, but he never felt a need to learn to drive, nor did Cassie.

My grandmother's life offered many hardships by today's standards, but also much joy and laughter. She lived to be 84 years young. Never losing her great wit or Irish brogue, she watched her children grow to be productive citizens, and definitely left footprints in the hearts of all that knew her.

Until Next Time….

NICK PAPADAKOS

Byron Volunteer Fire Department, Brentwood News, *September 1957, Collection of East Contra Costa Historical Society (c/o Carol Jensen and Robert Ruddick, Dec. 18, 2020) Left to Right: Oliver Armstrong, Henry Ricioli, Mike Granados, Sam Howard (kneeling, Nick Papadakos, Gus French, Fire Commissioner (standing on truck), Stanley Pereira, Assistant Chief (in cab), Elmer Armstrong (on stretcher), Everett Hammond (kneeling), James Hannum (standing)*

How nice it is be able to recognize someone in the community who has been an active part of Byron all his life. So often people like Nick Papadakos are never aware of the fact that their neighbors appreciate the energy and effort they have put forth to make our community a better place to live.

Nick resides on Byron Highway in the home his parents, Antonia and Sam Papadakos, purchased in 1912. He attended the Byron School, located next to the Congregational Church on Holway Street and later attended Liberty High School. He has great memories of growing up in Byron when Main Street was filled with businesses; the Southern Pacific tracks were traveled constantly (trains stopping in Byron four times a day); and you seldom saw a stranger in town. He has resided in the same location, except for the time he spent in Korea in the early 1950s with Uncle Sam.

In 1947, Nick graduated from high school and by 1950 he decided that it was important that he put his energy into the community. He joined the Byron Volunteer Fire Department. When Nick first joined the department they had two engines: a 1937 Jimmy and a 1947 Dodge. The Fire Station was located on Main Street in the building that houses the Byron Bethany Irrigation District today. In the 1950s, the department responded primarily to grass fires, an occasional structure fire and, on rare occasions, an automobile accident. Today, when the fire department responds to a call it is primarily a medical call, Next, it responds to automobile accidents. Occasionally, it puts out a grass fire. On rare occasions it responds to a structure fire.

The present Fire Station was built in 1956 on land donated by Josephine and Louis Souza. Nick and the other volunteers were involved in developing the grounds and improvements to the facility.

Nick became Assistant Chief of the Byron Fire Department in 1959 and was promoted to Chief in 1968. During his tenure as Chief, Nick witnessed an unbelievable amount of change to the town of Byron and the Fire Department. The department was well respected by Byron's citizens. It was reassuring to know the volunteer firefighters were there in a time of crisis.

While Nick was with the department there were two train derailments in 1981 and 1989, numerous large grass fires, the burning of Liberty Union High School, and the introduction of medical calls for the fire department. The Byron department became the second fire station in the county to purchase a semi-automatic defibrillator. Nick served a total of 40 years and 6 months in the Byron Fire Dept.

In 1956 Nick went to work for DuPont Chemical as a Control Room Operator. He retired in 1981 and devoted more time to the Fire Department.

Nick was involved with not only the growth of the Fire Department but was also a key player in other aspects of the Byron community. He served on the Byron Chamber of Commerce Board of Directors for, was active in the Byron Native Sons, and is presently serving his community as a member of the Byron MAC. He has been actively involved politically for many years. Nick fights for what he believes in and always has Byron's best interest at heart.

ELLEN HOSIE LADD

In collecting information for my columns I haunt libraries, old newspapers, miscellaneous public records, and find data where I can, but the most fun is chatting with old timers. Each interview is special. In all the interviews that I have done none is more touching than the time I spent with Ellen Hosie Ladd.

Ellen was born in her parents home on May 24, 1897 in Byron. She left this life 98 years later on July 25, 1995, having left footprints on many hearts and definitely a mark on the world she lived in. I was amazed at Ellen's memory. She described Doctor Hammond, Tobe LeGrande, and Renny Plumley as if she had seen them the day before. She told stories of her school days and life in Byron when it was little more than a hamlet.

Her parents were Thomas and Thirza Hosie. Thomas was the son of James Hosie, who brought Tom to California from Scotland in 1870. Thirza was the daughter of Ellen and George Washington Tully Carter. George Washington Tully Carter came to California from New York via wagon train in 1852.

The Hosies and the Carters both settled in Byron in 1876. Thirza Carter and Tom Hosie both attended the Excelsior School. This school building still stands on the corner of Highway 4 and Marsh Creek Road. They were married in September 1895.

Tom Hosie drove the "butcher wagon" for Mr. Sloan's Butcher Shop which was located on Main Street in Byron. Tom would load the wagon with fresh meat several times a week and travel from farm to farm and sell his pork or beef. Mr. Sloan gave Tom the Butcher Shop a few years after Tom and Thirza were married.

Tom Hosie was an industrious man. He was involved in several businesses. He drove stage for the Byron Hot Springs for several years. In 1906 he built and operated a skating rink that was located on Hosie Lane. Many of the old-timers have great memories of this rink. The floor was made of 3/4" maple hardwood.

In 1908 Tom went to work for Standard Oil. His first position with the company was in the pipeline department as a line walker. He would walk from Byron to Banta and check the pipeline for leaks. He later became a fireman in the Standard Pumping Station that was located on Marsh Creek Road, near the railroad. The Hosie family lived in the company housing at the pumping station. The house is still standing.

George Washington Tully Carter, Ellen's grandfather, was an assemblyman in the California State Legislature from 1880 to 1884. He published the "Gyascuitus", a humorous sheet, in Benica in the 1860's, and he wrote for several newspapers. He was an adventurer and has a wonderful history.

While living in the Byron area, he was a keyplayer in the community. Carter was instrumental in establishing Union Cemetery. The first cemetery in the Byron area was located on Will's property (corner of Marsh Creek Road and Highway 4) across from the Excelsior School. Carter and several other men relocated six bodies from the Wills site to property donated by Colburn Preston. This is the site where Union Cemetery is located today.

Carter served on the Excelsior School Board, was active in the Grange and the Point of Timber Farmers Protective Club, and was a charter member of the AOUW Lodge. Very little happened in the Byron region between 1876 and 1885 that Carter was not involved in. He operated threshing machines in the summertime all up and down the San Joaquin Valley. He moved to the Fresno area around 1885.

When I interviewed Ellen she talked about Byron in the early 1900's. Her description made a chapter of Byron's history come alive for me. There were three warehouses for hay and grain. The

Southern Pacific Depot, with living quarters up stairs for the railroad agent, was located on Main Street directly across the street from the Byron Hotel, operated by Major and Mrs. Grey. The hotel was located next to where the Byron Post Office is today. There was a barbershop run by Constable Tobe LeGrand; three saloons; Holway, Clas Peers, and Frerichs; two blacksmith shops, Armstrong's and Franks; two general stores, Plumley's and Grunauer (the Post Office was located in Grunauer's Store) and a restaurant run by Tobe LeGrand and Sadie Plummer. There was even a 4 x 6 jail located at the end of Main Street where a trucking company is today.

Byron offered its residents a weekly newspaper, "The Byron Times", published by Harry Hammond; the Bank of Byron; several churches, the Congregational, Methodist and Seventh Day Adventist; a local athletic club; the Byron Concert Band; a skating rink; a Chinese laundry; an ice cream parlor; a butcher shop; a bakery; and more. Byron had a volunteer Fire Department and several Fraternal organizations that met at the Odd Fellows Hall. There was a doctor in town, Doctor James Hammond, that cared for Byron residents and the ranchers in the area. Most births were assisted by Mrs. Silvas, the towns mid-wife. Judge Krumland's office was located in the back of Plumley's Store.

Ellen was living in Byron when the first electric lights and the telephone came to town, the Byron Bethany Irrigation System was installed, the automobile replaced the horse drawn carriage, and the Byron Hot Springs was in its heyday. She recalled the train stopping in town several times a day and remembered well the townspeople. Ellen shared great stories about local politicians, businessmen and neighbors.

Ellen's memories offered me an opportunity to peer through a window in time into Byron on the other side of yesterday. Each story she told was unique but none more touching than the story of her first trip out of Byron. She told of going to the top of Mount Diablo with her Sunday School class. She had traveled into the foothills near town to cut a Christmas tree, but it was a dream come true to venture to the top of the mountain that she had viewed on the distant horizon.

Reverend and Mrs. Thomas Green loaded six young people into their chevrolet and headed down the dirt road that hugged the mountain side. They went back and forth and round and round, with short hair-pin curves every few hundred feet. When they finally arrived at the top of the mountain they looked down at the breathtaking view below. Ellen could pivot around and see five counties. As far as she could see, the world she knew was spread out beneath her. San Francisco, Oakland, the Bay, Stockton, and the valley between the mountain ranges. She could see Byron, which compared to the overall view seemed but a grain of sand.

Ellen sat on top of a rock and the wind blew cold as she held her coat tightly around her. She peered out at the cities and towns in the valley with rivers appearing as white ribbons and roads as black ribbons, and the snow capped Sierras in the distance. "There I was, just one small speck of humanity looking down on it all, and I wondered, and I still wonder if God looks down on all his great world as I looked down from the top of Mount Diablo?"

There are still remnants of the Byron that Ellen described. The Odd Fellows Hall (today, a restaurant), Frerich's Saloon (today, Byron Station), Claus Peers Saloon(today, Wild Idol),and the Methodist Church, to name a few.

Parts of Ellen's story were taken from her autobiography, which she wrote in 1981.

Ellen Hosie Ladd, and the others of her generation will surely be missed. I consider it an honor to have had the opportunity to spend time with this caring, thoughtful lady. The early settlers of the area produced a bumper crop of wondrous stories, and I thank Ellen for sharing many of these with me. It makes me sad to see the footprints of the pioneers disappear under the concrete of progress. Until Next Time....

BYRON HOLIDAY YARD, A FAMILY EVENT
MARGUERITE HEISOR DeBORBA

In Byron there is a yard that has become noted for its wonderful holiday displays. Marguerite DeBorba lives on Byron Highway, next to the Byron Methodist Church, and has been decorating her yard for almost forty years. On Halloween, Christmas, and Easter, Mrs. DeBorba's yard comes alive with the spirit of the season.

Mrs. DeBorba started setting up her display many years ago when her late husband, Joe DeBorba, suggested that she make a manger scene in their front yard because she already had a pet lamb and family dog to go with it. Each year since then, the display has grown.

People come from all over the county to admire her front yard, which is loaded with lights, ghosts, pumpkins, and witches in October, and nativity scenes or Easter bunnies during other holidays. Mrs. DeBorba said young couples that bring their children today tell her that they remember their own parents bringing them when they were kids. She said the children seem to respect the displays. There has never been any vandalism. She said that she does occasionally find a little gift on her steps or a card from a child thanking her for her efforts.

Family and friends have helped build many of the displays and collect the decorations. Each year her collection just seems to grow. She remembers being able to store her holiday treasures in a few boxes. Now she has a storage van on the ranch just for her huge collection of decorations. When asked why she does it, her reply was, "I love the kids. I do it or them. I just enjoy seeing the looks on their faces!"

For many years Mrs. DeBorba did most of the display herself, but today it is a family affair. Her 4 children, 16 grandchildren, and 23 great grandchildren have become involved in setting up the display, a project taking four to five days.

Marguerite DeBorba has lived in Byron all her life. In fact her grandfather, John George Adam Heiser, came to Byron from Germany in the 1880s and was a shoemaker in town. Her father was born in Byron in 1882 and farmed the Byron foothills. Marguerite and her father both attended Byron Hot Springs School.

Marguerite was born on the family farm near the Byron Hot Springs. She has great memories of Byron when it was in its heyday. When the trains stopped in town several times a day, the streets were filled with businesses like the Bank of Byron, the *Byron Times* newspaper office, and two active merchantiles. The neighbors all knew each other and where quick to help in a time of need.

BETHANY

Once upon a time there was a thriving little community named Bethany in the southwest corner of San Joaquin County, between Byron and Tracy.

As early as the 1850's, the area was known as Burns' Landing (named for Maurice Byrnes). Later it was renamed Mohr's Landing in honor of John Mohr, a German immigrant. In 1856, Edward Carrell and John O'Brian discovered coal near Tracy, in the Corral Hollow region, and needed a shipping point on the San Joaquin River for their diggings. A wagon route was developed between the mines owned by the Pacific Coal Mining Company and the landing, which was owned by John Mohr. Between 1856 and 1861, eighteen hundred tons of coal were shipped from Mohr's Landing to San Francisco.

Mohr's Landing became the supply center for early settlers; wheat farmers shipped grain, the Pacific Coal Mining Company shipped coal, and supplies were delivered from Stockton and San Francisco. All went well until the "Great Flood of 1862," when Mohr lost everything. The rains began on January 4, 1862 and did not let up until January 11; a total of 49 inches of rain fell in one week.

After the flood, Mohr decided to relocate to higher ground and in the late 1860's, he built a hotel to accommodate travelers through the area. Mohr sold general merchandise, food and drink, and he also put up and fed travelers passing through the region. In 1878, the San Pablo & Tulare Railroad decided to build a route from Martinez to Banta, and Mohr donated the right-of-way through his land, provided that the railroad agreed to build a station near his hotel. The town was renamed Bethany, probably from the biblical locality in Palestine.

The San Pablo & Tulare Railroad Company spent several years installing tracks, with their engineering corps, survey crews and laborers pitching their tents along the route. The coming of the railroad paved the way for progress and changed the early settlers' way of life, as well as the pace of their lives.

The first train through Bethany was on September 18, 1878, and the community immediately started to grow. The area drew wheat farmers, dairymen and early settlers interested in reclaiming the rich farmland along the river. By 1880, Bethany was a booming little hamlet offering residents a general mercantile owned by James Hutchins, a post office, a liquor store, a blacksmith, a wagon maker and a saloon/hotel known as Bethany House. John Mohr owned and operated the smithy and the hotel.

The railroad built facilities to house their station manager and section crew in Bethany during the early 1880s. Soon other businesses moved to town: a second blacksmith, a butcher shop, a church, a grain warehouse, a dance hall and shoemaker.

Claus Schlictman and his family moved to Bethany in 1893, purchasing the general store from James Hutchins and operating it until 1943. Schlictman was a key player in the town for half a century. He was the community's unofficial mayor, the storekeeper, postmaster, and "banker" for the Chinese employed to work on the levees and in the fields. They would bring their wages to him to be sent via money order to China.

The well water in town was too alkaline to drink, so the railroad regularly brought in a tanker of water that was emptied into a cistern for the use of everybody in town. Townsmen also collected rainwater for drinking. Prior to 1917, the residents of the Bethany area practiced dry farming, depending on Mother Nature to water their crops. In 1914 landowners from the Byron and Bethany districts met at a rousing public meeting and voted to move ahead with the installation of an irrigation system. A great project was begun. The Byron-Bethany Irrigation Company was formed, and officers were elected. After extensive investigation it was decided that ten thousand acres would be subject to irrigation. The water would be diverted through a dredged channel from Italian Slough. The first pumping station would be established on Bruns Hill with two canals, one furnishing water to the Byron lands and the other providing irrigation to the Bethany properties. In 1917 the first water flowed through some of the newly constructed canals.

John W. Lund's Holt Steam Harvester

Bethany established its importance over several decades as a shipping point for hay, grain, and sugar beets, but by the late 1920s businesses had closed and most residents had relocated. The towns of Byron and Tracy were booming and offered schools, libraries, banks, newspapers, fraternal organizations and more. In 1929 the only business listed in Bethany was Claus Schlictman's General Mercantile. The Bethany Post Office closed on January 31, 1940. Today nothing remains of the town of Bethany but an occasional mention of this little village in the chapters of our past.

Until Next Time….

MARSH CREEK SPRINGS PARK

If you lived in East Contra Costa in the 1920's, 30's, 40's and 50's, you probably spent time at the Marsh Creek Springs Park. I have many fond memories of school picnics, birthday parties, and family gatherings at the park.

Gerould L. Gill purchased 90 acres of swampy undesirable land on Marsh Creek Road in 1927. It is located on the eastern slope of Mount Diablo six miles from Clayton and twelve miles from Byron. Gill developed the site into one of the most popular recreational parks in the Bay Area. By 1940 his holding had increased to 210 acres.

Gerould Gill was a native Californian, born in San Joaquin County, raised on a ranch, and educated in Oakland. He spent his early years doing steel work, shipbuilding, drapery, and interior decorating. When he first moved to Contra Costa County and told people he was going to build a recreational resort that would attract thousands of tourists from far and wide, many laughed at him. But as he began to develop his property, Contra Costans sat up and took notice.

Gill personally supervised the development of his dream park. The facility offered visitors a variety of entertainment. There were two swimming pools and a wading pool for children, numerous cabins, picnic areas, four baseball diamonds, a large dance pavilion, several play grounds, snack bars, along with wonderful hiking trails, and a miniature steam railroad. Gill built a stable with more than fifty saddle horses to serve riding enthusiasts. Bridle paths laced the grounds. Guests could spend the day or rent a cabin.

*Scene of Marsh Creek Springs
from a special Development Edition of the Byron Times*

Marsh Creek Springs offered guests an extraordinary opportunity to enjoy the natural wonders of the area. My husband, Bill, and his family spent at least one week each summer camping on the grounds in the early 1950's. He tells great stories of catching frogs in the creek, climbing on wonderful rock formations, picking wildflowers, climbing the wild oak trees, and hiking through the poison oak. He remembers dancing at the pavilion and meeting other young people from all over the bay area.

Picnic at Marsh Creek, July 1888

When I was in elementary school one of the highlights of the year was the Annual Byron School Picnic. This event was held at the end of the school term at the Marsh Creek Springs Park. Students kindergarten through eighth grade and their families would spend one day in late May doing foot-races, riding horses, swimming, playing baseball, having sack races, and celebrating the coming of summer vacation. My memories of those wonderful picnics where the whole community was involved are definitely a part of my childhood that I hold dear.

At one time the grounds entertained 5000 people arriving in 1200 cars on a single weekend. In 1938 the park had an attendance of more than 138,000 guests.

In 1957 a storm hit the area and sent a twelve foot torrent of water down Marsh Creek destroying the park. The Gill family rebuilt the facility but it was destroyed by another flood in 1962. John and Eloise McHugh purchased Marsh Creek Springs Park in 1964.

Marsh Creek Springs Park was the dream of Gerould L. Gill which left memories in the hearts of several generations of young people from our area. Until Next Time....

REFLECTING ON THE HOT SPRINGS

As you drive through Byron today, it is difficult to imagine the bustling community that existed a hundred years ago, nor can we look at our local history without noting the impact the once famous Byron Hot Springs had on the area in those early years.

Geologically, the Byron area is a floodplain characterized by its alkaline soil. The area is of volcanic origin overlaid by layers of recent sediment. More than fifty hot springs bubbling from subterranean passages near Byron testify to this volcanic origin.

Artifacts of the Yokuts and Miwok Indians have been found in some of the springs, leading to the conjecture that Indians associated the springs with the supernatural and probably offered these items as gifts or sacrifices to the springs. A Spanish explorer, Captain Pedro Fages (1772), is given credit for the first written history of the area and it is believed the Indian tribes used the hot springs into the 1800's.

Records indicate that the first Anglo-American to make use of the springs for therapy was an unknown traveler who, while passing through the area in the dead of winter, was surprised to find hot water bubbling up through the frozen ground. Having heard stories of marvelous cures wrought by mud baths, he proceeded to enlarge the opening of one of the springs and bathe, and then continued on his way greatly invigorated.

Through this original traveler word spread and others learned of the marvelous waters. Before long many traveled to the springs in search of relief from rheumatism and other ailments. Eventually a crude bathhouse was erected and several of the springs were dug out and lined with rocks to serve as tubs for the mud baths.

Orange Risdon Jr., founder of Risdon and Coffey Ironworks of San Francisco, became interested in the springs in 1863 as a possible commercial source of salt. Risdon filed on 160 acres of land around the springs and deposited a warrant made out to Estaban Mansanares (private in the New Mexican Volunteers, War with Mexico) with the U. S. General Land Office. He received a patent on the land signed by President Andrew Jackson on October 2, 1865. A salt evaporating plant was erected on the site, but this venture was unsuccessful and Risdon decided to develop the springs as a health resort.

Lewis Mead, Orange Risdon's nephew, became involved in the resort. He built a bathhouse over the sulfur spring which soon became very popular. Four short years later, in 1872, the resort had gained so much popularity that a ten-room house was built to accommodate visitors.

In 1878, the railroad was completed through Byron and the resort became easily accessible to visitors from all over California. With the new depot in Byron, the Hot Springs established a stage line from town to the resort. Some years later the Byron Hot Springs was to have its own depot.

In 1885, after the death of Risdon, Mead became owner of the resort and later leased it to Amanda Gallagher who is credited with building bathhouses over several of the springs and instigating many other improvements to the site.

Between 1885 and 1887, Mead built the Mead home (this building is still standing and in fairly good repair); installed ten to twelve feet of good earth over the salt basin; and erected countless other buildings. By the end of 1887, he had developed a beautiful semitropical garden with evergreen trees, palms and flowers. The grounds were beautifully landscaped with walks lit at night by gas lamps. Mead had succeeded in creating an oasis in the midst of an alkaline desert.

The first hotel, built in 1889 for $50,000, was a three-story wood building with a large verandah extending along its full length, with several cottages placed at locations convenient to the hotel for the accommodation of families or large parties. The original hotel, several cottages, laundry, gas plant and ice plant were destroyed by fire on July 25, 1901.

The second hotel was constructed during 1901 and 1902 at a cost of $150,000. This building was a three-story stucco structure facing east with broad verandahs that extended along the front and two sides of the building, offering guests a panoramic view of the San Joaquin Valley. The Byron Hot Springs helped weave the rich fabric of Byron's history.

Until Next Time….

A MECCA FOR TOURISTS FROM EVERY PART OF CALIFORNIA

Nestled in the foothills two miles south of Byron in quiet solitude, the Byron Hot Springs spa still shows signs of its former opulence, although time has erased most of the evidence of this once world-famous resort.

The springs were famous for their mineral waters. Originally, California Indians used the springs and considered them a sacred place. Accustomed as the Indians were to sweat houses, these ready-made hot mud and hot water baths were greatly appreciated; they bathed in the hot peat holes and drank from the hot saline and sulfur springs for health reasons. Not long after the arrival of white men in California, trappers and gold seekers discovered the refreshing spring baths.

In 1861, R. O. Risdon, founder of the Risdon Ironworks of San Francisco, became interested in the location. Risdon's original interest was to explore the salt deposits in the area and build a salt plant. He erected a salt evaporating plant at the springs, but the plant was not successful. Exploration and future development of the property were turned over to Risdon's nephew, Lewis Risdon Mead, in 1863. Mead discovered more than fifty springs or outlets from subterranean passages that ranged in temperatures from 52 to 140 degrees F.

Mead immediately began developing the springs as a health resort. A bathhouse was built over the sulfur spring in 1868 and soon became quite popular. By 1872, the resort attracted so many visitors that a ten-room house was built to accommodate guests. The railroad came though the area in 1878, providing transportation for people from the bay area which assured the future of the resort. Under Mead's direction, guest cottages, bathhouses, and beautiful gardens were established with some of the springs developed for drinking, and others used as mud baths.

After two hotels were destroyed by fire (in 1901 and 1912), a large brick hotel was built in 1913. The shell of the third and final hotel is one of the only remaining landmarks of this wonderful chapter of Byron's history.

With the passing of time, a pool house, lawns for croquet, tennis courts, shuffleboards and a stable of horses were added to the resort. There were fountains, outdoor and indoor swimming pools, and a gazebo where a string quartet would play in the afternoon. The walls of several of the buildings were decorated with inlaid marble mosaics.

Byron Hot Springs drew people from all over the United States and Europe to bask in the warm sunshine and soak in its healing waters. Doctors of the period recommended the springs for relief of indigestion, ailments of the stomach and liver, rheumatism and gout. Guests had their choice of fifteen different mineral springs from which to drink, as well as fresh drinking water which was piped from Mount Diablo to the resort.

In 1915 the U.S. Geological Survey printed a volume entitled "Springs in California" that described the springs and gave their mineral content. The five principal constituents were sodium, potassium sulfate, chloride and carbonate along with traces of fifteen other minerals.

In its heyday during the 1920's and '30's, the Byron Hot Springs was a vacation spot and favorite get-away for the rich and famous. Jack London came to the springs to write, enjoy privacy and spend time using the healing waters. The Spreckels family and the Crockers, and other wealthy families maintained year-round rooms or cottages. Charlie Chaplin, Gary Cooper, Clark Gable and Norma Jean Baker (Marilyn Monroe) frequented the resort often. However, just as the depression brought the country to its knees, it also brought trouble to the Hot Springs. A series of arguments and lawsuits among the resort's owners resulted in the closing of the resort in 1938.

Camp Tracy, a prisoner-of-war interrogation center, was one of the best-kept secrets of World War II. The once luxurious resort was purchased by the government in 1941, and used from 1942 to 1945 to house German and Japanese prisoners. According to the National Archives records of 1944, during the busiest year of the center there were 908 Japanese and 48 German military personnel received there. Prisoners were brought to Byron from East Garrison, a screening facility on Angel Island in San Francisco Bay. After being processed and interrogated at Camp Tracy, most of the enlisted men were forwarded to Camp McCoy, a prisoner facility in Butte, Montana.

During the closing days of the war, orders were sent to close the camp, and on August 14, 1945, instructions were received to "dispose of the premises known as Byron Hot Springs, consisting of 209.27 acres respectively, together with improvements thereof." Camp Tracy was dismantled lock, stock and barrel. Microphones and interrogation equipment were removed, along with much of the original beauty of the resort. The property was immediately declared surplus by the Army Corps of Engineers and listed for sale.

The grounds lay fallow for three years, and in December 1948 it was announced that the resort had been sold to the Greek Orthodox Church for $105,000. A week later the buildings were dedicated as the first mission of the church in the United States. During the next twelve years, the grounds were used to carry on missionary work, house orphans and the elderly, as a retreat for church members from all over the state, and as the center for all church business. By 1960, the church had decided to sell due to the high cost of maintaining the facility and grounds.

Since 1945, Byron Hot Springs has changed hands a number of times, with each owner entertaining a dream of restoring the resort to its original condition. So far, the high costs of rebuilding the structures and grounds have made the dream an impossibility. Meanwhile, sparrow hawks hover over the ruins, jackrabbits nibble at the bases of palm trees planted over a hundred years ago, and ghosts from the other side of yesterday still linger in the winds.

Our older generations remember well the glamour and fantastic wealth of the pleasure and health seekers passing briefly through Byron on their way to the mineral springs. They enjoyed the tennis and croquet courts, golf course and a life-style very different from the average Byron resident. Having grown up on a ranch very close to the Hot Springs, I remember playing on the grounds as a child: swimming in the old wooden pool and sleeping on the rooftop of the hotel, telling ghost stories on a warm summer's night. Once again I am reminded of the wonders of our past. Until Next Time....

HOT SPRINGS VACATION 1905

Tucked into the foothills at the base of Mount Diablo about two miles from the town of Byron, there was one of the greatest and most interesting health spas in America in 1905, the Byron Hot Springs. The Springs were considered a fashionable place for vacationing Hollywood movie celebrities, socialites, and ailing people from all over the world. They took advantage of the mud baths, mineral baths, and curative waters. Many guests from the Bay Area went to relax, dine, and enjoy the recreation offered by the resort.

Weekend visits were very popular in the early 1900's. Southern Pacific offered special rates ($3 round trip ticket) for weekend excursions. Guests would board a train in San Francisco and arrive at the Hot Springs within a couple of hours. Many San Francisco businessmen would come on Friday evening and leave Monday morning thoroughly refreshed by the tonic waters and invigorating baths in time to reach their office when the day's work began.

There was a long palm lined drive connecting the resort to the Southern Pacific railroad. Guests were picked up at Byron Hot Springs Station and traveled through a tropical park of ferns, evergreen trees, palms, and flowering plants. There were rose covered cottages, fish ponds, fountains, gazebos, impressive drinking springs, and beautifully manicured gardens encompassing the modern Spanish style hotel which could accommodate two hundred guests.

The three story hotel was built on high ground in 1902, facing East, offering a wonderful view of the San Joaquin Valley and Coast Range, as well as the beauty of the immediate surroundings. There were spacious verandas along the entire front and two sides of the building and every guest's room offered a magnificent panorama. The building was considered very modern for the times. Each room offered electric light, gas light, steam heat, and electric call bells. Many of the rooms had full toilet accommodations, and some offered private bathrooms where hot mineral water was delivered directly from the springs in addition to hot and cold water. In 1889 Lewis Mead, owner of the resort, discovered natural gas on the site. Mead took advantage of it, and by the early 1900's, the entire resort was heated and illuminated by gas. At the same time, freshwater wells at the northeastern foot of Mount Diablo were tapped allowing running water to be piped to the resort.

The hotel offered a Post Office (opened in 1889 and discontinued in 1930), telegraph and telephone, and a resident physician located in the main foyer. A spacious airy dining room offered the best service available with an exceptional cuisine. Fresh meats, fish, and vegetables were delivered daily by train from the Bay Area. Eggs, poultry, and locally grown vegetables were purchased from farms near the resort. Milk products were produced on site at the Hot Springs Dairy where resort employees milked twenty cows delivering the fresh milk and cream to the kitchen staff.

Guests could stay in the main hotel for $3 a day or in one of the cottages for $2.50. These rates included free use of all the springs and baths. Consultation with the resident physician as to the proper use of waters and baths were also available to all guests and involved no additional charge. People who were not staying at the resort could obtain baths at a rate of $1 per bath.

The primary attraction of the resort was it's curative properties of mud and mineral baths and waters. Peat mud baths were claimed to be effective in cases of gout, rheumatism, and sciatica. The belief was that the baths would dilate the blood vessels of the skin and relieve congestion in the deeper parts of the body. With the aid of the resident physician and a skilled attendant, a guest would immerse into hot mud up to their neck for approximately fifteen minutes.

Sulphur Water Baths were available in a building that had been erected directly over a sulphur spring. These baths claimed to soften and beautify the skin. Hot Mineral Spring Baths were taken in porcelain tubs in the bathing section of the hotel itself. Water was pumped to these tubs from the Hot Mineral Spring where it flowed at a temperature of 122 degrees. The primary result from enjoying the mineral bath was to relax the guests entire body.

A Hot Salt Water Spring supplied guests with a liquid which induced a normal action of the bowels. Many of the old timers I've interviewed remembered the use of this solution when they were growing up.

The Liver and Kidney Spring was diuretic and slightly laxative, offering relief in diseases of the liver, kidney, and bladder. It further claimed to relieve patients suffering of gout, rheumatism, neurasthenia, sciatica, malaria, diabetes, and lumbago.

The Byron Hot Springs Resort not only offered guests treatment and relief from their ailments but also was a facility designed for general recreation and entertainment. Visitors were offered horseback riding, buggy riding or driving through the countryside. Billiards, shuffle-board, golf, lawn croquet, tennis and other outdoor and indoor amusements were also offered. They could swim in the Gas Plunge, an indoor swimming pool, that was 44 feet long and 20 feet wide with a depth of 4 to 8 feet and built directly over a sulphur spring. This pool maintained a temperature of 88 degrees and had a constant flow of water passing through completely changing the water several times a day. A swim in this pool claimed to soften the swimmers skin and allow wrinkles to disappear before their eyes.

There were glass enclosed verandas where guests could sit in the warm sun and play cards, board games, or read. On weekends, evening dances were held in the great open square in front of the hotel. A number of cottages were built for large parties or families that desired the seclusion a hotel couldn't provide. It was not uncommon for a wealthy family to rent a cottage for the summer. According to an article in the Contra Costa Gazette 1908 "More than 5000 people visited the Springs an average of over 400 a month."

Long before the commercial development of the springs, their curative powers were recognized by the Indians. They bathed in the bubbling mud and drank the mineral waters which they believed to have supernatural powers. Evidence has been uncovered indicating that an Indian encampment was once located near the springs. Information about the springs spread by word of mouth and travelers passing through this region of California began visiting the site. In 1865, Orange Risdon, Lewis Mead's uncle, received a land patent for a quarter section of land. The location catered to guests for more than sixty years. There were numerous cottages, three hotels (1888, 1902 and 1913) and an endless list of out buildings built on the site between 1865 and 1938 when the resort closed. (Two hotels burned.)

The once famous and picturesque Byron Hot Springs have crumbled into ruins through the years. Today barn owls nest in the palm trees, most of the original buildings and gardens are gone, and over the years the grand old resort that was so famous during it's heyday has disappeared with the passing of time. Numerous developers have attempted to revive the site, but to date only the shadow of this famed California resort remains. Until Next Time….

PRISONERS OF WAR AT BYRON HOT SPRINGS

The once luxurious Byron Hot Springs Resort, nestled in the foothills two miles south of Byron, closed its gates in 1938. By 1941, the beautiful resort that had been a favorite haunt for Hollywood celebrities was showing signs of neglect. The buildings were in need of paint, and the once elegant gardens were overgrown with wild wheat and thistles.

According to National Archivist James O'Neill, shortly after the bombing of Pearl Harbor, Frank Knox, Secretary of the Navy, proposed to the War Department that two joint Army-Navy prisoner-of-war interrogation centers be established, one on each coast. Several locations on the West Coast were considered. In 1942, the U.S. Government purchased Byron Hot Springs to be used as an interrogation center for German and Japanese prisoners of war during World War II. The facility was referred to as Camp Tracy. Preparations for occupancy were completed in December 1942, and the first prisoners to be interrogated arrived a few weeks later. Byron was selected because it was isolated, yet close to San Francisco, the existing structures were sound, and the cost of acquiring the property was low.

The Byron Hot Springs camp was originally intended as a Japanese interrogation center, but due to the paucity of Japanese prisoners during 1943 and '44, Germans were also confined there. In 1945, it was used exclusively for the interrogation of Japanese prisoners. During the two and a half years the center was in operation, a total of 252 Germans and 3,234 Japanese were interrogated. High-ranking enemy officers who passed through included Rear Admiral Kojima Hideo, Japanese naval attaché in Berlin, and German Generals Gustave Von Vaerst, Karl R. M. Buelowius, Peter Bernard Koechy and Willibald Borowetz.

As the facility could only house 44 prisoners at one time, the Prisoner of War Processing Center at Fort McDowell (Angel Island) was used to segregate those prisoners deemed worthy of intensive debriefing for shipment to Byron Hot Springs. These prisoners were delivered to the camp by closed car, usually guarded front and rear, and in some instances they were blindfolded en route to guard the identity and location of the Byron Hot Springs center. A prisoner's internment at the Byron facility could last from a few days to several weeks or months, depending on the prisoner's cooperation and the amount of information he was believed to possess. There was no set amount of time that each prisoner would be interrogated. After interrogation at Camp Tracy, enlisted men were forwarded to Camp McCoy, Wisconsin, and officers to a facility at Butte, Montana.

As a general rule, prisoners were asked questions about their home lives, friends and families. These questions often led to inadvertent admission of the desired information. Some prisoners even went so far as to draw detailed diagrams of enemy vessels and facilities.

The four-story brick hotel and much of the surrounding grounds were bugged extensively. Microphones were installed in false ceilings of the prisoners' rooms and throughout the prisoner recreation area at the rear of the building. According to declassified documents released on April 1, 1980, from the National Archives in Washington D.C., the basement of the hotel was used as the central recording point. Listeners were on duty at all times, and all prisoner conversations as well as interrogation conversations were recorded. False partitions in some rooms also provided listening space behind walls. The first floor contained the officers' quarters, mess hall, officers' club and kitchen. The second floor held officer's quarters and interrogation rooms, and the third floor contained prisoners' quarters. The hotel was surrounded by two fifteen-foot-high fences, one inside the other, with towers at each corner manned around the clock by heavily armed guards.

Prisoners were well fed and clothed. They were permitted daily recreation as well as rest periods and were allowed to receive mail under certain restrictions. They were furnished with tobacco, toothpaste and personal items, and when kept at the interrogation center for over six days, were allowed ten cents per day with which the camp welfare officer purchased commodities for them at the post exchange.

Except for the mental anguish of captivity, long hours of boredom, uncertainty as to what was happening or would happen next, life at Camp Tracy was actually relatively pleasant. Food was good, interrogation sessions often featured relaxed, informal conversation, and copious quantities of beer, whiskey, cigarettes and reading material were readily available.

The area inside the inner fence of the prison enclosure, known as the interrogation center, which was operated by the Chief of Military Intelligence; the outer area was the general compound. The general compound was reserved for barracks, mess halls, dispensary, dental clinic, laundry, guard house, storehouses, telephone exchange, barber shop and recreation hall. There were approximately 250 U.S. officers and enlisted men stationed at Camp Tracy, and over 3500 prisoners interrogated there between 1942 and 1945.

While the army owned Byron Hot Springs, they remodeled the hotel, a pump house, a firehouse and eleven cabins, built a garage and installed underground sewer lines.

Camp Tracy was declared surplus property after the war in Europe. Orders came to close the interrogation center August 13, 1945, and to dispose of the 209-acre facility. The interrogation center was dismantled lock, stock and microphones, and with it went much of the original beauty of the resort. The grounds lay fallow for three years, and in December 1948 it was announced that the Greek Archdiocese of North and South America Missions purchased the property for $105,000. During the next twelve years, the grounds were used to carry on missionary work, house orphans and the elderly, and as a retreat for church members from all over the state.

Time has erased most evidence of the Byron Hot Springs, but if the walls of that old brick hotel could speak—what wonderful tales they could tell! Vern Allen, one of my most favorite uncles, was stationed at Camp Tracy during its days as a POW camp and was instrumental in helping me fill in the details for this chapter of our past. Thank you, Uncle Vern!! Until Next Time....

DISCOVERY BAY

DISCOVERY BAY TIMELINE

1500's—1600's.....California Indians roamed East Contra Costa County. The area where Discovery Bay is located was marsh land. Much of this region was covered with tules and abundant in wildlife.

1772......Spanish explorers led by Captain Pedro Fages traveled through East Contra Costa.

1820s & 1830s.....Trappers and Mountain Men arrived in the Delta region in search of the beaver, mink, and otter that inhabited the rivers and streams. Jedediah Smith and Joseph Walker were setting their traps on the periphery of the great marsh.

1900—1966.....Frank A. West and Eugene L. Wilhoit of Stockton and Veronica Baird owned Byron Tract. The Byron Tract was primarily farmed, producing large quantities potatoes, onions, sugar beets, corn, wheat, and barley.

1912.......Reclamation District #800, known as the Wilhoit District, was declared legal and valid.

1920—1960.....The West-Wilhoit Hog Feed Lot was in operation in Byron Tract.

1966.......Weldwood Structures Division of U.S. Plywood owned the land. They had a catfish farm on the site managed by Jorgen Lunding.

1967.......U.S. Plywood and Bixland Inc. took plans for Discovery Bay to the Contra Costa County Planning Commission. Discovery Bay was originally going to be named Riverlake.

1967......Jorgen Lunding, project manager for U.S. Plywood and Bixland, is credited with officially naming the project Discovery Bay.

1968......Champion Paper Products merged with U.S. Plywood.

1968......Grading for Lido Bay, the first bay in Discovery Bay, began.

1969......William Baldwin and Title Insurance & Trust bought the project.

1970......Burt Davi and William Baldwin formed Veronica Development Corporation.

1970..... The first Discovery Bay lot was sold. Deep water lots sold for $12,000 at that time.

1972......Andy DeVine's raspy voice promoted the development. He was heard on local radio stations saying, "If I could be a kid again..." The first home was built in Discovery Bay.

1972......Archie and Merle Grant became the first official residents of Discovery Bay. There was no water, electricity or gas at that time, so they lived in their camper for the first month.

1973.......Boykin Investment bought the development.

1973......1,443 acres were rezoned so the project could expand.

1975......The first meeting of the Discovery Bay Property Owners took place at Liberty Union High School (March 22). There were approximately 100 homes.

1976......Discovery Bay Yacht club held their first meeting on July 16. The first board of directors: Ott Evje, Lea Achey, Jack Mackrodt, Billy Roach, Jean Davis, Fred Roach, and Harry DeVoto.

1976......The Discovery Bay Volunteer Fire Department established.

1977......Ken Hofmann, of Hofmann Construction, purchased Discovery Bay. In April 1978 Hofmann built model homes on upper Willow Lake. These original homes started at $68,950.

1978.....The Discovery Bay Inn opened by Frank & Tommy PiJuan. The Inn offered a gourmet restaurant located at Highway 4 & Discovery Bay Blvd.

1978.....Hofmann built the first condominiums.
1979.....Street delivery of mail began.
1980.....The Discovery Bay Fire Station was dedicated.
1980.....The Census reported 1297 residents in 639 homes.
1981.....The Discovery Marina had its grand opening, with Jim Plunkett as celebrated guest.
1981.....Phase one of the Discovery Bay Landing Shopping Center opened.
1982.....The Discovery Bay Elementary School opened with four classrooms. The Byron Union School District enrollment was 350 students.
1983.....The Discovery Bay Lion's Club organized. The first Discovery Bay Lion's Club Boat Show was held in May with Ed Cornell as chairman.
1984.....Ground was broken for a champion eighteen hole golf course. The golf course takes in 400 acres and was designed by Ted Robinson.
1985.....Discovery Bay Corvette Club founded with fifteen charter members.
1986.....The Discovery Bay Country Club opened July 4th.
1987.....The Discovery Bay Yacht Club grand opening for the club house took place.
1988.....Cornell Park, between Discovery Bay Blvd. and Willow Lake Road, was dedicated and named for Ed Cornell.
1989.....Discovery Bay originally drew buyers looking for a week end getaway. By 1989 the population shifted to about 75% year-round homeowners.
1989.....Discovery Bay Chamber of Commerce was organized.
1989.....Discovery Bay had their first Art, Wine & Jazz Festival.
1992.....Discovery Bay Municipal Advisory Council (MAC) was established on February 25th. with Joe Philbrick as chairman.
1992.....Byron Delta Lions Club was chartered.
1992.....The Delta Community Presbyterian Church held their first services in their brand new facility on Willow Lake Road.
1997.....The Discovery Bay Community Services District (CSD) was formed on November 17th. with Bill Slifer serving as the first chairman. The CSD has direct control of the Sanitation Distict 19, which controls water and sewer facilities for Discovery Bay and Centex Homes.
1997.....The Golden State Corvette was founded September 1997.
2000.....Discovery Bay officially registered with the state as "Town of Discovery Bay". Until Next Time....

DISCOVERY BAY MOTTO:

"LIVE WHERE YOU PLAY....DISCOVERY BAY"

DISCOVERY BAY HISTORY

The construction of Discovery Bay was started in 1968 when large excavation equipment was moved on site to excavate Lido Bay, the developments first bay. The concept for the Discovery Bay Development and the first steps of the project began in 1964. The original plan was to use land bordered on the north by Indian Slough, on the east by Old River, and on the south by Italian Slough. The original name of the development was Riverlake. It would be a recreational community of bays dug from the delta farmland, then filled with water by breaking the levee of Indian Slough. It took the original developers years of meetings with county, state, and federal agencies before actual construction could begin.

Borden Highway to Stockton across Byron Tract

Long before Discovery Bay was ever thought of, the tract of land covered in upscale homes today was noted for the large staple crops it produced. The area between Byron and Old River was known as Byron Tract. About 3465 acres were owned by Frank A. West and Eugene L. Wilhoit of Stockton, and 3000 acres belonged to Veronica Baird. In the early 1900s the property was protected by huge levees, with a modern irrigation and drainage system on most of the land. This section was planted with potatoes, corn, onions, beans, sugar beets, and barley. By 1920 West-Wilhoit had established a large hog farm on their holdings. Their hogs were fed corn and barley that was grown on the property.

The southern portion of Byron Tract was known as the Baird Estate. Veronica Baird, a resident of New York, was the mother of Mrs. William Sproule, wife of the president of the Southern Pacific Railroad Company, and William Baldwin's great grandmother. This extensive estate was leased to the McCormack Brothers, contracting farmers, of Rio Vista. It was planted primarily in barley in the 1920s and 30s.

In 1966 Weldwood Structures Division of U.S. Plywood and Bixland Inc., under the direction of Jorgen Lunding, the projects manager, entered into a joint venture arrangement to sell recreational lots. Lunding is credited with naming the project "Discovery Bay". By 1968 U.S. Plywood merged with Champion Paper Products, and by the end of that same year, decided to sell the project to William Baldwin, an adjacent property owner.

Following the paper work for this project is difficult at best. Baldwin entered into a joint venture arrangement with Title Insurance and Trust in Southern California. They could not reach an agreement, so in 1969 their contract was cancelled.

Baldwin then went into partnership with Burt J. Davi, a civic leader from Pittsburg. They formed Veronica Development Corporation (named for Baldwin's great grandmother Veronica Baird). Discovery Bay lots opened for sale in October 1970, complete with a colorful tent as a sales office. Salesmen in jeeps took potential buyers to sites where the bays were to be built. Andy Devine commercials and the Old Savannah paddle boat were used to promote the project. Landlocked lots sold for about $9,000 and deep water lots ran about $15,000.

In 1973, the project was sold by Baldwin and Davi to a Southern Investment group named Boykin Investments. Boykin held the property until 1975 when it went into default on its purchase agreement. There were about 100 homes in Discovery Bay at this time. Baldwin and Davi got the development back and formed the Dominion Properties Company. Although Bank of America, Wells Fargo, and Union Bank had originally been the lenders in the early 1970s, Wells Fargo became the sole lender.

In 1977 the property was sold to Ken Hofmann of the Hofmann Company. With the Hofmann Company in charge, the pace quickened rapidly. Prospective home buyers camped over night to be the early birds getting first choice of newly constructed homes on Willow Lake. In 1978 Hofmann built a small condominium project and Windard Bay, the final deep water bay.

On July 4th, 1981 the Discovery Bay Marina had its grand opening complete with Jim Plunkett shaking everybody's hand.

By 1988 two thousand acres of land had been developed with eighteen deep-water bays, Discovery Bay Marina, Willow Lake, a swim and racket club, a shopping center, and a championship 18 hole golf course with a private 21,000 square foot clubhouse.

It's hard to imagine the fields of barley or potatoes that once grew on Byron Tract. Today we find a beautiful upscale community on the Delta, a community designed for people who want to live on the water. Until Next Time….

Discovery Bay Golf Club

THE DELTA

HISTORY OF THE DELTA

The Delta is made up of many islands surrounded by sloughs and rivers, which are all part of the great Sacramento and San Joaquin river system, an area well known to boaters and fishermen for years. A great deal of land throughout East Contra Costa was once covered with water much of the year, with ponds two miles across in some areas. One reason for the marshy landscape was that the rivers would overflow their banks every spring and leave water pooled on the surrounding land.

River paddle wheeler "Napa City" Owned by Larkin Transportation Co.

This marshy land was covered with tules and during the fall and winter huge flocks of ducks and geese flew over the marshlands. From October through March millions of snow geese, Canadian geese, pintail ducks and cinnamon teal filled the skies. Early settlers said there were so many ducks and geese overhead they blocked out the sun.

The redwing blackbird, great blue heron and whistling swan could also be seen along the waterways, and California beaver and otters were in abundance.

The riverbanks looked like jungles; heavy growth of trees like willows, Fremont poplar, Oregon ash, white alder, valley oak and cottonwood mixed with wild grape, blackberry, rose vines and poison oak grew into huge tangled masses. The rivers abounded with hundreds of thousands of fish during the fall and spring salmon run. Huge white sturgeon, river perch, western suckers and Sacramento pike could be found year-round.

As settlers began arriving in the 1850's and '60's, they recognized the value of the rich Delta soil and reclaimed the desirable farmland with the construction of levees, canals and islands.

The islands of the Delta are mostly man-made. They were formed by dredging the river bottoms and constantly piling up the mud and silt to form levees. These islands varied in size, from less than one acre to a few that are several thousand acres. More than 70,000 acres of Delta wetlands have been reclaimed, creating 55 man-made islands with more than 1,000 miles of waterways.

The first levees built were constructed by Chinese laborers using primitive, back-breaking methods.

Around 1850, large numbers of Chinese entered California, escaping from a thirteen-year revolution and the resulting political turmoil in China. Thousands of Chinese were brought into the area to work on the levees, and hundreds of others left railroad gangs to join them. Records were not kept of the total number of Chinese laborers, but the work force was huge. The laborers toted soil by hand using buckets and wheelbarrows. They worked sixteen hours a day, six days a week, receiving a meager $30 for their efforts. There were many laws restricting land ownership for immigrants and these laws were strictly upheld.

Eventually the Fresno Scraper was developed. It was a massive, horse-drawn shovel with big handles and a dumping catch which was used for work on the levees as well as the early East Contra Costa roads.

With the arrival of the Gold Rush, paddlewheel steamers traveled through the Sacramento and San Joaquin Rivers from Sacramento to San Francisco and further north to Red Bluff. History notes that ships would go as far south as Firebaugh carrying cargos of vegetables, fruit, grain and livestock. Many of these early ships were wood burners, using wood cut from the riverbanks into four-foot lengths as fuel, with the burners consuming as much as a cord of wood an hour. By the late 1860's coal taken from mines in the area replaced the wood.

During the 1850's a system of charting local channels and clearing obstructions from the rivers began. Most ships of that era drew only four feet of water. In 1850, Congress passed an act allowing the sale of the Delta islands, resulting in many early settlers purchasing tracts for as little as one dollar per acre. Most transportation for early residents of the Delta was via boat, including mail delivery and shopping.

In 1860 Mr. Stone reclaimed the land originally known as Stone Tract and now known as Bethel Island. It was not until the 1890's, when Dutch Slough was dredged to the east meeting Sandmound Slough, Taylor Slough was dredged south to meet Dutch Slough, and Piper Slough was dredged south meeting Sandmound Slough, that Bethel Island actually became an island.

Stone Tract was known for its dairies and the grain grown on the island in the early days. Levees of the period were inadequate, resulting in periods of flooding that made life on the tract a constant adventure. In 1901, the tract was renamed Bethel Island, after Frank and Anne Bethell.

From 1851 to 1861, the construction of the first levees and reclamation of the land were accomplished by individual landowners with the use of Chinese labor. From 1861 until 1866, the state legislature appointed a board of "Swamp and Overflow Land," to oversee the reclamation. The various county boards of supervisors assumed the commission in 1866, and in 1915 they also assumed Reclamation Districts 102, 107 and 183. These early districts had all been formed in 1894 for the purpose of raising money to build new levees around the island.

During the early days, Bethel Island was used exclusively for agriculture. Then, during the 1930's, hunters and fishermen established a weekend colony near the old wagon bridge over Dutch Slough. At the end of World War II the island became popular for boating and other recreational sports.

It wasn't until 1946 that Bethel Island enjoyed electricity or telephones, and the only bridge onto the island was still one lane wide. By 1947, the island had established a post office, with Ethel Boxel as the first postmaster. Prior to this time the mail was delivered to a row of mailboxes just over the bridge at Riverview Road. Gutters, curbs and sidewalks were not installed on the island until the 1970's.

In researching the history of the Delta a person can't help but be impressed by the hardships early settlers overcame. These settlers were primarily free-spirited, hardworking men and women that shaped development of the Delta as we know it today. Men like Stone and Bethell definitely left footprints in the chapters of our past. Until Next Time….

EAST CONTRA COSTA LANDINGS

The early history of East Contra Costa is rich with many wonderful stories, but none more interesting than the landings of the Delta. You can't look into the chapters of the past in this region without seeing references to Marsh Landing, Babbes Landing, Iron House Landing and Point of Timber Landing.

In the 1850's and 1860's the early settlers of the East Contra Costa area were primarily wheat farmers. Wheat seed was planted in the autumn. It lay in the ground all winter, and the winter rains softened the hard soil. In the spring the wheat sprouted, and under the hot summer sun the grains of wheat were ready to harvest.

The wheat was stored in large warehouses, then loaded on barges and schooners at one of the local landings and shipped to Carquinez docks or Port Costa where it was loaded onto larger vessels bound for ports all over the world.

Some of the early landings were formal docks. Others were less formal locations along the river where a farmer could stack his product for a ship to pick up and take to market.

MARSH LANDING:
Doctor John Marsh built Marsh Landing on the San Joaquin River in the 1840's. This was the first landing built in the area and Marsh was probably the only user since there were few other settlers. This landing was located at the eastern end of the sandy bluff above Antioch. Marsh had built a cottage on the site and a warehouse in which to store his supplies.

Marsh shipped his products (cattle, vegetables, and grain) to the port in Antioch and then on to market. In 1849, when the Gold Rush hit, Marsh saw an opportunity to supply goods to the mining towns. He built a long pier at Marsh Landing to accommodate the numerous trading ships carrying fresh meat, vegetables, grains, and fruit to the gold diggings. Here he saw a source of wealth greater than the digging of gold itself. Once he received $10,000 for one large shipment of cattle. The first mail delivery to Antioch was dropped off at Marsh Landing and then transported to town.

IRON HOUSE LANDING: Fassett and McCauley built this landing for Martin Hamburg. It was located five miles east of Marsh Landing on Dutch Slough at the junction of a small slough about two miles northeast of Oakley. On some old maps of the area this slough is identified as Iron House Slough.

The Iron House Landing was abandoned when Fred Babbe bought out Hamburg and built Babbes Landing.

BABBES LANDING: Fred Babbe came to California from Prussia in 1850 in search of gold. In 1854 he bought a three hundred acre farm in the Iron House District on a site that is about six miles east of what today is Antioch. The area was primarily swamp and overflow land and would often flood from high tide waters. He spent less than $30,000 reclaiming the land by building a levee around his farm that was five to seven feet high and approximately twenty five feet wide at the base.

He later built a canal 2,838 feet long, 42 feet wide, and approximately seven feet deep. This canal allowed 100 ton vessels to come to Babbes Landing to pick up grain and produce for the San Francisco markets. Shipping records show that Babbes Landing handled between 3,000 and 4,000 tons of grain each year.

Babbes Landing was located at the north end of Sellers Avenue on a dredged waterway that came off Dutch Slough. During its heyday this landing was one of the major grain shipping points in this region of California. Much of the grain shipped from here went by boat to grain warehouses in Port Costa that shipped worldwide.

When Babbes Landing was no longer used as a shipping point it became a horse farm where race horses were raised. Frederick Babbe sold the landing to Henry Dutard in 1894.

In the early 1900's the property changed hands several times. Central Shuey Company of Oakland established a large dairy. Next, Golden State Milk Company of San Francisco bought the dairy. Then, San Joaquin Farms took over. And in 1946 Oscar Burroughs bought the site and added it to the Burrough's Bros. Dairy which was located adjacent to the site.

POINT OF TIMBER LANDING: Local farmers decided to build Point of Timber landing in the 1860's. Prior to this time they were hauling their grain over dusty dirt roads to Babbes Landing or all the way to Antioch by wagon. The landing was located on Indian Slough across from where Discovery Bay is located today.

Josiah Wills was one of the principals in the building of the landing, and J.B. Greer built the first large grain warehouse at the landing site.

The Point of Timber Landing was burned in the winter of 1881-82 by tule fires. Local farmers again banded together forming Point of Timber Landing Company, and built a new landing in 1884. The new site offered a canal almost a mile long, thirty six feet wide, and four and one half feet deep.

In 1893 Captain C. W. Lent and his young wife traveled to California across the Mohave desert by train. The train was derailed by a sand storm, and the baggage coaches caught on fire destroying everything the young couple owned.

Captain Lent was an engineer who moved to the Delta to do reclamation work. He operated the first floating pump in the area establishing his main base at Point of Timber. Lent was instrumental in operating the Point of Timber Landing Company for many years.

Train service in East Contra Costa at the turn of the century was poor, and it was practically impossible to get to Stockton and back in one day. Captain Lent ran a passenger boat which took East County residents from Point of Timber Landing to Stockton and back.

Captain Lent made the trip to Stockton by boat every Saturday carrying 15 to 25 passengers. On Sunday he ran excursions for picnic parties from the landing to a sandy beach on the Delta that was ideal for fishing, swimming, and picnicking.

The early landings of the Delta definitely left footprints in the pages of our past.
Until Next Time....

TRACTS AND ISLANDS OF THE DELTA

Prior to reclamation of the Delta, the inland waterways were a vast marsh, cut by snag-filled, tidal-influenced waterways. The tidal action is less noticeable today, due to the water flows regulated by a network of upstream dams on the rivers and their tributaries. The area was covered with tules and the riverbanks were thick with trees and bushes.

Modern history of the Delta begins with reclamation. The Swamp and Overflow Act of 1850 gave title of 320 acres per person to those who would reclaim the land. By 1859 the limit was raised to 640 acres and by 1871 most of the land was spoken for.

Bradford Island: This 2,051-acre island was originally owned by J. W. Bradford. C. C. Webb purchased 130 acres from Bradford in 1869 for $100 and constructed Fisherman's Slough. In 1898 the Bradford Reclamation Company was formed to reclaim the land. George Sima, a Japanese farmer, was the first to grow potatoes on the island and later became known as the "Potato King" of the Delta.

Coney Island: Originally known as the "Gem of the Delta," this 935-acre island was first reclaimed in 1893. The Righetti family of San Francisco acquired the island and planted barley and asparagus. Coney Island flooded in 1918.

Franks Tract: This plot contains about 3,449 acres, only 397 of which are above water. In 1902, the Franks Reclamation Company owned the entire tract. Fred C. Franks of Antioch was the largest landowner. Originally known as Hall Tract, Franks Tract was flooded in 1936 and 1938. In 1955 the state legislature appropriated $300,000 to buy the tract, creating Franks Tract State Recreation Area, a popular destination for boaters and fishermen.

Grand Island: The first reclamation project in the Delta was done by Josiah Green and Reuben Kercheval on upper Grand Island in the early 1850s. The Fallman family acquired this island in 1869.

Holland Tract: California Delta Farms acquired this 4,060-acre tract from John Hurd in 1907. Delta Farms, under the direction of Lee Phillips, used clamshell dredges to build high levees and cut deep-water channels. The island is noted for crops of onions, potatoes, beets, celery and asparagus. There is a marshy lake on Holland Tract known as Big Lake.

Hotchkiss Tract: William J. Hotchkiss purchased 2,300 acres of this tract in 1904. County record books show that in 1916, William Hotchkiss received 1,317 acres for $10 per acre from the Central California Canneries of Oakland. He planted potatoes, beans and sugar beets. Part of Hotchkiss' holdings later became the Dal Porto Ranch.

Jersey Island: This 3,471-acre island was once known as "Queen of the Delta." It was reclaimed by Hagan and Davis in 1860. In 1900 the Jersey Island Packing Company acquired the island. The island flooded in 1906. The largest single field of celery ever planted was grown on 1,600 acres of this island in 1918.

Orwood Tract: H. Rindge and Lee A. Phillips, founders of California Delta Farms, reclaimed this 4,138-acre tract in 1907. Phillips traveled to Holland to observe the construction of dikes and returned to build levees around Orwood Tract.

Palm Tract: This 2,436-acre tract was originally owned by Frederick H. Rindge, who farmed the tract, planting primarily corn and barley.

Quimby Island: W. C. Wright and F. A. Quimby reclaimed this 769-acre tract in 1914. The island flooded in 1936 and 1938. The rich peat soil of this island produced crops of sugar beets, barley and corn for many years.

Sherman Island: Named after Sherman Day, United States Surveyor-General, this tract was reclaimed in 1865. Sherman was the first tract in the Delta to be completely enclosed with an artificial levee. The levee was 47 miles long, with a width of twelve feet at the base and it ranged from three to three and a half feet high. Crops raised on Sherman Island included wheat, potatoes, barley and onions. During Prohibition, lower Sherman Island provided a fine location for a bootleg liquor industry well hidden within the wilds.

Ferry Crossing

Veale Tract: This 1,298-acre tract was owned by Richard R. Veale in the 1870's. (Veale's son was elected sheriff of Contra Costa County in 1896, a job he held for more than forty years.) Balfour, Guthrie Co. and then I. L. Borden acquired Veale Tract. Borden spent thousands of dollars improving the land's productivity, using tractors to break up the ground to a depth of fourteen inches.

Webb Tract: This 5,490-acre tract is the largest island in East Contra Costa. Crops raised on this site include potatoes, corn, sunflowers, barley and sugar beets. In 1935 Webb had almost 5,000 acres planted in wheat when a fire raged across the island, destroying the entire crop and burning the peat dirt. The entire island had to be flooded to put out the burning peat fire. Until Next Time….

A CRUISE THROUGH THE DELTA

The rivers and sloughs of the Delta create a fantastic lowland system of water throughout the great basin of Northern California. In 1772, Fray Juan Crespi and Pedro Fages with their expedition party looked down from the top of Mount Diablo and saw two great rivers, a vast valley of sloughs, and fertile peat bogs flourishing with natural vegetation. These were the first white men to record the discovery of the Delta, their journals spoke of a "great inland lake that stretched farther than the eye could see, abounding with game, fish and fowl of all kinds."

Crespi was the first to write about wildlife in the East Contra Costa region of California, which provided ample food for Native Americans living in the area. Early explorers were impressed with the hundreds of waterways, variety of game, and the great stands of tules. They came to California to establish missions and seek out treasurers for their King. It is ironic that, eighty years later, the rivers they first saw from Mount Diablo would bear great treasures of gold.

Few frontiers were more interesting or colorful than those of the Delta. The waterways became main trails and by 1790 the Delta began to support a growing fur-trading industry. In 1827, Jedidiah Smith, an American adventurer, was trapping beaver, otter, and mink on the periphery of the giant marsh. Smith led a group of Americans into California by land; the route was long, crossing hot deserts and high mountains. Within the next few years fur trappers were a familiar sight on Delta waterways which were rich with beaver. Ships began navigating the Sacramento and San Joaquin rivers transporting supplies for upriver settlements and trading for huge numbers of animal skins.

When the Gold Rush struck California in 1849, thousands of men arrived in the Golden State to seek their fortune. The Delta rivers provided a means for exploring, prospecting, and settling the land. In many cases steamboats replaced dusty wagons, picking up where the ocean going ships unloaded their cargo and passengers. Between 1848 and 1850 California's population grew from 15,000 to 93,000.

The increasing use of hydraulic mining (the use of high-pressure jets of water to expose gold ore) in the 1860s changed the face of the Delta as mud, sand, and gravel washed from Sierra foothills flowed into rivers and downstream into the Delta, choking channels and raising the bottom of the estuary.

By 1860, many of the young men who originally came to California in search of gold began to settle in the Delta Region and farm. The Delta's rich soil and federal laws encouraging reclamation of swampland prompted settlers to drain and reclaim the marshlands.

These early Delta farmers had many problems to overcome. Their land was constantly being flooded. Chinese immigrants provided the great labor pool required for the massive human effort to build the first levees. They were shipped in by the thousands and many hundreds more came from the railroad-building gangs. The Chinese also helped work the rich farmlands.

During the second half of the 19th century enormous progress was made in developing the Delta as an agricultural paradise. New techniques were tried as part of the reclamation efforts. First the famous Fresno scraper (a huge horse drawn scraping shovel), then, mechanical power was applied to dredging, levee building, and land clearing. Pumps were introduced in 1876 to control water levels on reclaimed land.

By 1880, the amount of reclaimed area was 100,000 acres; by 1900, it had reached 250,000 acres. By the 1930s almost 450,000 acres had been reclaimed. Other changes were also taking place in the Delta. New species of fish were being introduced. American shad, striped bass, and white catfish were introduced in the Delta to share the waterways with existing salmon and other fish.

The new fish species flourished and between 1873 and 1910 as many as 21 canneries were built to process fish taken from the Sacramento and San Joaquin Rivers. An estimated 25% of all warm water and anadromous sport fishing species and 80% of the state's commercial fishery species inhabit or migrate through the Delta.

The Delta is still critical to the state's overall water picture. It is the heart of California's two largest water delivery projects, the State Water Project and the Federal Central Valley Project. Since the 1940s Delta rivers have transported water to the projects' pumps. From there Delta water is transported to cities in the Bay Area, and to more than 15 million people in Southern California. Two thirds of the state's residents rely on the Delta for at least a portion of their drinking water.

Today as we travel through the waterways of the Delta there are touches of nostalgia around every bend. Sometimes it's an old piling or two from an old landing or dock, sometimes the remains of an old hull or a broken down shack on a tulle island, yet the rivers and sloughs still flow quietly along as they did on the other side of yesterday.

BETHEL ISLAND

BETHEL ISLAND TIMELINE

The timeline below offers a glance into the development of Bethel Island from a time when Native Americans collected tules for baskets to a time when sportsmen flocked to the island to enjoy fishing and boating.

Early 1800's...Bethel Island was a huge marsh, interlaced with streams and covered with tules and willows which absorbed the spring and winter floods.

1860.....Mr. Stone reclaimed the land known as Bethel Island today under the Swamp and Over flowed Act of 1855. This site became known as Stone Tract.

1870.....Major William K. Bethell purchased land from Stone. The land was used to grow feed for the dairy herd on the island.

1871.....Jesse Cheney purchased land on Stone Tract from Bethell.

1878.....Stone Tract land value was set at $5 per acre according to Contra Costa County Assessors records; and Bethell & Company owned 2,200 acres, while Haggin & Davis owned 3,773 acres.

1880.....Sand Mound School was established. This one room school house was located on the west side of Bethel Island Road at Gateway Road.

1890's...Bethel Island became an island when Dutch Slough was dredged to the east to meet Sandmound Slough, Taylor Slough was extended south by dredging to meet Dutch Slough, and Piper Slough was extended south to meet Sandmound Slough.

1894.....Majority of landowners appoint a board to oversee the building of a new levee around the land and reconstruct the old levee.

1898.....Stone Tract was renamed Bethel Island when the County Board of Supervisors sold a strip of land 45' wide for a road to Frank and Anne Bethell.

1902.....William T. Sesone became holder of a large portion of the island.

1907.....The island suffered a devastating levee break.

1911.....Reclamation District 799 was declared valid by the courts and William Shafer served as chairman of the Board. Shafer resigned in 1912 and William J. Hotchkiss was elected to the position in 1913.

1913.....Judge E. A. Bridgeford built his home in the middle of the island. Bridgeford raised prize cattle and ran a dairy. During the 1940's the house was converted into a restaurant, named Mounds Club. This house in recent years was the office of Wes Anderson Engineering.

1915.....Reclamation District 1619 was organized under a part of Swamplands District #1 and parts of Districts 102, 107 and 183.

1916.....William Josephus Hotchkiss acquired 1,317 acres of Bethel Island to grow potatoes, beans, and sugar beets.

1918.....Judge E.A. Bridgeford organized the Bridgeford Company, which was a group of livestock breeders and dairymen. Bridgeford had a large herd of Holstein-Friesian cattle and started one of the first dairies in the area.

1918.....Bethel Island bridge, a one lane wood-planked structure, was built over Dutch Slough.

1920.....Sand Mound School closed and was moved to the Iron House School on the corner of Sellers Avenue and Cypress Road where it was used as a classroom.

1927.....A farmer was installing a floodgate in the levee and left the project unattended. During the night high tide came rushing through the excavation, washed out the levee and flooded the island.

1928.....Federal revenue agents raided an operating still on the island allegedly owned and operated by the son of a prominent area landowner. Newspapers said the operation supplied area bootleggers on a "gigantic scale".

1929.....High tides and rain broke the levees and flooded the island. The levees were repaired, and the island was pumped out and farming resumed.

1930's...Bethel Island became a fishing paradise and a favorite haunt for sportsmen looking for a prize winning striped bass.

1930....Blanche and Jack Farrar moved to Bethel Island to farm. They cleared a eucalyptus grove near the Bethel Island bridge to make a recreation area. Farrar's Park was on a site between the bridge and Stone Road. This became one of the area's favorite recreation sites. The park offered guests a picnic area, sandy beach, and cabins. The charge was twenty five cents per car and five cents per person.

Farrar Park

1937.....Before the original debt from the 1929 levee repair was paid off, the levees again broke and the landowners, overwhelmed by the second disaster, gave up and let the river reclaim what was originally its own. A 3,600 acre lake was created, known as Frank's Tract Lake.

1938.....Warren "Cap" Remsburg built the first boat harbor on the Island (near the bridge). Cap had 14 rowboats that he rented for $1 a day.

1939....Three hundred yards of the choicest top soil in which plants of many varieties were planted was taken from Bethel Island to Treasure Island during the Golden Gate International Exposition.

1945.....Connie and Flo Klein created Bethel Harbor.
1945.....Frank and Ted Andronico (brothers) built Frank's Marina. They offered a boat rental service, renting boats for $1.50 per day.
1945.....Judy and Rose Hribernik established a motel.
1946.....Bethel Island gets electricity.
1947.....Ethel Boxel became the Island's first postmaster. The post office was located in the back of the E & E Cafe, owned and operated by Ethel and Ed Boxel.
1947.....The Island gets its first firehouse. It was a war-surplus quonset hut placed on a site donated by Leroy Thomas. Charles Maxwell was the first fire chief.
1948.....Cypress Road and Bethel Island were connected. Prior to 1948 to get to Bethel Island you had to take Rose Aveune from Oakley to Cypress Road, then Jersey Island Road, and finally east along Dutch Slough Road to the one lane wooden Bethel Island bridge. A new bridge was also built in 1948 replacing the one lane wooden bridge that had been built thirty years earlier.

Marina Boulevard

1948.....Gene and Ada Krigbaum came to Bethel Island and built a dry-dock.
1948.....The island got its first telephones.
1949.....Leroy Thomas donated the land for the Bethel Island Scout Hall.
1949.....Julian Hribernik opened a hardware store.
1955.....Frank's Tract Lake was purchased by State Parks and Beaches Department of the State of California for $300,000.
1960.....Reclamation District 1619 converted to Bethel Island Municipal Improvement District.
1961.....The first edition of *Voice of the Delta* was published and edited by Ross Draper.
1961.....The Boat House Lounge was established when Ace Tennis converted a boat repair building into a bar and constructed the bar in the shape of a boat.
Until Next Time....

BETHEL ISLAND

When the Delta was first explored by white men it was a huge marsh cut by snag filled and tide influenced waterways. The low lands were covered with tules and willows. The valley oak was dominant, but there were also huge sycamore, laurel, willow, elderberry, locust, and cottonwood trees covering the land. Large flocks of pelicans, ducks, geese, and cranes were common in the lagoons and tule swamps. The rivers were filled with an endless supply of fish and beaver, muskrat, and otter were also bountiful.

Local Indians, in a primitive fashion, farmed the rich soil. They used the tule reeds to construct boats, homes, and baskets. The Indians lived a good life, and mother nature supplied them with an abundance of fish and game. During the winter months they moved into the foothills away from the waterfront.

By 1850, during the gold rush days, paddlewheel steamers ran between San Francisco and Sacramento, as well as Stockton. Many of those ships were woodburners using river oak and pine cut in four foot lengths and collected at the rivers edge. Some comsumed as much as a cord of wood per hour. Long before the railroads arrived or there were adequate roads in this region of California the river was used as the primary means of travel.

What made the Delta was its people. It was people that reclaimed the land. They built dikes and levees, dug the channels, created river ports and landings, and defied Mother Nature herself. When the waters swelled over the banks of the rivers to reclaim what was hers, it was the people that rebuilt the levees and started all over again. Early settlers purchased large tracts of land as early as 1855 for one dollar an acre throughout the Delta region. By 1878 land values had increased to $5 an acre.

In 1860 Mr. Stone reclaimed the land where Bethel Island is located today. Stone acted under the Swamp and Overflow Act of 1855. The island was originally known as Stone Tract and didn't actually become an island until the late 1890's when Dutch Slough was dredged to the east to meet Sandmound Slough. Taylor Slough was extended south by dredging to meet Dutch Slough, and Piper Slough was extended to meet Sandmound Slough.

In the early days, Stone Tract was known for the rich soil that grew cattle feed and grains and for the dairies that were established there. The land yielded hay and grain that was transported to market by barge.

Major Willaim K. Bethell purchased a large tract of land (approximately 3500 acres) from Mr. Stone. In 1871 Bethell sold part of his holdings to Mr. J.Cheney. Apparently the name was changed from Stone Tract to Bethel Island in 1898 when the Board of Supervisors sold a strip of land forty five feet wide for one dollar to Frank and Anna Bethell for a road. Why the second "l" was left off no one knows.

The first residents of Bethel Island received their mail and supplies by boat delivery. They were very isolated from the other communities of East Contra Costa County.

Reclamation District 1619 was established in 1915 as part of the Swamplands District #1, 102, 107, and 183. These earlier districts had been formed in 1894 to raise funding for levee maintenance. Reclamation District 1619 became the Bethel Island Municipal Improvement District in 1960.

In 1916 William J. Hotchkiss acquired 1,317 acres on Bethel Island to grow potatoes, beans, and sugar beets. About the same time Judge E.A. Bridgford purchased property and established a cattle ranch.

A single lane wooden bridge made out of 2 by 12 planks was constructed in the 1920's. The

Farrar family cleared a eucalyptus grove and established a recreation area near the bridge. This was Bethel Island's first recreation related enterprise. Many old timers in the area recall picnics, swimming, and Sunday afternoons at Farrar Park.

By the 1940s hunters and fishermen had established a week end colony near the old wooden bridge. After World War II, hunting and fishing cottages began to spring up on the periphery of the island. Sportsmen, fishermen, and boat enthusiasts had discovered the peace, and quiet, and solitude that Bethel Island offered and came in droves. It wasn't until 1946 that Bethel Island got electricity. In 1948 they got telephone service. On August 16,1946 the first Post Office was established in the rear of the E&E Cafe with Ethel Boxel as postmaster. Prior to the coming of postal service, residents received their mail in a row of boxes nailed to a fence near the bridge. With the arrival of these services the population of the island increased to a point where the one lane bridge had to be replaced. The building of the new bridge marked a turning point in Bethel Island's history. The first post office was built, stores were constructed, and facilities were established to offer complete boat launching, fishing, and other recreational activities.

Bethel Islands early postal service

Modern Bethel Island has about 3000 acres. It is assumed, that before reclamation, Stone Tract was about 6,000 acres which could have included land known today as Hotchkiss Tract.

Today Bethel Island is the most densely populated island in the Delta and offers complete services for permanent residents as well as weekend visitors. The island is often referred to as "the heart of the Delta". Until Next Time....

BETHEL ISLAND FIRE PROTECTION DISTRICT TIMELINE

1945.....After World War II, permanent residents moved to Bethel Island. Prior to that it had been totally owned by agricultural concerns.

1945.....Franks Tract became a State Park with fishing & recreational facilities.

1946.....Electricity brought to Bethel Island.

1947.....Bethel Island Fire District formed. County Board of Supervisors appointed Fire Commissioners. Bethel Island acquired its first fire engine—a 1930s-era American LaFrance. It was housed at Farrar Park Garage on Stone Road. Charles Maxwell named Fire Chief.

1947.....June 16—Bethel Island Firemen's Club organized. Charter members: Fire Chief Charles Maxwell, Assistant Fire Chief Clarence Shotswell, Ed Stone, Bill Andrews, Edwin Boxill, Art Hollander, George Duda, Johnny Duda, Julian (Judy) Hribernik, Bob Cunningham, Ben Tomlin, Tommy Tomlin, Jimmy Mattis, Edwin Drewick, Floyd Mathers, Bill Crossman, Fred Kee, and Leonard Burrow. All were required to be members of the Contra Costa Firemen's Association. Club officers elected were: President—Fire Chief Charles Maxwell, Vice President—Assistant Fire Chief Clarence Shotswell, Secretary-Treasurer—Edward H. Stone.

1947.....July 29—Second meeting of the Firemen's Club held in the Bel Isle Club (the fire phone was located at the end of the bar next to the back door of the Bel Isle and the firehouse was located just behind it).

1947.....November 7—Edward Stone resigned as Secretary-Treasurer. George Duda elected to replace him.

1948.....January—a surplus World War II Quonset hut was purchased to serve as the fire station. It was located on land donated by property owner Leroy Thomas, a Berkeley attorney. Volunteers completed work on the fire station after several months, only to have a huge windstorm destroy it four days later. A contractor was hired to rebuild the station.

1948.....May 21—Special meeting of the Firemen's Club held for the purpose of requesting the removal of Fire Commissioners Harry VonKosky, F. J. Hollander, B. Sanman, and (unknown first name) Beard and replacing them with Lawrence Mehaffey, Frank Andronico, Bill Crossman, and M. Gregory. Request was made to County Supervisor Trembath.

1948.....June—the first Bethel Island Firemen's Ball was held.

1948.....August 9—Bethel Island Improvement Club donated fire hose to the Fire Department. Clarence Shotswell (Assistant Fire Chief) resigned and George Duda resigned as Secretary-Treasurer. Bill Crossman, Sr. accepted temporary position of Secretary-Treasurer until election could be held.

1949.....Bethel Island Fire Department acquired a World War II "Command Car" for use as an emergency medical response vehicle.

1949.....August—Charles Hall succeeded Charles Maxwell as Fire Chief. Chief Hall appointed Floyd Mathers as Assistant Fire Chief.

1949.....September 26—E. A. Tomlin elected Secretary-Treasurer.

1949.....December 5—Bethel Island Firemen's Club had a total of $551.93 in its treasury. Lawrence Mehaffey was Secretary of the Bethel Island Fire Commissioners.

The first Bethel Island Volunteer Fire Department begins operation in a 2-door WW II Quonset Hut.

1950.....Bethel Island Fire Protection District Board of Commissioners included Ted Andronico, M. Gregory, and Bill Crossman.

1950.....February 7—Meeting room moved from right corner of firehouse to the front of the building. Work done by firemen volunteers.

1950.....February 21—Firehouse siren (that could be heard all over the island and called volunteers to duty) was tested at 8:00 p.m. on the first and third Mondays of the month.

1950.....March 6—Floyd Mathers resigned from Firemen's Club. Ben Tomlin elected to serve as Assistant Chief.

1950.....March 20—Firemen's Club invited all Fire Commissioners to attend meeting to discuss threats of the volunteers to resign. Commissioners at that meeting accepted the resignation of Chief Charles Hall and appointed Floyd Mathers as Fire Chief and Ben Tomlin, Assistant Fire Chief.

1950.....May 1—Leonard Burrows named new secretary of the Bethel Island Firemen's Club.

1951.....Living quarters were added to the fire station Quonset hut for volunteers to use.

1952.....A 1952 International Pumper fire engine was purchased (it was the fire district's first new engine).

1955.....Robert Cunningham was hired as the first part-time paid Fire Chief. Later Sam Scovel was hired as part-time paid Assistant Fire Chief.

1960.....Bethel Island Fire Commissioners were Ed Hill, Julian (Judy) Hribernik, Les Hauan, and Ted Andronico.

1960.....A concrete-block addition was added to the fire station to serve as an office and living quarters. A surplus military water tender was added to the fire department's apparatus.

1963.....A new 1962 International Pumper fire engine was purchased.

1968.....Radio Emergency Associated Communication Teams (REACT) organized on Bethel Island by Bruno Markel to assist BIFPD in emergency situations.

1969.....October—Bethel Island Fire Protection District Commissioners were: Judy Hribernik, Ted Andronico, Bob Gromm, Jerry Joseph, and John Thieme. BIFPD was unique in that it was the only district in the area to have two paid full-time employees: Fire Chief Sam Scovel and Assistant Fire Chief Joe Reas. The volunteers included Leo Whitener (Captain), Earl McMullen (Lieutenant) and 23 others.

1971.....Bethel Island Fire Department serviced 195 calls for the year (including 40 resuscitator calls).

1971.....December—Bethel Island Fire Department acted as escort service for Santa. Fire Chief Joe Reas drove Santa on a tour of the island before delivering him to Scouts Hall to see the children.

1971.....December 31—Bob Gramm's "Musings While Crossing the Bridge" column in the *Brentwood News* noted that the Bethel Island Fire Department did not have a single call for the New Year's Eve time period.

1972.....Joe Reas served as Fire Chief. The Bethel Island Fire Commissioners met on the first Thursday of the month.

1972.....February—the Bethel Island Boy Scouts, under the direction of Scoutmaster Carl Landgren, Jr., built house number signs to be placed on all residences of Bethel Island as an aid to the Fire Department.

1972.....March—Bethel Island Fire Department appreciated the support of the residents in a program of attaching red stickers with important emergency phone numbers to their phones for ready access.

1972.....June—The Fire Department had 3 resuscitator calls in one weekend (none were fatal).

1972.....September—Bethel Island Firemen's Club resumed hosting the Firemen's Ball. Jack Whitener appointed Fire Chief.

1975.....Bethel Island Fire Department acquired a new 1975 International Pumper to be used as its first responding engine.

1975.....A third full-time employee was hired. Paid employees work week was reduced from 84 hours to a standard 56 hour week.

1977.....Fire Chief Joseph (Jack) Whitener announced that the Bethel Island Fire Protection District underwent testing for its insurance rating. Ratings were numbered 1 to 10 by insurance companies to determine residents' insurance premiums. Tests rated the fire district as a Class 7 and only 88 points short of a Class 6 rating. Assistant Fire Chief was David Wahl.

1979.....A 22-foot Boston Whaler with a fire pump and emergency medical system was purchased for $20,000 in revenue collected at fund raisers and from donations. It was the department's first fire-rescue boat.

1980.....A 1980 water tender (2,000 gallon) was added to the department's equipment.
April 10—Bethel Island Fire Department, aided by Knightsen Fire Department assisted the U. S. Coast Guard in rescuing a family of five whose sailboat struck a barge near Webb Tract.

1982.....April 22—Fifteen reserve firefighters turned on their radio monitors in protest. Their complaints were against Fire Chief Jack Whitener and fire department policies. They presented a 9-page list of those complaints.

1982.....May 6—Fire Commissioners (Chairman Julian "Judy" Hribernik, Howard Holmes, Les Burke, and Ralph Waller) held a meeting with the reserves declaring them no longer employees. Charles Drolette, President of the United Firemen of Bethel Island, declared reserves fear retaliation from Fire Chief Whitener if they reapply to serve as reserves. County Supervisor Tom Torlakson appointed DeRoyce Bell of the County Administrator's office to act as coordinator of a panel to study the Bethel

1982.....Island Fire Protection District. (Report was to be presented to the Fire Commissioners at their July 1 meeting—results of the report are unknown).

1983.....Three new fire engines were purchased—one was a Type 1-1,250 GPM Pumper and two were Type 4-4WD wild land engines.

1984.....Bethel Island Fire Protection District had 35 reserve firefighters and three full-time paid officers: Fire Chief Joseph (Jack) Whitener, Assistant Chief David Wahl, and Bob Lindgren. Delores Hauan served as a part-time Secretary (this position was expanded to full-time in 1999) and James Coleman served as mechanic.

1984.....Fire Commissioners were: Chairman Howard Holmes, Julian (Judy) Hribemik, Ralph Waller, Jackie Fleming and Ralph Richardson. The fire station was located at 3045 Ranch Lane.

1987.....Jack Whitener was still Fire Chief.

1990.....The Fire Department acquired a 1966 3,500 gallon International water truck for $1.00 from the City of Antioch. It was refurbished to serve as the department's second water tender. The additional supply brought ISO (insurance) ratings to Class 5.

1990.....A second fire-rescue boat (a 22-foot Boston Whaler with 599 gallons per minute pump and monitor) was put into service.

1993.....The Fire Department deleted one full-time position and began staffing the fire station with paid-on-call volunteer firefighters.

1996.....October 23—The Fire Department established Contra Costa County's first part-time paramedic/firefighter program that served as non-transporting first responders and re-established 24-hour station coverage.

1997.....Staffing of the Fire Department included 3 full-time (2 uniform and 1 clerical) personnel, 17 paid-on-call firefighters and 45 part-time paramedic/firefighters.

2002.....November—Bethel Island Fire Protection District merged with East Diablo Fire District and Oakley/Knightsen Fire District to form East Contra Costa Fire Protection District. Bethel Island was staffed with two full-time firefighters. The Bethel Island Fire Commission was abolished.

2003.....May—Bethel Island residents said "farewell" to the Bethel Island Fire Department, which was headed by Fire Chief Dave Wahl, with beer and wine tasting, an art show featuring local artists, and an evening of dancing, food and extraordinary Chocolate Extravaganza to thank the volunteers for their years of dedication.

BETHEL ISLAND FIRE PROTECTION DISTRICT HISTORY

Bethel Island is approximately six square miles of land located nine miles east of Antioch, California. Until the end of World War II, the island was predominantly a farming community controlled by Reclamation District 1619. The Reclamation District had been formed in 1915 under the auspices of the California Water Code.

A few fishing "shacks" were erected in the 1930s, but summer homes, permanent residences, and boat harbors did not materialize until after World War II. Thus began conflicts between large agricultural landowners and the new residential owners on how to assess the Reclamation District's levee maintenance and island drainage. This is one reason the island was nicknamed "Battle Island." The island did not receive electricity until 1946. The first reliable phone service followed and in August, 1947, Bethel Island opened its first United States Post Office.

With the arrival of permanent residents, the need for a local fire department became urgent. Thus, in 1947, the Bethel Island Fire Protection District was established by Contra Costa County. The County Board of Supervisors appointed five local Fire Commissioners. Charles Maxwell was named Fire Chief and Clarence Shotswell was appointed Assistant Fire Chief; the department acquired a 1930s-era American LaFrance fire engine; about a dozen local residents signed up to be volunteers; the Bethel Island Firemen's Club was organized and the department was up and running.

The fire engine was originally housed at Farrar Park Garage. In January, 1948, the department purchased a surplus World War II Quonset hut to serve as its fire station. A Quonset hut is a

The proud founding volunteers of the Bethel Island Fire District display their fire engines and equipment in front their firehouse.

lightweight prefabricated circular structure of corrugated galvanized steel. These structures were used during the war. Its name derives from the site of its first manufacturer, Quonset Point, in Davisville, Rhode Island.

The structure was located on a lot donated by Leroy Thomas, a Berkeley attorney, who owned several pieces of property on Bethel Island. Eventually, additions were added to this building allowing for living quarters for some firefighters and a meeting room for the Bethel Island Firemen's Club. Over the course of the years, several new fire engines were purchased as well as used water tenders and two Boston Whalers that served as the department's fire-rescue boats.

In 1955, the Bethel Island Fire Protection District hired a part-time fire chief and assistant fire chief. By 1969, there were two full-time employees in addition to the volunteers. A third full time employee was hired in 1975. After 18 years (in 1993) one of these positions was eliminated, but a clerical position was added. The fire department established Contra Costa County's first part-time paramedic/firefighter program in October, 1996. The volunteers served as non transporting first responders.

In 1982, almost all of the reserve volunteers turned in their radio monitors in protest and compiled a list of complaints they had about the supervision of the fire department. At a meeting in May, 1982, the Fire Commissioners declared the reserves were no longer employees of the district.

County Supervisor Tom Torlakson appointed DeRoyce Bell of the Contra Costa County Administrator's office to assemble a panel of interested parties to address the complaints. Several articles were printed in the news media about the controversy. The panel was to issue its findings at a meeting scheduled for July 1 (the results of that report are not known).

Some of the Fire Commissioners who served the Bethel Island Fire Protection District over the fifty-five years of its existence included (listed in alphabetical order, not by time of service): Theodore Andronico, Les Burke, Bill Crossman, Sr., Jackie Fleming, Robert Gromm, Lester Hauan, Ed Hill, F. J. Hollander, Howard Holmes, Julian (Judy) Hribernik, Jerry Joseph, Lawrence Mehaffey, Ralph Richardson, John Thieme, Harry Von Kosky, and Ralph Waller.

Among the Fire Chiefs and Assistant Fire Chiefs who served the fire district were (in alphabetical order, not by time of service): Robert Cunningham, Charles Hall, Floyd Mathers, Charles Maxwell, Joe Reas, Sam Scovel, Clarence Shotswell, Ben Tomlin, David Wahl, and Joseph (Jack) Whitener.

In November, 2002, the Bethel Island Fire Protection District merged with the East Diablo (Brentwood and Byron) Fire District and the Oakley/Knightsen Fire District to form East Contra Costa Fire Protection District. With the formation of the merged district the Bethel Island Fire Commission was abolished.

As a farewell to the dedicated volunteers, paid-on-call firefighters and the leaders of the Bethel Island Fire District, the residents of Bethel Island staged a day-long event in May, 2003 that included an art show by local artists, a beer and wine tasting event, and an evening of dancing and dining to show their appreciation for the years of service.

KNIGHTSEN

KNIGHTSEN TIMELINE

The town of Knightsen was founded in 1898 when the Santa Fe Railroad made it's preliminary survey through the area. Knightsen has played an important role in the history of East Contra Costa. Listed below is a timeline of events that took place in Knightsen.

1776....Juan Bautisti de Anza, a great Spanish explorer led his men through the Knightsen area. With him was Father Font, who made maps and kept a dairy every day. Font's diary described the landscape, the wildlife, and the Indians living in the area.

1840's & 50's...The Tule Lane area near Knightsen was used by John Marsh vaqueros for their annual rodeo.

1865.....Lazarus Barkley, a native of Iowa, settled on 160 acres where the town of Knightsen is today. He farmed this land for more than twenty years before selling to George Knight.

1868.....Eden Plain School, a one room school house, was built on the John Pierce ranch. Miss Mary Lockhart was the first teacher. Classes were held at this site for thirty eight years. This school merged with Knightsen School in 1912

1869.....Christian Heidorn came to Knightsen from Germany.

1880.....First almond trees in the area were planted by M.A. Walton, L.G. Barkley, W.F. Pierce, and Oscar Smith.

1883.....George Washington Knight, a native of Maine, purchased 110 acres from Lazarus Barkley. This site would later become the town of Knightsen

1894.....Richard R. Veale of the Eden Plain District was elected sheriff for the county, a position he held until 1928 fro more than 40 years.

1898.....Knightsen first appeared on the survey maps of the San Francisco San Joaquin Railway (later the Santa Fe).

1899.....George W. Knight became the first postmaster and immediately built a building to be occupied by the new post office and a grocery, the first store in Knightsen. Knight was post master for thirteen years.

1900.....The Santa Fe Depot was built. It was designed by W.B. Storey Jr.. The first trains ran through Knightsen.

1902.....William Redmond became the town's first blacksmith.

1904.....Henry Heidorn established Heidorn General Merchandise.

1904.....George Knight exhibited Klondike Almonds that had been grown in Knightsen at the St. Louis Exposition.

1905.....A new Eden Plain School was built closer to Knightsen on Delta Road near Knightsen Ave. Four acres were purchased for the new school site. The new structure was completed June 1906, at a cost of $7,000 for the building and the grounds. The school had three classrooms and a full basement. This building was replaced in 1936 when a new Knightsen School was built.

1906.....Walnut Grove Farm, owned by Ernest and Benjamin Burrough was established. This later became Burrough's Brothers Dairy.

1908.....Hotchkiss Tract flooded.

1910.....Ted Ohmstede moved to Knightsen at the age of three with his family. He graduated from Liberty in 1927; became Justice of the Peace in 1951; was well known for his work with the youth of East County. In 1965 the LUHS sports field was named in his honor.

1911.....Gottlieb (better known as George) Somerhalder, a native of Nebraska settled in Knightsen, where he farmed for many years. Somerhalder died in 1953.
1912.....Veale Tract of 1700 acres was sold to California Reality Company of San Jose for $140,000.
1913.....Electricity came to town.
1916.....Record breaking shipments of celery shipped via the rails from Knightsen.
1917.....89 young men from Knightsen signed the roll for the draft (WW1).
1917.....Six dairy farmers in the area shipped a daily average of 2,500 gallons of bulk milk on the Santa Fe rails. The six dairies were : Fox, Stone Bros., Bridgeford, Burroughs Bros., Emerson, and Hotchkiss.
1917.....Cornelius L. "Sodie" Kriem became station master at the Santa Fe depot. He served in this position until 1938

Knightsen Dairies shipped 2500 gallons of milk daily - 1917

1918.....Knightsen Farm Center was organized. The first meeting was held on the second floor of the Heidorn Store. The first officers were Benjamin Burroughs, president; Henry Heidorn, vice president; Lillian Fotheringham, secretary; Gottlide Somerhalder, director. The organization built their clubhouse in 1922.
1918....Henry W. Heidorn became Justice of the Peace.
1919.....The Orwood Bridge opened.
1920.....Knightsen Irrigation District formed (April 1921 a $650,000 bond issue was passed to finance the district). The following directors were chosen: Joseph Minta, E.B.Sellers, H.W. Heidorn (the district's first president), Frank H. Estes, and Byron Grigsby. Dr. Bailey was elected assessor, A.H Shafer collector, and A.E. Bonnickson treasurer.
1920.....John N. Kristich built a concrete pipe manufacturing plant on the southeast corner of Delta Road and Knightsen Ave. In 1926 Kristich sold pipe used by the Knightsen Irrigation District for $170,000, and Byron Bethany Irrigation District bought pipe valued at $25,000.

Krislich Pipe Plant - 1922

1922.....Farm Bureau Center was built. George and Christina Knight, for whom the town was named, sold for $10 in gold, lots 8, 9, 10, and 11 of block 2, for the club house.

1924.....The Knightsen 4-H Club was founded. Paul Somerhalder was the organizations first leader. It is one of the oldest clubs in Contra Costa County. The group conducted an active learning program for the children of Knightsen.

1925.....Harold Bloomfields vineyards near Knightsen yielded forty tons. Bloomfield had sixteen acres in Tokay vines, of which ten were three year old vines and six acres were two years old.

1926.....Knightsen Irrigation Company consolidated with Brentwood and Lone Tree to create East Contra Costa Irrigation Dist.

1931.....Myrtle Pikron replaced Henry Heidorn as Knightsen's postmaster.

1931.....George Knight, who founded Knightsen, died at the home of his daughter Addie F.   f.

1931.....Johnny Schneider of Knightsen won the title of World's Champion All-Around Cowboy by sweeping the finals at a rodeo in Los Angeles.

1936.....The new Knightsen School was built on Delta Road.

1936.....The Knightsen Garden Club was founded by Lillian DeVlieger.

1940.....The Knightsen School had an enrollment of 123 students.

1940.....Rena Ohmstede was librarian at Knightsen Library.

1945.....June Bunn started teaching at Knightsen School where she taught for 37 years, retiring in 1984.

1946.....The town of Knightsen had the first dial telephones in Eastern Contra Costa. There were 18 phones served out of the Knightsen exchange.

1951.....Ted Ohmstede became Justice of the Peace.

1952.....The volunteer fire department formed with fourteen original volunteers. The first fire chief was Stan Duff, grandson of George Knight. Sam Somerhalder was first captain and Angelo Ghigliazza first lieutenant.

1958.....Jerry Cocco became Knightsen Volunteer Fire Dept fire chief.

1963.....Mrs Irene Hamilton, owner of the Sportsman Club tavern, provided in her will that $25,000 be given to the Knightsen School District for the use and benefit of young people and children in said school district. These funds were used to build the school swimming pool.

1968.....Judge Ted Ohmstede died of a heart attack.

1972.....The Santa Fe Station was demolished.

1994.....The Knightsen Town Advisory Council (K-TAC) was established on March 8th..
   Until Next Time....

KNIGHTSEN FOUNDED IN 1898

The town of Knightsen was founded in 1898 when the Santa Fe Railroad began a preliminary survey through the area to determine where tracks would be laid and which right-of-ways should be purchased for a line into Stockton. The railroad spent a year and a half grading the road bed and laying tracks expecting the first passenger and freight trains to arrive during the spring of 1900.

Knightsen's first buildings were the Santa Fe station house, a railroad station, and a pumping plant to supply locomotives with water and supplies. Harvey Rook was the first Santa Fe Railroad agent assigned to Knightsen. He later married George Knight's daughter.

The Santa Fe Railroad originally wanted to name the site Meganos after John Marsh's Los Meganos Ranch that once covered much of East County. Settlers in the area preferred the name of Knightsen after the George Knight family which stood to lose a portion of their farm land for construction of the railroad. To assure the town would be named Knightsen residents wrote to Washington DC and secured a post office under the name of Knightsen before the railway construction was completed. During the winter of 1899 George Knight was commissioned as postmaster of the new town named after his family (a position he held for thirteen years). He immediately built a post office and grocery store, the first retail establishment in Knightsen. Soon to follow was an

asparagus packing plant built by the Lynon Brothers which during harvest season would load and ship two to four freight cars full of asparagus stalks daily.

As early as the 1880's settlers planted the first almond trees, and dairymen had established their dairies in the Knightsen area. Some of these men were:
M. A. Walton, L.G. Barkley, W.F. Pierce, and Oscar Smith. By the 1890's George Knight, Thomas Murphy, William Shafter, John Byers, and W. W. Sterling were also producing almonds, apricots, grapes, and alfalfa. Prior to establishment of the railroad, farmers shipped their milk and cream to market on the same vessels which transported fruit and nut crops from Babbes Landing, a channel off Dutch Slough at the north end of Sellers Avenue. With arrival of the railroad these growers and dairymen had easier access to transportation for their crops and milk to market. There were six main dairies shipping a daily average of 2,500 gallons of bulk milk to Bay Area markets. The Stone Brothers established the first large dairy followed by Fox, Bridgeford, Burroughs Brothers, Emerson, and Hotchkiss. During the 1920's Knightsen was one of the largest milk shipping depots in the state of California.

Knightsen residents found they could board a train at eight in the morning bound for Stockton, spend the day shopping and attending to their business, then return home by five in the evening.

In the early 1900's the town of Knightsen consisted of Henry W. Heidorn's general store, a post office, Art English's Saloon, Frank Stone's Imperial Cafe, William Redmond's Blacksmith shop, the Santa Fe Depot, several warehouses, and a respectable number of residents. The residents of Knightsen established a small park in the middle of town consisting of a lawn, colorful flowers, and several eucalyptus trees where townsmen could sit and visit on a warm summer's day enjoying the delta breeze. A tall flag pole was erected in the middle of town where school children often presented patriotic programs. By 1913, electrical lights were installed, and the citizens could boast about their business district.

In 1920, after an overwhelming election, the Knightsen Irrigation District was formed to irrigate 10,000 acres of local farm land. The project cost $650,000. The first board consisted of Henry Heidorn, president; Adrian Shafer, assessor and controller; A.E. Bonnickson, treasurer, C.H. Noyes, secretary, and directors John Minta, Edwin Sellers, George Smith, Frank Estes, and Byron Grigsby. However, before completion of the project the district had become part of the East Contra Costa Water District.

The change from dry farming to irrigated fields brought many changes to the area. John N. Kristich, a pipe manufacturer from King City, established a branch of his firm in Knightsen. The concrete pipe manufacturing plant was located next to the railroad tracks, south of Delta Road, and across the street from Knightsen School. In the 1920's Kristich was one of the largest manufacturers of concrete pipe in California. Kristich made $170,000 worth of pipe for Knightsen Irrigation District, and $25,000 worth of pipe for the Byron-Bethany Irrigation District.

The Knightsen Farm Bureau was organized in 1918. Their first meetings were held on the second floor of Heidorn's Store, with Benjamin Burroughs as president; Henry Heidorn, vice president; Lillian Fotheringham, secretary; and George Somerhalder, director. The organization built a hall in 1922 on three lots donated by George Knight, which later became the heart of the community. Over the years the hall has been used for school graduations, dances, weddings, political functions, school plays, holiday celebrations, church services, a safe haven for flood victims, and an endless list of other events.

Knightsen has a wonderful history and has definitely left its mark on East Contra Costa County. Until Next Time....

GEORGE W. KNIGHT

In the beginning, the land was vast and ageless. Eventually came the Native Americans. Then, there were explorers and fur traders who paved the way for pioneer families. They came, slowly at first, and by the 1860s East Contra Costa was dotted with settlements and wheat fields from the foot of Mount Diablo to the river. This rich fertile land drew thousands of young men from the east who were searching for a place to settle and raise their families. George W. Knight was one of these men.

George W. Knight, credited with being the founder of Knightsen, was born in Chelsea, Maine, January 20,1843. His parents, John and Adeline Knight, had a farm where they raised apples and corn. Typical of that era in America, all the Knight children worked on the family farms. George learned first hand about horticulture, valuable lessons he would use all of his life. George knew he wanted to be a farmer. He had read about the climate in the West and had dreamt of farmland where you wouldn't have to wait until late spring, after the winter snows had melted to plant your crops. He dreamt of land that was fertile without pine trees and rocks.

At the age of twenty three, George moved to Massachusetts where he worked for several years before sailing to California in 1874 with his cousin via the Isthmus of Panama. Prior to settling in Contra Costa he worked on harvesters and hay presses in Santa Barbara, San Francisco, Marin County, Livermore, and Antioch. While working in the Livermore Valley, George had an opportunity to spend time in the foothills. Many years later he told a story of walking to Brushy Peak and looking out over the beautiful valley that lay below and saying, "That's the place for me to own a farm and build my home." By 1883 he had saved enough money to purchase 110 acres from Lazarus Barkley (my great grandfather's brother) and begin farming. The farm was located where the town of Knightsen is today.

George first planted wheat and hay. He worked hard and within a few years reaped the bounty of his harvest. He soon had saved enough to purchase the 80 acres adjoining his farm from the Veale family and expanded his crops to include a few acres of almonds.

In 1885 George Knight met and married Christina Christensen, a native of Denmark. She was the daughter of Johan and Anna Christensen. They were married in Antioch and honeymooned in San Francisco, which they traveled to by river boat.

Addie Knight Duff, George Knight's daughter, spoke to the Historical Society in 1971. The following is quoted from her— "One day a couple of surveyors for the Santa Fe Railroad Company came to see my father and told him they were going to survey his property for a railroad to run from Oakland to Stockton and on down south. They wanted to pass through his two large fields. Well, that displeased my father very much to have his two big fields cut in half. So he offered to give them enough land for a passing track and a station if they would move further west and cut off only the corner of his ranch. So they did, and this corner is now Knightsen."

Addie went on to tell about how the town got it's name. "In gratitude for the donation of land, the Superintendent of the Santa Fe named the town Knightsen using my father's name and the 'sen' off my mother's maiden name, which was Christensen."

In 1899 the Santa Fe laid it's track and by 1900 the first passenger and freight trains were running. Harvey Rock was the first railroad agent to be assigned to the new station. Rock later married one of George Knight's daughters. The first buildings erected in the new town were the Santa Fe section house, a railroad station, and a pumping plant to supply the locomotives with water. These facilities were soon followed by a general store and post office built by Knight, who was appointed the first postmaster. The general store was run by Neimeyer and Carston. The Lynon brothers built an asparagus packing plant. During asparagus season they would load two to four railroad cars full of stalks each day.

Knightsen grew. Businessmen came to town and established stores to meet the needs of area residents. Within a few years, Mr. Silva built a barber shop, John Cautrell established a saloon, Frank Stone built and operated the Imperial Cafe, and Sam and Bill Redmond erected a blacksmith. A small park containing a lawn, colorful flowers, and several eucalyptus trees was added. Knightsen was a thriving little town, and George Knight and his family were key players in all that transpired there.

The Knightsen region was noted for it's almonds, apricots, and other fruits including many vineyards. The community also became well known for the its dairies that produced thousands of gallons of milk and cream that were shipped to points throughout the Bay Area.

Knight donated the three lots for the Farm Bureau Building, served on the Eden Plains school board for fourteen years, and was Knightsen postmaster for thirteen years.

George Knight is remembered as a progressive and energetic farmer. He promoted the Klondike almond and displayed samples at the St Louis Exposition in 1904. He lived to see Knightsen become a prosperous agricultural center. He died in Brentwood in 1931 at the age of 87.

Until Next Time….

SAMUEL & SARAH SELLERS

Samuel and Sarah Sellers came to East Contra Costa County in 1860 via Cape Horn. Samuel was a native of Pennsylvania and Sarah was born in New York. Samuel tried his luck at gold mining in Mariposa prior to purchasing one hundred and sixty acres in the Iron House District (between Knightsen and Brentwood).

The Sellers, like many of the area's pioneer families, farmed the rich soil and reaped the bounty of their harvest. Samuel cleared the land and planted wheat, depending on nature for his crops' development. Raising grain was the largest industry in Contra Costa County during the 1860's, with early settlers experimenting with other crops, including fruits and vines. The Sellers planted pears, apples, peaches, pomegranates, olives, figs, almonds and apricots—in fact, they tried almost everything.

Cultivation and manufacturing of silk was introduced on the East Coast as early as 1771. The 1880 census shows the gross annual value of American manufactured silk goods to be millions of dollars with the operation of 18,467 looms. In 1861 Louis Prevost of San Jose became the first Californian to attempt raising silkworms and cocoons.

Feeling their land was especially adapted to the production of endless quantities of silk, Samuel and Sarah planted a grove of three thousand mulberry trees in the Iron House District and erected a cocoonery near the grove, constructing and maintaining it according to the strictest scientific principles of the era, giving a great deal of care to the worms between infancy and maturity as well as addition to raising the cocoons. They were among the few farmers in California heavily involved in the production of silk. Mrs. Sellers exhibited samples of reeled, raw and floss silk in different colors.

By the early 1880's Sarah Sellers became a renowned authority on silk cultivation and was an active member of the California Silk Culture Association. Mrs. Theodore Hittell, secretary of this organization, visited the Sellers farm and wrote a detailed report about the visit. The following details are quoted from this report.

"I went last Thursday, by rail, to Brentwood, which is near Antioch. From Brentwood a wagon road leads to Mrs. Sellers' house, which is surrounded with a grove of about three thousand mulberry trees, covered with fine, healthy leaves, and loaded with pink, white and black mulberries. Mrs. Sellers had hatched, from an ounce of eggs, about thirty thousand silk-worms, which were feeding in a room adjoining her kitchen. When the temperature of the feeding room falls below 70 degrees, she avails herself of the heat of the kitchen stove to bring it up again. I examined the worms; they were ferociously devouring the leaves of the mulberry, and were all in a healthy condition. She feeds them four times a day. She informed me that after the fourth molting one feeding does very well at ten o'clock at night."

"The feeding-room is a room generally used as a store room. On two of its sides are frames containing shelves, one above the other, made of rough wood, with laths across and covered with cloth, on which the leaves are spread and the worms distributed. Each shelf is three and a half feet wide. There is a window and one door in the room, which are opposite each other, so as to make ventilation easy. In the middle of the day the thermometer rose to 95 degrees, and then the worms were the liveliest; but the healthiest temperature is about 75 to 80 degrees."

"From what I saw I am entirely satisfied that millions upon millions of silk worms can be raised without any great trouble in California, and particularly, that they can be raised easily and conveniently, in remunerative quantities and at inconsiderable expense, by small farmers and comparatively poor people."

Samuel and Sarah maintained a display of cocoons and silkworms that attracted considerable attention from visitors to the county fair in Pacheco in 1878.

The Sellers planted their roots deep in the fertile soil of East Contra Costa. The family name can be found in church, school and fraternal organization records. Sellers Avenue is a constant reminder of a pioneer family that settled this land 136 years ago. Their son George Sellers owned one of the finest orchards in this region of California, growing primarily walnuts and apricots. He also served for many years as deputy sheriff under Sheriff Veale and was a member of the school board. Edith Agnes Sellers, Samuel and Sarah's granddaughter, was the first graduate from Liberty Union High School in 1905. She later became a high school teacher in Salinas.

As I research the pages of our history I find that families like the Sellers underwent incredible hardships to travel to this region of California and establish themselves in this new land, leaving footprints in the chapters of our past. Until Next Time....

Iron House School
Sarah Sellers was the first woman elected to a school board in the State of California

SHERIFF VEALE'S
RECORD OF ACHIEVEMENTS

The chapters of East Contra Costa's history would not be complete without the story of Richard R. Veale, who for 40 years served as county sheriff. Veale started his career in 1894 when the county was still wild and untamed. In those early days almost every lawbreaker was known as a gunman, and Veale's territory reached from the lowlands of the Delta, which was in its first stages of reclamation, to the foothills and Mount Diablo, where caves and numerous small valleys made perfect hideouts.

During his 40 years as sheriff, Veale had numerous miraculous escapes, arrested many desperate characters, and sent many of them to the penitentiary.

As a prominent resident of the county once said "The school, the church, and the home have all found Richard R. Veale a bulwark of strength, a monument of untiring energy, dependable at all times, and first to the front when duty calls, yet ever kind, consistent and considerate—a man!" (quoted from a 1924 edition of the *Byron Times*)

Veale was born in Solano County on March 27, 1864, and moved with his family to the Eden Plain District of Contra Costa County in 1868. His father, who raised stock and was an early wheat grower in the area, had come to California in 1855 via the Isthmus of Panama, settling in Solano County before moving to the Brentwood area.

Richard Veale followed in his father's footsteps and became a prominent farmer as a young man. He had the distinction of being the first farmer in the county to use modern and up-to-date methods such as the steam plows and harvesters he used on his 800-acre farm four miles from Brentwood.

Veale became interested in local and state politics at an early age. He attended state conferences, and served on the State Republican Committee.

When Richard R. Veale was thirty years old he was elected sheriff for the county. He was connected with many notable cases, including the capture of the criminal who stole over $300,000 worth of gold bullion from the Selby Smelting Company and hid it in the bay.

He was very involved in all aspects of the community. He was an active member of many fraternal organizations in the region: Knights Templars; the Royal Arch Chapter of Masons; the Elks; the Odd Fellows; the Eagles; the Native Sons; the Woodmen; the Moose; the Redmen; U.P.E.C.; the Knights of Pythias; and the Rebekahs. He served for twenty years as secretary of the Sheriffs of California Association.

His political interests are reflected in the fact that he was a delegate to the National Republican Convention several times. He also was the Contra Costa representative to the 1916 Panama-Pacific Exposition in San Francisco

Richard Veale married Mary E. Martin on November 11, 1890. To this union there were six children: Robert, William, Leila, Mortimer, Miriam and Leona.

Richard Veale was a dominant factor in the progress of Contra Costa County. There were few notable public projects that he didn't take a prominent part in. Men like Veale built the foundation on which the West was established. Until Next Time....

FREDERICK BABBE
EARLY LANDING DEVELOPER

Frederick Babbe was born in Holstein, Prussia, in 1823 and came to the New World in search of gold in 1850. In 1854 he purchased a three-hundred-acre farm in the Iron House district, a site about two miles northeast of Oakley, and started building Babbe's Landing. This landing replaced a landing known as Iron House Landing that had been built by Fassett and McCauley for Martin Hamburg on property further downstream. Babbe's land was primarily swamp and overflow land that would often receive high tide waters and flood.

Fred Babbe spent more than $30,000 reclaiming his land by building a levee around the property that was five to seven feet high and approximately twenty-five feet wide at the base. He later built a canal 2,838 feet long, 42 feet wide and approximately seven feet deep. This canal was deep enough for one-hundred-ton vessels to navigate and dock at his landing.

Babbes Landing

Babbe's Landing, located on Dutch Slough, at the north end of Sellers Avenue, was one of the primary shipping points during East Contra Costa's grain-growing era. (On old maps Dutch Slough is referred to as Iron House Slough.) Wheat was stored in large warehouses, then loaded onto barges and schooners at Babbe's or other local landings and shipped to docks in Martinez or Port Costa, where it was then transferred to larger vessels bound for ports all over the world. Shipping records show that Babbe's Landing shipped between three and four thousand tons of grain each year.

When Frederick Babbe first settled in the Delta region he found a land covered with tules and valley oak and teeming with wildlife: bear, tule elk, wildcat, antelope, otter, mink, raccoon, beaver, muskrat, fox, skunk, opossum, rabbit, waterfowl, quail and more. The waterways furnished salmon, bass, pike, perch, crayfish, catfish, shad, croppie, sturgeon, thicktail chub, freshwater clam and freshwater snail. There were also huge sycamore trees, and on the riverbanks you could find laurel, willow, elderberry, cottonwood, buckeye, and wild grape.

Johanna Babbe, Fred's daughter, married Andrew Portman and they farmed 1,240 acres between Veale Tract and Knightsen, an area known today as Reclamation District 799.

At one point when Babbe was experiencing financial difficulties he took Robert G. Dean on as a partner. Dean had worked for Balfour, Guthrie Co. for many years, was the first president of the Bank of Brentwood, and was financially connected to several early businesses.

Babbe's Landing became a horse sanitarium, or grazing farm, for the purpose of breeding race horses as well as a rehabilitation center where horses could recover from foot injuries received on the cobblestone streets of San Francisco. Henry Dutard, a well-known grain and commission merchant from San Francisco, purchased the property in 1897 and subdivided the Brentwood Horse Sanitarium into sections. These sections were further divided into box stalls for stallions, paddocks, departments for brood mares, jockey stables and other buildings to accommodate the farm's needs.

Dutard dredged the canal deeper and used the old landing for delivery of the tons of hay necessary for horse feed. He also created an irrigation system to supply the pastures with water during the summer months and a pumping system for use during the winter to expel excess rainwater into the river. Dutard's superintendent, Frank Nugent, lived on site and oversaw the day-to-day business of the farm.

Around 1912, Dutard sold the farm to Central Shuey Company, a large dairy in Oakland. The next owner, Golden State Milk Company of San Francisco, enlarged the dairy and operated it for many years.

During the 1930's, the property again changed hands, becoming San Joaquin Farms, owned by Turnbull and Gray. It was then sold to the Kenner brothers of Utah. In 1946 Oscar and Jeanie Burroughs bought the site and expanded the Burroughs Brothers Dairy, which was located next door.

B. R., W. P., and E. C. Burroughs (Oscar's father and uncles) had settled in the Iron House District in 1907. They purchased 320 acres and established a modern and progressive dairy farm. Milk from the dairy was marketed not only in East Contra Costa, but also in Oakland, San Francisco, Stockton, Fresno, Richmond, San Mateo, San Jose, Sacramento and Pittsburg.

The landings of East Contra Costa County played an important role in the lives of early settlers. Although barges were used primarily to transport crops to market, they also often made deliveries and carried families to and from the city. The rivers are still lined with many rotted remains of pilings that, at one time, supported landings and wharves built in the days when riverboats reigned supreme. After construction of our current network of roads the trucking industry took over the monumental task of transporting farmers' produce to market. Until Next Time....

THE CHRISTIAN HEIDORN FAMILY
KNIGHTSEN PIONEERS

Christian Heidorn came to California in 1868 when he was twenty seven years old from Hanover, Germany, via New York and Cape Horn. He was an early pioneer of the Knightsen area. In 1871 he purchased two hundred and forty acres and began his farming operations, growing primarily wheat which he shipped to market via Babbes Landing. By the 1890's his holdings had increased to more than eight hundred acres dedicated to wheat, nuts, and fruit as well as a fine productive vineyard.

Christian claimed a wife from his native land. He married Dorthea Stoverson, who was seven years his junior. They had three children, two girls and a boy. Henry W., married Helen Johnston, Emma, married Thomas White, and Edna, married Sam Hill. Christian died in 1908 at the age of 60.

The Heidorn family was actively involved in all aspects of the early development of East Contra Costa and Christian Heidorn's descendant's names can be found peppered throughout the chapters of our history. Henry W. Heidorn, Christians' son, owned and operated, Heidorn General Merchandise, which he opened in 1904. After receiving his early education locally, Henry attended college in San Francisco. Following college he found employment with several merchandise stores in San Francisco, Crockett, and Antioch prior to opening his own establishment in Knightsen. Henry also served the community as Judge and Justice of the Peace. He helped organize the Knightsen Irrigation District, served on the Knightsen School Board, and was Postmaster for Knightsen for many years. Henry was a fruit grower as well as serving as deputy county assessor for the fifth district. He was also heavily involved in several local fraternal organizations holding offices in the Masons, Odd Fellows, and Independent Order of Foresters.

In 1909, the Byron Times Booster Edition praised Henry Heidorn for his productive vineyard, consisting of 15,000 Zinfandel grape vines describing Henry as a progressive businessman with his eye on the future.

According to front page headlines of a 1907 Byron Times, Emma, Christian's daughter, married Thomas White on December 27. Thomas White was superintendent of the Solway Land Company. The newlyweds honeymooned for a month in Canada. Emma became a full partner with her brother, Henry W. Heidorn, in the Heidorn Mercantile business in Knightsen. She helped with the bookkeeping and many aspects of the business plus raised two boys.

Thomas White managed the Heidorn Ranch in Knightsen, and is also remembered for his involvement in maintenance of the county roads in the area. In the early days the roads were dirt and gravel. After months of hard rain each winter the roads became rutted and impassable. It was each farmers responsibility to maintain the roads near his property. The Contra Costa County Public Works Department would supply the equipment, usually a Fresno scraper, and the land owner supplied the manpower and horses to repair his section of the road. It was Thomas Whites job to care for the equipment and insure that it was delivered to the next land owners property and that it was subsequently used.

Edna Christina Heidorn Hill, for whom a Brentwood School is named, was Christian Heidorn's youngest child. She was fifteen years younger than her sister Emma. As a child Emma spent endless hours tutoring her baby sister, which explains why Edna had completed high school and San Jose Normal School by the time she was sixteen. By 1912 she was teaching at Eden Plain School in Knightsen where she had been a student herself years earlier. She claimed that when she took over her first class room she had students older than she was and definitely larger, as Edna was only 5' 1/2" tall. Edna became principal of Eden Plain School in 1914. Between 1930 and 1937 she was superintendent of Brentwood Schools, then returned to the classroom until her retirement in 1964. On May 15, 1955 the Brentwood Primary School was renamed Edna Hill School to honor Brentwood's most distinguished educator.

In 1920, Edna Heidorn Hill's husband, Sam Hill, purchased the Brentwood News. Sam was not only colorful in his writing but also very controversial. While her husband was editor and publisher of the newspaper, Edna had the opportunity to pursue a second career as a reporter and columnist.

Edna Hill was very active in the community. One of her primary interests was the history of East Contra Costa. She was a charter member of the East Contra Costa Historical Society and was editor of that organization's newsletter for many years. Edna compiled a huge amount of information about the early history of the Diablo Valley. She planned to write a book on the subject. Unfortunately she died in 1975 with her history book unfinished, a great loss to us all.

A story in regard to the Heidorn family would not be complete without mentioning that Christian Heidorn had a brother, Henry, who also immigrated from Germany in 1869 and settled in East Contra Costa County. He was a hard working and successful wheat farmer on Lone Tree Way. Henry Heidorn and his family were also key players in the early development of the area.

It is families like the Heidorns that were instrumental in the development of education, libraries, irrigation, business, and farming in this region of California. Until Next Time....

*Photo around 1900
the Heidorn Home
on Sellers Avenue
Mrs Maria Heidorn,
Edna Heidorn Hill
Chris Heidorn,
Mrs Emma Heidorn White*

OAKLEY-KNIGHTSEN FIRE PROTECTION DISTRICT TIME LINE

1920.....Businessmen of Oakley purchased two chemical fire extinguishers pulled by hand to the site of fires and a flat-bed wagon with about 10 milk cans full of water to recharge the fire extinguishers. This was the only fire equipment in the community.

1924.....Fire destroyed several buildings (including the Dal Porto Hotel) on Main Street in Oakley. Shortly thereafter the Oakley Fire Department was organized with Anthony Dal Porto named Fire Chief. The Dal Porto family purchased Oakley's first fire equipment, a used fire engine from Oakland.

1924.....The first fire station was located on Main Street next to the Oakley Theater.

1942.....Oakley Fire Department acquired its second fire engine—a 1940 Chevrolet with 350 gallons per minute capacity. The first engine was returned to the Dal Porto family.

1948.....Oakley Fire Department acquired its third fire engine with 500 gallons per minute capacity.

1952.....June 16—Knightsen formed a volunteer fire department as a branch of the Oakley Fire Protection District. The 1940 Chevrolet engine was transferred to the Knightsen fire station. There were 14 original volunteers. Stanley Duff, grandson of George Knight (founder of Knightsen) was named Fire Chief, Sam Somerhalder became Captain, Angelo Ghigliazza was named Lieutenant, and Richard Winter was designated as supervisor and trainer. The fire station was located on Santa Fe Railroad property on the main street of the town.

1952.....December—Oakley-Knightsen Fire Department started a tradition of taking Santa Claus around the towns to distribute oranges and candies to the children. This tradition continued for over 50 years.

1953.....Anthony Dal Porto retired as Fire Chief. Carl Gott was named to replace him. There were nine volunteers at this time.

1953.....November—Oakley firefighters were given permission by the Dal Porto family to renovate a vacant beauty shop on Acme Street to serve as a meeting room.

Knightsen Fire Department Engine Number 1 is a 1940 Chevrolet Van Pelt fire engine.

1957.....July—Oakley fire station was relocated to Acme Street on land donated by Anthony Dal Porto. The building included a dormitory, bath and shower, plus stalls for two engines. The fire department purchased a new fire engine with 1,000 gallons per minute capacity.

1958.....Knightsen Volunteer Fire Department named Jerry Crocco as Fire Chief.

1961.....May—Harry Hobbs, resident of Knightsen, began a fund-raising drive to build a new firehouse in Knightsen.

1963.....William Smith succeeded Jerry Crocco as Fire Chief of the Knightsen Volunteer Fire Department.

1963.....June—the first meeting was held in the new Knightsen firehouse. The station was outfitted with another new 1,000 gallons per minute fire engine.

1964.....Oakley Fire Station added two more bays to accommodate the fire engines and a pickup truck that was used by the officer in charge of a fire to carry emergency medical equipment.

1969.....October—Fire Commissioners for the Oakley-Knightsen Fire Protection District were: Charles Cekola, Tony Dal Porto, Walter Duff, Art Honegger, and Ray Michelotti. The district's Fire Chief was Carl Gott, Assistant Chief in Oakley was Joe Tovar, Assistant Chief in Knightsen was Bill Smith, Captains in Oakley were Manuel Tovar and Angelo Garcia, Captains in Knightsen were Arthur Somerhalder and Sam Somerhalder, Lieutenants for Oakley were Harry Armstrong and Rudy Duran, and in Knightsen, Lieutenants were Tony Berumen and Angelo Ghigliazza. In addition to these men, there were 13 firefighters in Oakley and 14 in Knightsen.

1970.....Bob Pastor succeeded William Smith as Fire Chief of the Knightsen volunteers. Smith became the training officer.

1971.....Oakley Fire Department purchased a 4-wheel drive fire engine with a 600 gallon per minute capacity.

1972.....October 31—DeVlieger's Knightsen Sunflower Seed Company's building burned to the ground. Readers Digest claimed it was the largest fire at one time. Twenty volunteers battled the blaze for over 22 hours; the Knightsen School swimming pool was drained (it was the nearest water supply); damage to the building and machinery was estimated to be $150,000, and the new crop of sunflower seeds lost was valued at $350,000.

1973.....February 1—Five volunteers and one fire engine responded to a fire behind Oakley School which destroyed about 50% of a maintenance building, several hand tools, paint, plumbing supplies, and a riding lawn mower, in addition to a brand new cabinet and eight chairs. Damage estimated at $17,500.

1980s...East County Soroptimists raised $5,000 to purchase the Oakley/Knightsen Fire Department a "Jaws of Life."

1984.....February—Oakley-Knightsen Fire Protection District Commissioners were: Evo Baldocchi, Ken Crockett, Rico Cinquini, Ray Michelotti, and Chairman Vince Jesse. The fire district extended from Bethel Island to the John A. Nejedly Bridge and south to Sunset Road. Fire Chief was Joe Tovar and Assistant Chiefs were Manuel Tovar (Oakley) and Bob Pastor (Knightsen). There were 27 volunteer firefighters in Oakley and 20 in Knightsen.

1984.....August 25—Oakley-Knightsen Fire District was aided by Brentwood and Bethel Island departments in fighting a fire that destroyed the Hydroponics Farm on Sellers Avenue near Delta Road.

1988.....Oakley-Knightsen Fire Protection District purchased two Chevrolet Blazers for Assistant Fire Chiefs Manuel Tovar and Bob Pastor to use.

1989.....The Fire District purchased a 1,500 gallon per minute fire engine, a one-ton wild land unit and a medical-rescue van.

1990.....Another rescue van and one-ton wild land unit were purchased to be housed at the Knightsen fire station. The Knightsen fire station added two additional bays to accommodate the new vehicles.

1991.....The fire department volunteers consisted of one Fire Chief, two Assistant Fire Chiefs, twelve Captains, and thirty-six firefighters.

1993.....Emily Cutino retired from the Fire Department after serving as fire dispatcher since 1970.

1994.....Oakley and Knightsen fire stations were absorbed into the Contra Costa Fire Protection District over the objections of the volunteers. Full-time union firefighters replaced the volunteers.

1998.....November 3—Drop-off in the department's efficiency caused the abandonment of the merger with the Contra Costa Fire District and the newly independent department became officially the Oakley-Knightsen Fire Protection District.

1999.....January—a used 1,250 GPM diesel fire engine was acquired by the Knightsen station from the Moraga-Orinda Fire District.

1973.....Knightsen fire station added a 4-wheel drive pickup/pumper for use in vegetation fires.

1974.....June 24—Carl Gott retired after 33 years of service. Joe Tovar was named Fire Chief to succeed him and Manual Tovar was appointed Assistant Fire Chief. There were 25 volunteer firemen in Oakley and 18 in Knightsen. They were paid $10 an hour for responding to calls.

1977.....April 22—the Continente packing shed erupted in flames at 4:00 a.m. Before the fire was extinguished, several Santa Fe boxcars were also destroyed.

1977.....June 26—the Knightsen fire station celebrated its 25th anniversary. Of the original 14 volunteers in 1952, four still remained on the department. Fire Chief was Bob Pastor and there were 20 volunteer firefighters.

1978.....April—Insurance Service Office (ISO) tested the Oakley/Knightsen volunteers and fire hydrants. Their report improved the District's rating from Class 5 to Class 4 (Class 1 being the highest rating possible).

1978.....June 12—Oakley Middle School's multi-cultural room was destroyed by fire suspected to be arson. Over $30,000 worth of damage was done.

1979.....February 24—Bill Smith retired as Knightsen's training officer. Installed as officers for the Knightsen Firemen's Association were: President Dave Stoeffler, Vice President Ray Gilmore, Secretary-Treasurer Sam Somerhalder, Training Officer Allen Roderick, and Sergeant-at-arms Ken Sheppard.

1980.....July—Oakley station had 24 volunteers and Knightsen station had 19. The volunteers ranged in age from 21 years to 67 years.

1982.....September—Watches were awarded to six members of the Oakley Fire Department for serving 20 years or more. Oakley Firemen's Association President was Paul Urenda.

1982.....September 3—Longtime Oakley volunteer Peter Ghigliazza was memorialized by Oakley-Knightsen Fire Department when two fire trucks led his funeral procession.

1982.....September 10—David Sommer (19) of Oakley was arrested for burning 12 vehicles in Oakley on July 25 and July 26.

1983.....The fire district purchased a 1,250 GPM Ford cab-over fire engine and a 1,000 GPM all-wheel drive International to replace the 1942 and 1948 engines.

OAKLEY

OAKLEY TIMELINE

1860.....Samuel C. Sellers settled in the Oakley area. He built his home in 1861.

1862.....Iron House School was organized by Sarah Sellers. This was the first school east of Antioch. Sarah was on the first Iron House Board of Trustees and the first women in the state to serve on a school board.

1886.....Miwok Indian skeletons found in the Big Break area.

1887.....James O'Hara, a native of Maine, settled in the Oakley region. The land he bought was a government-grant. It was covered with chaparral, live oak, and wild daises. He purchased this land from the government for $5 an acre. O'Hara died in 1912.

1889.....James O'Hara organized the Almond Growers Association of East Contra Costa County. He cultivated and cleared the land, and planted 80 acres of almonds. Later he added 160 acres in nuts and fruit trees, and by 1912 owned 7,000 acres.

1890.....Alden Nathan Norcross at the age of 62 traveled to California from Boston and settled in the Oakley Area. He later became partners with Randolph Marsh and helped plot the town of Oakley. Norcross donated the land for the first Oakley School and the Methodist Church.

1896.....Dr. J. W. Ellis started a medical practice in the area. He remained in the area until 1904.

1896.....Iron House School built a second building on a one acre lot on the corner of Cypress & Sellers across from a large metal storage shed known as the iron house, hence, the school name. This second structure cost the district $1,600 to construct. The property was deeded to the school district by Edward Emerson.

1897.....Randolph C. Marsh purchased property in the area. Marsh was a Civil War veteran from Ohio. He came to California in 1875 where he farmed in the Petaluma area. He purchased 12 acres of sandy soil that became the township of Oakley.

1897.....Santa Fe was given land for railroad. James O'Hara, Andrew Walker, B. F. Porter, and Randolph Marsh deeded a right of way to the railroad with the understanding that they would erect a depot where the proposed town of Oakley would be. Marsh also negotiated for a half mile of side track to enable local farmers to pack and ship their products for market.

1898.....The town of Oakley was plotted by Marsh and Norcross.
1898.....Marsh gave Joseph Jesse a free lot on the condition that Jesse establish a mercantile store, the first store in town.
1898.....The Oakley Post Office was dedicated November 1st with R. C. Marsh as first postmaster. For the first eight months the mail was delivered from Antioch daily by cart. Later it came from Brentwood. The first letter addressed to Oakley, California arrived September 9, 1898. It came from the Postmaster General in Washington DC.
1899.....Edward Bryner (Frank Stonebarger's cousin) planted one of the area's first almond orchards. It was located where the O'Hara School is today.
1900.....The Santa Fe Railroad comes to Oakley. The first train arrived on July 1, 1900.
1900.....Joseph A. Jesse opened the first general store in town. The lot was given to Jesse by Marsh. The store was 26' x 40' with a cellar.
1900.....John Augusta purchased the first business lot in town and established a blacksmith shop. His Blacksmith shop was a primary gathering spot for local farmers when they came to town.
1900.....The loganberry was introduced to the Oakley area by Rev. C. S. Scott, who brought the plants from Southern California.
1902.....Joseph A. Jesse was appointed deputy sheriff by Sheriff Veale. He held this position until 1918 without pay. He was later elected constable of the 17th Judicial Township where he served until his death in 1944.
1903.....Oakley School established. Prior to 1903 all of the children in the area attended school at Iron House. Oakley's first teacher was Susie McAravy. The first classes were held in a little green building in the middle of town. The first Oakley School building was actually built in 1904 on O'Hara Ave. In 1904 there were 15 students. The land was donated by Norcross.
1905.....The Oakley Hotel was built.

Oakley Catholic Church - 1908

1905.....The Oakley Cash Store, owned by Frank Silva and Jerry O'Meara, operated from 1905—1911. The Oakley Cash Store was so named because it sold strictly for cash, and had no charge accounts.

1905.....The first Oakley Jack Rabbit Bar-b-que. This activity became an annual event. At the first event there were over 2000 people in attendance. And the community dedicated a flag pole they had received from Washington DC.

Oakley Women's Club - 1918
Members rolled bandages for World War I Veterans

1906.....The Victor Parachini family settled in the area. He was foreman for James O'Hara and farmed his own land. He was one of the first directors of East Contra Costa County Almond Growers Association.

1908.....Live Oak School was built. This school closed in 1924 and most of the students then went to Antioch to school. This school was sold at public auction for $100.00

1908.....Oakley's second Methodist Church was erected. The first church was located 2 1/2 miles southwest of town. A. N. Norcross donated the land to build the church.

1908.....The Catholic Church was built in Oakley on land donated by O'Hara two years earlier. Father Riley was the first priest. The Church moved to O'Hara Ave in 1926 with Father Warren the acting priest. Before 1908 Oakley Catholics had to travel to Antioch for Mass. It was an all day trip because of bad roads. The Church is named Saint Anthony's. It was the original church built on the corner of Fourth and Ruby. The present church on O'Hara Ave was built in 1955. Worthy to note, the church tower still uses the same bell that was used in 1908.

1908.....William Henry Carpenter moved to Oakley. He was a storekeeper and farmer.
1908.....Salvador Dal Porto moved to town from Jackson. He built a hotel and several other businesses. The Dal Porto family were key players in establishing the town.
1909.....Rural postal delivery was established.
1910.....A. G. Ramos opened a store specializing in making harness of all kinds, whips, lap robes, and blankets.
1910.....Oakley had a Farmers Club with 50 members.
1910.....The Oakley Hotel was built by Salvador Dal Porto.
1911.....M. A. Farrell moved to town and opened a second mercantile store where he sold feed and hardware.
1913.....Oakley's first library was established. The library was in Mrs. Farrell's general store. They had 300 books which had been donated by local residents and the county branch library.
1913.....The Oakley Women's Club was established with Mary O'Hara as founder. The first meetings were held in Mrs. Farrell's general store. There were approximately 30 charter members. This group was originally known as the Ladies Improvement Club.
1913.....Joseph Augusto (John's brother) moved to Oakley and managed Adams Lumber.
1914.....Dr. Weatherbee started his practice.
1915.....G. Continente bought 600 acres and developed vineyards in the area.
1916.....The Oakley Women's Club purchased the Congregational Church building and established a club house and public library. The clubhouse was located on the corner of Acme Street and Second Street.
1917.....Ninety One young men from Oakley signed the roll for the draft (WW1).
1917.....Roman & Santa Morales came to Oakley. They left Spain in 1913 stopping in Hawaii for several years before moving on to Oakley where he farmed. He was one of the first Spanish to settle in the area. He died in 1970.
1920.....The Bank of Oakley was established in August. Mr. J. Shaw was the first manager. The bank closed in 1930.
1922.....Street lights were installed.
1922.....Alex Murdock was elected Justice of the Peace, a position he held until 1934
1924.....Fire struck Oakley burning most of the businesses in town.
1924.....Grace & Karl Gehringer came to town to teach 4th and 8th grades. Karl eventually became principal of Oakley School. The Gehringers taught in Oakley Schools for twenty four years and lived in the Oakley Hotel. Gehringer School was named for these dedicated educators in 1956.
1925.....Frank Stonebarger moved to area. He was a farmer and a great supporter of Liberty High School. The new gym on the Liberty campus was dedicated in his honor.
1926.....The First Holy Ghost Festival was held, established by the Portuguese residents. This group built the Flor do Oakley hall in 1928.
1926.....Ed & Muriel Leal had a meat market next to the Oakley Hotel until 1966.
1928.....There was a break in the levee north of town flooding 2 1/2 square miles. This area was never reclaimed creating what we know as Big Break today. It was originally farm land.
1930....Another fire struck downtown. This blaze was not as large as the 1924, fire but several businesses downtown were lost (June 22).
1936.....Oakley School District unionized with Sand Mound, Jersey Island, Bradford, and Iron House school districts.
1940.....Mrs. L. S. Burkhalter was librarian at Oakley Library.
1940.....New Oakley School was built on Norcross Lane at a cost of $96,000. There were five

hundred and one students and fifteen full-time teachers.
1941.....Haster England moved to Oakley and established the Signal Station & restaurant on the corner of O'Hara Avenue and Main Street. Nellie England, Haster's wife, had a taxi service from 1948 to 1959.
1941.....A. W.. Biglow was constable of Oakley from 1941 to 1946 when he died. Biglow was followed by Ernest Taylor. Biglow was a Spanish-American War Veteran and a very active member of the Masons.
1943.....A citizen's committee was assembled to promote local improvements and adopted a five year program that called for better streets, natural gas, dial telephones, street signs, and the formation of a sewer district.
1945.....The Oakley Sanitary District was established. Hasten England, Tony Dal Porto, Tony Vengley, Joseph Augusta, and Jess Mello were the first board members. In 1946 residents of Oakley authorized a $30,000 bond for the construction of sewer lines. The County Sanitary District was established in 1967 The district became the Ironhouse Sanitary District in 1992.
1947.....A local newspaper, *The Oakley Observer* was established with George Banks the publisher.
1947.... Ernest Taylor ws named as Justice of the Peace.
1947.....The Oakley Parent Teacher Association was established. Nellie England was the founder.
1948.....The Oakley Harvest Roundup was held for two years. This festival offered residents a parade,. a bar-b-que, games for kids, a Bass Derby, a free dance and more. The event was organized by the Oakley Sportsman Club.
1949.....Vada Carlson purchased the Oakley Observer from George Banks and renamed the newspaper East Contra Costa Observer. This paper was later to become the Diablo Valley News, owned by Doc. Smith.
1950.....Oakley's first shopping center was established.
1954.....The Oakley Chamber of Commerce founded. Victor Parachini was one of the first presidents.
1955.....Oakley water treatment plant went into operation. In 1981 a 2.5 million gallon water tank was added.
1956.....Gehringer School was built.
1972.....Iron House School moved to the Emerson Ranch and was converted to a residence.
1983.....The Oakley Municipal Advisory Council was formed. Members of the council were appointed by the Board of Supervisors. It was the first MAC in Contra Costa County.
1985.....The first annual Oakley Wine adn Jazz Festival was held at Cline Cellars Winery (discontinued in 1989). This event was sponsored by teh Oakley Chamber of Commerce.
1986.....Miwok skeletons found in the Big Break area. An Ohlone pestle for grinding grain and acorns was found near Vintage Parkway.
1990.....O'Hara School and park were built.
1990.....The first annual Almond Festival was held at O'Hara Park.
1999.....Oakley incorporates and becomes a city.
Until Next Time....

OAKLEY HISTORY

Evidence shows that the first residents of the Oakley area were Indians of the Miwok, Yokut, and Ohlone Tribes. In recent years camp sites, burial grounds, and many artifacts have been found. In 1986 several Miwok skeletons were found in the Big Break area and an Ohlone pestle, a stone tool for grinding grain and acorns, was found in 1992 near Vintage Parkway.

During the 1700's when California was part of Spain, Captain Pedro Fages passed through this region of California recording the first history of the area.

Doctor John Marsh was the first Anglo settler in Contra Costa County and arrived on the scene in 1836. He built a riverboat freight landing on the San Joaquin River in the 1840s near what is now Oakley. This was the first landing built in the county. In the early days, before the arrival of adequate roads and the railroad, the rivers acted as the primary means to transport goods. Much of the material to build John Marsh's home, the Stone House, were delivered to Marsh Landing and transported by wagon to the building site on Marsh Creek Road. Marsh Landing was very important to the early development of Oakley and the surrounding region.

Most people thought that the sandy soil in this section of Contra Costa County was not good for farming. It was covered with chaparral, oak trees, coyotes, and jack rabbits. When the first settlers arrived wildlife was plentiful in what was then a wilderness. Flocks of wild ducks, geese, white swans, and pelicans could be seen along the waterfront. Great droves of wild horses, elk, deer, wild boar, and an occasional bear passed through enroute to the river.

Early settlers of the area were laughingly referred to as Sandlappers as it was said that "Only jack rabbits and coyotes can thrive here". Within a few years Oakley's orchards were blooming, and the little town was booming and no longer was anyone making fun of the settlers. James O'Hara was one of the first settlers in Oakley when he arrived in 1889. He purchased seven hundred acres of government-grant land for five dollars an acre. Most of this land he later sold to other settlers for fifty dollas an acre. He knew the common belief was that the sandy soil of the area was only good for growing chaparral and oak trees. It took his insight and the planting of nut trees and grapes to prove the sandy soil was good for growing crops.

Andrew Portman was one of the first settlers to reclaim delta lands by building levees. He hired Chinese laborers for about twenty five cents a day to pack wheelbarrows full of dirt into long mounds high enough to retain the tidal waters. He then planted hundreds of acres of wheat, alfalfa and hay in the rich peat soil.

In 1897 Randolph Marsh purchased twelve acres of land and planned a town. Marsh is credited with naming Oakley for the trees that occupied a large portion of the natural landscape. However, there is a great story about how Oakley was almost named Dewey. It seems that Randolph Marsh and another settler, Joel Wightman, couldn't agree on the towns name. Wightman wanted to name the new community after Admiral George Dewey, a hero of the Spanish American War, and Randolph Marsh wanted to name it Oakley. They decided to play a game of cribbage. The winner of the game would name the town. Marsh won, and Oakley was officially named.

Alden Norcross joined Randolph Marsh in futher developing Oakley when they purchased an additional nineteen acres and plotted the town. They recorded the maps, and Oakley was founded.

The first business to be established was a mercantile built by Joseph Jesse. Marsh agreed to give Jesse the land for free hoping that with one store built it would encourage others to come. He was right. There was soon a blacksmith shop, saloon, hotel, railroad depot, barber shop, and more. Some of the first merchants were John Augusto, Jerry O'Meara, Henry Jansse, Frank Silva, William Carpenter, and Arnold Van Kathoven.

Oakley's boundaries at the turn of the century were Dutch Slough on the north, on the east Marsh Creek, and to the south sand hills covered with chaparral.

On July 1, 1900 the first Santa Fe train stopped in Oakley. The Santa Fe Railroad provided the spur needed for agricultural growth of the area and afforded local farmers a means of transporting their products to market.

Oakley's first school was the Iron House School organized in 1862 by Sarah Abbott Sellers. Iron House was the first school east of Antioch. The Oakley School opened in a tiny building downtown in 1903 and was moved to a schoolhouse on O'Hara Avenue between Acme and Ruby Streets the following year. In 1904 fifteen students were enrolled at the school and by 1920 the school had been enlarged to three rooms with a teacher for each room plus a principal, Edith Dal Porto Berta, and an enrollment of fifty students.

In 1908 Salvador Dal Porto, a boarding house operator from Jackson, settled in Oakley. Dal Porto was instrumental in the development of Oakley's business district. It didn't take long before the town had two social halls, four churches, two saloons, a barber shop, two grocery stores, a blacksmith shop, several warehouses, a bank, and many more business's. In 1910 Dal Porto purchased, remodeled, and enlarged the Oakley Hotel. In 1917 the Bank of Oakley was established.

The Ladies Improvement Club was organized in 1913 with Mary O'Hara serving as the first president. These women were instrumental in the development of Oakleys first library. A small library was first housed in Farrell's general store offering the residents of Oakley three hundred books. In 1916 the Ladies Improvement Club purchased the Congregational Church building for a clubhouse and public library. The Ladies Improvement Club later changed their name to the Oakley Women's Club.

In 1924 the Oakley Hotel and most of the businesses downtown were destroyed by a fire. Dal Porto rebuilt his hotel and several other businesses. He also installed a waterworks. He remained one of the towns most prominent citizens until his death in 1932.

By the 1930s there were packing sheds along the Santa Fe spur that shipped carloads of produce to eastern markets. During harvest time Oakley was filled with men that had come to work in the fields and packing sheds.

It took a special breed of pioneer to settle in the Oakley area. It was necessary to face long hot summers with winds blowing that would cover everything in sight with the local sand.
Until NextTime....

OAKLEY PIONEERS

When most of us reflect on history, we think in terms of great events and famous people who have played roles in building the nations of the world. Yet, it is clear history enables us to progress to all our tomorrows. Or, put another way, our past is the engine that drives our future, and our history is the road we are taking.

Chapters of Oakley's history are rich with stories of young idealistic pioneers that came west to build a new life for themselves and their families. It is impossible to not be impressed with the hardships they overcame, the can do attitude they displayed, and the determined outlook they had about their lives. They depended on each other and were quick to extend a helping hand to their neighbors.

There are many descendants of these original pioneer families still residing in the Oakley area. Some of these early settlers names will sound familiar because they can still be seen on local street signs.

RANDOLPH C. MARSH is noted in history as a roving Civil War veteran and the "Father of Oakley." Born in Ohio in 1838, he moved to Kansas in 1866 where he farmed for many years before traveling west to California in 1875. He first settled in the Petaluma area where he raised his family and tilled the land before actually relocating to Oakley.

Marsh purchased twelve acres of sandy soil establishing what we today know as Oakley. The town was named for trees that occupied a large portion of the areas natural landscape. Marsh gave the first business lot in town to Joseph Jesse to build a grocery store.

An interesting thing that Marsh did was to name the first five streets in town - Main, Acme, Ruby, Star, and Home - take the first letter of each and they spell MARSH.

After purchasing the original twelve acres, Marsh was joined by Alden Norcross in business. Together they purchased an additional nineteen acres of land (at that time at about $50 an acre) plotted out a town site and recorded the maps.

President Mckinley appointed Randolph Marsh as Oakley's first postmaster, a position he held for fourteen years.

JAMES O'HARA was a key player in the early development of the Oakley area. He was born November 8, 1840 in Bangor, Maine, the son of Henry and Ann O'Hara, both natives of Ireland. His father was a farmer and James worked on his father's farm until he was eighteen when he left home and traveled through the Southern States. James came west to California in 1860 where he found employment working for several different farms and dairies.

James O'Hara met and married Mary Hickey, a native of Massachusetts in 1885. The O'Hara's had four children, William, Anna, Elwin and Charles.

In 1887 James purchased 160 acres and later bought an additional 640 acres near Oakley for five dollars an acre. When he arrived in Oakley the land was covered with chaparral. During his life he cleared and farmed five sections of land and established the first almond orchard in the region. Much of the land he originally purchased for five dollars an acre was later sold for fifty dollars an acre to newcomers.

James O'Hara sold the land where the town of Oakley is located to Randolph C. Marsh. He donated the land for Saint Anthony's Catholic Church in 1906.

James O'Hara was actively involved in Oakley schools and the Catholic Church.

ALDEN NATHAN NORCROSS was born in Vermont, November 27, 1829. At twenty one he left his family farm for Boston where be became a prominent businessman. While residing in Boston Alden Norcross married Julia Landmaid, of Pittsfield, New Hampshire in 1861. This union produced six children several of which became key players in Oakley's history. It wasn't until 1890 at the age of sixty two that he decided to travel west to California (now that's a mid-life crisis!) where he settled in the Oakley area.

Norcross became Randolph Marsh's partner in several business transactions, one of which was to purchase land for the further development of the town of Oakley. There is still a street today bearing Norcross' name, and the history books tell us he also donated a half block of land for the first Oakley school and two lots for the Methodist Church.

Of the Norcross children, Bert LeLand Norcross was one of the first nut growers in the region. He planted walnuts and almonds, and by 1915 was shipping nuts to markets in San Francisco.

I am ever amazed at the ingenuity early settlers used to accomplish what seemed to be impossible. They turned undesirable sandy soil into fields and orchards producing an endless variety of crops They also built a bustling community on sand mounds once inhabited by jack rabbits and sage brush. They have truly left footprints in the sand we see today. There is much we can still learn from these courageous settlers. Until next time....

OAKLEY FIRE DEPARTMENT

When Oakley was first established in 1897, there was no fire department. The residents all stood ready to fight for their homes and businesses with buckets, shovels and wet gunny sacks. Such tools were feeble weapons against rampant flames, and as soon as they could afford it the Oakley residents purchased more effective equipment. For many years residents simply had a system where everyone in town assisted when there was a fire. They created a volunteer bucket brigade that dipped water from horse troughs located on Main Street or from the nearest well's hand pump.

In the early 1900's many small towns were plagued with fires. Oakley was no exception. There were numerous conflagrations between 1900 and 1920 and then, in 1924, several businesses on Main Street burned. The Dal Porto Hotel, John Augusto's Blacksmith and most of the downtown businesses were destroyed in the blaze.

As a result of the 1924 fire, Oakley businessmen and residents decided it was time to form a modern fire department. They determined the boundaries of the new district and decided what equipment they would purchase. It was resolved that the newly formed fire district would run from Neroly and Bridgehead Roads to the west, Neroly and Delta Roads to the south, Byron and Sandmound Roads to the east, and the San Joaquin River to the north.

Next, the fire committee purchased a used fire engine from Oakland and appointed Anthony Dal Porto as fire chief. Every able-bodied man in town became a volunteer when a fire struck.

As Oakley grew, so did the needs of the fire department. In 1942 the department acquired a second engine, a Chevrolet with a water capacity of 350 gallons, and by 1948 they bought a third. The third engine was also a Chevrolet and held 500 gallons of water. In 1948 the department decided to open a second fire station in Knightsen. The engine that had been purchased in 1942 was sent to the new station.

Anthony Dal Porto served as fire chief for 29 years, and in 1953 retired, turning the job over to Carl Gott. Chief Gott was determined to develop a well-trained volunteer fire department. Under his leadership the department got more professional. They formed an official volunteer fire department, originally having nine members. Volunteers were asked to attend classes about fire-fighting techniques and instruction on the proper use and care of equipment.

The fire station was originally located in the east end of the Oakley Theater building, a facility barely large enough to house the fire engine and supplies. By the end of 1953 the firemen decided they needed to locate a site where they could hold their meetings and training sections. The Dal Porto family owned a vacant building on Acme Street and graciously agreed to allow the department to use the building as a meeting place.

In 1957 a new Oakley Fire House was built, with space to house two engines, an office, conference room, dormitory, bath and shower. That same year the district purchased a new engine with a 1000-gallon capacity. There was a siren installed on the roof of the station, used to alert volunteers of a fire or emergency.

By 1960 it had become obvious that the eastern end of the district also needed more space and additional equipment, so a new station was built in Knightsen and a 1000-gallon pumper truck was added to their inventory.

Chief Gott served with the Oakley Volunteer Fire Department for thirty years. In 1974 he retired, recommending that Assistant Chief Joe Tovar be appointed to replace him, and that Manuel Tovar become assistant chief. By 1974 the Oakley station had twenty-five volunteers and Knightsen had eighteen. Until next time....

OAKLEY'S HOLY GHOST FESTIVAL

A Portuguese tradition, the Holy Ghost Festival held in Oakley each summer since 1927 is a wonderful chapter in the history of that community. It is a colorful social and religious event that dates back hundreds of years in the Azores Islands to the reign of Queen Isabel in 1332.

The festival, also known as Festa Do Espitio Santo, is held each year on the third Sunday of July and is dedicated to the Catholic Holy Ghost, the symbol of peace. Unfortunately, early records of the IDES men's Portuguese lodge were stored in the basement of Flor do Oakley Hall and destroyed in a flood about 25 years ago, so researching the early history of this organization or its festival was not easy. The story of this wonderful event remains in the memories of old-timers and the few newspaper articles I was able to locate.

As legend has it, Queen Isabel held the first festival. There are several stories about how the tradition started. One of these stories is: there was a horrible famine, the people of Portugal were starving, and Queen Isabel promised God if He would help her feed the people, she would give away all her jewels. Her cruel husband, King Diniz, saw her with something in her apron. It was the jewels. He asked her what was in the apron and she replied, "Roses, my lord." He grabbed her apron and out tumbled white roses - it was a miracle. It was winter and not the season for roses. The following morning two ships appeared in the harbor. Both ships were completely unmanned, one ship was full of grain and the other animals. The queen ordered that bread be made with the grain and that the meat of the animals be cooked for the poor.

Oakley's first Holy Ghost Festival was held in 1927, with Anna Silveira reigning as queen. The queen was selected by selling tickets to a dance held before the festival. The organizers of the 1927 event were Tony Silveira, Jim Pappas, Manuel Minta, Tony Fertado, Bob Rodriques and Tony Noia. In 1905, Oakley resident Lucy Lima was crowned queen at the annual Antioch Holy Ghost Festival.

The Holy Ghost Festival commemorates the charity of Queen Isabel and feeds the community each July at the Holy Ghost Celebration. The festival committee works for the whole year planning the following year's event. Cows are donated by local ranchers and dairymen to be used for the sopas (shredded beef in sauce) served at the feast. Others donate money and auction items to help sponsor the activity.

Ed Markus has overseen the preparation of the sopas for many years. Usually twelve cows are butchered by Alpine Meat and delivered to the hall two days before the feast. The committee spends hours cutting and cooking the meat.

According to Tony Gonzales, the Flor do Oakley Hall was built on three lots that were purchased from John Minta for $150 in 1927. Prior to the construction of the hall, the IDES met in a building near Big Break.

The Flor do Oakley Hall has played an important role in the Oakley community. This facility served as a theater, roller-skating rink and location of the annual Volunteer Firemen's Ball for many, many years. Hundreds of Oakley's youth received their eighth-grade diplomas on the Flor do Oakley stage and it was the site of innumerable school plays and Christmas pageants. Over the years there have been Citizen of the Year dinners, political gatherings, crab feeds, weddings and class reunions there and more.

The Flor do Oakley Hall has served as the heart of Oakley for many years. Until next time....

JOHN AUGUSTO & JOSEPH AUGUSTA
OAKLEY PIONEERS

Looking through the pages of Oakley's history, I find several early settlers who, full of energy and youthful enthusiasm, experienced discouragement and exerted enormous efforts to overcome adverse conditions. There are many interesting details in Oakley's past of men like John Augusto and Joseph Augusta who felt they could do anything and therefore tried everything.

John was born in the Madeira Islands on September 29, 1872, the son of Lawrence and Mary Augusta. As a child he traveled with his family to the Hawaiian Islands, where he acquired an education at St. Louis College of Honolulu. Following college John spent three years working for the Hawaiian Carriage Manufacturing Company learning the blacksmith trade. In 1892 he left Hawaii for the Americas in search of his fortune.

Arriving in San Francisco he labored as a blacksmith for a year, then moved on to Oakland and San Leandro for the next few years, still working as a blacksmith. In 1899, John Augusta married Ermina Fernandez Gonsalves, a native of Honolulu. They were blessed with five children: George, Hazel, Edward, Martha and Archibald.

In April of 1900, John heard of a new little community called Oakley, in eastern Contra Costa County, that had just appeared on the map. Realizing the possibilities of this newly developed area, and still in search of his fortune, John moved to Oakley. He purchased the first business lot in the newly plotted town, on the corners of O'Hara and Main Street, and immediately proceeded to build and outfit a blacksmith shop.

The blacksmith shop became a gathering place for early settlers where neighbors would meet and compare opinions on the weather and crops, and discuss local business politics. John was to spend the rest of his life as a key player in the development of the town of Oakley. John and Ermina's first two children, Hazel and Edward, were the first recorded births in Oakley.

As his blacksmith business grew, John expanded his holdings. He purchased and developed five more lots on Main Street as well as two larger parcels of land on which he planted orchards of nut and fruit trees. John Augusto became Oakley's first John Deere agent, specializing in the sale and repair of John Deere wagons, buggies and farm equipment. In 1924, several downtown businesses went up in flames, including John's blacksmith shop with a stock of new farm machinery.

John Augusto was an active player in all aspects of Oakley's growth, whether in business, social or political affairs. He was an active member of the Masonic Lodge and the Odd Fellows. He was one of the founders of the annual Fourth of July celebration first observed in 1905 that featured music, dancing, games, patriotic orations and contests for young and old alike. Old timers remember these celebrations fondly, particularly the jackrabbits which flourished in the area's dry terrain and were served as a main course at the barbecue. The festivities always began with John's "black powder explosion," a procedure where he ignited the black powder between two heavy anvils. John would also perform his "black powder" explosion at the request of the townspeople at their annual New Year's Eve celebration.

The Portuguese of the area began observing the Holy Ghost Festival in 1926 with a parade, feast, and religious services. The Augusta brothers, John and Joseph, were both instrumental in promotion of this event for many years.

John's brother, Joseph Augusta, and his wife Margaret settled in Oakley in 1913 and also became involved in the community's development. The brothers found they continually experienced difficulty with the mail because of the similarity of the their names, so John changed the spelling of his last name from Augusta to Augusto.

Joseph was employed by the California Packing Company and dealt in dried fruits and nuts prior to becoming manager of Adams Lumber Co. (Adams later became Sterling Lumber). With 44 years of experience in the lumber industry, he earned a reputation of being able to look at a set of house plans and accurately estimate the cost of lumber needed to complete the structure. People traveled from miles around to obtain his consulting services.

A truck scale located in front of Sterling Lumber was used to weigh produce before shipment out of Oakley. Over the years, as Oakley grew, the size of the scale increased. JoAnn Byer remembers the scale as being approximately forty feet long, and she remembers watching her grandfather, Joseph, weighing produce for shipment as late as ten o'clock some evenings.

Joseph Augusta, along with several other early Oakley businessmen, fought long and hard for curb and gutter improvements for the town. They often traveled to Martinez to attend meetings and address the board of supervisors for improvements to the town. Finally they won the battle, which was quite a progressive step for Oakley. Joseph was instrumental in the formation of the Oakley Sanitary District in 1945, and served on the first elected board for the district; he was a fifty-year member of the Odd Fellows, and an active member of the Masonic Lodge.

World War I Parade - 1917
Louise Augusta was crowned "Miss Liberty"

Joseph and Margaret had seven children: Mable, Myrtle, Louise, Lawrence, Leonard, Marjorie and Earl. Today there are grandchildren and great-grandchildren still residing in the area: Mable Dutra, Joseph's daughter; Betty Benn, his granddaughter; Peggy Benn Kelch, his great-granddaughter; Lisa and Dana Duncan, his great-great-granddaughters; and Laci Gonsalves, his great- great-great-granddaughter, all live in East Contra Costa. Joseph's daughter Louise and her daughter JoAnn Byer still reside in Oakley, and JoAnn's daughters, Nancy and Jacquelen, live in the area. Joseph's daughter Marjorie Chastek also resides in Oakley.

Laci Gonsalves is "sixth-generation Oakley"! Pretty remarkable in today's mobile world! Few young people are able to trace their family roots back 150 years, and even fewer see that much of their heritage in the community where they are raised.

From the beginning of time men have built pyramids, castles, and empires so their names would be forever before the future generations. John Augusto and Joseph Augusta did not build any pyramids, castles or empires, but they did build a monument in the hearts of loved ones that will last until the end of time. Their friends are everywhere and their buildings were made of love, respect and friendship. Until Next Time….

SALVADORE DAL PORTO

Salvadore and Maria Dal Porto were both born and reared in Italy. Salvadore was born near Lucca on November 5, 1865, and Maria on May 14, 1868. They were married in San Francisco in 1892 and settled in Jackson, where they operated a boarding house for gold miners working in the Kennedy Mine, before moving to Oakley in 1908. The Dal Portos had five children: Anthony, Frank, Ben, and twin daughters Lena and Edith. Their first home in the Oakley area was a small farm on Live Oak Avenue.

In 1910 they purchased the Oakley Hotel, which they remodeled and expanded to 32 guest rooms and a living space for their family. The hotel was Oakley's social center and a good place for traveling men to spend the night when passing through the area. Salvadore managed the hotel, Maria cooked, and the children all assisted in the general maintenance of the business. Maria's culinary talents were well known throughout the region. She cooked on one wood-burning stove and a kerosene stove, sending tempting aromas throughout the hotel. Lena and Edith waited on tables in the hotel restaurant and Ben and Frank ran the bar.

Ben established a saloon and pool hall in his parents' hotel, known as "Ben's Place," that was active for more than sixty years.

The Dal Porto family lived in the hotel until 1918, when they built a beautiful home on the corner of Ruby and Third Streets. In 1918 Salvadore hired Mr. and Mrs. Joe Brag to manage the hotel and dedicated his time to other enterprises. The hotel and several other Oakley businesses were destroyed by fire in 1924 and the Dal Portos rebuilt a new, modern structure to replace it in 1926. Salvadore hired Tenna and Gladys Sad to manage the new hotel and restaurant. The Sad family purchased the hotel in 1932 from Salvadore Dal Porto's estate.

The Dal Portos were key players in the early development of Oakley. Salvadore was one of the foremost leaders in the community for many years. He built the post office at a cost of $8,000; the Oakley Garage for $15,000; the Oakley Theater block, also costing $15,000; and the new Oakley Hotel at an expense of $50,000.

Anthony and Frank both served their country in World War I, Anthony in the Army and Frank in the Navy. After the war, in 1919, the brothers decided to open the Oakley Garage. The garage was originally a Ford agency, but in 1926 they changed to Chevrolet and also took over the distributorship of International Harvester trucks, tractors and farm equipment for Contra Costa County.

Frank pioneered an "open air" school bus operation that took Oakley students to Antioch High School from 1913 until 1933. He also drove a bus for the Oakley School District, with an accident-free record, for 36 years.

The Dal Porto family has definitely left footprints in the chapters of Oakley's past. This family was instrumental in the early development of the Oakley business district; active in the schools; built the town hall; had a large cattle ranch with Angus and Hereford stock; and even owned Oakley's first waterworks. Anthony Dal Porto was instrumental in forming the Oakley Fire District and was appointed the first fire chief. He was also elected to serve on the first board for the Oakley Sanitation District. Salvadore Dal Porto remained one of the town's most prominent citizens until 1932, when he was hurled to instant death when the truck on which he was riding collided with a Santa Fe freight train.

I can't help but wonder what Salvadore Dal Porto would think of Oakley today.
Until next time...

INDEX

A

Abbott, 65, 76, 89, 90, 110, 123, 134, 152, 292
Abney, 85
Abreu, 196
Achey, 242
Acrey, 179
Adams, 79, 150, 153, 289, 298
Aldrin, 147
Alexson, 192
Allen, 50, 69, 70, 73, 78, 79, 85, 86, 87, 91, 154, 223
Alphonse, 54
Ambrosino, 74
Anderson, 59, 69, 92, 140, 148, 151, 152, 158, 191, 197, 201, 256
Andrew, 207
Andrews, 30, 173, 205, 261
Andrieu, 105
Andronico, 258, 261, 262, 263, 266
Antino, 37
Antonocci, 89, 90
Arminio, 98
Armstrong, 26, 43, 63, 67, 79, 84, 106, 127, 142, 143, 156, 157, 160, 162, 163, 169, 172, 179, 181, 185, 188, 189, 195, 202, 209, 210, 212, 222, 223, 224, 227, 283
Ashe, 151
Augusta, 212, 287, 290, 297, 298
Augusto, 289, 290, 295, 297, 298
Avery, 78, 139

B

Babbe, 250, 278, 279
Babbes Landing, 25
Bacagallupi, 76, 97, 118
Bailey, 151, 269
Bainbridge, 66, 102

Baird, 242, 244, 245
Baker, 195, 236
Baldocchi, 283
Baldwin, 27, 242, 244, 245
Balfour, 59, 67, 77, 78, 96, 108, 122, 123
Banard, 151
Bancroft, 143
Banks, 290
Barber, 148
Barkley, 21, 23, 32, 78, 79, 82, 84, 92, 93, 99, 113, 114, 115, 116, 117, 118, 119, 138, 140, 143, 148, 149, 179, 268, 271, 273
Barnard, 89, 90
Barnes, 73, 91, 149
Bartheld, 42, 102
Bartleson, 18
Beaman, 105, 106
Bean, 15
Beard, 261
Beasley, 79, 91
Becerra, 79, 148
Beed, 151
Begin, 55
Belden, 18
Bell, 43, 264, 266
Benn, 42, 83, 105, 298
Berlington, 41, 156
Berry, 83, 84, 142
Berta, 287
Berumen, 283
Bessac, 86
Best, 127
Bethell, 248, 256, 259
Bidwell, 15, 18, 76, 156, 160
Biglow, 50, 290
Billingsley, 72, 149
Bird, 183
Birney, 107
Bisby, 87
Bixler, 68
Blaustien, 199
Blewett, 138, 140

Bloodworth, 98, 154
Bloomfield, 270
Bluman, 91
Blumen, 79
Bohakle, 73
Bohmen, 205
Boltzen, 25, 138, 140, 143, 147
Bonde, 73
Bonnickson, 32, 50, 51, 62, 74, 77, 79, 91, 139, 140, 144, 212, 269, 272
Borden, 17, 252
Bordes, 30, 33, 63
Borowetz, 239
Bovo, 55, 59
Bowerman, 43
Bowlin, 212
Boxel, 258, 260
Boxill, 261
Bradford, 251
Brag, 299
Brangwin, 124
Branscum, 196
Bray, 92
Brewer, 62, 76, 87, 121
Bridgeford, 191, 193, 256, 259, 269, 271
Briggs, 86
Brixey, 90
Bronzan, 69, 73, 79, 143
Brown, 95
Bruce, 204
Bryner, 72, 287
Bucholtz, 147
Buell, 139
Buelowius, 239
Bunn, 90, 176, 270
Burke, 264, 266
Burkhalter, 289
Burlington, 157, 206
Burness, 59, 147
Burns, 147
Burroughs, 250, 268, 269, 271, 272, 279
Burrows, 261, 262

Bush, 9
Bushby, 151
Butcher, 89
Byer, 21, 41, 73, 271, 298
Byrnes, 229

C

Cabral, 55, 61, 158, 198, 216, 217, 220
Cakebread, 20, 32, 33, 103, 104, 128, 199
Callaghan, 151
Calvin, 197
Cardiff, 79
Carey, 21, 23, 27, 32, 57, 76, 80, 81, 83, 118, 119, 142
Carlisle, 154
Carlson, 290
Carpenter, 128, 152, 289, 291
Carrell, 229
Carson, 23, 174
Carston, 274
Carter, 33, 226
Casey, 70, 138, 140, 153
Castello, 137
Castoro, 79
Castro, 17
Cautrell, 274
Cekola, 283
Chadwick, 5
Chaim, 70, 158, 169, 171, 199
Chamoures, 87
Champlin, 59, 236
Chase, 17
Chastek, 298
Cheney, 256, 259
Cheseldine, 152
Chick, 104
Chiles, 19
Chilson, 180
Christensen, 79, 139, 273
Cinquini, 283
Claghorn, 142
Cleaves, 71
Coan, 111
Coates, 62, 120, 121, 146, 154
Cocco, 270
Coffey, 233
Cogswell, 79, 92, 154

Coleman, 264
Collins, 83, 147
Conner, 209
Connors, 43
Consadine, 165
Continente, 139, 141, 289
Cook, 44, 82, 145, 147
Cooper, 236
Copland, 169, 170
Cople, 21, 32, 33, 156, 192, 218, 219
Corey, 139
Cornell, 243
Cowell, 114, 128, 129
Cowen, 97
Cox, 87
Craig, 139, 140
Crawford, 151
Crespi, 12, 160, 253
Crist, 167
Crocco, 283
Crocker, 30, 127, 236
Crockett, 283
Cross, 187, 205
Crosslin, 113, 196
Crossman, 261, 262, 266
Cumming, 30, 50
Cunningham, 79, 139, 261, 262, 266
Currier, 148
Curtis, 78, 79, 139
Cutino, 284

D

Dainty, 32, 33, 53, 67, 105, 106
Dal Porto, 134, 251, 282, 283, 289, 290, 292, 295, 299
Danielson, 78, 138, 139, 140, 142, 153
Darby, 99
Darling, 8
Davi, 242, 245
Davidson, 183
Davis, 63, 79, 80, 81, 112, 123, 128, 134, 151, 154, 242, 251, 256
Dawson, 19
Day, 251

Dean, 20, 27, 49, 59, 107, 108, 125, 144, 153, 279
DeAnza, 4, 12, 268
DeBorba, 195, 228
DeFermery, 152
DeMartini, 6, 70, 79
DePledge, 148
Dermody, 54
DeVine, 242, 245
De Vlieger, 270, 283
DeVoto, 242
Dewey, 138, 291
Dickey, 142, 152, 154
Dickhoff, 30
Diffin, 89, 99, 105, 120, 147
Dillion, 30
Diniz, 296
Dinney, 151
Ditmars, 85, 138, 140
Dixon, 86
Dodge, 59
Doherty, 172
Dohr, 176
Dolan, 183
Dominguiz, 79
Donaldson, 148, 193
Donner, 42, 203
Dowell, 92
Draper, 258
Drewick, 261
Drolette, 264
Drumm, 114
Drummond, 196
Duda, 261
Duff, 270, 274, 282, 283
Duhnken, 84
Duncan, 298
Duran, 283
Durham, 59, 87, 125
Dutard, 250, 279
Dutra, 298
Dwelley, 150, 151
Dwinell, 17
Dyer, 138

E

Eachus, 76, 86, 218
Earp, 174
Easton, 30

Eichler, 38
Eisele, 82, 142, 152
Eisenhower, 137
Elam, 139
Ellis, 286
Elsworth, 99, 105, 148
Emerson, 269, 271, 286, 290
England, 290
Engle, 157
English, 272
Eppinger, 50
Espercia, 152
Esterbrook, 76, 82, 83
Estes, 148, 214, 269, 272
Evje, 242

F

Fages, 4, 12, 76, 156, 160, 242, 243, 253, 291
Farrar, 257, 260
Farrell, 289, 292
Fassett, 249, 278
Fellows, 41, 207
Ferrill, 69, 79
Fertado, 296
Fetters, 135
Field, 148
Fisher, 79, 139
Fitzpatrick, 18
Fleming, 54, 199, 264, 266
Fletcher, 32, 99
Fly, 207
Font, 268
Forbes, 121, 148
Ford, 86, 147
Fortheringham, 157, 269, 272
Fortson, 223
Forward, 65
Foster, 111
Fox, 113, 269, 271
Frank, 169, 170, 227
Franke, 196
Franks, 251
Frederick, 136, 137, 208
Frederickson, 8
French, 83, 139, 140, 142, 145, 151, 195, 224

Frerich, 77, 148, 153, 166, 227
Fuss, 196

G

Gable, 236
Galvan, 9
Gambetta, 196
Gamble, 79, 139
Garcia, 16, 17, 283
Gardner, 43
Garin, 77, 78, 79, 132, 133
Garner, 85
Gassner, 6
Geddes, 19, 32, 105, 191
Gehringer, 152, 289
Geiser, 201
Gennasee, 173
Gessler, 74, 148
Geyser, 79, 201
Ghigliazza, 270, 282, 283, 284
Ghiselli, 79, 139
Gibson, 78, 111, 139
Gill, 73, 139, 231, 232
Gilmore, 284
Giusti, 195
Glosser, 42
Golden, 61, 62, 77
Golder, 94
Goldsby, 196
Gomes, 86, 138, 140
Gondon, 37
Gonsalves, 297, 298
Gonzales, 79, 139, 195, 295
Gore, 138
Gorham, 126, 134
Gott, 282, 284, 295
Graf, 143
Gramm, 263
Granados, 195, 224
Grant, 105, 114, 242
Gray, 279
Greathouse, 200
Green, 19, 87, 227, 251
Greer, 250
Gregory, 77, 145, 261, 262
Grennen, 83, 142
Griffith, 89, 90, 92, 93, 151, 153
Grimes, 119
Grisby, 97, 151, 269, 272

Gromm, 74, 263, 266
Grove, 50, 193
Grover, 41
Grueninger, 21, 148
Grunauer, 20, 34, 57, 61, 71, 76, 81, 83, 95, 142, 168, 169, 170, 171, 227
Guest, 37, 84, 104
Guinn, 106
Guise, 79, 139
Guthrie, 67, 122, 123

H

Haag, 212
Hagan, 251
Hage, 118
Haggin, 256
Hagmayer, 50
Hale, 58
Hall, 5, 59, 179, 261, 266
Hallman, 99
Hamburg, 249, 278
Hamilton, 270
Hammond, 23, 43, 53, 61, 91, 157, 158, 174, 175, 185, 186, 187, 195, 198, 199, 220, 224, 226
Hannratty, 85, 138, 140, 143
Hannum, 70, 90, 140, 195, 224
Hansen, 176
Hargis, 85
Harley, 212, 213
Harmon, 79
Harper, 222, 223
Harrer, 70
Harrison, 76
Hartwig, 154
Hatfield, 90
Hauan, 262, 264, 266
Hearst, 136
Heck, 50
Heidorn, 20, 32, 34, 50, 86, 119, 143, 170, 268, 269, 272, 280, 281
Heiser, 228
Helm, 106
Henderson, 27, 87
Hennessey, 54
Hertell, 43

Hester, 37
Hickey, 293
Hideo, 239
Hill, 73, 77, 78, 79, 86, 119, 139, 151, 262, 266, 280, 281
Hilliard, 151
Hinebaugh, 118, 119
Hiserman, 174
Hittell, 275
Hobbs, 283
Hoell, 195
Hoffman, 23, 32, 68, 202, 203, 212
Hofmann, 242, 243, 245
Holden, 78
Holeman, 85
Hollander, 261, 266
Holliday, 174
Holmes, 264, 266
Holt, 126, 127
Holway, 50, 61, 157, 158, 166, 178, 179, 194, 227
Honegger, 89, 150, 283
Hopper, 98, 139, 141
Horr, 50
Hosie, 41, 71, 72, 157, 169, 220, 226, 227
Hotchkiss, 251, 256, 259, 269, 271
Houston, 172, 189, 192, 193
Howard, 53, 61, 147, 195, 198, 199, 224
Hribemik, 258, 261, 262, 263, 264, 266
Hudson, 191
Hughes, 112
Hulbun, 98, 139, 141
Hummel, 91
Humphreys, 50, 62, 76
Hutchins, 229

I

Irons, 138
Irvan, 84
Israel, 35
Iverson, 222
Ivory, 144

J

Jackson, 233
Jacobsen, 90, 91
Jacoby, 158
Jansse, 77, 94, 138, 140, 151, 291
Jenson, 79, 139
Jerrisleu, 77, 120, 146, 147, 154
Jesse, 54, 72, 283, 287, 291, 293
Johnson, 148, 173, 195, 196, 197, 219
Johnston, 280
Jones, 41, 84, 152, 197
Jordon, 128
Joseph, 263, 266
Juarez, 37
Juett, 91

K

Kee, 261
Kelch, 298
Kelley, 74, 79
Kellogg, 156
Kelsey, 18, 19
Kelso, 176, 189, 195
Kenner, 279
Kennerly, 55, 176
Kenny, 53, 54
Kercheval, 251
Kerr, 183
Kidd, 79, 134
Kiefier, 98, 151
Kimball, 10
Kirkman, 77
Kitchen, 54
Klein, 257
Knight, 116, 268, 270, 271, 272, 273, 274, 282
Knox, 239
Koechy, 239
Kriem, 269
Krigbaum, 258
Kristich, 269, 272
Kroeber, 2
Kroner, 170
Krumland, 134, 157, 158, 163, 167, 169, 176, 177, 181, 188, 189, 195, 199, 227
Kynoch, 86

L

Ladd, 226, 227
Landgren, 263
Landmaid, 294
Lane, 78, 138, 139, 140
Laredo, 195
Lawrence, 92, 151
Leal, 289
Lee, 70, 98
LeGrand, 61, 167, 184, 189, 198, 226, 227
LeGrange, 17
Leighton, 74, 79, 91, 148, 232
Lembi, 70, 158
LeMoin, 78, 92, 118, 139, 148, 191
Lemyre, 87
Lent, 25, 250
Lesher, 87
Lewis, 70, 152, 158, 159
Lima, 296
Lincoln, 104
Lindberge, 147
Lindgren, 264
Lindsey, 9, 85
Lipman, 156
Lockhart, 268
Logan, 59, 62, 77, 92, 94, 96, 124, 125, 144, 146, 151
London, 236
Longwell, 200
Lopez, 195
Lucas, 195, 221
Luddinghouse, 59
Luhrsen, 179
Lund, 230
Lunding, 242, 245
Lyman, 15
Lynon, 271

M

MacArthur, 147
Mackrodt, 242
MacLeod, 59
Madigan, 121
Magbuhos, 152
Maggi, 159
Maggiore, 150, 154
Maiocco, 69
Mandrell, 138
Mann, 197

Mansanares, 233
Mansfield, 148
Markel, 263
Markus, 296
Marsh, 2, 10, 13, 14, 16, 18, 29, 33, 35, 36, 37, 43, 62, 67, 68, 73, 76, 104, 129, 156, 160, 249, 271, 286, 287, 291, 293, 294
Martin, 38, 108, 120, 191, 277
Martinelli, 54
Mass, 41
Mathers, 261, 262, 266
Mathews, 17, 87
Mattis, 261
Maxwell, 258, 261, 265, 266
McAravy, 287
McCabe, 21, 27, 32, 34, 53, 54, 156, 190, 201, 206, 207
McCauley, 249, 278
McClarren, 69
McClelland, 88, 90, 131, 151, 154
McCormack, 244
McCoy, 50
McCurley, 72, 141
McDonald, 197
McGillvray, 143
McGuire, 183
McHenry, 42, 74, 105
McHugh, 232
McKinley, 293
McLaughlin, 30
McMillian, 152
McMullen, 263
McNamara, 55
McPoland, 139
Mead, 55, 233, 234, 235, 236, 237
Mehaffey, 261, 266
Mehrlens, 50
Mello, 290
Mendez, 89, 90
Merit, 148
Merriam, 90, 130
Messer, 179, 195
Metez, 91
Michelotti, 283
Middleton, 163, 176, 189

Miguel, 159
Milet, 143
Miller, 84, 85, 150
Minta, 269, 272, 296
Mitty, 53, 54
Modin, 192
Moffatt, 151
Mohr, 229
Monroe, 143, 146, 236
Montgomery, 49
Moody, 6, 62, 63, 76, 105, 106, 116
Mooney, 54
Moore, 79, 81, 139, 169
Moores, 89, 151
Morales, 37, 289
Morchio, 134, 189, 190
Moreno, 16, 17
Morgan, 21, 23, 32, 83, 89, 97, 104, 111, 142, 151, 212
Morgans, 70
Morrill, 79, 139
Mott, 76, 82, 83, 142
Mozart, 147
Murchio, 98
Murdock, 91, 289
Murietta, 174
Murphy, 20, 100, 148, 271

N
Nail, 73, 79
Nash, 70, 77, 145, 151
Nebergall, 91
Neimeyer, 274
Netherton, 21, 32, 34, 62, 76, 86, 172, 214, 215
Neubert, 86
Nicholson, 105, 106
Noble, 69, 152
Noia, 73, 296
Norcross, 286, 287, 288, 291, 293, 294
Noriega, 13, 14, 29, 67, 156, 160
Norris, 133
Norton, 35
Noyes, 147, 272
Nugent, 279
Nunez, 216, 217

Nunn, 79, 89, 90, 91, 138, 139, 140, 143, 152

O
O'Brian, 229
O'Brien, 109, 142, 143
O'Conner, 54
O'Hara, 50, 53, 54, 68, 286, 288, 289, 292, 293, 294
Ohmstede, 268, 270
Olivas, 16, 17
Olney, 78, 152, 154
Olsen, 61, 62, 77, 94, 143
O'Meara, 89, 92, 130, 138, 151, 288, 291
O'Neill, 239
Ordway, 30, 127
Oyer, 140

P
Painter, 138, 140
Palmer, 79, 139
Papadakos, 159, 184, 195, 196, 197, 224, 225
Pappas, 296
Parachini, 288, 290
Parsons, 151
Pastor, 197, 283, 284
Patterson, 43, 156
Patton, 196
Peacock, 207
Peak, 37, 84
Peale, 147
Pearce, 65
Pedersen, 91
Peers, 84, 156, 162, 165, 166, 167, 189, 227
Pendry, 114, 117, 149
Penn, 113
Peppers, 78, 123
Percy, 165
Pereira, 195, 196, 224
Peres, 30
Perkins, 111
Petersen, 78, 142, 143, 149, 153, 192
Peterson, 143, 158, 192, 196, 199
Philbrick, 243
Phillips, 139, 140, 251

Pierce, 74, 79, 101, 268, 271
PiJuan, 242
Pikron, 270
Pimental, 30, 53, 55
Planchon, 148
Pledger, 91
Plimpton, 71
Plumley, 23, 32, 41, 61, 72, 111, 158, 168, 169, 176, 179, 180, 188, 198, 199, 202, 226, 227
Plunkett, 243, 245
Poertner, 139
Porter, 148, 286
Portman, 279, 291
Powell, 104, 208
Pratt, 189
Prelli, 120
Preston, 20, 32, 41, 76, 79, 151, 156, 157, 203, 206
Prevost, 275
Prewett, 32, 67, 109, 110, 147, 152
Pulver, 151
Purcell, 176
Putman, 79

Q
Quesada, 85
Quimby, 251

R
Rademacher, 196
Rahmedorff, 157
Ramirez, 120
Ramos, 151, 289
Ransome, 4
Reali, 55
Reas, 263, 266
Reddick, 85
Redenbaugh, 195
Redmond, 272
Reed, 139, 141, 195
Regelman, 195
Regill, 148
Reichmuth, 90
Reitz, 197
Remsburg, 257
Renner, 179
Retting, 176

Reynolds, 69, 125, 147, 158, 195
Richardson, 27, 32, 34, 41, 156, 157, 163, 172, 189, 203, 205, 212, 264, 266
Richart, 73, 151
Ricioli, 159, 195, 224
Righetti, 251
Righter, 30
Riley, 288
Rindge, 251
Risdon, 156, 233, 234, 235
Rist, 54
Rixon, 93, 138, 139, 140, 143
Roach, 242
Robinson, 37, 243
Roderick, 194, 284
Rodrick, 198
Rodrigues, 195
Rodriques, 143, 296
Roehm, 79
Rogers, 135, 147, 169, 195, 216
Rolando, 72, 97, 98, 139, 141, 151
Rolph, 90, 130, 187
Rook, 271
Root, 59
Rosa, 192
Rosas, 43
Rose, 197
Ruetenik, 143
Ruiz, 79
Russell, 50, 139, 223

S
Sad, 152
Sadler, 85
Salts, 164
Sanders, 50
Sanford, 36, 76, 88, 90, 133
Sani, 195
Sanman, 261
Santana, 55
Santos, 61, 166, 167, 169, 189, 195, 198, 199, 201
Sargent, 61, 62, 77, 94
Sargentina, 143, 152, 191
Sattler, 134
Saunders, 99
Saxouer, 59, 192

Scanlin, 196
Schermer, 6
Schlictman, 229, 230
Schmidt, 59
Schneider, 270
Schnittker, 91
Schwendel, 104
Scoggin, 142
Scott, 287
Scovel, 262, 263, 266
Seabury, 106
Selders, 79
Sellers, 32, 34, 50, 51, 65, 67, 77, 269, 272, 275, 276, 281
Sequeira, 191
Sesone, 256
Shafer, 20, 41, 62, 66, 89, 97, 101, 102, 119, 146, 151, 269, 271, 272
Shanks, 82
Sharafanowich, 73, 74, 79
Shaw, 59, 289
Sheddrick, 83, 142
Shellengerger, 99, 148, 152
Sheppard, 284
Sherbian, 173
Sherfy, 74
Shipley, 84
Shoemaker, 147, 151
Shotswell, 261, 265, 266
Sibrian, 17
Silva, 69, 78, 92, 139, 143, 274, 288, 291
Silveira, 296
Sima, 251
Simmons, 138
Sinclair, 59
Slatten, 74, 79
Slifer, 243
Sloan, 226
Smith, 103, 139, 141, 161, 214, 223, 242, 253, 268, 271, 272, 283, 284, 290
Somerhalder, 269, 270, 272, 282, 283, 284
Somers, 35
Sommer, 284
Souza, 30, 159, 195, 225
Spidel, 191

Spiering, 138, 140, 143
Spiess, 152
Sprawlings, 99
Spreckle, 236
Sproul, 55, 244
Stanford, 143, 150
Stanton, 138, 139, 140
Starr, 30, 126, 127
Steel, 80
Steingrant, 81
Sterling, 271
Stewart, 98
Stinmetz, 176
Stoeffler, 284
Stone, 76, 144, 153, 248, 256, 259, 261, 269, 272
Stonebarger, 79, 287, 289
Storey, 268
Stornetta, 41, 74, 195, 196
Stoverson, 280
Strang, 179
Stuart, 207
Sullenger, 23, 99, 114
Sunol, 30
Sutter, 19
Sweeney, 98
Sweetser, 185
Swicegood, 154
Swift, 148
Sykes, 139, 140

T
Taylor, 32, 34, 68, 156, 172, 192, 203, 204, 205, 206, 212, 290
Templeton, 91
Tennant, 109, 110
Thieme, 263, 266
Thomas, 18, 54, 169, 189, 191, 195, 220, 221, 258, 261, 266
Thompson, 186
Tibbetts, 193
Timms, 148
Tisch, 152
Tomlin, 261, 262, 266
Torlakson, 264, 266

Torres, 97, 98
Tovar, 283, 284, 295
Trembath, 261
Trembley, 77
Tuck, 15
Tucker, 195
Turnbull, 279

U
U'Geni, 79
Uren, 84
Urenda, 284

V
Van Buren, 99
Van Hom, 158
Van Kathoven, 291
Van Pelt, 195
Van Sant, 71
Veale, 20, 41, 69, 85, 119, 252, 268, 269, 276, 277, 287
Vengley, 290
Verne, 182
Viala, 30
Vilchez, 83
Vivian, 103, 104
VonderAhe, 151, 152
Von Konsky, 143
Von Kosky, 261, 266
Von Vaerst, 239

W
Wagenet, 147
Wahl, 263, 264, 266
Walker, 12, 242
Wallace, 59, 70, 76, 78, 83, 84, 89, 92, 98, 100, 106, 125, 131, 138, 140, 142, 145, 146, 147, 148, 152, 154
Waller, 264, 266
Walton, 268, 271
Warmcastle, 37, 84
Warner, 3
Warren, 55
Watson, 37, 70, 77, 78, 84, 92, 133, 150, 154

Wayne, 147
Weatherbee, 289
Webb, 251, 252
Weber, 18, 19, 111
Wedgewood, 138, 139, 140, 143
Weeks, 79, 89, 151
Weihe, 100, 158
Weller, 6
Wells, 92, 143
Welsh, 81
West, 242, 244
Weyand, 85
White, 70, 158, 191, 195, 280, 281
Whitehouse, 105, 106
Whitener, 263, 264, 266
Wickham, 104
Wightman, 199, 291
Wilder, 42, 203
Wilhoit, 242, 244
Wilkening, 20, 41, 56, 61, 156, 161, 162, 164, 165, 166, 167, 179
Wilkerson, 194
Williams, 17, 36, 69, 88, 90, 131
Williamson, 147
Wills, 24, 27, 41, 250
Wilson, 24
Winger, 143
Winning, 119
Winter, 282
Wiseman, 42
Wittenmeyer, 49
Wolf, 113
Wooley, 148
Worden, 85
Wright, 26, 50, 86, 193, 251
Wristen, 50, 79, 119, 134, 148

Y
Yelland, 110
Young, 130

Z
Zarro, 197

ABOUT THE EAST CONTRA COSTA HISTORICAL SOCIETY & MUSEUM

The East Contra Costa Historical Society, founded in 1970, is an all-volunteer, non-profit organization whose mission is to collect, maintain, preserve, and protect historical artifacts and information of cultural and historic value relative to the area of eastern Contra Costa County, California.

The Society's museum, the Byer/Nail House, is maintained and preserved to promote public awareness, education, and appreciation of the heritage of East County. It is a two-story 1878 home furnished with period rooms capturing domestic economy in the late 1800s. The museum is located in Knightsen Township, near the City of Brentwood, just 50 miles east of San Francisco. Its collection tells the story of small town and agricultural life along the San Joaquin River Delta.

You will enjoy our exhibits, self-guided tours, curated programs, and living history events. The Society provides a showcase of photographs, artifacts, farm equipment, and other pioneer living furnishings for the visiting public. In addition, we offer an interactive educational program tailored to kindergarten through high school students. The Society's archive of documents and images provides local historians and genealogists with a great historical resource. The periodic newsletter chronicles local historical incidents of note and calendars of upcoming community events. A selection of local history publications is available for sale.

The East Contra Costa Historical Society welcomes all to join our organization. We are located at 3890 Sellers Avenue, Knightsen, California 94548. Our mailing address is P. O. Box 202, Brentwood, California 94513. Please contact us for more information and our seasonal hours. Our website is http://EastContraCostaHistory.org, telephone number (925) 634-0917 and email Info@EastContraCostaHistory.org. We welcome your visit.

ABOUT THE AUTHOR

Kathy Armstrong Leighton is a 5th generation resident of eastern Contra Costa County. Her Armstrong and Barkley ancestors both homesteaded properties along the Byron foothills and Vasco/Mount Diablo range. Her interest in history began with curiosity in family genealogy and expanded into research into the life and times of local pioneers.

Over the years, Kathy has interviewed pioneer descendents, municipal judges, bar keeps, and war veterans. Family journals, archival research and manuscripts have filled in many gaps in memory and provided substantiating facts. Many of these interviews lead to articles in the local *Brentwood News, East Bay Times, Discovery Bay Clipper,* and *Oakley Gazette* newspapers from 1990 to 2000. In these articles we learned a lot about the communities of Brentwood, Byron, Oakley, Knightsen, Discovery Bay and Bethel Island.

These articles have spanned the range of fraternal organizations, volunteer fire departments, reclamation districts, crop reports, levee breaks, and more. Kathy's byline, "Footprints in the Sand," was a historical human-interest piece eagerly read every week. She concluded each article with the phrase, "Until next time…" and her loyal readers could not wait.

This revised and expanded edition of her 2001 publication, *Footprints in the Sand*, includes an additional 21 articles and new images not in the original edition. The index has also been enhanced. It now includes topic areas such as fire companies, fraternal lodges and events in addition to family names. This 200-page, local history book will provide enjoyable reading for both long-time residents and an excellent introduction to the community for recent resident new to their new San Joaquin Delta home.

www.ingramcontent.com/pod-product-compliance
Lightning Source LLC
Chambersburg PA
CBHW080725230426
43665CB00020B/2623